PENGUIN CLASSICS

# THE DIVINE COMEDY · 2
## PURGATORY

DANTE ALIGHIERI was born in Florence in 1265 and belonged to a noble but impoverished family. He followed a normal course of studies, possibly attending university in Bologna, and when he was about twenty he married Gemma Donati, by whom he had four children. He had first met Bice Portinari, whom he called Beatrice, in 1274, and when she died in 1290 he sought distraction by studying philosophy and theology and by writing *La Vita Nuova*. During this time he became involved in the strife between the Guelfs and the Ghibellines; he became a prominent White Guelf and when the Black Guelfs came to power in 1302 Dante, during an absence from Florence, was condemned to exile. He took refuge first in Verona and after wandering from place to place, as far as Paris and even, some have said improbably, to Oxford, he settled in Ravenna. While there he completed the *Divine Comedy* which he had begun in about 1308, if not later. Dante died in Ravenna in 1321.

DOROTHY LEIGH SAYERS translated *The Song of Roland*, in addition to Dante's *Divine Comedy*, for the Penguin Classics. She graduated with first class honours in French from Somerville College, Oxford, in 1915. In 1916 and 1918 she published two volumes of poetry. Her first novel appeared in 1923 and she later wrote thirteen more books of fiction including *The Nine Tailors*, a fascinating novel about campanology. She also wrote religious plays, notably *The Man Born to Be King*. She died in 1957.

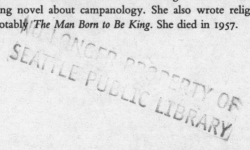

# THE COMEDY

## OF

# DANTE ALIGHIERI

## THE FLORENTINE

\*

## CANTICA II

# PURGATORY

## ⟨IL PURGATORIO⟩

\*

## TRANSLATED BY
## DOROTHY L. SAYERS

\*

PENGUIN BOOKS

**PENGUIN BOOKS**

Published by the Penguin Group
Penguin Books Ltd, 27 Wrights Lane, London W8 5TZ, England
Penguin Books USA Inc., 375 Hudson Street, New York, New York 10014, USA
Penguin Books Australia Ltd, Ringwood, Victoria, Australia
Penguin Books Canada Ltd, 10 Alcorn Avenue, Toronto, Ontario, Canada M4V 3B2
Penguin Books (NZ) Ltd, 182–190 Wairau Road, Auckland 10, New Zealand

Penguin Books Ltd, Registered Offices: Harmondsworth, Middlesex, England

This translation first published 1955
27  29  30  28

Printed in England by Clays Ltd, St Ives plc
Set in Monotype Bembo

*Dimmi che è cagion per che dimostri
nel dire e nel guardare avermi caro.
Ed io a lui: Li dolci detti vostri
che, quanto durerà l' uso moderno,
faranno cari ancora i loro inchiostri.*

Purg. XXVI. 110–114

*Maps and diagrams*
*specially drawn for this edition by*
*C. W. Scott-Giles*

# CONTENTS

The reader's attention is drawn to the cut-out
Universal Clock to be found between
pages 350 and 351.

MOUNT PURGATORY

# INTRODUCTION

OF the three books of the *Commedia*, the *Purgatorio* is, for English readers, the least known, the least quoted – and the most beloved. It forms, as it were, a test case. Persons who pontificate about Dante without making mention of his Purgatory may reasonably be suspected of knowing him only at second hand, or of having at most skimmed through the circles of his Hell in the hope of finding something to be shocked at. Let no one, therefore, get away with a condemnation – or for that matter a eulogy – of Dante on the mere strength of broiled Popes, disembowelled Schismatics, grotesque Demons, Count Ugolino, Francesca da Rimini, and the Voyage of Ulysses, even if backed up by an erotic mysticism borrowed from the Pre-Raphaelites, and the line "His will is our peace", recollected from somebody's sermon. Press him, rather, for an intelligent opinion on the Ship of Souls and Peter's Gate; on Buonconte, Sapìa, and Arnaut Daniel; on the Prayer of the Proud, the theology of Free Judgement, Dante's three Dreams, the Sacred Forest, and the symbolism of the Beatrician Pageant. If he cannot satisfy the examiners on these points, let him be to you as a heathen man and a publican. But if he can walk at ease in death's second kingdom, then he is a true citizen of the Dantean Empire; and though he may still feel something of a stranger in Paradise, yet the odds are he will come to it in the end. For the *Inferno* may fill one with only an appalled fascination, and the *Paradiso* may daunt one at first by its intellectual severity; but if one is drawn to the *Purgatorio* at all, it is by the cords of love, which will not cease drawing till they have drawn the whole poem into the same embrace.

There are perfectly understandable reasons for the common reader's neglect of this tenderest, subtlest, and most human section of the *Comedy*. One must, of course, allow, in Protestant countries, for a widespread ignorance of, and half-unconscious resistance to, the whole doctrine of Purgatory. But this obstacle is, I think, only a minor one.[1] The head and front of the trouble is the persistent influence of that popular superstition which – originating in the

---

1. Those who are not quite clear about what the doctrine is, or at what point in its development Dante comes, will find a short exposition of it on pp. 54–61 at the end of this introduction.

## Introduction

eighteenth century along with the vogue for Gothick gloom and Tales of Horror [1] – has fastened upon Dante the title "Poet of Hell". This, reinforced as it is for us by a similar superstition about Milton, encourages the credulous to suppose that a Dante out of Hell is a Dante poetically out of his element, and that the *Purgatorio* and *Paradiso* are not only less characteristic of their author than the *Inferno*, but also inferior in workmanship. The only thing to be said about that is that it is not true. Bulk for bulk, there is in Dante's work as a whole more joy than grief and far more charity than hatred; his abiding characteristic is not gloom but "pure intellectual light fulfilled with love".[2] And in the matter of sheer artistry, the second *cantica*, by comparison with the first, displays a livelier invention, increased architectural skill, greater freedom of handling and technique, a smoother and more assured mastery of the verse. There are moments of clumsiness in the *Inferno*, awkward transitions and improvisations, an unevenness of texture here and there, passages that are tentative or derivative, as of a writer fumbling to grips with a partly recalcitrant material; not till about the ninth canto does the poem begin to shake itself loose from these initial hesitations; and almost to the end it shows a slight tendency to throw up detached episodes and lyrical flashes imperfectly integrated with their context.[3] The *Purgatorio* is, from the start, much more firmly consolidated; the poet is doing exactly what he chooses, as he chooses, and when he chooses, with perfect awareness throughout of what he is doing. Whether, of course, we like what he is doing

1. Prior to this period there is no trace in English literature of any such exclusive concentration upon the *Inferno*, as may be seen by reference to vol. i of Paget Toynbee's *Dante in English Literature* (Methuen, 1909).
2. *Para: xxx.* 40.
3. Consider, for example, the bald catalogues of names in *Inf.* iv. 55–60, 121–9, 136–44, by contrast with *Purg.* xiv. 97–108 or *Para.* xvi. 88–108, where the whole passage is coloured by the emotions of the speaker; the improvisation in *Inf.* vi. 25–7 of the "sop to Cerberus", and the still more awkward improvisation of the girdle in *Inf.* xvi. 106–8; the ambiguous treatment of the Beasts (personified qualities) in *Inf.* i. 31 *sqq.* and the contrasting skill with which the conventional symbols (personified virtues, books of the Bible, images of Rome, the Empire, etc.) of *Purg.* xxix. 82–154, xxxii. 109–60 are distinguished from the natural symbols by being framed off in a masque or pageant; the ominous ease with which the Francesca, Ulysses, and Ugolino episodes lend themselves to extraction as detached "beauties"; and the comparative lack of motivation for the lovely description of the Mincio in *Inf.* xx. 61–81.

depends upon what we think a great narrative poem should be. If we look upon it only as a matrix from which to extract a few lyrical gems, discarding the setting as dull or worthless, then no doubt we shall prefer the *Inferno*, which lends itself more readily to such treatment. But that only means that we do not really like great narrative poems as such, and that we admire the *Inferno* for its weak points rather than for its strong.

There is another reason why we may not approve what Dante is doing in the *Purgatory* – a reason succinctly phrased by one critic in the poignant cry: "Then the sermons begin." There are long passages which can only be classed as didactic poetry – versified statements of plain theological or scientific fact; these are more numerous in the *Purgatorio* than in the *Inferno*, and still more numerous in the *Paradiso*. The inhabitants of Hell are not remarkable for any great interest in morals or divinity – naturally enough, since they have "lost the good of the intellect"; they pass their eternity in a bustle of purposeless activity and have no use for thinking. And since there are twenty-four circles to be hastened through, over a very rough road amid a perpetual and distracting clamour, Dante and Virgil themselves have but little leisure for improving conversation.[1] This, after all, is as it should be. It is not while undergoing the foretaste of damnation that one can engage in abstract speculation; it is much if one can endure and come through unscathed. Only when one has squeezed out from Hell's suffocating bottle-neck to "look once more upon the stars" can the mind resume its discursive and contemplative functions, and the vast intellectual movement of the *Commedia* begin to be unfolded in direct speech without a figure.

That is why "the sermons begin" on the slopes of Mount Purgatory and not before. But even if there were no "sermons" – if Dante had omitted from the *Purgatorio* the half-dozen or so great discourses on Love, Free-will, the nature of the Soul, and so forth, which are didactic in form as well as in content – we should still have to come to grips with the intellectual substance of the poem. For the truth is that we can, if we choose, read the *Inferno* as a simple tale of adventure, without greatly caring what it is all about. To be sure, we shall

1. "Discourses" of this kind do occur in the *Inferno*; e.g. the passage on Holy Luck in *Inf.* vii. 73–96, and the lengthy exposition of the different kinds of sins in *Inf.* xi. 22–111.

not get very much out of it that way, beyond a few purple passages and the satisfaction of a slightly morbid curiosity. Still, it can be done. But that method will not work very well with the *Purgatorio*, still less with the *Paradiso*. To enjoy these last two books we must take them seriously. And to do so we must discard a number of assumptions which have in these latter days become almost second nature to us.

We must, for instance, dismiss the notion that there is something called "pure poetry", whose values subsist and can be appreciated in isolation from the subject and meaning of the work. This idea is no longer very modern, but it was fashionable some thirty years ago, and its ghost still haunts the by-ways of criticism. We must also abandon – and this is perhaps more difficult – the distinction we have grown accustomed to making between "poetical" and "prosaic" subjects. This artificial distinction, though there are already signs of its appearance in the seventeenth century, was quite unknown in earlier ages, and has only petrified into rigidity within living memory. In the present writer's childhood, "didactic poetry", like "rhetoric" (of which didactic poetry is a department) was still a descriptive term and not a term of abuse. From Lucretius to Wordsworth, and indeed as late as Browning and Bridges, a writer was free if he chose to use verse as the medium for instruction, demonstration, and argument, and in that medium to handle morals, philosophy, science, or any other material belonging to human experience. The assumption that verse should occupy itself exclusively with the personal, the emotional, and the introspective is so recent that one may fairly call the "unpoetic subject" the invention of the Romantic Revival. Yet it has so laid hold of the popular imagination that quite intelligent writers not only take it for granted in their estimate of contemporary literature, but also project it backwards upon periods to which it has no sort of appropriateness. To take a typical case: H. A. L. Fisher, quoting from the *Paradiso* Beatrice's description of the experiment with three mirrors,[1] observes:

[1] "Take three mirrors, and set two of them at an equal distance from you, and the third between the two, a little further from the eye; and, as you stand facing them, have a candle behind you, so placed that its light falls upon the mirrors and is reflected from them all. You will then see that although the more distant image of the flame is smaller than the others it is just as bright as they are" – *Para.* ii. 97–105. Compare what Lascelles Abercrombie rightly

Now this passage, the versification of which is a wonderful piece of dexterity, is pure prose. No modern poet would dream of introducing a chilly slab of scientific lecturing into the body of a passionate and mystical poem.[1]

And he offers this and similar passages[2] as proof that "the poet was without humour".

Let us grant that statements of scientific truth so lucid and unemotional as this are rare in modern verse. The fact remains that to a medieval reader the whole of Fisher's comment would "seem drunken lunacy". The imputation of lack of humour would leave him quite bewildered, since for the life of him he would not be able to conceive what humour had to do with it one way or other. The expression "pure prose" as applied to the *content* of a passage would have no meaning for him; and he would strongly object to the epithet "chilly", protesting that to him scientific knowledge was a matter of warm, not to say burning, interest. He would readily agree about the dexterous versification – and indeed Dante's sinewy, compact, and epigrammatic style is eminently adapted for the marshalling of complex facts into orderly sequences[3] – but he would altogether fail to see why this praise should be surrounded by a faint aura of reprobation. As for the mixture of passion, mysticism, and science in one and the same poem, he would highly approve it, as imparting an agreeable variety and comprehensiveness to the work. It would never occur to him that he ought to keep his head, his heart, and his religious experience in water-tight compartments, or that a poem might not properly appeal to all of them in turn. It is only the twentieth-century reader who is disconcerted by having to break down the Victorian bulkheads in order that his partitioned-off personality may flow together again.[4] The easiest way to do this

---

calls the "Dantesque image" of the twenty candles in *The Borderers*, Act iii, l. 1512; and Browning's image of the alloy in *The Ring and the Book*, Bk. i. 18–30.

1. H. A. L. Fisher: *A History of Europe* (Edwin Arnold, one-vol. ed., 1936), p. 286.

2. Such, presumably, as *Purg*. iv. 1–12; xv. 16–21; xviii. 49–69; xxv. 37–57; xxviii. 97–114, etc.

3. *Purg*. xviii. 49–69 is an outstanding example.

4. "A poetry which excludes the searchings of reason and the promptings of the moral sense is by so much the less impassioned, the less various and human, the less a product of the whole man at his full imaginative height" – C. Day Lewis: *The Poetic Image* (Cape, 1947), p. 133.

is to forget about the distinction between "prose" and "poetry", and to approach the *Comedy* as though it were a serious and intelligent novel – which, in fact, it is. For in the fourteenth century, the allegorical poem was precisely what the novel is to-day – the dominant literary form, into which a writer could pour, without incongruity, everything that he had to say about life and the universe.

The *Purgatorio*, like the *Inferno*, is – necessarily – concerned with souls who are suffering the penalty for sin. A good deal of ink and argument have consequently been expended from time to time in speculation as to why Dante's Purgatory is not simply his Hell in reverse. Nothing, obviously, would have been neater and easier than to build up all three *cantiche* on the basis of the Seven Capital Sins, punished in Hell in order of heinousness, and purged in reverse order in Purgatory, while in Heaven the seven opposing virtues should receive their appropriate rewards. There are indications in the *Inferno* that Dante himself may originally have contemplated making a shorter poem on these ingenuous lines, but if so, he abandoned the project before the end of the seventh canto, and incorporated the work that he had already done into a much wider scheme. For a poem on the grand scale, so tedious and repetitive a classification clearly would not do. Excellent theological justification can be produced for the threefold arrangement actually adopted; but the overriding reason for it is that Dante was not an engineer but a poet addressing a reading public, and therefore obliged both to be interesting and to satisfy his own artistic conscience. He is the most symmetrical of poets; but the symmetry of art is like that of nature, and is produced, not by a dead uniformity, but by a correspondence and balance of parts. The problem, as it presented itself to him, was not how to make Purgatory a "hell in reverse", but how to avoid doing so: how to provide the desirable variety and surprise in two long poems whose subjects were so fundamentally similar.

Accordingly, the "seven-sins" classification which lurks behind Cantos III–VII of the *Inferno* was discarded (if indeed it was ever really contemplated), and the classification into sins of Incontinence, Violence, and Fraud adopted in its place.[1] The victims of Lust, Gluttony, Avarice, and Wrath already dealt with were relegated to the

1. See *Inf.* Canto xi and Images.

suburbs of Upper Hell, and the nether abyss was opened up behind the barriers of Pride and within the walls of the City. On the other hand, this plan may have been intended from the start. Being based on classical sources, it is manifestly appropriate to a tour conducted under the guidance of Virgil, and although it does not formally invoke ecclesiastical authority it is not irreconcilable with it; moreover, it is in a manner foreshadowed and figured by the appearance of the Three Beasts in Canto I. It has the further great advantage that the use of two distinct systems of classification emphasizes the essential distinction between Hell and Purgatory: in the former, *acts of sin* produce their cumulative effects, the soul remaining at the lowest point of degradation to which it has unrepentantly willed to descend; in the latter, the *stain of sinfulness* is cleansed, the penitent soul shedding off successively all those imperfections which cling to it against its better will. Hell is concerned with the fruits, but Purgatory with the roots, of sin.

In any case, whether the arrangement of the *Inferno* as we have it was the offspring of first or second thoughts, we are still brought up against the problem with which we started; the *Purgatorio* must again exhibit souls who are suffering the penalty for sin, and the poet must somehow contrive to avoid a mere repetition of his effects.

The device which would immediately suggest itself to any modern moralist is not employed by Dante, or at least only in a very modified form. Purgatory is not related to Hell as Borstal is to Dartmoor: no intrinsic difference is made between remedial and retributive punishment. The pains of Purgatory are in themselves very like those of Hell, and some of them are but little lighter. The penitent Proud, like the impenitent Hypocrites, ceaselessly walk their appointed round bowed down by heavy weights; the penitent Lustful, like the impenitent Heretics, endure the torment of fire and heat immeasurable by earthly standards. The sole transforming difference is in the mental attitude of the sufferers. Dante has grasped the great essential which is so often overlooked in arguments about penal reform, namely, the prime necessity of persuading the culprit to accept judgement. If a man is once convinced of his own guilt, and that he is sentenced by a just tribunal, *all* punishment of whatever kind is remedial, since it lies with him to make it so; if he is not so convinced, then *all* punishment, however enlightened, remains merely vindictive, since he sees it so and will not make it otherwise. It has been well said by a great saint[1] that the fire of Hell is simply the light of God as experienced by those who reject it; to those, that is, who hold fast to their darling illusion of sin, the burning reality of holiness is a thing unbearable. To the penitent, that reality is a torment so long and only so long as any vestige of illusion remains to hamper their assent to it: they welcome the torment, as a sick man welcomes the pains of surgery, in order that the last crippling illusion may be burned away. The whole operation of Purgatory is directed to the freeing of the judgement and the will. Hell is the fleeing deeper into the iron-bound prison of the self – for the damned also, after their manner, seek their own torment:

> ... *the fire*
> *Of heavenly justice stings and spurs them so*
> *That all their fear is changed into desire.*[2]

Purgatory is the resolute breaking-down, at whatever cost, of the prison walls, so that the soul may be able to emerge at last into liberty and endure unscathed the unveiled light of reality. To this end:

> ... *heavenly justice keeps desire*
> *Set toward the pain as once 'twas toward the sin.*[3]

There is no difference in the justice; the only difference is in the repudiation or acceptance of judgement.

The accusation of cruelty, so often urged against the *Purgatorio* as well as against the *Inferno*, is therefore without meaning or relevance. Whether in Hell or in Purgatory, you get what you want – if that is what you really do want. If you insist on having your own way, you will get it: Hell is the enjoyment of your own way for ever. If you really want God's way for you, you will get it in Heaven, and the pains of Purgatory will not deter you, they will be welcomed as the means to that end. It must always be remembered that for Dante, as for all Catholic Christians, man is a responsible being. The dishonouring notion that he is the helpless puppet of circumstance or temperament, and therefore not justly liable to

1. St Catherine of Genoa. For all this doctrine, see Von Hügel: *The Mystical Element of Religion* (Dent, 1923), or in *Readings from Friedrich von Hügel* (Dent, 1929), Section: "The Soul of a Saint".

2. *Inf.* iii. 124–6.    3. *Purg.* xxi. 65–6.

punishment or reward, is one which the poet over and over again goes out of his way to refute. That is why so many of the "sermons" in the *Purgatory* deal with the subject of Free Will. When every allowance is made (and Dante makes generous allowance), when mercy and pity and grace have done all they can, the consequences of sin are the sinner's – to be borne, at his own choice, in a spirit of sullen rebellion or of ready acquiescence.

The contrast between Hell and Purgatory is therefore, in its essentials, a contrast of spiritual mood – a contrast, one may say, of atmosphere. And from the very first lines of the *Purgatorio*, Dante strikes the new, contrasting note, and strikes it ringingly:

> *For better waters heading with the wind*
> *My ship of genius now shakes out her sail.*

For many theologians, including St Thomas, Purgatory was imagined as a region bordering on Hell and rather like it; for some of the older visionaries, Hell and Purgatory were the same place of gloom, and all sinners endured the like torments, the only difference being that the sufferings of the saved were temporal and those of the damned, eternal. Dante will have none of this. The lowest part of his Purgatory is as remote from Hell as the surface of Earth from the Centre; its summit soars beyond Earth's atmosphere to a height no eye can reach. Hell is black, confined, stinking, noisy, and suffocating. The great Mountain of Purgatory rises in a pure sunlit solitude out of the windswept southern sea where never man set sail; nothing disturbs its calm, and the silence of its lofty spaces is scarcely broken save by the murmur of prayer and the crying of angelic voices; only when a soul is released to its triumph does the whole Mount quake and thunder with the shout of jubilee. And by night and day the flaming hosts of Heaven, which never were seen in Hell – the undimmed sun, the moon like a burnished mazer, the starry habitations of the Zodiac – wheel round the alien pole through a sky that knows no clouds. The whole landscape is washed in with a sweet and delicate austerity. At the Mountain's base, reeds and sand; the illimitable ocean in the dawnlight; the changing of the sky from orient sapphire through rose and gold to blue; the tang of the clean sea-breezes. On the lower slopes, which lie within earth's atmosphere, grass, with great ridges and outcrops of rock, and, nestling between two spurs of the Mountain, the secluded, scented, song-haunted, angel-guarded Valley of the Rulers, suddenly touched in with strong and vivid colour:

> *Gold and fine silver, crimson and ceruse,*
> *Wood yellow-lustrous, clear cerulean dye,*
> *Indigo, fresh-cracked emerald's brilliant hues,*
>
> *Matched with the foliage and the flowers that lie*
> *Heaped in that lap, would faint, as minor faints*
> *Beneath its major, and show dim thereby.*
>
> *Here nature had not only plied her paints,*
> *But had distilled, unnameable, unknown,*
> *The mingled sweetness of a thousand scents.*

But once past Peter's Gate and beyond the sphere of air, the hues of living nature vanish. Except for the two supernatural trees and the mysterious cascade on the Eighth Cornice, the Mountain is naked rock to the summit; "*Et statuit super petram pedes meos* – He brought me out of the horrible pit, out of the mire and clay, and set my feet upon the rock and ordered my goings."

And there, at length – when we have passed through the fire of the last cornice, when we have drowsed through the last enchanted night, sheltered by the rock-cleft, and

> *... through the narrow gap seen star on star*
> *Bigger and brighter than they'd ever been,*

when we have dreamed the last dream, and climbed the last steep ascent – there is the Forest.

We started from a Forest and we arrive at a Forest – not now the Dark Wood, "rude and rough and stubborn", whose memory chills the blood, but the Other Forest – the one from which we should have set out if Man had never sinned. Green and cool and fragrant with flowers, murmurous with bird-song and babbling brook and tree-tops rustling in the wind that moves with the turning worlds, holding fast its secret of repatriation and renewal, this is the place that all mankind remembers. This is the forgotten innocence, thrust back by the trauma of Adam's guilt into the unconsciousness of all his seed, the image of which troubles the imagination of some children and all poets with intimations of immortality. Do not at once turn to the end of the poem and look it up: the right way is to come to it, as the poet wanted us to come to it, "Forth of the steep, forth of the narrow ways", at the end of the enormous journey. And when you get there, remind yourself that this[1] is "grim Dante" writing, out of the depths of his fierce heart, of the vision that had haunted him from the beginning of his New Life. It is not Dante the pilgrim alone but also Dante the poet who is glad to be quit of Hell, and who experiences a renewal of delight on issuing forth from

> *... that dead air*
> *Which had oppressed my bosom and my sight.*

When, at the beginning of the Cantica, he exclaims: "Now from the grave wake poetry again!" he sincerely means what he says; and as he nears the end of it his song rises like a fountain. The *Purgatory*, with its freshness, sparkle, and gaiety, its tenderness, its journeying in hope, and its reunion of true lovers after estrangement and separation, is the very stuff of fairy-tale and quintessence of all the romances, handled with all the classical restraint which its author had learned from Virgil. When we have read it, we find it necessary to modify the accepted associations of the epithet "Dantesque". Whenever Dante is moved he writes like an angel – but angels are not all of one kind: between the *Inferno* and the *Purgatorio* we pass from the imagery of Michelangelo to the imagery of Fra Angelico.

Within the all-pervading atmosphere of "delight renewed", the change of outlook defines itself with endless subtlety. Courtesy is everywhere the key-note.

> *What different passes these from those we knew*
> *In Hell! for there with hideous howls of pain,*
> *And here with singing, we are ushered through.*

Here are no Charon, no Minos "horrible and girning", no Phlegyas or Minotaur to be coerced with "words of power". The "courteous porter" at Peter's Gate cries "Welcome!", the Angel of the Cornice "spreads his vans" in a gesture of salutation and divine humility. Virgil, mightiest among the Lost, greets the lowest and least among

1. (As may unworthiness define – for any translation wrongs it.)

these Blessed with an exquisite deference: "Spirits elect", "spirits formed for bliss". Dante – he who tore Bocca's hair from his scalp and mocked the prayer of Alberigo – shows to the penitent Blind on the Cornice of Envy the extreme of considerate delicacy. The spirits respond in like manner, lavishing on Virgil a reverent and admiring love whose pity leaves no wound; on Dante, a joyful wonder at the great grace vouchsafed him, which bears no trace of grudging. Eagerly they beseech the prayers of the living man and wish him God-speed upon his journey; readily they answer questions and supply helpful information; willingly they name themselves and their companions – not, like the horrible people in Caïna and Antenora, in order to denounce and defame one another, but anxious to admit their own failings and to yield the palm to others. In Hell, community is lost, or perverted into antagonism; but all Purgatory is united in the bonds of mutual goodwill and of goodwill to earth and Heaven. Not that its goodwill takes the form of an indiscriminate tolerance: the rebuke of sin is delivered on the Cornices as astringently as in the Infernal Circles, with a more sensitive perception and an acuter grief. But between the Church Expectant and the Church Militant there is exchange of love and prayer, and community of aspiration toward the Church Triumphant.

One consideration alone sets limits to the generous friendliness of the Penitent, and even for this they abound in polite apology. If Dante is (as always) disposed to linger in conversation, it is now not Virgil but the shades who urge him on his way. Hell and Heaven are eternal states, but the life of Purgatory, like that of earth, is a temporal process, and time is of its very essence. "Quick, quick! let not the precious time be lost!" is the constant cry, not only on the Cornice of Sloth, but throughout the Mountain. Every moment spared to Dante is a distraction from the blissful pain ("I call it pain; solace, I ought to say") – a distraction which, even for charity's sake, must not be prolonged out of measure. Dallying is a postponement of beatitude; even, in a sense, a robbery of God, who looks for the home-coming of His own. "Zeal to be moving goads us so that stay we cannot"; "Now go; I am reluctant to allow thy longer stay; thy presence stems my tears"; "Time's precious, and I make too long delay"; thus they excuse themselves. Thus, on the Cornice of the Lovers, the shades who press close to look on Dante are "scrupulous not to o'erstep the flame". As, in C. S. Lewis's book, the devil Screwtape angrily explains to Wormwood, "they *embrace* those pains; they would not barter them for any earthly pleasure."[1] That is the mark of Purgatory, the thing which Hell cannot understand, and which turns to folly earth's fumbling attempts to discriminate between retributive and remedial punishment. Their desire is turned to the torment as aforetime to the sin; they suffer no coercion but their own unwavering will: "my heart is fixed, O Lord, my heart is fixed."

It is, of course, open to anyone to say that the whole idea is morbid and exaggerated – open even to those who think nothing of queueing for twenty-four hours in acute discomfort to see the first night of a musical comedy which lasts three hours at most, which they are not sure of liking when they get there, and which they could see any other night with no trouble at all. Heaven offers only joy eternal and inexhaustible, and offers it once and for all. It is a question of value and proportion.

> *Reader, I would not have you turn, dismayed,*
> *From good resolves, for having heard me say*
> *How God ordains our debts should be repaid;*
>
> *Heed not the form of the affliction – nay,*
> *Think of what follows; pray you, think, this woe*
> *Cannot, at worst, outlast the Judgement Day.*

Thus Dante, knowing his world, and with a certain agreeable candour.

On this journey, from height to height of Christian paradox, Dante is accompanied and sustained by Virgil. It is frequently asserted, by people who ought to know better, that according to Dante the natural perfection for which Virgil stands is sufficient of itself to guide the soul as far as the Earthly Paradise. On the contrary, Dante takes the utmost pains from the very start to make it plain to the reader that this is not so. Even in Hell, Virgil had to be commissioned by Beatrice; even there, he had to invoke powers greater than his own; even there, he could not force the gates of Dis without divine assistance; nevertheless, there he speaks with authority. Here,

1. *The Screwtape Letters*, p. 159.

it is otherwise. He commanded Charon; he approaches Cato with obsequious deference, and even for this he is tartly rebuked: "Flattery is out of place here; if a heavenly Lady has sent you, that is enough." He is again rebuked by Cato for loitering, and challenged again by the Angel at Peter's Gate (where, having learned his lesson, he immediately produces his credentials). He does not know the way; he does not know the Rule of the Mountain; he repeatedly admits that his understanding of these high matters is partial and limited; he will even accept encouragement and advice from Dante. He is sensitively aware that he is only here, as it were, on sufferance, and shows a pathetic eagerness to explain to the "elect spirits" that his dwelling-place is Limbo and not Hell. Though he never loses his dignity he remains a little, so to say, self-conscious about his position. He is indeed still necessary to Dante; he is his "contact" in the world of spirits, lending him eyes to behold the "secret things"; he sustains and heartens him for the steep ascent; his teachings lay the foundation for the loftier revelation to come – he is the "preparation of the Gospel" here as in the world of the living. Yet the love and honour which Sordello and Statius make haste to pay him, his own grave and generous kindness, his new-found humility, and his increasingly warm and tender relations with his pupil, do but make us the more acutely aware of him as an alien here and an exile. Symptomatic at once of the enhanced affection and the diminished authority is the free use of his proper name; he who in Hell was, almost invariably, "master", "leader", or "lord" is now called, as often as anything else, simply "Virgil".[1]

All this serves to bind the charm of Virgil upon us like a spell. We had always known, of course, that there was a point beyond which Virgil could not go – he warned Dante of that at their first meeting. But Dante had almost forgotten it, and so had we: throughout the nightmare of Hell, Virgil had seemed the one unshifting point of security, steadfast as the rocks and, somehow, equally permanent. We share the shock and the sudden sense of desolation, when, as the Easter sun rises over Purgatory, we see Dante's shadow lie solitary on the slopes of the Mountain, and think for a moment that he and

[1]. The actual frequency of the titles, in the orginal, is: "maestro", *Inf.* 70, *Purg.* 25; "duca", *Inf.* 59, *Purg.* 24; "signore", *Inf.* 4, *Purg.* 2; "Virgilio", *Inf.* 5, *Purg.* 24. He is also called "dottore" twice in the *Inf.* and once in the *Purg.*

we are abandoned. The golden voice reassures us:

> ... *"Why wilt thou*
> *Always mistrust? Believ'st thou not I come*
> *Still at thy side and lead thee even now?"*

And then, with a wistful melancholy which belongs no less to the historical Virgil than to the *lachrymae rerum*[1] which he sang and to the unsubstantial perfection of this world which Dante's Virgil symbolizes:

> *" 'Tis vesper-tide already where the tomb*
> *Yet holds the body in which I once cast shade:*
> *Naples received it from Brundisium."*

The stroke is masterly, for the allegorical as well as for the literal sense. There is a moment in the life of the convert, there have been moments in the life of the Church herself, when it seems as though the embracing of the Christian life must involve the total "naughting" of all the natural powers and of every human interest. *"Quid Athenae Hierosolymis?* – What part," asked Tertullian, "has Athens in Jerusalem?" But it is not really so. Virgil will go at our side as long as time shall last – though subject at every step to those eternities which supersede because they contain and transcend him. And while he is with us, we love and honour him the more delicately because we know we hold him on so brief and frail a tenure. It is arguable that when the Humanists "shook off", as people say, "the trammels of religion", and discovered the things of this world as objects of veneration in their own right – as though Virgil could indeed in his sole power lead men to the Earthly Paradise – they began to lose the finer appreciation even of the world itself. Thus to the Christian centuries the flesh was holy (or *sacer* at least, in one or the other sense), and they veiled its awful majesty; to the Humanist centuries it was divine in its own right, and they exhibited it. Now, it is the commonplace of the magazine-cover; it has lost its *numen*. So, too, with the cult of knowledge for its own sake, declining from the Revival of Learning to the Brains Trust. Virgil without his heaven-born commission is only ourselves; and we cannot long venerate the familiar self. Familiarity breeds contempt, and con-

1. "The tearfulness of things."

tempt, despair: we are back before the Gates of Dis and face to face with the Gorgon. The condition of honouring Virgil is to remember what he is, and what we are:

> *Already stooping to my lord, he made*
> *To kiss his feet; but: "Brother, do not so,*
> *For shade thou art, and look'st upon a shade."*[1]

Technically, however, these premonitions of bereavement, this new and pathetic emphasis on Virgil, and this deepening of our affection for him, do but multiply tenfold the difficulty of the artistic task which Dante has set himself. Swapping horses in mid-stream is proverbially a perilous business; and nothing is as a rule more fatal to the maintenance of the audience's interest in a narrative or dramatic action than the disappearance, half-way through, of a sympathetic and important character. No poet ever took a greater risk than Dante when, at the emotional peak of his story, he swept away Virgil and set Beatrice in his vacant place.[2] A less courageous artist would have tried to let us down gently, soft-pedalling Virgil a little as we near the summit of the Mountain, and weaning us imperceptibly away from him. But Dante, with a serene confidence in his own powers, does precisely the opposite. He, whose impeccable poetic tact evaded so many minor hurdles over which lesser men have come crashing, evades nothing here. He builds his obstacle as high and wide as he can, and rides for it with a high heart and sheer consummate horsemanship. He brings it off – though, it may be, only just. But that he does bring it off, I am sure, because the more

1. The curiously swift process by which the cult of "Virgil" for his own sake tends to lose interest in the object of its veneration is exemplified in the history of Western Painting, where attention is seen to be focused successively upon: (*a*) (Pre-Humanist period): the body as symbol and vehicle of spirit (about 15 centuries); (*b*) (Post-Humanist Period): (1) bodies in themselves; (2) bodies as emotive stimuli; (3) bodies as patterns of light, form, texture, etc.; (4) light, form, texture, etc. as patterns in paint; (5) paint in itself; (6) abstracts (about 5 centuries). A parallel development takes place in poetry.

2. Euripides took a similar risk, and perhaps less successfully, in the *Hippolytus*, when he killed off Phaedra and brought in Theseus to carry the last scenes of the play. I say "perhaps", because we have to-day a good deal more sympathy than a Greek audience had for erring wives and considerably less for male chastity; so that we are very poor judges of how it was likely to strike a contemporary.

often we read the passage the more inevitably "right" it seems. It is not one of those *tours de force* which are impressive at first sight, and afterwards show flaws in the handling; it is a thing which, when the first shock is over, convinces us that it is done with perfect mastery, and could not possibly have been otherwise.

It is interesting to see how it is done. The appearance of Beatrice has been, of course, prepared throughout the poem. From time to time Virgil has pronounced her name and held out the expectation of meeting. It is a spur to greater effort:

> "... *on this mount's high crest*
> *Thou shalt behold her, smiling and in bliss.*"
>
> "*O sir," said I, "let us make greater haste!*
> *I can, indeed – I'm much less tired already.*"

Sometimes it is a promise of deeper spiritual satisfaction, openly emphasized:

> "*So much as reason here distinguisheth*
> *I can unfold," said he; "thereafter, sound*
> *Beatrice's mind alone, for that needs faith*" –

or slipped in, as it were, casually at the end of a long discourse, with a hint of delightful and intimate conversations to come:

> "*And this same noble faculty it is*
> *Beatrice calls Free Will; if she thereon*
> *Should speak with thee, look thou remember this.*"

The name of the beloved is the apple to lure her lover through the fire and the courage that strengthens him to bear its burning; the eyes of Beatrice, "bright with bliss", shine to him through that last great speech in which the lips of Virgil crown and mitre him and then are silent for ever. And after that, there is an interlude, during which we give ourselves over to the enchantment of the Forest.

A voice is heard singing; a Lady appears – alone, and gathering flowers. Is this she? No. As in the courtly *Romance of Tristan*, this miracle of beauty, lovelier than Cytheraea at her loveliest, is but her handmaiden: it is not yet she. The Lady is gracious; she talks of the Golden Age of which the ancient poets sang – perhaps they were not wrong – perhaps they were indeed remembering Eden. Dante looks round to see if Virgil has heard this tribute – Yes, Virgil is there, he has heard, he smiles, we are reassured.

Then slowly, from the mysterious depths of the Forest, come the lights, and the singing, the great mysterious pageant unfolding itself, with the triumph-car in its midst, drawn by the Gryphon, the "Twy-formed ambiguity", the sacramental image of the God-Manhood. And now, exalted upon the car, amid the angels and the showering roses, as it might be the Holy Host Itself, veiled, yet known instantly, unchanged and unmistakable, stepping straight out of Dante's past into his present, there appears that which makes his flesh shake and his blood hammer in his veins. With a line of Virgil's verse upon his lips, he once more turns to seek the strength and stay who never has failed him yet – and Virgil is not there.

And at this point Dante, boldly anticipating the cry of protest which trembles on his readers' lips, says firmly:

> *And not for all that our First Mother lost*
> *Could I forbid the smutching tears to steep*
> *My cheeks, once cleansed with dew from all their dust.*

It was Virgil who had cleansed his cheeks, far down below upon the sandy shore of the Island. And while we are remembering this, the voice of Beatrice breaks in upon us:

> *"Dante, weep not for Virgil's going – keep*
> *As yet from weeping; weep not yet, for soon*
> *Another sword shall give thee cause to weep."*

And for a canto and a half she heaps reproaches upon him, showing no mercy, hammering him into such a state of speechless tears and misery that we feel we cannot bear to see any grown man so publicly humiliated. But she goes on and on until she breaks him – and with the snapping of the tension and the plunge into the sundering stream, we realize how taut that tension has been. For when he stands before her on the other bank, we discover that Lethe water has had its effect upon us too. We have done the very thing we could have sworn we should never do – we had, for the moment, quite forgotten Virgil.

As the scene was ushered in, so it is ushered out, with a formal masque, the actors in which are the conventional personified abstractions of simple allegory. The trick of the thing lies in its formal structure: the slow, very slowly quickening tempo of the preparation; the interposition between Virgil and Beatrice of the long lyrical interlude (the longest sustained lyrical passage in the entire work); the careful setting and framing of the central scene between two highly elaborate and artificial masques; the astounding dramatic swiftness of the actual change-over; the sheer weight and drive of the scene itself; and the fact that, in this crucial passage of the story's action, literal and allegorical meanings are so closely and intimately fused that it is possible, and at the first reading inevitable, to take it throughout at the purely human level. It is a man and a woman meeting, after a long estrangement for which he is to blame; she is justly indignant, and he finds nothing to say for himself. She is the Sacrament of the Body, she is divine Theology, she is the vehicle of Grace, she is the Body of Christ in the Church – but all these identities are summed up in the single identity of her person:

> *"Look on us well; we are indeed, we are*
> *Beatrice...."*

Having said that, she has said everything.

When we examine the structure of these concluding cantos of *Purgatory*, it is more than ever evident that we are in the hands of a born dramatist. Had he lived at a time when drama was the dominant form, the plays of Dante might be holding the stage to this day. His work has all the marks: the solid planting and setting of a dramatic action; the brisk economy of the dialogue; the instinctive avoidance of scenic incongruities; the sure recognition of the *scène-à-faire*; the knack of relieving a situation with a touch of high comedy; the ability to establish character in a line or two; the rejection of ramblings and embroideries; the knowledge of when to stop. It is this compact and sinewy quality in his narrative which holds the reader's attention. Other medieval poems delight by their surface texture; his, by its architecture.

The mere fact, however, that the interest is here so forcibly concentrated upon the literal and personal aspects of the story makes it peculiarly important for us to approach the scene without period preconceptions. And for the English reader, with his mind full of vague expectations gathered from his own literature and art, it is often difficult to discern the features of the real Beatrice beneath the veil – one might say, the shroud – cast over them by the Pre-Raphaelites. In the works, written or painted, of D. G. Rossetti and his circle, reference to the *Purgatorio* and *Paradiso* is rare and, as it were, reluctant; their brooding fancy, obsessed by images of longing and loss of death, poured itself readily into the mould of the *Vita Nuova*, and, overflowing upon actuality, identified the figure of the transhumanized Beatrice with that of the melancholy and consumptive Elizabeth Siddal. The tone is uniformly elegiac, the emphasis upon parting rather than upon reunion. But if we come to the *Comedy* expecting to encounter the Beatrice of *Dante's Dream*, *Beata Beatrix*, or *The Blessed Damozel*, we shall receive a shock – pleasurable or otherwise according as we prefer to connect love with the will to life or the will to death; in either case, severe. The beatified lady displays no romantic languor: her bearing is energetic, and the language in which she welcomes back her prodigal lover is crisp and forcible, not to say tart. Her love for him – for it is love, and the poet means us so to understand it – expresses itself, woman's fashion, in a mixture of exasperated reproach and practical charity. Dante has been in desperate peril – entirely by his own fault; she has exerted herself to extricate him; having got him back safe, she rounds upon him with a hearty scolding, before forgiving and smiling upon him and leading him homeward into bliss.

It is interesting to see Rossetti, in the final stanzas of the poem called *Dante at Verona*, recoiling from this image of an active felicity:

> Ah! haply now the heavenly guide
>  Was not the last form seen by him:
>  But here that Beatrice stood slim
> And bowed in passing at his side,
> For whom in youth his heart made moan
> Then when the city sat alone.

> Clearly herself: the same whom he
>  Met, not past girlhood, in the street ...
>   ... But indeed
> It may be memory might recall
> Last to him then the first of all –
> The child his boyhood bore in heed
> Nine years ...

It may be memory might; but if so, its operations ran counter to the whole intention of his poem. For if there is one thing which emerges emphatically from the text, it is that Dante desires no substitution of the past for the present, no flight back into infancy, no eclipsing of the glorified reality by the former earthly image. "Clearly herself" she is, and remains, in that dramatic moment of meeting: between the Florentine girl and the "heavenly guide" there is no solution of continuity. Only, the new is better: even the dim and distant apprehension of it is more satisfying than the fullness of mortal vision:

> *And there, beneath her veil, beyond the stream,*
> *Her former self, methought, she more outshone*
> *Than here, with others, she once outshone them.*

Her unveiled beauty passes the wits of poets to communicate; and as it rises from sphere to sphere of Heaven it glows with an ever more radiant splendour. So Dante says: if he says it, it is because he means us to believe it, and our refusal does him no honour.

But there are others besides Rossetti who find belief difficult. Every generation of readers is liable to fasten upon the poet of another age its own peculiar associative obsessions; and there are nearly always hooks in his work on which such associations can plausibly be hung. Modern fashions in perversity, without abandoning the identification of sexual love with the will to destruction, have blocked the way to sanity at the more cheerful and domestic end of the corridor with a bogey called the "mother-image". Between these two obstructions, any poet who ventures to write about a woman can be securely trapped, and Dante is no exception. Miss Maud Bodkin, for example, has expressed herself on the subject in the following ominous words:

To the mischief-working egoism so often present in the parent-child relation we have become so sensitive that when we recognize it in the vision of Dante there is apt to be a moment of recoil, the intensity of which is perhaps the measure of our spontaneous sympathy with Freud's teaching. ... The mother-imago had perhaps a part to play in the activity of creative minds of Dante's age that it can no longer fulfil for minds of our own time. ... Within my own experience it is only as I relate the dialogue and description of the vision to the movement of the poem in its completeness that I can pass beyond the feeling of revulsion against what seems the dominance in the mind of Dante of the mother-imago. ...

After a reference to the *Eumenides* of Aeschylus, she adds:

> The mother-imago, thus transformed to embody an inward aspiration, and ideal of the good life [the "City-ideal"], possesses a hold upon the deep springs of instinctive energy that enables it to encounter and withstand the power of the imago in its phase of tyranny and terror.[1]

How seriously are we to take these statements? I think we must allow them considerable weight, though I believe them to be rather exaggerated so far as the common reader is concerned. If the mere suggestion of a "parent-child relation" has become revolting to us, so that we must sterilize the concept of motherhood in the political associations of the city-state before we can cleanse it from associations of "tyranny and terror", then the situation is a parlous one, both for literature and for life. Moreover, a little thought will show that every corridor in the Palace of Art is similarly made impassable by the images of Oedipus, Electra (though Lot's Daughters would make a better group), Tamar, Pylades, Ganymede, Sappho, Pasiphaë, and other assorted allegories, so that there is no conceivable human relationship which has not been involved by this latest "treason of the clerks" in an ambiguity that unfits it for honest use. Rare indeed are those who can contrive to enter the world without being born of woman; and most of us find ourselves surrounded with domestic and social contacts of one kind or another. Between the bishops who assure us that the family is the one and only seed-bed of all the virtues, and the psychiatrists who warn us that it is a hotbed of all the vices, we hardly know how to advise any child to enter upon the hazard of existence. Meanwhile, the poets, nervous of using the great traditional archetypes lest they should provoke repulsion or misunderstanding, and driven to invent new ones at the risk of not being understood at all, are rendered tongue-tied by self-consciousness. The critic also, dealing with older poets for whom "perhaps" the fundamentals of human society provided

---

1. Maud Bodkin: *Archetypal Patterns in Poetry*, pp. 182, 183, 185. I have chosen this work to illustrate my argument because of its outstanding quality and wide critical influence. There are many others from which I might have quoted in the same sense.

creative material, is in a cleft stick: he must either write his author down a psychopath or himself a simpleton: and professional critics cannot afford to be thought naïve.

Now it is perfectly true that, in a fallen world, every natural institution, and indeed every natural virtue, bears within itself the seeds of its equal and opposite perversion. That is precisely why the upper Cornices of Purgatory are devoted to the purgation of a too-eager love of the Secondary Goods. Those who deify the family, in disregard of Christ's reiterated warnings,[1] are from the Christian point of view equally in error with those who deify sex, or power, or pleasure. But what the opposite party is in danger of forgetting is the doctrine, well known to the Schoolmen, that it is evil which is a parasite upon the good, and not the other way round. Only good can originate anything: evil can only deform and corrupt the good already existing. The error lies in accepting the perversion as the norm, thus involving the image itself, with all its associations good or bad, in that repulsion to which Miss Bodkin so candidly admits.

Let us at once agree that Dante does use the mother-image with respect to Beatrice, and more than once – though not so persistently as he uses the father-image with respect to Virgil. It would even be possible to argue that the disappearance of Virgil at the very moment of Beatrice's appearance symbolizes Dante's unconscious desire to eliminate a tenderly loved father in favour of a tyrannous and terrifying mother.[2] Certainly the tone of Beatrice's reproaches wakes an echo only too desolatingly familiar in the days of our childhood: "What have you been up to? ... Why? ... Have you any excuse? ... Come now, be your age – look me in the face and speak the truth.... How many times have I told you? ... The moment my back is turned you get into mischief.... Are you sorry? ... Really sorry? ... Very well, then, stop crying and wash your face, and we will say no more about it." We may also note that at one point[3] the mother-image is used with respect to Virgil, in connexion, this time, not with terror but with refuge and escape from terror. We may infer that Dante recognized, and did not

1. E.g. *Matt.* xii. 47–50; *Matt.* x. 37; *Luke* ix. 59–60.
2. I say "it would be possible", because that kind of thing is very easy to do, and it is most important not to seem naïve; but I do not seriously propose to do anything of the sort.
3. *Inf.* xxiii. 37–42.

dislike, a certain maternal quality in the woman he loved, and that he thought of a mother as a being who could be rather formidable when one had been naughty, but full of practical help and comfort when one was in danger or distress. We need not be concerned to deny the dominance, or at any rate the presence, of the "mother-imago" in the figure of Beatrice, but only to ask why it is there. One explanation is that "Dante's love for Beatrice, the Florentine maiden, seems to have had an infantile character"[1] – or, to put it bluntly, that he was a milksop. Another possible explanation is that he was one of those rare men who know what their wives and other female belongings really think about them. The question is worth examining, because it involves a great deal more than the psychology of any one man, however great a poet.

Let us begin by reminding ourselves that Dante was nurtured upon the poetic doctrine of Courtly Love. That doctrine, arising out of the conditions of a feudal society, did not, strictly speaking, represent an attitude to sex. It did not (directly at any rate) determine your behaviour to your wife, or to your trull. In its origin, it was a devotion – part amorous and part worshipful – to a particular lady who in rank and culture was your acknowledged superior, and who was addressed normally as *"madonna"*, but frequently also, among those Provençal poets with whom the cult started, by the masculine title *"midons* – my liege".[2] It postulated, therefore, a subservience and humility on the man's part, which was extended to cover his general behaviour to all ladies, though not by any means necessarily to all women. He took orders from his lady, but his wife and daughters took orders from him; if by any chance he succeeded in marrying the object of his worship, she ceased to be his liege-lady and became his servant. The courtly convention, running counter as it did to ecclesiastical and civil sanctions, was always anomalous and felt to be so; and at the best of times a good deal of extravagance entered into the manner of its expression. Yet it was a genuine power and a genuine inspiration; it was the most important factor in adjusting the earlier sordid and unbalanced relations between man and woman, and it influences our whole conception of those relations

1. Bodkin: *op. cit.* p. 190.
2. Similarly, before Queen Elizabeth II came to the throne, she was "our Princess"; but since her accession she may rightly say of herself, in the phrase used by Queen Elizabeth I, "I am your Prince."

down to the present day. But although it eventually produced an attitude to sex, it began as a specialized attitude to a particular person – a fact that we shall need to remember.

And, with all its extravagance, the doctrine of Courtly Love is so far realistic that it assigns all the amorous fuss and to-do, all the tormented philosophy of love, to the male. He presents his pierced and burning heart on a plate, wreathed round with elegant devices: the lady (who has a pretty taste in such matters) considers it critically and either approves it or waves it away. It may be death to him, but to her it is a pastime. That, at all events, is the theory, and it is very sharply distinguished from certain later theories – particularly that of the Romantic Revival or Byronic period. And art and literature, as well as experience, bear witness that on the whole woman's preoccupation is not with the subtleties of love but with the practical problems of marriage and household. Women are interested not in sex, but in love-affairs; not in passion but in people; not in man but in men. Whether this difference between the sexes is organic or merely occupational has yet to be proved. But it is very observable that whereas there has been from time immemorial an Enigma of Woman, there is no corresponding Enigma of Man. When women write or talk (and they have always talked pretty freely) one gets the impression that Man as such is an open book to them: their problem is to do their best with the individual males presented for their attention. The sentiment, "Man's love is of man's life a thing apart; 'tis woman's whole existence" is, in fact, a piece of male wishful thinking, which can only be made to come true by depriving the life of the leisured woman of every other practical and intellectual interest. Lovers, husbands, children, households – these are major feminine preoccupations: but not love. It is the male who looks upon amorous adventure as an end in itself, and dignifies it with a metaphysic. The great love-lyrics, the great love-tragedies, the romantic agony, the religion of beauty, the cult of the *ewig Weibliches*, the entire mystique of sex is, in historic fact, of masculine invention. The exaltation of virginity, the worship of the dark Eros, the apotheosis of motherhood, are alike the work of man; the Fatal Woman is his discovery (and so, indeed, is the Fatal Man: Faust and Don Juan, Lovelace and Manfred are not of woman born). If we search the pages of serious literature for the woman-made male counter-

parts of Helen and Cleopatra, Dido and Delilah, of Salome, of Cly-
temnestra, of Guinevere, Isolde, and Morgan le Fay, of Dolores
and the Gioconda, of Lamia and Ligeia and Lilith, of Manon Les-
caut, Ann Whitefield, and all the devouring women who have pur-
sued their devastating way through a shambles of broken hearts and
broken lives, we shall find but a brief list, almost beginning and end-
ing with the comparatively harmless figure of Mr Edward Fairfax
Rochester.[1] To this characteristically masculine theme the character-
istic feminine counter-theme is that which makes itself heard with
a peculiar clarity in mid-movement as it were between *Clarissa
Harlowe* and *Don Juan* and even from the heart of leisure: "Had you
behaved in a more gentlemanlike manner ..." "She remembered
that he had yet to learn to be laughed at."[2] When I say that the
accents of Dante's Beatrice have much in common with those of
Elizabeth Bennet, I intend a compliment, not only to the poet's cen-
tral and abiding sanity, but also to the sensitive accuracy of his femi-
nine psychology. "Had you behaved in a more gentlemanlike
manner ..." Yes, indeed.

The Beatrice of the *Vita Nuova* is the radiant miracle of a young
man's passionate fancy; the Beatrice of the *Commedia* is seen with

1. Take, for example, this typical sentence from Marcus Cunliffe's
*Literature of the U.S.* (Pelican Books, 1964, p. 288), which might be paralleled
from a hundred other sources: "She [a character in a novel of William
Faulkner's] is more than a shiftless poor-white girl with an illegitimate
baby: she is *the huge warm trap of womanhood which awaits all men*" – and try
to produce a "masculine counterpart" to the phrase I have italicized, which
shall be equally trite, familiar, and acceptable to the sex not concerned.

Or contrast, in Jung's psychological system, the rich, poetic, and magical
content of the *anima* in the male with that ascribed to the corresponding
*animus* in the female – so desiccated, impoverished, and lacking in any touch
of the numinous that it might appear to have been artificially patched
together for the sole purpose of completing the symmetrical pattern. (See,
e.g., Frieda Fordham: *An Introduction to Jung's Psychology*, Pelican Books,
1953, pp. 54–8.)

Jung himself has been struck by the odd literary lacuna indicated above:
"The figure of the animus, the man in the woman, is equally paradoxical.
... It is a curious fact that no woman of talent has succeeded in producing
an adequate picture [of it]. It may be that a woman's animus writes her
novels for her, and thus escapes portrayal" (*The Integration of the Personality*,
Routledge and Kegan Paul, 1952, p. 23). That is, of course, a comfortable
way of accounting for it. Jung claims to have found "a clever and accurate
picture" of the animus in a novel by a male author; but what the soldier said
is not evidence.

2. Jane Austen: *Pride and Prejudice*, chaps. 34, 58.

adult eyes, and is more maturely and completely a woman. The poet of the *Purgatorio* was, after all, neither child nor boy, but a grown man with a wife and four children of his own; the late Charles Williams was wont to remark that there was probably more of Gemma in Beatrice than Dante himself quite knew. Nevertheless – and this is where both Rossetti and the "mother-imago" theorists are right about the facts – the two Beatrices are one Beatrice, because all the Dantes are one Dante. "*Una donna m'apparve* – there appeared to me a lady": and in the shock of that meeting all times rush together; the child and the youth are instantly and vividly alive in the fifty-year-old man. This is the poet's pre-eminent gift, his freehold and foretaste of eternity. So fresh, so convincing, so directly felt and communicated is the impact of that meeting that it is sometimes difficult to remember that no such encounter ever in fact took place. It is vision or imagination; but Dante persuades us that it happened, because as he wrote he felt it happen, and all his responses were alive to it. He never, like Wordsworth, lost his childhood; for him the "glory and the dream" never faded into "the light of common day". At no point does he need to look wistfully back, or to set the compensatory advantages of age against those of his vanished youth: everything that he ever was is with him to the end; he does not *remember* what he once felt, but whenever he wills to feel it he feels it again, unaltered and undimmed. When and because Wordsworth lost touch with his own younger self he ceased to be a supreme poet and we deplore the fact as much as he did. But Dante, who never lost touch, grew in wisdom and stature to the end; why should we deplore that?

Yet between the "parent-child" image in Dante and the bogey-image of Freudian myth there is a profound difference, and it is not hard to see what that difference is. We have only to remember (and here we can most cordially agree with Miss Bodkin) that the "mother-imago" passages must be studied in relation to "the movement of the poem in its completeness." There will then be no need to invoke the laws of Athens, to release Dante from a tyrannous fixation. Bear in mind first of all that throughout the poem Dante is passing judgement on Dante. If Beatrice rebukes Dante the pilgrim for his childish tears and terrors, reminding him caustically that he is not a child but an adult and responsible man, it is Dante the poet who puts those words in her mouth. She does not encourage any flight from reality or "retreat to the womb"; and if she does not, then he does not. In the second place, the gravamen of the charge against the "parent-child relation" is possessiveness: that, like that of the succubus with the lover, it is a relation of devourer and devoured. But if we pursue our researches into the *Paradiso* we find that Beatrice shows no desire to possess Dante: she takes him with one hand only to give him away with the other. "Look on us well; we are indeed Beatrice";[1] "Not only in my eyes is Paradise";[2] "Look on me, what I am; thou hast seen things which make thee mighty to endure my smile";[3] "Why does my face so enamour thee that thou turnest not to look upon the company of Christ's people?"[4] The rhythm of that movement is unmistakable: "I am myself; I am not everything; I am but a type of that which is greater than I; turn from the type to the Archetype." When she has completed her work for her lover, she quietly hands him over to St Bernard, herself returning to her own joy in everlasting contemplation of the "Eternal Fountain". She is not the heavenly mother, nor even the heavenly mistress, so much as – and this figure also is Dante's[5] – the heavenly schoolmistress, who having seen her pupil safely through his examination, goes on her way rejoicing. She looses him into freedom – even from herself – and he is willing to be set free. With grateful love he praises her, in words which establish her as a type of the Incarnate,[6] and then abandons himself to the contemplation of that Image in which all other images are included and fulfilled; Christ our Father, Christ our Mother, Christ our Lover and Spouse, Christ our Friend, Christ our Brother, Christ our Child – Christ the one Archetypal Pattern, of whom all patterns and all relationships are but the ectypes, and concerning whom St Augustine said: "I am the food of the full-grown; become a man and thou shalt feed on Me." The "movement of the poem as a whole" is towards that central Image, nor can it be interpreted otherwise than by reference to that movement, which carries all the minor motions with it as the tide carries the running and returning of the wave.

And here it is seen to be especially relevant that Christianity,

1. *Purg.* xxx. 73.   2. *Para.* xviii. 21.   3. *Para.* xxiii. 46–8.
4. *Para.* xxiii. 70–3.   5. *Para.* xxv. 64.   6. *Para.* xxxi. 80–1.

which very notoriously makes use of the Parental Image, is insistent to deny that God's love is "possessive" in the sense complained of. God does not, in the manner of the Gnostic's Absolute Being, desire the absorption of the many in the One; His love is anxiously directed to confirm each individual soul in its own identity, so that, the nearer it draws to Him, the more truly it becomes its unique and personal self. This, by the mouth of Beatrice, Dante categorically affirms to be the aim of Creation: "Not that He might acquire any advantage (*bene*) for Himself, for that is impossible, but that His splendour, shining back to Him, might be able to declare: *I am* (*subsisto*) ... did the First Love unfold Himself into new loves."[1] It is the jealousy for the independence of the creature that prompts the means for man's redemption: "For God was more generous in giving Himself, to enable man to raise himself again, than if He had by His own power remitted [the consequences of the Fall]."[2] This redemption is open to every man, individually, to accept or reject, because his will is free, and God will not usurp it. To make a great boast about defying Omnipotence is bombastic and absurd: it is a thing that any fool can do, since his freedom is itself the act of Omnipotence.

This character, which has also been called the "scandal", of particularity, stamped upon Christianity, is of its very essence, and governs all the imagery of its poets. Because of it, Dante's encounter with an individual living woman can be made the image of the soul's encounter with a personal living God. The Infinite came once into the finite as a single and particular Person; the company of His elect is made up of single and particular persons, each having single and particular relationships with Himself, and with each other. If we try to efface from the Christian revelation the brand of singularity, then what we shall have left is not Christianity at all. The symbolism of the *Commedia* will be unintelligible to us unless we remember this basic principle, which at every level runs counter to contemporary notions of what a religious revelation should be. Another quotation or two from Miss Bodkin's book will illuminate our modern difficulty. Here it is at the human level:

The famous lines with which the drama of Faust closes live in poetic tradition as expressing that aspect of the woman archetype which we

1. *Para.* xxix. 13–18.       2. *Para.* vii. 115–17.

have studied in its first great embodiment in Dante's *Commedia*.

> *Das Ewig-Weibliche*
> *Zieht uns hinan.*
> (The Eternal Feminine
> Draws us up yonder.)[1]

Possibly, even more in the case of a woman than of a man reader, there is a negative reaction to be eliminated, against what seems extravagant adulation of an individual person, before one can fully respond to Dante's conception of a personal love transfigured to become a way of ascent to Heaven.[2]

Now, the first thing to be said about these two passages is that they are mutually contradictory. Personal love for *a* woman, and a diffused idealism about Woman-in-general are two different things; they may or may not coexist in the same person – if they do, either the second is a mere overflow and by-product of the first, or the first is a mere by-product of the second and is destroyed by it. But the question is: which is the redeeming power? In Dante's case there is no possible doubt about it: the redemption is in the personal love. I do not, in fact, find in his work any vestiges of "*Ewig-Weiblich*" mystique: there is the one Lady, there are a number of subsidiary and individual ladies; but of mere Femininity as a power for good or evil there is no more trace than in the Gospels. Further, I am not convinced about the "woman reader". I think that, as I have indicated before, the average woman of intelligence is fairly ready to believe in the value of a personal relationship, but the idea of a peculiar *mana* attached to femaleness as such, deriving as it does from primitive fertility-cults and nature-magic, is likely to strike her as either nonsensical or repellent.

Beside these two passages let us place a third, which tackles the problem at the divine level:

Poetry makes no claim to historic truth; the Gospel story does make this claim. Poetic faith, even when serious and adequate, in the myth of Shelley, or in the allegory of Dante, need assert no more than that satisfying expression has been given to impulses and ideals active within our experience. Adequate faith in the Gospel story must assert, some would urge, that the selfless love and compassion, joined with perfect insight, that makes the glory of our moral ideal, became, once

1. Bodkin, *op. cit.* p. 142.    2. Bodkin, *op. cit.* p. 142.

*Introduction*

for all, incarnate within the temporal series. Through the identification of the historic Jesus with the transcendent and eternal religious object, it has been argued, "the Christian, and he alone, can find a solution to the paradox of the inherence of eternity in time and of the absolute in the finite" (Christopher Dawson: *Progress and Religion*). It is, I think, rightly urged that so far as this paradox has been solved for imagination and feeling, it is through the Christian image of God in man. Yet, in my mind, the reference of the image to a certain point in the historic series is not essential to this conciliation, and to such minimum of faith as may sustain the moral life.[1]

Taken thus together, the two passages on Beatrice and the passage on Jesus display the same trend: the flight from the concrete, individualized, historical, and mystical into the abstract, generalized, mythical, and magical – a trend only too faithfully reflected (especially in the third excerpt) in the imprecision of vocabulary and style. It is not our business at the moment to inquire whether a diffused incarnation of attributes is in fact more poetically inspiring than a real baby in a real manger, or whether such cautious "minimum of faith as may sustain the moral life" was quite what Dante had in mind when he brought the three Theological Graces dancing at the wheel of his Lady's triumph-car. But we must clearly understand that to the medieval mind this whole trend could only appear as a retrogression into the infantilism of pagan ignorance. Thirteen Christian centuries had toiled to bring conscious order out of subliminal chaos; to replace the female principle and the Great Mother by the personal operation of the Mother of God; to bind the legends of dead-and-risen deities to a place and date: "suffered under Pontius Pilate ... and the third day rose again"; to drag the dark images of fable and fancy into the daylight of history and reason. The Christian formula is not: "Humanity manifests certain adumbrations of the divine", but: "*This* man was very God." On that pivot of singularity the whole Christian interpretation of phenomena uncompromisingly turns.

From our recent reversal of the Christian process in these matters there results the quite peculiar connotation which modern criticism gives to the words "real" and "reality". It locates "reality" almost exclusively in the instinctive, the unconscious, or the anti-rational, discounting what the poet actually said in favour of what (it is supposed) his words "really" convey. Thus, Virgil was "really" on Dido's side against Aeneas; Satan is Milton's "real" hero; Dante's "real" sympathies are with Francesca and Farinata: everything that these poets explicitly say to the contrary – even though that contrary may be involved in the very stuff of their chosen theme and expressed in their most magnificently inspired verse – is hypocrisy, or a concession to the conventions, or, perhaps, the rationalization of some other "real" but unavowed feeling, such as cruelty, envy, or a sense of inferiority. The line between pagan and Christian values is here very sharply drawn, even in the same generation of critics. Thus, Miss Bodkin offers as a hypothesis concerning Dante's Francesca, that she "gives expression to that *instinctive basis of adult love* that is lacking, or inadequately represented, in Beatrice";[1] Charles Williams, on the other hand, says precisely: "The formal sin here is the adultery of the two lovers [Paolo and Francesca], the poetic sin is *their shrinking from the adult love demanded of them*, and their refusal of the opportunity of glory."[2] For the one, the "basis of adult love" is instinct; for the other, a deliberate act of the will. There can, of course, be no doubt that Dante shares the instinct and (to that extent) sympathizes with the sin: the condemnation is pronounced by his considered judgement. But which is the "real" Dante – the sympathizer or the judge? Dante himself would not have hesitated: and if you had said, as Beatrice says to him, that a good deal of his own conduct belied his judgement, he would have retorted, not that he was justified in acting down to his "real" feelings, but that he was to blame for not acting up to his "real" convictions. But if you were to go on to ask him whether instinct was not the basis of adult love, he would quite certainly reply: "Instinct is the basis of *all* love, and is without error so far as it goes. We have an instinctive love (*amor naturale*) for whatever is good and pleasing. But to follow instinct without the control of the judgement is the mark of childishness. The business of the judgement is so to order the natural affections that our pursuit of the lesser good is subordinated to that of the greater; and this is rational love (*amor d' animo*). Inasmuch as God is more real than any of His creatures (since His reality is absolute,

1. *Op. cit.* p. 204.
2. *The Figure of Beatrice*, p. 118 (italics mine in both cases).

theirs conditioned by His) our love for God partakes of the greater reality of its object. Because of sin, which perverts judgement, the rational love may err; but it is more 'real' in us than instinctive love alone, because more fully human, the rational soul being the substantial form which distinguishes man from the animals."

This much we know he would have said, for he has said it – notably in the *Purgatorio*.[1] He would probably have approved our adding a caution against trying to distinguish a "real" Dante, made up of unconscious instincts and appetites, from an "artificial" Dante, made up of conscious reason and will – as though the faculties had independent existence apart from the person who exercises them. We may for convenience speak of them so, by way of an allegory or fiction; but in fact they are only "accidents existing in a substance."[2] There is but one Dante, who feels and desires and wills, and rationally judges himself: "one single soul complete, alive and sensitive and self-aware."[3]

To the baffling complexity of human motives Dante is very much alive, as we shall see when, in the *Paradiso*, he comes to deal with the "absolute" and the "conditioned" will.[4] But he would set about finding the "reality" – that is, the basic truth – of a man, not by separating the conscious from the unconscious, or instinct from reason, but by observing the permanent orientation of the whole personality – by seeing what "good" it is that the will persistently pursues, despite all deviations due to error, inconstancy, or pressure of environment. Guido da Montefeltro, dying in complacent reliance upon an absolution not earned by contrition, discovers that he had never truly wanted God;[5] Buonconte da Montefeltro, dying unabsolved with the name of Mary on his lips, discovers that he had never truly wanted anything else.[6] So, when Dante himself has confessed to Beatrice his sins of unfaithfulness and has plunged in the waters of Lethe which drown all memory of error, he says to her with naïve bewilderment: "I do not remember that ever I estranged

---

1. Cantos xviii, xix, xxv: see notes *in loc.*
2. *V. N.* xxv. "A person ... might be perplexed by the way I talk about Love, as though he were a thing in himself, and not merely an intelligent substance (i.e. being), but a corporeal substance. Which thing, according to the truth, is false, for Love exists, not as a substance but as an accident in a substance."

3. *Purg.* xxv. 74–5.
4. *Para.* iv. 73 *sqq.*   5. *Inf.* xxvii. 67 *sqq.*   6. *Purg.* v. 94 *sqq.*

myself from you." And, fundamentally, he is quite right: his love for Beatrice and what she stands for is the one instinct to which his will and reason had always fully assented.

The point to which my argument tends is this. Like the great religion which (in the scholastic sense) "informs" its matter – makes it, that is, the kind of thing it is – the *Commedia* is at the same time intensely personal and magnificently public. Consequently it does not yield much fruit to analysis along the lines either of "free association" (involving the atomization of the personality) or of "private symbolism" (involving the atomization of society). Dante's experience is personal, but it is not in the least private; it is universal, and he intends it to be thus understood. He is a poet in the ancient tradition, talking not to himself but to mankind at large. Whether any poet, even the most modern and post-Freudian, has ever really succeeded in so drugging his judgement as to present us with a totally unselective series of the images thrown up by the "stream of consciousness" is perhaps open to question; we can be sure that Dante did no such thing, and that he took good care not to. Every image emerging over the threshold would be subjected to the careful and conscious scrutiny of the Censor, to see whether it represented truth not for him only but for his readers. Even when he portrays himself in his book we must proceed with caution; for that portrait is not himself, but his judgement of himself, which (whether or not it is biased or mistaken) is without any doubt at all deliberately distorted for artistic ends, so that we take for unconscious self-betrayal what in fact is intentional caricature. For a great stylist, and especially a great stylist in the classical tradition, is always more subtle than we think. As "Q" once put it:

Though personality pervades style and cannot be escaped, the first sin against Style as against good Manners is to obtrude or exploit personality. The very greatest work in Literature – the *Iliad*, the *Odyssey*, the *Purgatorio*, *The Tempest*, *Paradise Lost*, the *Republic*, *Don Quixote* – is all

> Seraphically free
> From taint of personality.[1]

We must come, then, to Beatrice with an open mind, prepared to see what the poet chooses to show, and to accept as his "real" inten-

1. Sir A. Quiller-Couch: *On the Art of Writing* (C.U.P.), p. 213.

tion that which he has backed with the whole power of his art, and the labour of a lifetime. Of all the loves he had known – and the witness, internal and external, is that he had known love in many kinds, including the "dark Eros" and the *"debito amore"* [1] – this is the one which, with will and judgement assenting, he declares to be a revelation of divine truth. It is not the febrile anguish of the death-Eros, in which possession forever mocks desire; nor yet the simple and affectionate exchange which does not look beyond possession. It is in fact not concerned with possession one way or the other, though it may survive loss. It is a love whose joy – and therefore its fulfilment – consists in the worshipful contemplation of that which stands over and above the worshipper. True to its origins in courtly love, it finds its entire happiness in being allowed to do homage to its acknowledged superior.

This an equalitarian age finds hard to stomach. It is, of course, bound up with the whole doctrine of Hierarchy which dominated Western thought to the end of the seventeenth century, and which will receive fuller exposition when we come to the *Paradiso*. But it is also bound up with a metaphysic of love which we no longer take for granted. If earthly love, as such, is but a type and an overflowing of our innate (though it may be unrecognized) desire for God, then it is inevitable that there should always be something in its nature which transcends and eludes possession. During the last fifty years or thereabouts we have come to believe that the basis of all love is sexual, and that therefore any and every love which does not issue in sexual satisfactions is warped in its nature and in its effects. And by our belief we make it so, for we bring to bear upon the unfortunate lover all the relentless one-sided pressure of our current critical assumptions. But when Dante loved it was otherwise. The denial of a physical desire was not then looked upon as a solecism, nor had the achievement of happiness been erected into a moral obligation. The lover who had set his heart upon the unattainable suffered, no doubt, the usual bodily frustrations, but he was not haunted by a guilty sense of personal failure and social inadequacy. He was not despised as an escapist; nobody told him that he was maladjusted, or hinted that there was something seriously wrong with him if he was not uproariously releasing his repressions at every turn. On the

1. "The love which is due [from a husband to a wife]." *Inf.* xxvi. 95.

contrary, he was admired and commended. Whatever his private distresses, he could feel that his public conduct was irreproachable. He was sustained by his whole culture.

Our present distrust of "idealism" in all its forms is partly due to a very proper sense (which Dante shares) that soul and body are an integrated complex whose substance we divide at our peril. And it is exceedingly true that an idealistic love which is not firmly related to its divine archetype is fraught with dangers, since it may lead to a destructive self-worship – a Narcissus-projection of our own ego upon the object of desire, and the extinction of all reality in fantasy. This is no new discovery. It is because he is so well aware of that very danger that Dante has placed the dream-image of the Siren at the entrance to those last three cornices where Excessive Love is purged.[1] There is no more insidious enemy of the true Beatrice than the false Beatrice who bears to her so deceptive a superficial likeness. The two are distinguished most readily and surely by their effects – the false image turning for ever inwards in narrowing circles of egotism; the true working for ever outwards to embrace the Creator, and all creation. For the present, it is perhaps enough to remember that every man or woman who (sincerely meaning it) has ever said: "Darling, you're marvellous!" has, if only for a brief ecstatic moment, known love as Dante knew it. It is this quality of wondering adoration – Dante calls it *stupore*, and sometimes *umiltà* – which makes love of this kind so fit a poetic symbol for that which it figures in the *Comedy*. The Beatrician vision is the beholding of the universal hierarchy in the "intellectual light" of the ecstatic moment. The Beatific Vision is the eternalizing of that moment in the contemplation of that Perfection beyond which nothing greater can be conceived for desiring.

Having written thus far, I find that I am overtaken by a doubt. In view of the very general sympathy which our contemporary critics extend to men like Keats and Coleridge, whose love was unfulfilled,

1. See Canto xix and Images. The distinction between the Siren and Beatrice is one with which Coleridge was later impelled to wrestle. "The business of the Imagination was not to generate chimaeras and fictions – the *imaginary* – but to 'disimprison the soul of fact'." Basil Willey: *Nineteenth Century Studies* (Chatto & Windus, 1949, p. 25. Penguin Books, 1964, p. 33).

and who lamented the fact in no uncertain terms, is it possible that what we resent in Dante is not his suffering but his serenity, not the nostalgia but the triumphant coming-home? What right has he to rejoice in defiance of the rules we have laid down for rejoicing, or to persist in remaining more than a mile high despite every critical effort to diminish his embarrassing stature?

"Well, I shan't go, at any rate," said Alice: "besides, that's not a regular rule: you invented it just now." "It's the oldest rule in the book," said the King. "Then it ought to be Number One," said Alice. The King turned pale, and shut his notebook hastily. "Consider your verdict," he said to the jury, in a low, trembling voice.

The trouble about that, as readers of *Wonderland* will remember, is that the poor little jurors are almost squeezed out of the jury-box.

From all that I have been saying so far, the reader might well conclude that he can hope to enjoy the *Comedy* only if he jettisons all his most cherished convictions, whether about life or about literature. Up to a point, that is true, but only up to a point. It is not necessary to discard all the rules in the book; merely to exercise a certain wholesome scepticism about those which were "invented just now". A "historic sense" in criticism is good and valuable in so far as it reveals to us the situation in which, so many centuries ago, men of like passions with us found themselves, and enables us to interpret their behaviour. It is mischievous in so far as it encourages us to dismiss our forebears as the mere creatures of a period environment, and therefore wholly unlike us and irrelevant to us or to present realities. Our best cure for over-indulgence in the "period-sense" is a hair of the dog that bit us – the realization, that is, that to-day is a historic period like any other. Those preferences which appear to us self-justified out of all argument belong to a period attitude, no less (if no more) than the corresponding preferences of fourteenth-century people. Our successors will speak of "the Neo-Elizabethans" precisely as we speak of "the Victorians", and in the same tone of voice; "depth-psychology" will take its place in their museums alongside of "faculty-psychology"; "faith in the future" will seem to them as reprehensible as "nostalgia for the past" does to us; and their journalists will use "twentieth century", as ours use "medieval", by way of a handy term of abuse for such crudities, cruelties, and superstitions as they may happen to disapprove. We cannot, after all, have it both ways. If all truths are period products, then our own standards offer no secure basis for passing judgement on those of former ages; if any truths have claims on universality, then every claim, old or new, requires to be examined on its merits. And it is interesting to observe how certain of these, which at one time seemed as thoroughly exploded as that of the Tichborne Claimant, have a way of reappearing at the bar of history to have the cause retried and the sentence modified or reversed.

A typical example of this periodicity of critical judgement is offered us by Dante's philosophy of government, and his conception of the perfect State. In the hey-day of liberal theology and of democratic nationalism, the centralized Dantean world-empire, with its elaborate dual control by Church and State, seemed antiquated beyond rejuvenation. Commentators dutifully expounded it, along with the Ptolemaic astronomy, as something necessary to the understanding of the *Comedy*, but with a vivid consciousness that, in the one case as in the other, the whole controversy had been settled for good, and settled otherwise. Two global wars, the appearance of at least two vigorous bids for a single secular world-domination, and the disquieting doubts felt in consequence about nationalism, democracy, and liberalism in all its forms, have tended to unsettle that settlement, with the result that critical attention has of late again been focused upon Dante's political theory. It is once more a living issue, and for that very reason, the present-day reader is likely to find less difficulty in grappling with this aspect of the *Purgatorio* than with some of the others.

It has been said of Coleridge that for him "at all stages of development politics and religion were inseparable."[1] That is equally true of Dante – though it does not mean that either of them tried to make a religion of politics. The word I should like to emphasize here is "development". When the poetic mind is stirred to concern itself with political questions, the first impulse is, very frequently, towards direct action, or – if that, for any reason, proves impracticable – at least towards the writing of direct political propaganda.

1. Humphrey House: *Coleridge* (Rupert Hart-Davis, 1953).

Dante in exile first broaches the theory of government in the *Convivio*, and a little later, excited by the advent of Henry VII, feels himself called to be a political leader, and writes the *De Monarchia* and the political *Letters*. Similarly, Milton reacts to the Great Rebellion, Wordsworth to the French Revolution, Stephen Spender to the Spanish War – to cite but three names from our own literary history. But it is difficult for poets to remain acceptable or contented party men; they ask too many questions.

... unless (as sometimes happens) they abandon poetry for the new-found cause, their very espousal is liable to become a passionate criticism, while they make their imperative and embarrassing demands.

Thus Spender, in a candid passage of a candid book.[1] The poet questions, and as he questions, his first enthusiasms undergo modification and development. Whether, as in Dante's experience, the cause is defeated, or, as in Milton's and Wordsworth's, its triumph leads to disillusionment and depression of spirits, the issues are seen to be too complex for settlement along rigid partisan lines. The second impulse is often, therefore, a recoil from political action and a return to poetical expression, involving a restatement of the original thesis within a wider frame of reference. In place of pamphleteering we have *Paradise Lost* and *The Prelude*; the *De Monarchia* is superseded by the *Commedia*. In some of the recent publications on Dante's political philosophy there has been a tendency to overlook this characteristic development, and the consequent attempt to make the scheme of the *Comedy* square at all points with that of the earlier works has not been altogether successful. This comparative examination is outside the scope of the present commentary; those who are interested may be referred to Professor d'Entrèves' interesting study,[2] in which the development of Dante's thought is fully recognized. Between 1311 and 1321, the scales in which Dante held the balance of power between Church and Empire are seen to have tilted unmistakably to the side of the Church. Not, indeed, that he ever ceased to maintain the immediate derivation of the Imperial power from God, or to deprecate direct interference by churchmen in secular affairs; but that he came to realize more and more vividly

1. Stephen Spender: *Life and the Poet* (Secker & Warburg, 1942).
2. A. P. d'Entrèves: *Dante as a Political Thinker* (Clarendon Press, 1952).

.the entire dependence of the "felicity of this present life" upon the beatitude of the life to come. Virgil, in short, must receive his commission from above, and ascend the Mountain only under the spiritual discipline of "those who are of Paradise". As ever, the signification of the poem is to be seen most clearly and unmistakably in the movement of the images.

The theory of the Two Powers, each equally of Divine appointment and operating each in its own sphere, was by no means peculiar to Dante, still less a subversive innovation of his own. The use, on the one hand, of his writings by Protestant polemic as a weapon against the temporal claims of the Papacy, and on the other, the placing of the *De Monarchia* upon the Index at a time when those claims were being most extravagantly urged, have combined to make posterity oblivious of how traditional and indeed orthodox the theory actually was. The whole subject has been greatly clarified for the general reader by Fr Lecler's book (now happily available in English), *L'Église et la souveraineté de l'état*,[1] which shows how closely Dante's theory coincides both with the ancient conception and with the position taken up by modern Roman theologians. It is true that Fr Lecler says:

We may at once set aside the theory of Dante [as expressed in the *De Monarchia*; he, too, ignores any development between that work and the *Commedia*] according to which the Pope is in duty bound to give enlightenment and advice to the Emperor, whilst the Emperor is obliged to show the Pope the reverence due from an eldest son to his father; for here we have no more than a *directive* power ... that of a simple spiritual father whose authority is not exercised by command but merely by suasion.[2]

1. Joseph Lecler, s.j.: *The Two Sovereignties* (Burns, Oates, and Washbourne, 1952).
2. *Op. cit.* p. 74. Dante's actual words are: "Wherefore man had need of a twofold directive power according to this twofold end, to wit, the supreme pontiff, to lead the human race, in accordance with things revealed, to eternal life; and the emperor, to direct the human race to temporal felicity in accordance with the teachings of philosophy. ...
"The truth concerning [the derivation of the monarch's authority immediately from God, and not via the intermediation the Holy See] is not to be received in such narrow sense as that the Roman prince is subordinate in naught to the Roman pontiff; inasmuch as mortal felicity is in a certain sense ordained with reference to immortal felicity. Let Caesar, therefore, observe that reverence to Peter which a first-born son should observe to a father, so that illuminated by the light of paternal grace he may with greater power

Yet Fr Lecler's own conclusion differs but little from Dante's:

> The primacy of the spiritual can no longer be conceived like [*sic*] in the Middle Ages, as being equivalent to an external and direct domination over secular affairs. This primacy involves the right to rule, but it is a rule over souls, an authority which directs them and enlightens them in regard to the Christian principles of social life – the Church's rights can even be thought of as including a power over temporal things, but it is in this case an oblique and indirect power, a power which only affects earthly states and institutions in virtue of the sway which she still holds over the hearts of men and of the after-effects which spring therefrom.[1]

Indeed, if we bear in mind the medieval conception of the authority investing a father, we may well feel that, even in the *De Monarchia*, it is Dante who, of the two writers, makes the higher claim on behalf of the spiritual sovereign.

The difficulty of adjustment between a spiritual authority claiming absolute rule over men's consciences and a secular authority claiming absolute rule over their actions scarcely made itself felt in Ancient Rome, where the Emperor was, *ex officio, pontifex maximus,* and religion a department of State; though the beginning of trouble became manifest when the Imperial rule was extended over Jewry, and a rigid theocracy found itself at loggerheads with the civil power. "Is it lawful to give tribute unto Caesar or no?" The Divine answer, while it accorded emphatic recognition to Caesar, yet did, in a sense, but restate the problem by laying bare its moral foundations. The early Church, while drawing the line at Emperor-worship, even of the most formal kind (for which abstention she was duly persecuted), was otherwise anxious to prove herself in all respects a good citizen, and tended, when cases of possible conflict presented themselves, to avoid occasions of giving offence. Christians, if they remembered their calling and status as a divine society, should, for example, settle disputes peaceably among themselves and not invoke the secular jurisdiction of the Imperial courts. In all matters that did not involve a real violation of conscience, they should submit themselves to the powers that were, since these were

---

irradiate the world, over which he is set by Him alone who is ruler of all things spiritual and temporal" (*De Mon.* III, xvi. T.C. translation).
1. *Op. cit.* p. 83.

ordained of God. The situation, though always perilous, was sim-
plified by the fact that, while they had the choice between keeping
and breaking the laws, they were not called upon either to make or
enforce them. But when, under Constantine, Christians ceased to
be a persecuted minority and found themselves invested with the
responsibilities of government, the latent tension between the City
of God and the City of this World became apparent, for it now
existed within one and the same society. From this time onward
the relations between the ecclesiastical and secular authorities could
not but be delicate and complex and the subject of much conflicting
theory. The difficulty of precisely delimiting their respective spheres
of action was all the more subtle when the membership of the
Church was co-terminous with that of the State. The issue is more
clear-cut when, as in many parts of Europe to-day, the Church has
to reckon with a State the majority of whose members are not
Christian even in name, and which does not claim to derive its auth-
ority from a God whom it repudiates. But the division of the Middle
Ages was a division within the conscience of Christendom itself.

In Europe the decay of the Western Empire during the Dark
Ages made it easy and natural for the Roman See – the one centre
of stability amid the general chaos – to claim, and to some extent
exercise, control over the medieval monarchies. But there were
never lacking theologians – St Thomas among them – who, basing
their teaching upon the *Politics* of Aristotle, maintained that the
secular power belonged to the natural order and took its origin
from the law of nations, "which is a human law". The Christian
revelation did not abolish the natural order nor cancel the human
law; neither did it render the rule of pagan kings unlawful, even in
Christian times and over Christian subjects. St Thomas declares:

> As it was the function of secular princes to issue positive decrees
> based on Natural Law, with a view to the common temporal good,
> so it was the function of the rulers of the Church to frame spiritual
> laws for the general welfare of the faithful.[1]

And he delimits these functions thus:

> The spiritual power and the secular power both derive their origin
> from the Divine Power. This means that the secular power is subord-

1. *S.T.* II.II^ae, q. 147, a. 3c.

inate to the spiritual power in the measure decreed by God, that is to say, in all matters concerning the salvation of souls; for in such things it is more profitable to obey the spiritual rather than the secular power.[1]

If we compare these two statements with those already quoted from the *De Monarchia*, we shall see that Dante, though with a more picturesque style and rather more vehemence (he was, after all, engaged in writing political propaganda), is following the Angelic Doctor fairly closely; and it seems probable that he did not intend to go beyond him.[2] He was, however, facing a rather different situation. In another place St Thomas says:

The secular power is subject to the spiritual as the body is subject to the soul. It is for this reason that there is no usurpation when the spiritual superior intervenes regarding those particular temporal matters in which the secular power is subject to him.[3]

No one need cavil at that. But the question is, which, precisely, are those particular temporal matters? It seemed to Dante that the spiritual superior, in the person of Boniface VIII, was intervening where he should not, and that there was, in fact, usurpation. He was indignant about this, not only on account of the secular disorders produced by clerical interference in politics, but because he saw the danger of political corruption in the Church, and the risk the Papacy ran of losing the substance of spiritual power in grasping at the shadow of the temporal. On the other hand, the neglect of the Emperor to maintain the unity of the West had left the door open to the menace of an aggressive nationalism, whose leading exponents were liable to redress the balance of sovereignties in Europe after a fashion that could benefit nobody but themselves. To imagine, as some have done, that Dante's anti-clericalism was anti-Catholic was and remains only another piece of period wishful thinking: he saw clericalism as an imminent threat to Catholicism. He had no power to stay the march of events, and the Imperial remedy he proposed was perhaps never practical politics; but his

---

1. In II *Sent.*, dist. 44, q. 2, a. 3, ad 4.
2. It is true that his conception of the Roman nation as an "elect people" prompts him to attribute peculiar sanctity to the Roman *Code Law*, and almost to equate it with the *Lex Humana* (see Table, Appendix p. 346); but that is an error of a slightly different kind.    3. *S.T.* II.II[ae], q. 60, a. 6, ad 3.

warnings contained the elements of true prophecy. Did he not himself see the tragedy of Alagna,[1] and the carrying away of the Holy Sée into the "Babylonish captivity" of Avignon, under the domination of Philip the Fair?[2] And the repeated and passionate denunciations of the clergy for snatching at the reins of empire, and of the royal house of France for its hectoring and rapacious insolence towards Christ's Vicar, all culminating in the ugly pageant of Church and Empire which leaves the Woman on the Beast corrupted and maltreated in the giant hands of a brutal secularity – these passages in the *Purgatorio* have an interest for us which is not merely historical. We have seen persecuted churches, and attempts at making the churches into tools for tyranny; we have seen uneasy concordats between the Two Sovereignties, and one or two experiments in the direction of the theocratic State; above all, we are now aware, as formerly we were not, of the situation which results when secular power is emancipated from all religious sanctions. It is now less easy than it once was to dismiss Dante's political passages as "tedious and frigid allegories" erected over the tomb of a controversy long dead and forgotten.

The doctrine of Purgation, the doctrine of Divine Love made known in the transfigured Creation, the doctrine of the Two Sovereignties, the doctrine of the "single soul complete" with its complex of Instinct and Free Will – these are the cardinal points upon which the action of the *Purgatorio* turns; the subjects of its "sermons" and the motive powers of its allegory. It is perhaps only when we try to disentangle them and consider each one separately that we become aware how closely they are in fact interconnected, and how astonishing is the skill with which they are woven into a single developing narrative action. That which at first sight may appear to be irrelevant or digressive turns out, as we pursue our way up the Mountain, to be but a necessary stage in a continuous process; from each new knot of "perplexity" new lines of understanding successively unfold, until the whole is seen to make up one complex and coherent pattern with all its parts interdependent and corresponding. No-

1. See *Purg.* xx. 86–90 and note.
2. See *Purg.* xxxii. 151–60 and note.

thing is easier than to begin vast and complicated works of art, and to devise impressive endings presents little greater difficulty; but to construct their middle parts in such a way that no loose ends are left behind and no unprepared situations lurk ahead, and to keep the story and the poetry going all the time – this is the test of great architectural art. The world is littered with unfinished masterpieces whose makers have failed to survive this test; but the *Comedy* is not one of them. There are, of course, readers who have not stayed the course; but for that there are, as I have tried to show, reasons which are not of Dante's making. What is astonishing is that among those who know and love the poem as a whole there should be so many who find the middle third the most attractive part of it. That is a thing which very rarely happens. The general tendency of long poems is to sag in the middle, or to become entangled in their own complexity. What saves the *Commedia* is its rigid simplicity of outline, the austere functionalism of all its parts, and the passionate intellectual integrity of the man who made it.

Of the present translation of the *Purgatorio* there is not much to say that I have not already said in my Introduction to the *Inferno*. I have kept the same aims in mind, except that I have allowed myself rather fewer metrical roughnesses and eccentricities in this second Cantica, in the endeavour to match my style to the greater smoothness and ease of the original. In the philosophic passages, however, I have tried at all costs to be as exact as possible, since no neatness or slickness in the verse will excuse an imprecise use of technical terms; the provision of elegant periphrases for such uncompromising expressions as "substantial form" or "the prime appetibles" is as unpardonable as calling oysters "succulent bivalves" – moreover, it may easily entail bad reasoning, mental confusion, heresy, and perhaps (who knows?)

> Twenty-nine distinct damnations,
> One sure if another fails.

I have done my best to elucidate the more crabbed and difficult passages in the Notes, and sincerely hope that I have not fallen into any disastrous errors. I can but apologize for the resulting formidable bulk of the Commentaries to certain cantos. In commenting on the finer theological points, there appear to be only two possibilities: a brief definition, as technical as the text itself and equally unintelligible to the general reader; or a lengthy explanation, in terms of cats and cabbages and other familiar phenomena, to show what the problem or doctrine in question really means, and what its consequences are in daily experience. Of these alternatives, I have not hesitated to choose the latter; the book is so arranged that the reader can easily skip any explanations in which he is not interested. Two or three arguments about alternative readings and disputed interpretations, of no interest except to professional critics, have been banished to Appendices, where those who enjoy "trundling in the dismal joust" can roll stones to their hearts' content.

I find that there are two schools of thought about the pronunciation of the name "Beatrice" – some preferring to give it the full four syllables of the Italian, and others to speak it in the plain English way (though nobody, I think, nowadays joins with Chaucer in calling Dante "Dant"). It is probably a question of what one has been accustomed to hear from childhood. In order that nobody shall be irritated at some crucial and moving moment of the poem by having to reform a habit of speech which long use has consecrated, I have (at infinite trouble and expense) so arranged the verse that in nearly every case *either* pronunciation will yield a passable scansion. In the one or two passages where I could not by any ingenuity squeeze in more than three syllables I have used the form "Beatrix".

## PURGATORY: THE DOCTRINE

The doctrine of Purgatory, while not resting upon such explicit and reiterated Scriptural authority as the doctrine of Hell, is of early Patristic origin, and seems to have been first clearly formulated by the Alexandrian Fathers. Thus Origen, in the second century, commenting on Our Lord's words, "thou shalt by no means come out thence till thou hast paid the uttermost farthing",[1] interprets them as a reference to Purgatory, and explains: "These souls receive in

---

1. *Matt.* v. 26.

prison, not the retribution of their folly; but a benefaction in the purification from the evils contracted in that folly; a purification effected by the means of salutary troubles."[1] St Augustine (354–430), though inclining at times to the older Jewish-Christian belief that the soul passed the time between death and Doomsday in a state of suspended animation, in *The City of God* definitely accepts the idea of Purgatory as an extension and completion of the purifying trials of earth: "As for temporal pain, some endure it here and some hereafter, and some both here and there; yet all is past before the Last Judgement."[2] It will be noticed that in both these pronouncements the emphasis is laid upon the purgative rather than on the penal aspect of punishment; and the official declarations of the Church of Rome take the same line, affirming (Confession of Faith of Michael Palaeologos, A.D. 1267, and by the Decree of the Council of Florence, A.D. 1429) that souls in the Intermediate State "are purged after death by purgatorial or cathartic pains." This, the traditional and correct balance of the doctrine, is maintained by Dante throughout the *Purgatorio*.[3]

Those who are interested in the complex question of penance and punishment would profit greatly by studying the chapters devoted to the subject by St Thomas Aquinas in the *Summa*. I shall presently quote a long and important passage from him; but it will perhaps be better to begin by giving, in the simplest possible terms, an example which I have already used elsewhere.[4]

Suppose that, in a fit of rage, or through carelessness, you have destroyed a valuable vase belonging to a friend. The effect of this act is to disturb the friendly relations between you, and to bring matters back to normal it is necessary that you should be (*a*) sorry, and (*b*) forgiven.

1. Origen: Treatise on Prayer, xxix, 16. Cit. Von Hügel: *Mystical Element of Religion* (Dent, 1923): II. 233.
2. *De Civ. Dei*, xxi. 13.
3. In the period immediately subsequent to this, there was a tendency in the Western Church to reverse the emphasis by stressing the purely legal and mechanical aspect of "satisfaction". This led to various abuses (e.g. the sale of indulgences and the traffic in expiatory masses) which shocked the conscience of the Reformers. If Dante's teaching appears more "modern" and liberal than that of his successors, it is not because he was "a Protestant before his time", but because he was following the older Catholic tradition.
4. *Introductory Papers on Dante* (Methuen, 1954), p. 79 sq.

The first necessity is that you should "accept judgement" – i.e. admit that you are in the wrong. The vase did not "come to pieces in your hands", and nobody else knocked it out of them: your own ill-temper or your own negligence is alone to blame. When you have frankly admitted this, to yourself first and then to your friend, you have performed the first of the three parts of Penance, viz. *Confession*.

The next necessity is that you should both *be* sorry, and *say* that you are sorry, for what you did, and for the fault that caused you to do it; and that you should ask to be forgiven. This is the second part of Penance, viz. *Contrition*.[1]

When this is done, your friend forgives you, and good relations are restored.[2] You are now, without any further act, free of the *guilt* of your evil act: in technical language you have "purged the *culpa*".

Two things, however, remain: the vase is still broken, and you yourself are still liable to attack by the rage or negligence which caused the trouble in the first place. Technically, you have still to "purge the *reatus*". This leads you to the third part of Penance, viz. *Satisfaction*, and calls for two further acts: *reparation* to your friend and *amendment* in yourself.

Note that if you are really sorry, these are acts which you will *wish* to perform. For the value of the damaged property you are indeed legally responsible, and the owner could sue you for it. But even though you have been forgiven, you will want to "make it up to" your friend as best you can; and you will also be particularly anxious to rid yourself of any tendency to fall into the same fault again.

Now, when we sin, we always wrong God, and usually our neighbour as well. Our acts of confession, contrition, and reparation have therefore to be made, not only to God, but to the injured human parties and also to the Church in general. The setting-right of the wrong done is our duty to our neighbour; the bestowing of expiatory alms, offerings, and so on is the outward token of our wish

1. I have placed Confession and Contrition in this order, because it is the order used by Dante (*Purg*. ix. 94–102). Some writers put Contrition first; but it seems logically necessary to admit that the fault is yours before you can be sorry for it. In practice, the two acts are simultaneous and inseparable.
2. We need not consider the case of an unforgiving friend, since the friend we are concerned with is God, who is always ready to forgive.

to pay reparation to the Church. But reparation to God is a different matter. Just as (in one sense) it is impossible for us to injure the infinite and immutable Omnipotence – in the sense, that is, of doing Him any personal damage, so (in the same sense) it is impossible for us to offer reparation or compensation to Him, since all that we have is His already. The only "property" of God's which we can really harm is ourselves; and the only offering we are able to make to Him is again ourselves, mended and made presentable at whatever cost. Thus, in this unique case, reparation and amendment are the same thing.

True, no individual repentances, nor the sum of them, can totally restore mankind as a whole; neither can any human "satisfaction" be wholly disinterested: our best amends are always partly in our own interests. We are all too much involved in the common guilt – part wrongers and partly wronged – ever to be sure of a perfectly pure motive for what we do. Mercifully, however, the whole burden of reparation has not been left on our shoulders. The full satisfaction for all mankind was made once for all by the one Man who, being Himself sinless, could offer Himself complete, receiving into Himself the total evil and returning the total good. What remains for us to do is to unite ourselves with that act of Atonement,[1] so that whatever in us is (comparatively speaking) innocent may be taken up into Christ's sacrifice in expiation of whatever is evil in ourselves and others.[2]

Since, as we said earlier, the mere acts of confession and contrition immediately purge the *culpa* of sin, it follows that a man living the Christian life in Grace will as a rule die free from actual

1. Dante's Atonement theology will receive fuller and more specific attention when we come to deal with *Paradiso* vii.
2. This is bound to raise in the reader's mind the whole question of suffering innocence, with which the *Purgatory* is, of course, not immediately concerned. This much may be safely said: (*a*) Any suffering of ours which is directly attributable to a particular sin of our own may be accepted by us as a purgative discipline for that sin, and being thus accepted and offered to God, will be accepted by Him as satisfaction. (*b*) Similarly, any suffering of our own which cannot be directly so attributed may be accepted by us as purgative discipline for other sins of ours whose immediate consequences we seem to have wholly or partly escaped; and if we accept and offer it so, God will likewise so accept it. (*c*) All unmerited suffering (including that of children and animals) is the participation of the creature in the sinless suffering of Christ, and is offered in Him and by Him for the sins of the whole world.

guilt. What is left to be done in Purgatory is the purging of the *reatus*, so far as there may not have been time or opportunity to do this on earth, and, especially, the cleansing of the soul from the *stain of sin*. By this is meant the damage done to the soul by the habit of sinfulness – the coarsening of fibre, and the clouding of the mind and imagination:

> I waive the quantum of the sin,
> The hazard of concealing;
> But och! it hardens a' within,
> And petrifies the feeling![1]

So long as there remains in the soul the least trace of consent to sin, this clouding and coarsening remain to fetter the will and judgement. Only when the clear sight and tender conscience are restored is the soul set free to stand before the unveiled light of the presence of God, which otherwise it could not endure. It is this which underlies Dante's great statement, that when the soul *feels* itself free, it *is* free.[2] Purgatory is not a system of Divine book-keeping – so many years for so much sin – but a process of spiritual improvement which is completed precisely when it is complete. "God is satisfied when we are satisfied."[3] We are now in a position to appreciate more exactly what St Thomas says about penalty and purgation:

> Two things [he says] may be considered in sin; the guilty act and the consequent stain. Now it is evident that in all actual sins, when the act of sin has ceased the guilt remains; for the act of sin makes man deserving of punishment, in so far as he transgresses the order of divine justice, to which he cannot return except he pay some sort of penal compensation which restores him to the equality of justice. Hence, according to the order of divine justice, he who has been too indulgent to his will, by transgressing God's commandment, suffers, either willingly or unwillingly, something contrary to what he would wish. This restoration of the equality of justice by penal compensation is also to be observed in injuries done to one's fellow-men. Consequently, it is

---

1. Robert Burns: *Epistle to a Young Friend.*
2. *Purg.* xxi. 61–6. Similarly, in this life, practising mystics reach a point where "the new life has triumphed [and] Mortification is at an end. The mystics always know when this moment comes. Often an inner voice then warns them to lay their active penances aside" – Evelyn Underhill: *Mysticism* (Methuen, 17th ed., 1949), p. 217, and examples in the following pages.
3. Charles Williams: *Figure of Beatrice*, p. 160.

evident that when the sinful or injurious act has ceased, there still remains the debt of punishment.

But if we speak of the removal of sin as to the stain, it is evident that the stain of sin cannot be removed from the soul without the soul being united to God, since it was through being separated from Him that it suffered the loss of its splendour, in which the stain consists. ... Now man is united to God by his will. Therefore the stain of sin cannot be removed from man unless his will accepts the order of divine justice; that is to say, unless either of his own accord he take upon himself the punishment of his past sin, or bear patiently the punishment which God inflicts upon him; and in both ways punishment has the character of satisfaction. Now when punishment is satisfactory, it loses somewhat of the nature of punishment, for the nature of punishment is to be against the will: and although satisfactory punishment, absolutely speaking, is against the will, nevertheless, in this particular case and for this particular purpose it is voluntary. ... We must therefore say that, when the stain of sin has been removed, there may remain a debt of punishment, not indeed of punishment absolutely, but of satisfactory punishment. (*S.T.* I.II$^{ae}$, q. 87, ad 7.)

It will be seen how closely Dante keeps to St Thomas's definition, and with how sensitive a skill he constructs narrative and images to illumine this apparently arid theme.

We may add here a few words to clear up a number of widely current perplexities and misunderstandings about Purgatory.

(1) Purgatory is *not* a place of probation, from which the soul may go either to Heaven or to Hell. All souls admitted to Purgatory are bound for Heaven sooner or later, and are for ever beyond the reach of sin.

(2) Purgatory is *not* a "second chance" for those who die obstinately unrepentant. The soul's own choice between God and self, made in the moment of death, is final. (This moment of final choice is known as the "Particular Judgement".)

(3) Repentance in the moment of death (*in articulo mortis*) is always accepted. If the movement of the soul is, however feebly, away from self and towards God, its act of confession and contrition is complete, whether or not it is accompanied by formal confession and absolution; and the soul enters Purgatory.

(4) The Divine acceptance of a repentance *in articulo mortis* does

*not* mean that the sinner "gets away with it" scot-free. What it does mean is that the soul is now obliged, with prolonged labour and pains, and without the assistance of the body, to accomplish in Purgatory the entire process of satisfaction and purification, the greater part of which should have been carried out on earth.

(5) The souls in Purgatory and the souls on earth are in touch with one another and can aid each other by their prayers. But it is wrong for the living to distract the dead from their task of purgation by egotistical and importunate demands for attention.

   *Note*: Attempts to keep souls "earth-bound" by magical or spiritualistic conjurations are wicked, and can only do them injury. Dante does not deal with this possibility, unless the solemn warning of the Angel at Peter's Gate (ix. 131–2) can, in the literal significance, be held to refer to it. If any saved soul is ever so recalled, it is most probably from the first stage of its journey, called by Dante "the shores of Tiber" and by others "the prison-house" or "the shadow-city"; and to encourage it to linger there is only to prolong its trials.

(6) Souls which have so persevered in virtue till the moment of death as to accomplish their whole purgation in this life, are not detained in Purgatory, but pass immediately into the 'Presence of God. These are the Saints.

   *N.B.*: Canonization is not (as Bernard Shaw implies in the Epilogue to *St Joan*) the award of an earthly honour, but the recognition of a Divine fact. There may be, and undoubtedly are, innumerable saints unrecognized and uncanonized.

The above is a summary of the Doctrine of Purgatory as generally held by Catholics. Not every item in it is *de fide*.

It is instructive to compare Dante's massive intellectual exposition with the crude popular version presented for our consideration, nearly three centuries later, in the first act of *Hamlet*. This latter is often the only context in which the average uninstructed English layman ever encounters the doctrine. Such a version is admirable for producing stage effects, but should not be accepted as a basis for theological argument. The results of dying "unhousel'd, disap-pointed, unaneal'd" are (in "grim Dante's" opinion) a good deal less drastic than "gentle Shakespeare" would lead one to suppose – always provided that Hamlet senior was really the virtuous Christian man that he is represented to be, and had not previously neglected his religious duties. His heathen insistence on remaining earth-bound until his murder is avenged is certainly rather suspicious, and might well justify his son's doubts as to his *bona fides*. Needless to say, the whole "revenge-motif", like the cognate "burial-motif", derives from pagan sources, and has no place whatever in serious Christian eschatology.

## PURGATORY: DANTE'S ARRANGEMENT

Since Purgatory is a place of systematic discipline, it is only to be expected that it should be more highly and more serenely organized than Hell. Even upon Hell, indeed, the medieval passion for order imposes a coherent classification and a rigid external symmetry. But within the circles thus ordered, the anarchy of evil goes, for the most part, its own chaotic way. The whirling banner in the Vesti-bule, the whirling wind in the Second Circle, the ghastly hunt of the Profligates through the Wood of the Suicides, the aimless fisticuffs of the Wrathful in the mud of Styx, the ceaseless to-and-fro of the Sodomites upon the Abominable Sand, the vulgar buffoonery of demons and damned alike in the Pitch of the Barrators, the restless change and interchange of forms among the Thieves, the blind crawling and creeping of the Diseased in the Moat of the Falsifiers are activities without rhyme or reason, which alternate only with a meaningless monotony or a sterile fixity. In all it does and is, damna-tion is without direction or purpose. Why not? It has nothing to do, and all eternity to do it in.

In Purgatory, although the circles are fewer and the classification much simpler, the symmetry of the whole is more elaborate, and the activity of each circle has a much richer content. As in the *Inferno*, Dante postpones his explanation of all arrangements until his pil-grims have accomplished a considerable part of their journey. From

## THE EARTHLY PARADISE

| | | |
|---|---|---|
| **UPPER PURGATORY** | Disordered Love of Good | Excessive Love of Secondary Good | Cornice 7 – The Lustful<br><br>Cornice 6 – The Gluttonous<br><br>Cornice 5 – The Covetous |
| **MIDDLE PURGA-TORY** | | Love Defective | Cornice 4 – The Slothful |
| **LOWER PURGATORY** | Love of Neighbours' Harm (Love Perverted) | | Cornice 3 – The Wrathful<br><br><br>Cornice 2 – The Envious<br><br><br>Cornice 1 – The Proud |
| **PETER'S GATE** | | Steps: | 3. Satisfaction<br>2. Contrition<br>1. Confession |
| **ANTE-PURGATORY** | Salvation in articulo mortis | Terrace 2 | The Late Repentant –<br>(a) The Indolent<br>(b) The Unshriven<br>(c) The Pre-occupied |
| | | Terrace 1 | The Excommunicate |

MOUNT PURGATORY

the point of view of straightforward narrative interest, his is undoubtedly the better way; but for the purpose of the commentator, who is obliged to annotate passages as and when they occur, it is easier to make the earlier sections of Purgatory comprehensible to the reader if the general lay-out of the Mountain is made clear from the start. In order to avoid encumbering the "Images" and the "Notes" with a great deal of unwieldy matter, I have thought it best to make a preliminary survey here, and to refer the readers to it as the story goes along. Anybody who prefers to read the poem, as Dante of course meant it to be read, without knowing from one canto to another what is coming next, can do so, ignoring both Introduction and Notes at the first run-through. Those who choose this course do Dante honour and therein do well.

Like the *Inferno* and the *Paradiso*, the *Purgatorio* is built up on a numerical system of $7 + 2 = 9 + 1 = 10$ (seven being the sacred number; 9 the square of 3, the number of the Trinity, and 10 the "perfect number"). There are 7 Cornices devoted to the purging of the Seven Capital Sins (again divided internally into $3 + 1 + 3$); preceded by the 2 Terraces of Ante-Purgatory, and followed by the Earthly Paradise at the Summit of the Mountain. To each of the Cornices is allotted a Penance, a Meditation, a Prayer,[1] a Guardian Angel, and a Benediction; while the ascents from one circle to another are, for the most part, each embellished by a Discourse on some scientific or philosophical subject.

### ANTE-PURGATORY

The two terraces of Ante-Purgatory are occupied by those who, in one way or another, failed to avail themselves in good time of the means of Grace, and so died unprepared or imperfectly prepared, repenting only *in articulo mortis*. Of all the "punishments" in Purgatory, theirs alone is wholly penal and imposed from without; and it consists solely in being obliged to wait for a fixed period of time before being admitted to the "cleansing pains" of Purgatory itself. During this waiting time, nothing that they themselves can do can avail to shorten the period of their detention: as, formerly, they

---

1. With the exception of Cornice 4, which is a special case.

would not, so now they cannot, help themselves. The period may, however, be shortened *for* them by the prayers of the living; for this punishment, just because it is merely penal, may be remitted by a simple act of Grace on God's part. So far as I know, Ante-Purgatory is of Dante's own invention.

*Terrace 1* is inhabited by the *Excommunicate*, who are detained for thirty times the period of their contumacy. (An act of last-minute repentance has, of course, already purged their *culpa*; otherwise they would not be on Mount Purgatory at all.)

*Note* that excommunication is itself not a sin, but a punishment for sin – although, if one has been excommunicated, it is obviously sinful to remain obdurate. If a man's sin has been so flagrant as to cause his excommunication he can either (1) hasten to repent the sin and seek reconciliation with the Church, in which case he will, after death, proceed immediately to Purgatory and not suffer detention; (2) remain in contumacy to the end of his life, but make a private act of contrition *in articulo mortis*; in which case he qualifies for Ante-Purgatory; (3) live and die excommunicate and unrepentant; in which case he goes, like other unrepentant sinners, to Hell, and there suffers for his sins in the appropriate circle – i.e. at the lowest depth to which sin has reduced him – (thus Frederick II, dying excommunicate, is found in the Circle of the Heretics). If by any chance an innocent man had been excommunicated in error, and had sought, without success, to obtain reconciliation, the excommunication would be without validity, and he would not be detained. It seems advisable to make this clear, since I find by experience that there may be misunderstanding about it.

*Terrace 2* is inhabited by those who, while remaining within the communion of the Church, delayed repentance until the moment of death. They are divided into (*a*) the Indolent, (*b*) the Unshriven, (*c*) the Preoccupied. For all these the period of detention is a period equal to the length of their earthly life.

PETER'S GATE

All souls entering Purgatory, whether directly on arrival or from the Terraces, pass through Peter's Gate, which is approached by the Three Steps of Penitence: Confession, Contrition, and Satisfaction. The Seven P's standing for the Seven Capital Sins (*Peccata*) are inscribed upon their foreheads by the Angelic Warder, and are erased, one by one, as the soul ascends by the Pass of Pardon, at the exit from each Cornice.

## PURGATORY PROPER

On the Seven Cornices of Purgatory Proper, the "punishments" are purgative rather than penal. Accordingly, as we have already seen, they are not terminated or remitted from without, but come to an end as soon as the cleansing is completed from within. The prayers of the living avail the penitent, not to "beg him off", but to help and sustain him in his task of purification so that the "wound of sin" may heal more quickly.

## THE SEVEN ROOTS OF SINFULNESS

What is purged upon the Cornices is not the *act* of sin, but the *stain* of sin, as defined above (p. 58 *sq.*). Accordingly, each Cornice is devoted to the purging of one of what are often called the "Seven Deadly Sins", but also (and less misleadingly for our purpose) the *Seven Capital Sins*.[1] These are the fundamental bad habits of mind recognized and defined by the Church as the well-heads from which all sinful behaviour ultimately springs. They may also be called: the *Seven Roots of Sinfulness*. In classifying sin under these seven main heads, the Church displays more subtlety and a profounder psychology than is sometimes supposed. It is, for instance, often asked: "Why does the Church not count Cruelty as a Deadly Sin?" The answer is that although cruelty is indeed (in one sense) a sin deadly to the soul that indulges in it, it is not a *root*-sin. No sane person is cruel for cruelty's sake: there is always, hidden behind the act and habit of cruelty, some other (often unacknowledged and unsuspected) evil motive. It is important (as many psychiatrists would agree) to discover what, in any particular case, the root of cruelty is. It may, in fact, derive from any one of the Capital Sins: from sheer selfish indifference to others' needs and feelings (Pride); from jealousy, resentment, or fear (Envy); from ill-temper, vindictiveness, or violent indignation (Wrath); from laziness, cowardice, lack of imagination, complacency, or irresponsibility (Sloth); from meanness, acquisitiveness, or the determination to get on in life (Avarice);

1. *Lat.*: *caput* = head: the "head and front of offending".

from self-indulgence and the wanton pursuit of pleasure (Gluttony); from perversions of sexual and personal relationships, such as sadism, masochism, or possessiveness (Lust). And so with other symptomatic sins. Even in this world, it is usually found insufficient to punish symptoms without an effort to discover the underlying spiritual disease. Here, however, the cure is often attempted by merely removing the occasion of discontent; in Purgatory it is necessary to cut deeper and eradicate the sin.[1]

We will now examine these Seven Roots of Sinfulness; and to this end briefly summarize Virgil's Discourse on Love,[2] which leads up to his exposition of the arrangement of Purgatory.

His argument rests upon the great Augustinian premiss that evil in itself is nothing and can originate nothing positive – not even sin. It can only be a parasite upon the good which God has created. Man has a natural impulse to love that which pleases him. This impulse, which is the root of all virtue, can be perverted, weakened, or misdirected to become the root of all sin. Thus, all the Capital Sins are shown to derive from love for some good, either falsely perceived, or inadequately or excessively pursued. Accordingly, the three Lower Cornices are devoted to the purging of *Love Perverted* (love, that is, directed to a false object), and the four Upper Cornices to the purging of Love which, though directed to an object legitimate in itself, errs either by *Defect* (Cornice 4) or by *Excess* (Cornices 5–7). (See table, pp. 202–3.)

## LOWER PURGATORY: LOVE PERVERTED

There is no actual existing person or thing that is not, in some degree, a proper object of love. The only wrong object of love is the love of *harm*, which results when love for object A is perverted into hatred for object B. Since God is the source of all good, to hate Him is a delusion and to harm Him is impossible; neither does anyone really hate or want to harm himself. In practice, therefore, *Perverted Love* is love of injury to one's neighbour, springing from the evil fantasy that one can gain good for one's self from others' harm.

---

1. Christians, of course, make this their aim on earth also; and the more they do about it here, the less they will have to do hereafter. The method has this further practical advantage, that when further occasions of trouble present themselves (as is their horrid way) they are rendered innocuous. •
2. *Purg.* xvii. 91 – xviii. 75.

*Cornice 1: Pride (Superbia)* (love of self perverted to hatred and contempt for one's neighbour).

*Cornice 2: Envy (Invidia)* (love of one's own good perverted to the wish to deprive other men of theirs).

*Cornice 3: Wrath (Ira)* (love of justice perverted to revenge and spite).

### MID-PURGATORY: LOVE DEFECTIVE

*Cornice 4: Sloth or Accidie (Acedia)* (the failure to love any good object in its proper measure, and, especially, to love God actively with all one has and is).

### UPPER PURGATORY: LOVE EXCESSIVE

One object, and one object only, is rightly to be loved "with all my heart, with all my mind, with all my soul, and with all my strength." Love for any other object must be so ordered as to remain subordinate to the love of God and the right hierarchy of the "secondary goods".

*Cornice 5: Avarice or Covetousness (Avaritia)* (the excessive love of money and power).

*Cornice 6: Gluttony (Gula)* (the excessive love of pleasure).

*Cornice 7: Lust (Luxuria)* (the excessive love of persons).

It will be noticed that, as in Hell, the warmer-hearted sins which involve exchange and reciprocity are at the top, and the cold egotism which rejects community is at the bottom.

### SYMMETRY OF THE CORNICES

On every Cornice the discipline of Penitence follows the same pattern, and comprises:

1. The *Penance* itself, appropriate to the sin, and taking the form either of
    (*a*) the patient endurance of the sin in its effects (Cornices 2, 3, 5), or
    (*b*) the practice of the opposing virtue (Cornices 1, 4, 6), or
    (*c*) both (Cornice 7).
2. The *Meditation*, consisting of
    (*a*) the *Whip*: examples of the opposing virtue, one of

which is always taken from the life of the Blessed Virgin, and the others from sacred and profane history alternately;

(b) the *Bridle*: deterrent examples of the sin itself, taken from sacred and profane sources, and usually corresponding in number and significance to those of the Whip.

3. The *Prayer*, taken from the Psalms or from the Hymns of the Church.

4. The *Benediction*, taken from the Beatitudes, and pronounced by

5. The *Angel of the Cornice*, who receives the soul when the sin of that Cornice is purged, erases the P (the brand of the sin) from its forehead, and directs it upward by the Pass of Pardon.

At the summit of Mount Purgatory is the *Earthly Paradise*, the place of Man's Innocence, "empty now, because of her fault who gave ear to the Serpent." It is from here that, if Man had not fallen, he would have entered upon the life of Perfection, in this world and the next. As it is, he has to start from "Jerusalem", the place of Man's Redemption, and so pass either by "the short way" (the way of the Saints) or by the long way through the Dark Wood and the vision of Hell, up the Mountain of Repentance to the regaining of his lost Innocence.

The innocence thus regained can never be exactly what it would have been if Man had not sinned. God wastes nothing – not even sin. The soul that has struggled and come through is enriched by its experiences, and Grace does not merely blot out the evil past but in the most literal sense "makes it good". The sin is not *forgotten*, either by God or by the soul: it is *forgiven*, and so made the occasion of a new and still more blessed relationship; redeemed Man is a creature more precious to his Creator than unfallen Man could have been. Accordingly, in Dante's Earthly Paradise, the soul has to drink of the twin streams of Lethe and Eunoë. The first destroys all memory of evil and the sin with it; the second restores remembrance of the sin, but only as an historical fact and as the occasion of grace and blessedness.[1]

1. Caution is needed here lest we find ourselves in the wrong place with Guido da Montefeltro. "Shall we," asks St Paul, "continue in sin that grace

# Introduction

## THE PHYSICAL ASPECT OF THE MOUNTAIN

When Ruskin inferred, from Dante's repeated moanings and groanings over the difficulties of the ascent, that the poet himself must have been but a poor mountaineer, he showed not merely an indifference to the allegorical significance of "The Way", but also a curious failure to appreciate the enormous scale of Dante's literal picture. And indeed, the descriptions given by some of the commentators – usually beginning: "Mount Purgatory is depicted as a truncated cone" – and their accompanying diagrams, which show something like a squat sand-castle, embellished with a series of short ladders, and an outsized tree at the top, are not exactly helpful to the imagination. The trouble about any diagram is, of course, that if it is to be contained upon a printed page, and also show details of the journey accompanied by legible captions, the scale is bound to be lost. We must think in terms of what Dante says himself, resisting firmly all efforts to confine him in neat little outlines and footnotes.

Let us remember, to begin with, that Mount Purgatory was made from that part of the Earth's interior, which "rushed up" (*Inf.* xxxiv. 121 *sqq.* and note) when Satan fell from Heaven, and left the Pit of Hell yawning to receive him. Its summit is therefore as far from the surface of the earth as the surface is from the centre: this means that, according to medieval calculations, the Mountain is something over three thousand *miles* high. If this is a little difficult to visualize, we may remind ourselves that when we have scaled the two lower Terraces and been carried up the steep cliff to the three steps before St Peter's Gate (*Purg.* ix), we have reached the place where no rain nor cloud nor snow nor wind ever comes: it is the limit of the Earth's atmosphere. It is here that the real ascent of

---

may abound? God forbid" (*Rom.* vi. 1). The reason is obvious: grace abounds when there is genuine repentance, and we cannot, as the logical demon so rightly observes (*Inf.* xxvii. 118–20), simultaneously will sin and repentance, since this involves a contradiction in terms.

Incidentally, a similar logical fallacy attends all ingenious proposals to "test the efficacy of prayer" by (for example) praying for the patients in Ward A of a hospital and leaving Ward B unprayed for, in order to see which set recovers. Prayer undertaken in that spirit is not prayer at all, and it requires a singular naïvety to imagine that Omniscience could be so easily bamboozled.

Purgatory begins: the seven great Cornices and the final stair to the Earthly Paradise at the top are all piled above it. Without troubling ourselves too much about precise measurements, we may say that the first two Terraces bring us to somewhere about the topmost peak of Mount Everest, and that after that we start climbing in earnest. The Mountain slopes up at an angle "very much steeper than 45°", while the Cornices themselves are incredibly narrow – eighteen feet at the most – and have no parapet. If by this time we are not already giddy, we may also take note that the Third Cornice has to be negotiated in a blinding fog; that the Fifth is so encumbered by prostrate bodies that it is difficult to pick one's way; that the Sixth is blocked at intervals by large trees; and that the Seventh and highest is occupied by a huge wall of flame, so that Dante has to creep cautiously along the extreme outer edge, "between the fire and the precipice". It is true that, above Peter's Gate, the ascent is by stairs and not by scrambling, and that, as the load of sin is gradually lightened by penitence, the going becomes easier and easier, until on the last stair it is as though the pilgrim's feet had wings. That does not diminish the tremendous scale of the poet's conception.

The first stages of the journey are the hardest, and indeed it is only here that Dante complains of difficulty and exhaustion. At the foot of the Mountain there lies a sandy shore, where only soft reeds can withstand the pressure of wind and tide. From this, a precipitous slope, about which we are told nothing except that there is grass upon it in places, leads up to the First Terrace. Thence we proceed by a narrow chimney up a perpendicular rock to the Second Terrace and there, scooped out in the face of the cliff, we find the flower-scented "Valley of the Rulers". The next ascent is so tremendous that Dante's mortal weight has to be carried up to Peter's Gate by heavenly intervention. Once through the Gate, there is the steep and narrow zigzag of the "Needle's Eye" before we emerge at length upon the First Cornice.

I need scarcely say that our little sketch-diagram on p. 62 makes no pretensions to either adequacy or accuracy. The wide and solitary shore, and the spacious Terraces, have had to be compressed almost to nothing, lest the Mountain should soar right out of the book. Moreover, in order to allow the whole ascent to be shown, the stairways have been bent back upon themselves in a way that

Dante did not intend. The actual compass position of the Poets at each stage of the ascent can be seen in the more severely geometrical plan on p. 340. Both diagrams, however, show clearly (what is frequently overlooked) that the face of the Mountain, from East to West, is traversed only *once* in the course of the poem. All the stairways are set upon the Northern side; on the Southern, sunless side, Dante and Virgil never set foot, although the souls of the Penitent, when mobile, run all the way round the Mountain.

The reader in the Northern Hemisphere is earnestly exhorted to remember that he is at the Antipodes, and not to get his compasspoints muddled up. Dante, though he had never in his life crossed the Line, has no moments of forgetfulness or confusion, which is more than can be said for most of us who live beneath the Wain. Readers in Australia, New Zealand, and South Africa will find that (for once, in a European literary classic) the Sun is in the right part of the sky.

D. L. S.

*September 1954*

# CANTO I

THE STORY. *Dante and Virgil, emerging from Hell, find themselves on the shore of the Island of Purgatory at the Antipodes. They are met by Cato, the guardian of the Mountain, who instructs Virgil to wash Dante's face in dew and to gird him with a reed in preparation for the ascent.*

For better waters heading with the wind
　My ship of genius now shakes out her sail
　And leaves that ocean of despair behind;

For to the second realm I tune my tale, 　　　　　　4
　Where human spirits purge thenselves, and train
　To leap up into joy celestial.

Now from the grave wake poetry again, 　　　　　　7
　O sacred Muses I have served so long!
　Now let Calliope uplift her strain

And lift my voice up on the mighty song 　　　　　10
　That smote the miserable Magpies nine
　Out of all hope of pardon for their wrong!

Colour unclouded, orient-sapphirine, 　　　　　　13
　Softly suffusing from meridian height
　Down the still sky to the horizon-line,

Brought to mine eyes renewal of delight 　　　　　16
　So soon as I came forth from that dead air
　Which had oppressed my bosom and my sight.

The lovely planet, love's own quickener, 　　　　　19
　Now lit to laughter all the eastern sky,
　Veiling the Fishes that attended her.

Right-hand I turned, and, setting me to spy 　　　22
　That alien pole, beheld four stars, the same
　The first men saw, and since, no living eye;

Meseemed the heavens exulted in their flame – 　　25
　O widowed world beneath the northern Plough,
　For ever famished of the sight of them!

28     Tearing my eyes away, I scarce know how,
       I turned me toward the other pole – our own,
       Whence Plough and all had wholly vanished now,

31     And saw hard by me an old man alone,
       Whose reverend mien commanded such respect,
       No father could deserve more from a son.

34     Flowing he wore his beard, and silver-flecked,
       Likewise his hair, whereof a double tress,
       Falling this side and that, his shoulders decked;

37     And those four holy stars so poured their rays,
       Gilding his looks with light, that I descried
       Him plain as though the sun shone in his face.

40     "What men are you, that 'gainst the hidden tide
       Have slipped the eternal prison-house?" he said,
       Shaking his honoured locks from side to side.

43     "Who was your guide? your lantern, when you fled
       The night unfathomed that, without surcease,
       Makes dark the infernal valley of the dead?

46     What! broken thus, the laws of the Abyss?
       Or can high Heaven have changed its ordinance,
       That you lost souls should seek my terraces?"

49     At this, my guide, with instant vigilance,
       Seized on me, and by hand and word and sign
       Composed my knees and brow to reverence;

52     Then answered: "Not my power, but Heaven's design
       Brought me; a lady stooped from bliss to pray
       My aid and escort for this charge of mine;

55     But since it is thy will I should display
       More fully how it stands now with our case,
       What will could be in me to say thee nay?

58     This man has not yet seen his term of days,
       Yet in his crazy wickedness he drew
       So near it, he had but short breathing-space.

61     So, as I said, I was dispatched to do
       My utmost for his rescue; nor appeared
       Any good way save this I've set me to.

I've shown him Hell with all its guilty herd,          64
   And mean to show him next the souls who dwell
   Making purgation here beneath thy ward.

How I have brought him through, 'twere long to tell;          67
   Power from on high helps me to guide his feet
   To thee, to see and hear and mark thee well.

Be gracious to his coming, I entreat;          70
   'Tis liberty he seeks – how dear a thing
   That is, they know who give their lives for it;

Thou know'st; for thee this passion drew death's sting          73
   In Utica, where thou didst doff the weed
   Which at the Doom shall shine so glistering.

None breaks for us the dateless law decreed,          76
   For this man lives, and Minos binds not me;
   My circle's that which sees thy Marcia plead

With her chaste eyes, O holy heart, to thee          79
   That thine she is, and thou wilt deem her so.
   For her sake, then, receive us favourably;

Through thy seven kingdoms give us leave to go;          82
   Great praise of thee I'll carry back to her,
   If thou disdain not mention down below."

"Marcia," said he, "when I lived over there,          85
   So pleased the eyes of me, that whatsoever
   She asked me, that I did, and did not spare.

Now that she dwells beyond the evil river          88
   She may not move me, by the edict made
   When I was taken thence – not now, nor ever.

But since thou sayest a heavenly lady's aid          91
   Moves thee and guides, these flatteries are misplaced;
   Ask in her name, that's all that needs be said.

Go, take this man, and see thou gird his waist          94
   With a smooth reed, and from his brow likewise
   Cleanse all this filth with which it is defaced;

He may not meetly go with clouded eyes          97
   Before the great First Minister to stand,
   Who is of those who are of Paradise.

100    All round this little island, on the strand
           Far down below there, where the breakers strive,
           Grow the tall rushes from the oozy sand;

103    No other plant could keep itself alive:
           None that bears leaf, or hardens in its prime
           And will not bend when wind and water drive.

106    Do not come back this way a second time;
           The sun's just rising; he will show a place
           At which the mountain is less hard to climb."

109    He spoke; and promptly vanished from our gaze.
           I rose without a word, and to my guide
           Drew near, and fixed my eyes upon his face.

112    "Follow my footsteps, little son; abide
           Close by me. Turn we round; this way," said he,
           "The plain slopes low to meet the encircling tide."

115    And the dawn rose triumphant, making flee
           The morning breeze before her; and far off
           I recognized the shimmering of the sea.

118    So we along that lonely plain did move,
           Like one who's lost the road and seems to go
           With wasted steps till repossessed thereof;

121    And coming to a place where dew can show
           Resistance to the sun, since day-long shade
           Keeps the earth cool and exhalation slow,

124    Gently upon the turf my master spread
           Both hands; and I, not taken unawares,
           But understanding what this purported,

127    Held up to him my face begrimed with tears;
           And so he brought my native hue once more
           To light, washed clean of hell's disfiguring smears.

130    When we had reached the solitary shore
           Which ne'er saw seaman yet who after found
           Skill to recross that sea by sail and oar,

> There, as Another pleased, he girt me round;    133
>     And soon as it was plucked – O, strange to say!
>     Just as it was, from that same spot of ground,
>
> The humble plant sprang up again straightway.    136

THE IMAGES. *Cato of Utica* (for whose history see Glossary) was for
the Romans, and also for the men of the Middle Ages, the accepted
type of the (natural) moral virtues. For the purposes of the *story*,
he is chosen to guard the approach to Mount Purgatory; since
the ascent of the Mountain is a moral progress in which the
natural virtues are purified and strengthened by Grace. Dante thus
emphasizes *allegorically* the Catholic assertion that Grace does not
oust or destroy Nature, but redeems and perfects it. The passage
about Marcia (ll. 85–90) makes it, however, clear that when nat-
ural morality is taken up into the Christian life, it cannot retain its
former attachments, but must spring from a new root and be
wholly reorientated.

When this has been said, there remain some puzzling factors
about Dante's treatment of this figure. Cato has been taken out of
Limbo, detached from his former associations and affections, and
set, until the end of time, on what may be called "Christian ter-
ritory". Yet there is no suggestion that he will ever himself climb
the Mountain which he guards; nor, although we are assured that
Cato's resurrection body will be a glorious one, is it ever specifi-
cally stated that he will eventually enter Heaven like the redeemed
pagans Trajan and Rhipeus (*Para.* xx. 103 *sqq.*). It may be, as J. S.
Carroll suggests, that in the Last Day he will return to become the
brightest and most authoritative inhabitant of the Elysian Fields in
Limbo, "giving laws there to the good in the hidden place", as
Virgil wrote of him (*Aen.* viii. 670). Certainly, Cato does not bear
about with him the atmosphere of Grace: when we compare him
with the souls actually redeemed in Purgatory, and still more with
the angel-guardians of the Cornices, we see that he lacks the inten-
sity, the exuberance, and the courtesy which are the marks of those
in Grace; he is, in a word, ungracious. He is a moral imperative,
founded in duty rather than in love: a preparation for penitence,
but not penitence itself; as such a very recognizable figure, and
acceptable enough if we concentrate on his *allegorical* function
rather than on his personal destiny as a character in the *story*.

*The Four Stars*. These typify the Cardinal Virtues (Justice, Prudence,
Temperence, and Fortitude) belonging to natural morality, and so

common to good pagan and Christian alike. These virtues are called "cardinal" (from *cardo*, a hinge) because all natural morality hangs and turns upon them.

*The Dew*. Before ascending the Mountain, Dante's face must be cleansed from the tears he shed in Hell. The penitent's first duty is cheerfulness: having recognized his sin he must put it out of his mind and not wallow in self-pity and self-reproach, which are forms of egotism. (Cf. also *Inf*. xx. 29–30 and note.)

*The Reed*. The reader will remember that Dante's original rope-girdle was thrown over the Great Barrier between Upper and Nether Hell, to call up the monster Fraud. (See *Inf*. xvi. Images.) He is now given a new one, made of the pliant reed which symbolizes Humility, as a safeguard against Pride, which is the head and source of all the Capital Sins.

NOTES. l. 7: *Now from the grave*, etc.: This is the first invocation, addressed to the Muses, and in particular to Calliope, the Muse of Epic Poetry.

l. 11: *The miserable Magpies*: the nine daughters of Pireus, King of Emathia challenged the nine Muses to a singing-contest. They were defeated, and changed, for their presumption, into magpies.

ll. 19–21: *The lovely planet ... that attended her*: Venus, the planet of love, was not actually in the constellation of Pisces (the Fishes) in the spring of 1300. Dante was probably misled by the Almanac of Profhacius (a perpetual calendar widely used in his time) which shows the varying positions of Sun, Moon, and Planets from day to day over whole cycles of years. In the Hebrew original, all the cycles begin in the year 1301; but in the Latin edition (which Dante would have used) they all begin in 1300, *except* those of Venus and the Sun, which begin in 1301. In some copies the error has been corrected by placing a "1" at the top of the column for Venus; others contain no indication of the discrepancy, while in yet others the date 1300 has been wrongly inserted. Since both the Hebrew and Latin prefaces state that *all* the cycles begin in 1300, anyone consulting an uncorrected copy to see where Venus was in March–April of that year would naturally look in the first column, and would find there that she was passing into Pisces at the end of the month; though in fact this was true, not for 1300, but for 1301. This seems the simplest explanation for the error; on the other hand, Dante may possibly have been following a traditional disposition of all the planets at the time of the Creation (cf. *Inf*. i. 37–40).

ll. 23–4: *that alien pole*, etc.: the South Pole, which, with its attendant stars, would have been visible to Adam and Eve in the Earthly Paradise at the summit of Mount Purgatory, but never seen again after the Fall and the Expulsion, when man's habitation was removed to the Northern Hemisphere. This statement would appear to exclude the supposition that Dante had heard of the Southern Cross from Marco Polo or other travellers. (It seems to have slipped his memory that in *Inf.* xxvi. 127–8 he had described Ulysses and his fellow-voyagers as seeing "the other pole with all its stars".)

l. 31: *an old man alone*: Cato. He was actually only 49 at the time of his death, so that Dante's description of him is not so much realistic as appropriate to his venerable character. His face is illuminated (ll. 37–9) by the cardinal virtues (but not by the stars representing the theological graces, which rise later, viii. 85–93).

l. 40: *'gainst the hidden tide*: the Poets had followed the river of Lethe *upstream* out of Hell (see *Inf.* xxxiv. 127–35, and note).

l. 53: *a lady*: i.e. Beatrice.

l. 58: *his term of days*: the death (literally) of the body and (allegorically) of the soul (cf. *Inf.* i. 25–7, 94–6).

l. 73: *thou know'st*, etc.: Cato committed suicide (see Glossary) rather than submit to Caesar's tyranny. This is another instance of Dante's ambivalent attitude to Caesar (see *Inf.* xxxiv and Images). Cato is not, like Brutus and Cassius, relegated to Hell as an opponent of the Empire; because of his devotion to political liberty he is here made guardian of the path to spiritual liberty. Neither does his suicide qualify him for Hell, since the heathen are judged by their own code, which did not necessarily condemn suicide. On this point Dante is quite consistent: he places no *Christian* suicides in Purgatory or Paradise and no *pagans* in the portion of Hell (Circle vii, Ring 1) appointed for the punishment of suicides (*Inf.* xiii).

l. 74: *the weed*: i.e. the body.

ll. 77–8: *Minos binds not me*: as a virtuous pagan, Virgil is not subject to Minos, the infernal judge. *My circle*: i.e. Limbo, which lies above the seat of Minos and the circles of Hell proper. (See *Inf.* iv and v and the map of Hell in that volume.)

l. 78: *Marcia*: the wife of Cato (see Glossary).

l. 82: *thy seven kingdoms*: the seven Cornices of the Mountain, on which the Capital Sins are successively purged.

l. 88: *the evil river*: Acheron (see *Inf.* iii. 70 *sqq.*).

ll. 89–90: *the edict made when I was taken thence*: Cato was presumably taken out of Limbo, and the edict concerning him made, at the Harrowing of Hell, when Purgatory was first established. The fact that Dante does not mention this in Virgil's account (*Inf.* iv. 52–63) of the Harrowing suggests that he had not at that time considered the use he was to make of Cato.

l. 98: *the great First Minister*: the angel at the gate of Purgatory (ix. 78 *sqq.*).

l. 133: *as Another pleased*: the mark of humility is submission to the will of another (Cato) or of Another (God). The phrase (*come altrui piacque*) first occurs in *Inf.* xxvi. 141, where the submission is involuntary, whereas here it is embraced by the will (cf. *John* xxi. 18).

# CANTO II

THE STORY. *The Ship of Souls arrives at the Island, steered by an Angel, and bringing a boat-load of the newly-dead from the mouth of Tiber to Purgatory. One of the souls is Dante's friend, Casella the Musician. He recognizes the Poet, and delights him and the other spirits by singing one of Dante's own songs. The party is broken up by Cato, who chides them for lingering and sends them about their business.*

The sun by now o'er that horizon's rim
   Was sinking, whose meridian circle stands
   With its mid-arch above Jerusalem,

While night, who wheels opposed to him, from sands    4
   Of Ganges mounted with the Scales, whose weight
   Drops in her hour of victory from her hands;

So that, where we were, fair Aurora, late    7
   Flushing from white to rose-vermilion,
   Grew sallow with ripe age and matron state.

And still we stood beside the sea alone,    10
   Like travellers uncertain of their way,
   Whose bodies linger while the heart hies on.

And lo! as sometimes at the approach of day    13
   Mars in the West across the ocean floor
   Glows through thick vapour with a dim, red ray,

Even so – God send I see that sight once more! –    16
   I saw a light come speeding o'er the sea,
   So swift, flight knows no simile therefor.

For a brief space I turned inquiringly    19
   Back to my guide; then looked again, and lo!
   Bigger and brighter far it seemed to me.

Then, from each side of it, there seemed to grow    22
   A white I-knew-not-what; and there appeared
   Another whiteness, bit by bit, below.

Now all this time my master spoke no word,    25
   Till plain we saw, those first two whitenesses
   Were wings; and knowing then what helmsman steered,

28    "Down, down!" he cried, "fold hands and bow thy knees;
        Behold the angel of the Lord! Henceforth
        Thou shalt see many of these great emissaries.

31    See how he scorns all instruments of earth,
        Needing no oar, no sail but his own wings,
        'Twixt shores that span so vast an ocean's girth.

34    See how each soaring pinion heavenward springs,
        Beating the air with pens imperishable
        That are not mewed like mortal coverings."

37    And near and nearer as he came full sail
        The bird of God shone momently more bright,
        So that mine eyes endured him not, but fell.

40    And hard on toward the shore he steered his flight,
        Borne forward in a ship that skimmed apace,
        Drawing no water, 'twas so swift and light.

43    Freehold of bliss apparent in his face,
        The heavenly pilot on the poop stood tiptoe,
        And with him full an hundred souls had place.

46    *"In exitu Israel de Aegypto,"*
        From end to end they sang their holy lay
        In unison; and so he brought the ship to.

49    He signed them with the blessed cross, and they,
        All with one motion, leapt upon the strand;
        Then, swiftly as he came, he went his way.

52    Those left behind seemed strangers in the land,
        Gazing about like men who test and try
        Some unknown thing they seek to understand.

55    The sun with his sure arrows had made fly
        The Goat from out mid-heaven, and far and wide
        Was shooting shafts of day all round the sky,

58    When those new folk caught sight of us, and cried:
        "Tell us, we beg, if you are able to,
        Which way will bring us to the mountain-side."

61    Virgil replied: "Belike you think us two
        Familiar with the place; it is not thus,
        For we are strangers here as much as you;

We've just arrived, a short while previous                    64
   To you, but by so steep and rough a road
   That this new climb will seem child's play to us."

Then, when they looked at me, whose breathing showed         67
   That I was still alive, each spirit's brow
   Grew pallid with surprise; and in like mode

As, when a courier with an olive-bough                       70
   Comes, bringing news, the townsfolk throng to hear,
   Jostling each other unabashed, so now

Did all those souls, so happy as they were,                  73
   Rivet inquiring eyes upon my face,
   Well-nigh forgetting to go make them fair;

And one I saw advance, all eagerness                         76
   To clasp me in its arms, whose looks expressed
   Such love as moved me to a like embrace.

O shades! vain visual shows no touch can test!               79
   Three times I felt my hands behind it meet,
   Three times they came back empty to my breast.

I think amazement in my face was writ                        82
   In changing colours, for the shade withdrew
   Smiling, and I plunged forward after it.

Gently it bade me cease; at once I knew                      85
   What man it was, and begged him to bestow
   One moment on me, and a word or two.

"As in my mortal bonds I loved thee, so                      88
   I love thee free; and therefore I will stay;
   I stay," said he; "but wherefore dost thou go?"

"O my Casella, in the hope some day                          91
   To come back here, I journey now," I cried;
   "But thou? What's caused thee all this long delay?"

"I am not wronged, if he who may decide                      94
   Both when to lade his vessel, and with whom,
   Hath oft refused me waftage," he replied.

"For the just will shapes his. But now, for some             97
   Three months he hath received without demur
   Any and all of us who wish to come.

100    So, when I sought that shore where first the stir
             Of the salt wave meets Tiber, he anon
             Graciously took me as his passenger.

103    Thither again his pinions bear him on,
             For to that spot all souls come presently,
             So be they sink not down to Acheron."

106    Then I: "If no new law prohibit thee
             Skill or remembrance of those songs of love
             Which once could charm all fevers out of me,

109    Beseech thee, sing; and comfortingly move
             My spirit, which in this dull body taking
             The long road here, faints with the toil thereof."

112    "*Love in my mind his conversation making,*"
             Thus he began, so sweetly that I find
             Within me still the dulcet echoes waking.

115    My master and I and all that spirit-kind
             That came to him, hung on those notes of his
             Entranced, as bearing nothing else in mind.

118    Stock-still we stood, intent no word to miss,
             When lo! that reverend elder, all at once
             Crying: "How now, you laggard souls! what's this?

121    Why all this dawdling? why this negligence?
             Run to the mountains, slough away the filth
             That will not let you see God's countenance."

124    Like as, when pigeons gather on the tilth
             To make a goodly feast of wheat or tares,
             Their pouting pride put by, a commonwealth

127    Of peaceful industry, if aught appears
             To scare them, off they go and quit their feeding,
             Driven by pressure of more urgent cares:

130    So, breaking from the song, I saw them heading
             Towards the slope, that new-found company,
             Like men who speed, nor know to what they're speeding;

133    And we went too, and no less hastily.

THE IMAGES. *The Ship of Souls.* The imagery of this canto hardly needs elucidation, but it is interesting to note the parallels and contrasts with the corresponding imagery in *Inf.* iii. The souls of the damned assemble on the bank of the River Acheron, and are ferried to Hell by the Demon Charon: the souls of the saved assemble at the mouth of the River Tiber, and are ferried by an Angelic Pilot across the whole width of the world to Purgatory. In each case, the ferryman selects his own boat-load. Charon plies an oar (which he uses, incidentally, to thump his passengers into submission): the Angel needs "no oar, no sail but his own wings". The damned, wailing and blaspheming, embark one by one (fellowship is lost); the saved sing their hymn in unison and disembark all together (fellowship is recovered).

NOTES. ll. 1–9: *The sun by now*, etc.: It is sunset at Jerusalem (in the Northern Hemisphere) and consequently sunrise in Purgatory (at the Antipodes). The Ganges, in India, is taken as lying on the eastern horizon of Jerusalem, and the Pillars of Hercules on the western. Since (as we know from *Inf.* i. 37) the Sun is in Aries (the Ram), Night is located in the opposite sign from him – that of Libra (the Scales). The Scales "fall from the hand of Night" when the Sun enters the sign, i.e. at the autumn equinox, when the nights become longer than the days (Night's "hour of victory").

l. 7: *fair Aurora*: the goddess of dawn. The white glimmer and the rosy flush of early daybreak are giving place to the yellow light of the rising sun.

ll. 17–24: *a light ... from each side of it ... a white I knew-not-what ... another whiteness bit by bit below*: Dante sees the ship coming up over the curve of the earth. The "light" is the glory about the head of the angel standing on the poop; the two white appearances which follow are the angel's wings; the "other whiteness" rising gradually into sight "below" is the body of the standing angel and, finally, the hull of the boat.

l. 42: *so swift and light*: This is the "lighter skiff" to which Charon referred in *Inf.* iii. 91–3, when he said that Dante should pass by "another road and other ferries".

l. 43: *freehold of bliss*: reading *per iscritto,* and rendering "as though a charter of bliss had been conferred upon him" (the text is disputed).

l. 46: *in exitu Israel de Aegypto*: "When Israel came out of Egypt", the opening verse of *Ps.* cxiv (*Vulg.* cxiii). In his *Letter to Can Grande,* Dante gives the literal, allegorical, moral, and anagogical (mystical) interpretations of this verse (see Introduction to *Inf.* pp. 14–15).

l. 56: *the Goat*: When Aries is on the eastern horizon the constellation of Capricornus (the Goat) is on the meridian. The rays of the rising sun have blotted out the starlight as far as mid-heaven, and are extending their brightness all over the sky.

l. 61: *Virgil replied*, etc.: It lends a homely touch to Purgatory to know that persons asking the way are liable, there as here, to receive the answer, "I'm a stranger here myself".

l. 67: *whose breathing showed*: in the diffused dawnlight of Purgatory, as in the gloom of Hell, the spirits know Dante to be alive by seeing him breathe (cf. *Inf.* xxiii. 88–9). Later, the poet's ingenuity will devise various other means of recognition.

l. 70: *an olive-bough*: traditionally carried by the bearer of good tidings.

ll. 80–1: *three times*, etc.: Dante is here imitating Virgil (*Aen.* vi. 700–2), who in his turn is imitating Homer (*Od.* xi. 204–8). In hell, Dante represents the shades as weightless (*Inf.* viii. 26–7, xxiv. 32) but palpable (*Inf.* xxxii. 76 *sqq.* etc.). In Purgatory, the shade of Casella is here represented as impalpable to Dante's grasp, though Dante can grasp Virgil (viii. 41), and the great spirits appointed to guide him can grasp and lift him (e.g. Lucy, ix. 59 and Matilda, xxxi, 100–101). The aery bodies (see *Purg.* xxv. 88–105) supplied to the shades are, in the Divine economy, made adequate to their necessary functions (iii. 31–2); here it is not necessary that Dante should embrace Casella, but rather desirable that he should be reminded of the difference in their conditions.

l. 90: *wherefore dost thou* (i.e. a living man) *go*: (i.e. by the way of the dead?).

l. 91: *Casella*: little is known of him, but the old commentators all agree that he was a musician, born either in Florence or Pistoia, who had set some of Dante's songs to music. Milton refers to the present passage in his *Sonnet to Mr H. Lawes*.

l. 92: *to come back here*: i.e. after death.

l. 93: *this long delay*: Casella had apparently died some little time previously, and Dante is surprised to find him only just arriving in Purgatory.

l. 97: *the just will*: i.e. God's will, to which the angel's will conforms.

l. 98: *for some three months*: The benefits of the papal indulgences granted to pilgrims in the Jubilee Year of 1300 were extended to the souls of those dying in that year. The Bull of Jubilee, though not promulgated till 22 Feb. 1300, was made retrospective to Christmas 1299 (the end of the year according to the style of the Roman Curia), so that by the date of Dante's vision it has been operative in Purgatory for "some three months".

l. 101: *Tiber*: The angel's vessel sets out from the port of Rome, the City of St Peter and central see of Christendom.

l. 106: *new law*: "the conditions of your new life".

l. 112: *"Love in my mind"*, etc.: Casella sings Dante's own *canzone*, *Amor che nella mente mi ragiona*, one of those included in the *Convivio*, for which he had presumably composed the setting.

# CANTO III

THE STORY. *The Poets climb the lower slopes of the Mountain, where Dante's solitary shadow, cast by the rising sun, poignantly brings home to him the fact that Virgil is only a shade. At the foot of a steep cliff they encounter the souls of the Excommunicate, detained upon this First Terrace of Ante-Purgatory, and converse with Manfred, who explains to them the law of the Terrace.*

Though in their hurried flight the shadows thus
    Were running scattered o'er the champaign wide
    Towards the Mount where Justice searches us,

4    I still clung closely to my faithful guide;
    How had I sped without his comradeship?
    Who would have brought me up the mountain-side?

7    He looked as though remorse had stung him deep:
    O noble conscience, clear and undefaced,
    How keen thy self-reproach for one small slip!

10    Now when his feet had put away the haste
    Which robs all actions of their dignity,
    My mind, till then in one strait groove compressed,

13    Expanded, letting eager thought range free,
    And I looked up to that great mountain, soaring
    Highest to Heaven from the encircling sea.

16    Fire-red behind our backs the sun was pouring
    Light on the slope before us, broken where
    I blocked the rays, my shadowy outline scoring

19    Black on the ground – I whipped about in fear,
    Abandoned, as I thought, beholding how
    I, and I only, made a darkness there.

22    My Comfort turned and faced me: "Why wilt thou
    Always mistrust? Believ'st thou not I come
    Still at thy side and lead thee even now?

25    'Tis vesper-tide already where the tomb
    Yet holds the body in which I once cast shade;
    Naples received it from Brundisium.

Though shadowless I go, be not dismayed,     28
  Nor marvel more than at the heavens, which fleet
  Their radiance through from sphere to sphere unstayed.

Bodies like mine, to bear pain, cold and heat,     31
  That power ordains, whose will forever spreads
  A veil between its working and our wit.

Madness! that reason lodged in human heads     34
  Should hope to traverse backward and unweave
  The infinite path Three-personed Substance treads.

Content you with the *quia*, sons of Eve:     37
  For had you power to see the whole truth plain
  No need had been for Mary to conceive;

And you have seen such great souls thirst in vain     40
  As else had stilled that thirst in quietness
  Which now is given them for eternal pain;

I speak of Plato, Aristotle – yes,     43
  And many others." Here he bent his head
  And moved on, silent, with a troubled face.

Meanwhile, we'd reached the mountain's foot – and dead     46
  Upright it rose, a cliff so steep and sheer,
  'Twould make the nimblest legs seem dull as lead.

The craggiest way, the most remote and drear     49
  Between Turbia and Lerici, you'd call,
  Compared with that, a broad and easy stair.

My master stopped: "Now, who can tell at all     52
  Which side," said he, "these ridges slope, to give
  A chance for wingless men to climb the wall?"

And as with downcast eyes contemplative     55
  He stood and searched his mind which way to go,
  While I gazed up and round about the cliff,

I saw a troop of spirits moving slow,     58
  So slow towards us on the left of me,
  'Twas hard to tell if they came on or no.

"Master," said I, "lift up thine eyes and see;     61
  Here come some people we can call upon,
  If thine own wisdom cannot counsel thee."

64    He looked, and said with frank delight: "Come on;
          They're slow – we'll go to meet this loitering band;
          And be thou steadfast still in hope, dear son."

67    When still they were as far – after we'd spanned,
          That is, what here we'd call a thousand paces –
          As a stone's cast from a good slinger's hand,

70    They all shrank up to the rough rock that raises
          Its towering height there, and stood huddling, checked
          Like one who walks perplexed, and stops and gazes.

73    "O souls peace-parted, souls already elect,"
          Virgil began, "by that same peace I pray
          Which, as I think, you eagerly expect,

76    Tell us, where slopes the cliff, to make a way
          That man may climb? For they who know its worth
          Fret most when time is wasted in delay."

79    Then, just as from the fold the sheep come forth,
          By one, by two, by three, and others go
          Timidly bunched behind them, nose to earth,

82    And what the first one does, the others do,
          Bumping against her if she stops, and wait
          Silly and meek, though why they do not know,

85    So of that flock most blest, most fortunate,
          I saw the leaders move as to come on,
          With modest looks and tripping step sedate;

88    But when they saw the radiance of the sun
          Broken upon the hillside as I came,
          And on my right saw the long shadow run

91    To touch the rock, they halted, drawing them
          Somewhat aback; and following these, the rest
          Not knowing why or wherefore, did the same.

94    "Before you ask me, let it stand confessed,
          This thing you see, that cleaves the falling light,
          Is a man's body, plain and manifest.

97    Be not afraid, for not without the might,
          Believe you well, of grace from heaven shed
          Does he come here and seek to scale this height."

90

Thus far my lord: the kindly people said:      100
   "Turn round then, go before us – that way, see!"
   And with their hands backhanded waved ahead.

And one began: "Whoever thou may'st be,      103
   Look backward as thou goest; consider, do,
   If, yonder, thou didst e'er set eyes on me."

I turned to him and took a careful view;      106
   Buxom he was, and blond, and debonair,
   Only he had one eyebrow cloven through.

When I had modestly confessed, I ne'er      109
   Had seen his face: "Nay, look!" quoth he, and on
   His upper breast showed me a fearful scar:

Then, smiling, said: "Manfred am I, grandson      112
   To Empress Constance: wherefore, grant me this:
   On thy return, pray go, and tell my own

Fair daughter, mother of the majesties      115
   Of Sicily and Aragon, the truth,
   Should any man report my tale amiss.

When I had suffered two strokes, mortal both,      118
   I sighed my soul out weeping unto Him
   Whose whole delight is always to have ruth.

My sins were horrible in the extreme,      121
   Yet such the infinite mercy's wide embrace,
   Its arms go out to all who turn to them.

And ere Cosenza's bishop ran to chase      124
   Me out, by Clement's orders, had he once
   Well read the word of God, and marked that place,

Still would the kind earth keep my body's bones      127
   At Benevento by the bridgehead, trenched
   And guarded by the heavy cairn of stones.

Now they tie tumbled by the wind and drenched      130
   With rain, beyond the realm, by Verde river,
   Where he translated them with tapers quenched.

Their curse cannot so damn a man for ever      133
   That the eternal love may not return
   While one green hope puts forth the feeblest sliver.

136    True, he who dies in contumacy and scorn
         Of Holy Church, though dying he repent,
         Must stay outside this barrier here, and mourn

139    Thirty long years for every year he spent
         In his presumption, save good prayers should gain
         Remission of his term of banishment.

142    See if thou canst not make me happy, then;
         Tell my kind Constance thou hast seen me; touch
         Upon this ban of exile – make all plain;

145    You people there can help us here so much."

THE IMAGES. *The Excommunicate*: Those who have incurred excommunication, and have thus been cut off from the sacraments, guidance, and fellowship of the Church, are condemned to wander "as sheep that have no shepherd" thirty times as long as their contumacy lasted upon earth. Although they repented in their last hour (otherwise they would never have reached Purgatory) they left themselves no time for formal reconciliation, and no opportunity to make satisfaction; satisfaction must therefore be made here, and their punishment (like all other *penal* inflictions in the *Comedy*) is simply the sin itself: the old self-banishment and the old delay. But, unlike the impenitent in Hell, they endure their suffering in hope and patience.

   No prayer is allotted to the Excommunicate – doubtless because of their severance from the Church.

NOTES. l. 9: *reproach for one small slip*: Cf. and contrast the passage in *Inf.* xxx. 142–4, where Virgil has rebuked Dante for a similar dawdling to listen. "The difference between [Virgil] and Dante is that the Florentine is delayed by the obscenity of Hell, the Roman only by the song of love in the island of purgatory: yet for that his self-reproach is as deep as Dante's had been, and Dante says, as Virgil had said, 'How little the fault!' But Virgil had said it aloud, and Dante does not; there are degrees in such things: it is not for Dante – Christian and capable of beatitude though he may be – to console Virgil. This certainly is one of the preludes to the inothering, to observe everywhere a proper courtesy. The great may have their faults: but our business is to remember their greatness and not cheapen it" – Charles Williams: *The Figure of Beatrice*.

   l. 18: *my shadowy outline*: the sun is now risen, and casts a defined shadow. Note the artistic skill which reserves this beautiful effect for the present passage, instead of squandering it on Dante's encounter with the shades in the previous canto.

l. 25: *vesper-tide*: It is 3 P.M. in Italy (where Virgil's body is buried): and therefore 6 P.M. in Jerusalem and 6 A.M. in Purgatory.

l. 27: *Naples received it from Brundisium*: Virgil died (19 B.C.) at Brundisium (Brindisi), in Apulia on the Adriatic coast, and his body was transferred by the orders of Augustus to Naples. His supposed tomb is still to be seen, on the road to Pozzuoli.

ll. 29–30: *the heavens ... unstayed*: the rays of the sun pass unobstructed through the aery body of Virgil as those of the outermost planets pass through the series of transparent spheres on which the inner planets are carried (see *Dante's Universe, Inf.* p. 292).

l. 31: *bodies like mine*: for the full explanation of the aery body, see below, Canto xxv. 88 *sqq*.

l. 37: *content you with the quia*: Aristotle, and, following him, the Schoolmen, distinguish between two kinds of demonstration: (1) the knowledge *that* a thing is, obtained by arguing *a posteriori*, from effect to cause: this is the demonstration *quia*; (2) the knowledge *why* a thing is as it is, obtained by arguing *a priori*, from cause to effect: this is the demonstration *propter quid*. In this life, finite minds cannot (ll. 32–6) know God as He is (in His quiddity), but only by His effects; and must therefore be content to know only the *quia* of His mysterious Providence.

l. 39: *no need had been for Mary to conceive*: Had it been possible for mankind to know all things *propter quid*, there would have been no need for the revelation in human terms by the Incarnation. And had Adam and Eve been contented with the *quia*, man would not have fallen, nor needed to be redeemed by Christ's death (cf. xxix. 23–30 and note).

l. 42: *which now is given them for eternal pain*: the pagan philosophers in Limbo eternally retain the desire of knowing God, without hope of fulfilment (*Inf.* iv. 41–2).

l. 50: *between Turbia and Lerici*: a village and town at the W. and E. extremities of the Genoese riviera, a district studded with steep and, in Dante's time, almost unscalable acclivities.

l. 61: "*Master*", *said I*, etc.: Note that here, in Purgatory, Dante is emboldened to offer Virgil suggestions about procedure, which are amiably received.

l. 65: *this loitering band*: these are the Excommunicate.

l. 68: *what here we'd call a thousand paces*: Dante means us to understand that distances in Purgatory are not commensurable with ours, but that if one thinks of about half a mile one will get the right impression.

l. 70: *they all shrank*, etc.: Having no leader, the souls are timid and uncertain: they are not merely perplexed, but terrified by Dante's shadow (ll. 88–92), and seem to find a living man as alarming as a ghost is to living men.

l. 112: *Manfred* (1231–66): natural son of the Emperor Frederick II, and grandson of the Emperor Henry VI and his wife Constance, was a pillar of the Ghibelline cause. At his father's death in 1250, he was ruler of Apulia and Sicily, and much beloved by his subjects. He was driven out by his legitimate brother, Conrad IV; but on the latter's death he in turn expelled his nephew Conradin IV; and in 1258 was crowned at Palermo. Pope Clement IV, however, excommunicated him as a Ghibelline and heretic, setting up in his place Charles of Anjou (*q.v.* Glossary), who in 1265 entered Italy with a large army, and in 1266 overthrew and killed Manfred at Benevento. After three days' search, Manfred's body was found by a camp-follower and brought to Charles, who granted him honourable burial, though not in consecrated ground, because he was excommunicate. He was, therefore, buried at the foot of the bridge at Benevento, under a cairn to which each soldier contributed a stone. But later, the Bishop of Cosenza, by command of the Pope, had the body taken up and deposited on the banks of the Verde (now the Garigliano) beyond the confines of the kingdom of Naples and the Church States.

Villani describes Manfred as "comely of his body and as dissolute as his father, and more so. He was a musician and singer, and delighted in the company of jesters, courtiers, and courtesans, and always dressed in green; he was very liberal and courteous and debonair (*di buon aire*), so that he was greatly loved and gracious; but all his life he was an Epicurean, caring neither for God nor His saints, but only for bodily pleasure. He was an enemy of the Church and the clergy". (*Chron*: vi. 46.)

ll. 115–16: *the majesties of Sicily and Aragon*: Manfred's daughter Constance married Peter III of Aragon, and had three sons who succeeded one another as kings of Aragon and Sicily (v. *subt.* vii. 115–20).

l. 121: *my sins were horrible*: Manfred was further accused (rightly or wrongly) of having murdered his father, his brother Conrad, and two of his nephews, and of attempting to murder his nephew Conradin. These charges are chronicled by Brunetto Latini in his *Livre dou Trésor*, which Dante had certainly read (*Inf*. xv. 30 and note).

# CANTO IV

**THE STORY.** *The Poets accompany the spirits of the Excommunicate till they reach a steep cranny in the rock-face. Here, quitting their guides, they climb to the Second Terrace of Ante-Purgatory. Virgil explains to Dante why, at the Antipodes, they see the Sun in the North. They meet with a group of the Late-Repentant, one of whom, the lazy Belacqua, tells them of the rule which governs that Terrace.*

When some one faculty, by its apprehension
    Of pain or pleasure, grows so clamorous
    That it commands the soul's entire attention,

Of all powers else the soul's oblivious –         4
    Which goes to show how false is the surmise
    That soul is kindled above soul in us.

Thus, when such things engage our ears or eyes     7
    As bend the soul towards them totally,
    Time passes, and we mark not how it flies;

For that which marks it is one faculty;         10
    Another, that which masters the whole soul;
    This one is bound, as 'twere, and that one free.

This truth I now experienced to the full,         13
    While to that spirit I hearkened marvelling;
    For lo! the sun had mounted up a whole

Fifty degrees without my noticing,         16
    When we arrived at where those souls all cried:
    "Here's what you seek!" in one voice chorussing.

Often the labourer fills a gap more wide         19
    With a little forkful of thorns, when the purple dye
    Darkens upon the grape toward vintage-tide,

A wider gap than the cleft my guide and I,         22
    He first, I after him, had to climb alone
    When that flock left us, bidding us good-bye.

You can mount up to San Leo, or to Noli scramble down,   25
    You can tackle tall Bismantova and clamber to the top
    On your two flat feet; but this way has to be flown;

28    You must fly with the plumes, I mean, and be lifted up
    On the wings of desire, still following at the back
    Of that great leader who gave to me light and hope.

31    So in we went and up through the stony crack,
    Wedged either side between the rock-walls sheer,
    Needing both hands and feet to grip the track.

34    And when we had scaled the cranny and got out clear
    At the high cliff's top on the slope of the open hill:
    "Master," said I, "where do we go from here?"

37    And he: "Let not one foot fall back, but still
    Follow on up the mountain, till we light
    On some good escort to assist our skill."

40    So high the summit, it outsoared the sight;
    So steep the slope, the line from centre straight
    Up to mid-quadrant is far less upright.

43    Soon I grew tired: "Don't go at such a rate,"
    I cried; "Dear father – see! I shall get stuck
    All by myself here if thou wilt not wait."

46    "My son," said he, "drag thyself onward – look!
    As far as there"; and, pointing up, he showed,
    Running all round that side, a ledge of rock

49    Not far above. His words were such a goad,
    I strained to follow, and with desperate pressure
    Crawled on – crawled up – and on the terrace stood.

52    Here we sat down, both facing East, to measure
    Our climb from where it started – for it's grand
    Thus to look back, and gives all travellers pleasure.

55    I turned mine eyes first downward to the strand,
    Then to the sun – and stared to see him go
    So that he smote us on the leftward hand.

58    The poet saw me gaping there, as though
    Dumbfounded, at the chariot of the day
    Driving its course 'twixt us and Aquilo;

61    Wherefore: "If Castor," he began to say,
    "And Pollux were in consort with that burning
    Mirror which up and downward casts its ray,

Thou wouldst behold the kindled Zodiac turning     64
   Yet closer to the Bears; if it did not,
   It would have strayed, its ancient path unlearning.

Come, recollect thyself and work it out –     67
   So: think of Zion and this mountain here
   As being so placed on earth that they have got

A separate hemisphere for each, but share     70
   The same horizon; thus, that road ill-tried
   By Phaeton the luckless charioteer,

Must, when it passes Zion on one side     73
   Pass this upon the other, as, if thou
   Hast a clear brain, thou wilt be satisfied."

"Master of mine," said I, "indeed I vow     76
   'Tis plain as plain, and never yet saw I
   So well what first perplexed me; namely, how

What one art calls the Equator of the sky,     79
   The median circle of the moving spheres,
   Which still 'twixt winter and the sun doth lie,

Stands North from hence as far as in past years     82
   The Hebrews saw it toward the Southern heat –
   For just that cause which in thy speech appears.

But let me ask thee now, how far our feet     85
   Have yet to walk; the hill soars up and goes
   Higher than my sight can soar to follow it."

"This mount is such," he answered, "that to those     88
   Starting at the foot it's hard in the extreme;
   The more they climb, the easier it grows;

Therefore, when the ascent of it shall seem     91
   Right pleasant to thee, and the going smooth
   As when a boat floats downward with the stream,

That will be journey's end, and then in sooth     94
   After long toil look thou for ease at last;
   More I can't say, but this I know for truth."

He'd hardly spoken when, from somewhere fast     97
   Beside us, came a voice which said: "Maybe
   Thou'lt need to sit ere all that road is passed."

100     At this we both glanced round inquiringly,
             And on our left observed a massive boulder,
             Which up till then we had not chanced to see.

103     This, when explored, revealed to the beholder
             A group of persons lounging in the shade,
             As lazy people lounge, behind its shoulder.

106     And one of them, whose attitude displayed
             Extreme fatigue, sat there and clasped his knees,
             Drooping between them his exhausted head.

109     "O good my lord," said I, "pray look at this
             Bone-lazy lad, content to sit and settle
             Like sloth's own brother taking of his ease!"

112     Then he gave heed, and turning just a little
             Only his face upon his thigh, he grunted:
             "Go up then, thou, thou mighty man of mettle."

115     I knew him then; and proved that, though I panted
             Still from the climb, I was not so bereft
             Of breath, I could not reach him if I wanted.

118     When I drew near him he would scarcely shift
             His head to say: "Nay, hast thou, really though,
             Grasped why the sun's car drives upon thy left?"

121     My lips twitched at the grudging speech, and slow
             Gestures. "Belacqua," I began, "I see
             I need not grieve for thee henceforward; no,

124     But tell me: why dost thou resignedly
             Sit here? Is it for escort thou must wait?
             Or have old habits overtaken thee?"

127     "Brother," said he, "what use to go up yet?
             He'd not admit me to the cleansing pain,
             That bird of God who perches at the gate.

130     My lifetime long the heavens must wheel again
             Round me, that to my parting hour put off
             My healing sighs; and I meanwhile remain

133     Outside, unless prayer hasten my remove –
             Prayer from a heart in grace; for who sets store
             By other kinds, which are not heard above?"

> But now the poet was going on before;                   136
>   "Forward!" said he; "look how the sun doth stand
>   Meridian-high, while on the Western shore
>
> Night sets her foot upon Morocco's strand."             139

THE IMAGES. *The Late-Repentant*: (1) *The Indolent.* The whole of the
Second Terrace is occupied by those who, while remaining in the
fold of the Church, yet for one reason or another postponed re-
pentance until their last hour (*in articulo mortis*). Like the Excom-
municate, they are punished by a delay, extending in this case for a
period equal to the length of their earthly lives. This first and low-
est group comprises those who have their own laziness to blame
for their procrastination, and who therefore spend their time sit-
ting about, enduring the indolence in which they used to indulge.
Like the Excommunicate, they have no prayer allotted to them:
even in this they must remain idle.

NOTES. l. 6: *that soul is kindled above soul in us*: Dante is here repudiat-
ing the theory (ascribed to Plato, and reproduced with some modi-
fications by the Manichaeans) that man possesses a plurality of souls,
each with its own organs. Aristotle combats this theory; and so does
St Thomas Aquinas (*S.T.* I.I$^{ae}$, q. 26, a. 3) giving among other reasons,
the fact that "when one operation of the mind is intense, it impedes
others, a thing which could nowise happen unless the principle of
actions was essentially one". This is Dante's argument here. (For the
full Aristotelian-Thomist doctrine of the three powers, Nutritive,
Sensitive, and Intellectual, blended to form "one single soul com-
plete", see *Purg.* xxv. 52 *sqq.* and notes.)

ll. 10–12: *that which marks it*, etc.: The general sense of the passage is
clear, but there is some ambiguity in the use of the words *questa* (this)
and *quella* (that). If, as in modern usage, *questa* means "the latter" and
*quella* "the former", the sense is: "the faculty which by its apprehen-
sion engages our whole attention is bound, or yoked, to the soul, and
that which marks the passage of time is disengaged". (Using a twen-
tieth-century analogy, we might say that the one is "in gear", the
other "ticking over idly in neutral".) But if, as in *Purg.* xxv. 52–4,
*questa* means "the first-mentioned", then the sense is: "the time-sense
is impeded and the other (the apprehending faculty) free to function."

l. 16: *fifty degrees*: the sun passes over 15° every hour; it is now 50°
above the horizon; therefore, sunrise being at 6 A.M., it is now about
9.30 A.M.

l. 24: *when that flock left us*: the Excommunicate could not, of course,

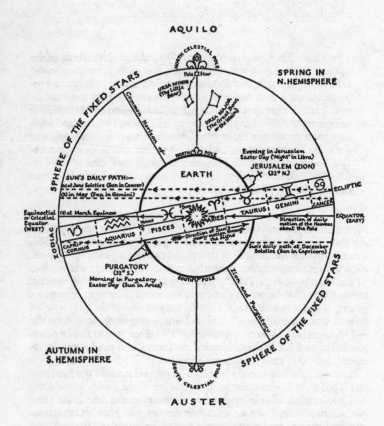

PATH OF THE SUN

Canto iv. 61-84

go up with the Poets, but had to wander round the First Terrace till their allotted time was accomplished.

ll. 25–6: *You can mount up*, etc.: *San Leo*: a small town on a precipitous ridge, in the ancient Duchy of Urbino; *Noli*: a little town at the foot of the Capo di Noli, which is now on the Corniche road, but in Dante's time could be reached only from the sea or by scrambling down steps cut in the rocks above it; *Bismantova*: on the highest peak of the mountains near Reggio, in Emilia.

l. 41: *the line from centre ... to mid-quadrant*: the angle of the quadrant is 90°; the gradient was therefore steeper than 45°.

l. 48: *a ledge of rock*: this is the Second Terrace.

l. 57: *so that he smote us on the leftward hand*: they were south of the equator, so that they saw the sun passing to the north of them; i.e. to their left, since they were looking east.

l. 60: *Aquilo*: the (quarter of the) North wind.

ll. 61–2: *Castor ... and Pollux*: "If it were June instead of March, and the Sun therefore in Gemini (the sign of the Twins, Castor and Pollux), which is further north of the equator than Aries, where the Sun is now, the kindled Zodiac (i.e. that part of the Zodiac in which the Sun is) would lie still nearer to the Great and Little Bears (*Ursa Major* and *Ursa Minor*, indicating the N. Pole) than it does at present." Just as in the N. Hemisphere the sun is lower in the sky (i.e. further *south*) in December, so in the S. Hemisphere it is lower (i.e. further *north*) in June (the antipodean winter) than it is at the equinoxes (March and September). See diagram, p. 100.

ll. 62–3: *that burning mirror*: the Sun, which receives the divine light from above (i.e. from the Empyrean) and reflects it upward to God and downward to the earth.

ll. 68–70: *think of Zion*, etc.: "Think of Purgatory as being at the exact antipodes of Zion (Jerusalem)." The horizon is here not, of course, the *visible* but the *astronomical* horizon: "a great circle of the celestial sphere, the plane of which passes through the centre of the earth and is parallel to the sensible [visible] horizon of a given place." (O.E.D.)

l. 71: *that road ill-tried by Phaeton*: the ecliptic, the sun's path along the Zodiac. (For *Phaeton*, see *Inf.* xvii. 107 and note.) The ecliptic always lies midway between any point on the earth and its antipodes.

ll. 79–84: *the Equator of the sky*, etc.: "The celestial equator (for we are now speaking in terms of the astronomical 'art'), always lies between winter and the sun (summer); so that when it is summer in one hemisphere it is winter in the other." Dante now grasps that he is at the antipodes of Jerusalem, with all the astronomical implications which Virgil has pointed out. He has confused the matter for us slightly by introducing an irrelevant time-element: "the equator is as far north of *us now* in Purgatory as it was south of the *ancient Hebrews in past years* at Jerusalem." It would, naturally, be equally far south of the inhabitants of Jerusalem in 1300 or at any other time. I suspect that Dante was not quite sure what to call the contemporary population of Jerusalem, in view of the Dispersion of the Jews and the Moslem occupation of Palestine.

ll. 88 *sqq.*: *This mount is such*, etc.: Virgil's generalization (that the life of penitence gets easier as it goes along) is elucidated in Cantos xii and xxvii.

l. 122: *Belacqua*: according to the old commentators, a Florentine maker of musical instruments notorious for his indolence, for which Dante, who knew him well, often used to rebuke him.

l. 129: *that bird of God*: the angel who guards the entrance to Purgatory proper (see Canto ix. 78 *sqq.*).

ll. 137–9: *the sun doth stand meridian-high*, etc.: it is noon in Purgatory, and in the N. Hemisphere Night stretches right across the inhabited world to its western limit in Morocco (see clock diagram between pages 350 and 351).

# CANTO V

THE STORY. *On their way up the Second Terrace, the Poets meet with a company of the Unshriven, and speak with the souls of Jacopo del Cassero, Buonconte da Montefeltro, and the lady known as La Pia (Piety), who tell their stories and ask for Dante's help and prayers.*

Already, parting from the shades, I'd passed
   On at my leader's heels, when one of those
   Behind me cried, pointing at me, aghast:

"Look on the left! meseems a darkness flows     4
   From him that climbs up last toward the height;
   And see how like a living man he goes!"

Hearing the words I paused and turned my sight     7
   Backward on them, and saw them stand and stare
   At me, me only, and the broken light.

Then said the master: "Why should this ensnare     10
   Thy wits, to slack thy speed? What does it matter
   To thee what they are whispering over there?

Follow thou me, and let the people chatter;     13
   Stand as a tower stands firm in time of trouble,
   Nor bends its head, though winds may bawl and batter.

He aims beside the mark whose fancies bubble     16
   One on another, driving back and drumming
   Each other out, so that his eye sees double."

What could I say to that, except: "I'm coming"?     19
   I said it – flushing somewhat to that hue
   Which may show cause why grace should be forthcoming.

Meanwhile, athwart the slope ahead, a crew     22
   Of souls passed over, singing, verse by verse
   Antiphonal, the *Miserere* through.

But when they saw that sunlight could not pierce     25
   My form, they changed their tune into an "Oo!"
   Long-drawn and breathless; then, like messengers

28     Deputed from their number, there came two
        Running towards us, crying: "Be so good,
        Pray, as to tell us who and what are you!"

31     "You may go back," my guide with promptitude
        Replied, "to those that sent you; and proclaim
        That this man's body is true flesh and blood.

34     If 'twas his shadow stayed you, as I deem,
        That answer will suffice them; let them pay
        Honour to one who can do much for them."

37     I ne'er saw vapours cleave their fiery way
        So swift through some young night undimmed of rain,
        Or clouds at setting of an August day,

40     But swifter still those two sped up again,
        And, when they got there, they with all that host
        Wheeled like a troop that rides and draws not rein.

43     "Right many are these who rush on us, disposed
        To beg a boon of thee," the poet said;
        "Do thou keep going; hearken as thou go'st."

46     "O soul, that with the limbs thy mother made
        Passest to joy," they cried as they came up,
        "Stay! just a moment bear to be delayed!

49     See if thou know but one of all our troop,
        To bear back news of him to yonder side –
        O why this haste? O why wilt thou not stop?

52     All we are sinners who by violence died,
        Sinners to our last hour; and then Heaven's grace
        Enlightened us and opened our eyes wide;

55     So, penitent and pardoning and at peace
        With God, we passed from that life into this,
        Heart-pierced with longing to behold His face."

58     "Look as I may, not one of you there is
        I recognize; but if I can do aught,"
        Said I, "to please you, spirits born for bliss,

61     Speak; I'll perform it, by that peace which brought
        Me here, thus greatly guided, to pursue it
        From world to world, where'er it may be sought."

"We need no oath," said one, "to bind thee to it;    64
  All count on thee for help – unless, indeed,
  The lack of power frustrate the will to do it.

So, speaking for myself now, I will plead:    67
  If e'er thou see the land which lies aligned
  'Twixt Charles's and Romagna, intercede

With those of Fano – since thou art so kind –    70
  To give me much good prayer, that I may look
  To purge my guilt, and leave the load behind.

There was I born; but the wide wounds whose stroke    73
  Spilled out the blood wherein my life held seat
  Were dealt me deep among Antenor's folk,

Where I had thought my safety most complete.    76
  'Twas he of Este did it – he being then
  More wroth against me than was just or meet.

Had I but fled towards La Mira, when    79
  Ambushed at Oriago, I'd be found
  Still in the company of breathing men.

But 'twas the marsh I made for; there, bogged round    82
  With mire, and tangled in the reeds, I fell,
  And saw my veins make pools upon the ground."

"Pray," said the next, "so Heav'n thy hope fulfil    85
  Which draws thee up the height, look pitying thou
  Upon these hopes of mine and aid me well.

Da Montefeltro once, Buonconte now,    88
  None cares for me – not Joan, nor any one;
  So among these I walk with downcast brow."

And I: "What evil chance, or violence done    91
  Drove thee away so far from Campaldino
  That thy last resting-place was never known?"

"O, at the foot," said he, "of Casentino,    94
  The stream called Archian runs, whose springs well out
  Above the convent in the Apennino.

There where its name is lost, I came on foot,    97
  Stabbed in the throat and fleeing; and as I fled
  My life-blood dabbled all the plain about.

100    There my sight failed me, and my last word sped
    Forth in the name of Mary; there headlong
    I fell; there left only my body dead.

103    'Tis truth I speak: proclaim that truth among
    Live men. God's angel took me, and Hell's fiend
    Shrieked out: 'O thief of Heaven, why do me wrong?

106    He's thine – one tear, one little tear could rend
    His deathless part away from me! the other –
    That's quite another thing, trust me, my friend!'

109    Thou knowest well the way damp vapours gather
    In air, and turn to water again, and spill,
    When, rising, they're condensed by colder weather.

112    He wedded intellect to the wicked will
    Which still loves harm; and moved the mist and wind
    By what his nature gave of power and skill,

115    Till the whole valley, when that day declined,
    From Pratomagno to the mountain chain
    Lay reeking, and the skies hung heavy and blind

118    So that the air teemed water, and the rain
    Fell, till earth could not hold it; every source
    And streamlet gushed full spate, and joined again

121    Into great torrents, driving their swift course
    Down to the royal river, tumultuous
    So in their rage, nothing could stay their force.

124    Then, at its mouth, the Archian's roaring sluice
    Found my stiff frozen body, and it swept me
    Into the Arno, and from my breast shook loose

127    The cross I made of me when the death-pangs gripped me;
    And rolling me down on its bed, over boulder and brae,
At length with its booty it girded and shrouded and heaped me."

130    The third soul followed on the second: "Pray,
    When thou returnest to the world," said she,
    "And art well rested from the weary way,

> Remember me, that am called Piety;                              133
> Siena made me and Maremma undid me,
> As well he knows who plighted troth to me,
>
> And set his ring upon my hand to wed me."              136

THE IMAGES. *The Late-Repentant:* (2) *The Unshriven.* This second group consists of those who were cut off in their sins by battle or murder, and so died unshriven. Since circumstances are partly responsible for their death, they occupy a slightly higher position than the Indolent, and have a prayer of their own; but they are still surrounded by the atmosphere of haste and agitation which attended their last moments.

NOTES. l. 24: *the Miserere*: this is the special Prayer of the Unshriven: *Ps.* li (*Vulg.* i), *Miserere mei, Domine* (Have mercy upon me, O Lord): one of the Seven Penitential Psalms.

l. 37: *vapours*: falling stars (l. 37) and summer lightning (l. 39) were attributed by medieval science to the presence of "fiery vapours" in the atmosphere.

l. 55: *penitent and pardoning*: in their dying moments they have made an act of (*a*) contrition for their own sins, (*b*) forgiveness of the sins of others, and are therefore at peace both with God and man.

l. 64: *said one*: This is Jacopo del Cassero, a Guelf of Fano, who offended Azzo VIII of Este and was murdered by his orders at Oriago, between Venice and Padua, when travelling from Bologna to Milan.

l. 69: *the land, twixt Charles's and Romagna*: Fano is situated between Romagna and the Kingdom of Naples, whose ruler was Charles of Anjou.

l. 75: *Antenor's folk*: the Paduans, so called from Antenor (for whom see *Inf.* xxxii. 88 and Images), the reputed founder of Padua. (See *Aen.* i. 242 *sqq.*)

l. 77: *he of Este*: Azzo VIII.

l. 79: *La Mira*: a town lying between Oriago and Padua, and belonging at that time to the Paduans.

l. 80: *Oriago*: In Dante's time the main road between Venice and Padua passed through La Mira, near Oriago, to the N.W. of the marshy tract known to-day as the *laguna morta* (the dead lagoon). Jacopo, either through losing his bearings or through fearing to trust himself to a Paduan town, left the high road and fled into the lagoon, where the reedy swamp trapped him and he was overtaken and stabbed.

l. 88: *da Montefeltro once, Buonconte now*: In Purgatory and Paradise, earthly titles no longer mean anything; the speaker *was* Lord of Montefeltro, but calls himself now only by his personal name (cf. the emperor in *Para*. vi. 10, "Caesar I was, and am Justinian"). Buonconte da Montefeltro, like his father Guido whose story Dante tells in *Inf*. xxvii (see *Inf*. Glossary and note on *Inf*. xxvii. 29), was a Ghibelline leader. He commanded the Aretines when they defeated the Sienese in 1288 at Pieve del Toppo (see *Inf*. xiii. 115 and note), and in 1289 led them against the Florentines at Campaldino, where they were defeated and he himself was killed.

In the *Comedy*, the deaths of the two lords of Montefeltro form, as it were, companion-pieces: the father being damned and the son saved at the last moment, the one by a false and the other by a true act of contrition.

l. 89: *Joan (Giovanna)*: Buonconte's wife.

ll. 91–3: *what evil chance*, etc.: Dante naturally displays particular interest at this point, since he himself had fought at Campaldino on the Guelf side (see *Inf*. Introduction, pp. 30–1). Buonconte was known to have been killed in the battle, but his body was never identified, and the story he tells is presumably of Dante's own invention.

ll. 94–6: *Casentino*, etc.: The district of Casentino (cf. *Inf*. xxx. 65) or Valley of the Upper Arno, is bounded on the W. by the mountains of Pratomagno (l. 116) and on the E. by the principal chain of the Apennines. The river Archian (Archiano) rises at the monastery of Camaldoli and flows into the Arno, dividing the Casentino from the neighbouring district of Bibbiena.

l. 97: *where its name is lost*: i.e. where it joins the Arno and so ceases to be called the Archiano.

ll. 109–11: *the way damp vapours gather*, etc.: medieval, based on classical, meteorological theory understood fairly well the phenomena of evaporation and condensation by cold.

l. 112: *he wedded intellect to the wicked will*: Angels are *intelligences* who have control over the elements, and this devil (or fallen angel) retains some part of the power native to his angelic nature. On the calamitous alliance of intellect and evil will see *Inf*. xxiii. 16 and *Inf*. xxxi. 55–7.

l. 122: *the royal river*: the Arno; the epithet denotes a river which flows into the sea, as distinguished from a tributary.

ll. 126–7: *shook loose the cross I made of me*: i.e. threw apart Buonconte's arms, which he had devoutly crossed upon his breast in the moment of death.

l. 132: *well rested from the weary way*: Characteristically, Dante depicts this solitary lady (for the other spirits mentioned are all male) as being the only inhabitant of Ante-Purgatory to show this self-effacing consideration for his health and convenience. She appears to have had no friend or relation left on earth who could be asked to pray for her.

l. 133: *that am called Piety: (La Pia)*: Pia dei Tolomei, daughter of a Sienese family, is said to have married Nello, or Paganello, dei Pannocchieschi, a Guelf leader, lord (among other castles) of the Castello della Pietra in the Maremma. Whether through jealousy or because he wanted to marry a richer heiress, Nello took her away to Pietra and there (in 1295) murdered her – some say by exposing her to the unhealthy air of the place (see *Inf.* xxix. 48 and Glossary); others, by throwing her from the castle window down a precipice; others say simply, "so secretly that nobody ever knew how." Since Dante classes her among the victims of sudden and unprepared death, he probably discounts the first of these theories.

l. 135: *who plighted troth to me*: she emphasizes the solemnity of the bonds uniting her to her murderous husband: she was first troth-plight and afterwards married to him. (Betrothal was a contract binding in law and in religion, which pledged the parties to one another and could not be dissolved without a formal dispensation. After a longer or shorter period, during which neither party was free to marry elsewhere, the marriage was celebrated and could be consummated.)

# CANTO VI

THE STORY. *After extricating himself from a whole crowd of the Un-shriven, who besiege him with requests for help, Dante asks Virgil about the efficacy of prayer, and receives an interim answer, the profounder aspects of the matter being referred to Beatrice for explanation. The Poets meet with Sordello, who affectionately hails Virgil as his fellow-Mantuan, and thus prompts Dante to denounce at some length the internecine quarrels which divide Italy, concluding with a savagely ironical passage of invective directed against Florence.*


The loser at the hazard, when the game breaks up,
    Sadder and sorrier lingers on alone,
    Re-plays each throw, and drinks of wisdom's cup.

4    Off go the others with the lucky one;
    This tries to catch his eye, that jogs his back,
    One plucks his sleeve with: "Think of me anon!"

7    He pushes through – tips Tom, remembers Jack –
    And where his hand goes out they melt away,
    Till in the end he's quit of all the pack.

10    So in that milling crowd was I that day,
    And, turning here, there, everywhere my face,
    Bought myself off with promises to pay.

13    There was that Aretine whom vengefulness
    At Ghin di Tacco's murderous hand pursued;
    There he who drowned while running in the chase.

16    There Frederick Novello pleading stood
    With outstretched hands; the Pisan too, whose fate
    Made good Marzucco show such fortitude.

19    I saw Count Orso; and that soul whom hate
    And envy severed from its flesh by force –
    For no crime done, it said; I'll name him straight:

22    Pierre de la Brosse; and ere she end her course
    Here, let the Lady of Brabant give heed
    Lest this procure her other mates, and worse.

So, being at length from all those spirits freed,      25
   Whose one prayer was that we should pray for them,
   And help them to grow holy with more speed,

"My Light," said I, "I think thou didst condemn      28
   Expressly, once, the thought that Heaven's decree
   Would bow to any prayer; and yet the theme

Of all these people's prayers is constantly      31
   That, and that only. Is their hope then vain?
   Or are thy words not fully clear to me?"

And he to me: "That which I wrote is plain,      34
   Nor are their hopes deceived, if thy wit skills
   With clear, whole sight to con this point again.

High justice does not stoop when love fulfils      37
   In one fire's flash the whole great payment owed
   By him that here in debt and bondage dwells;

But in that case I treated of, the load      40
   Might not be shifted; prayer had no effect
   Because the prayer was then disjoined from God.

These are deep waters; rest not there – reject      43
   Conclusion, till she show it thee who is
   Set as a light 'twixt truth and intellect –

I know not if thou understandest this:      46
   I mean Beatrice; on this mount's high crest
   Thou shalt behold her, smiling and in bliss."

"O sir," said I, "let us make greater haste!      49
   I can, indeed – I'm much less tired already –
   And look how the hill's shadow veils its breast."

"While this day lasts we'll march on straight and steady      52
   As far as maybe; yet the facts," he said,
   "Are other than thou think'st, and howso speedy

Our pace, thou wilt not reach the mountain's head      55
   Ere he return, who now is so far gone
   Behind the slope that thou dost cast no shade.

But see! a soul, all by himself alone,      58
   Looking our way; he'll guide us toward our goal,
   And show the quickest way to walk upon."

61     We came to him. O lofty Lombard soul,
       How stately didst thou bear thyself, avouching
       Scorn in thine eyes' slow glance majestical!

64     He said no word to us, but, gravely watching,
       Let us come on, and sat and eyed us there,
       After the fashion of a lion couching.

67     Yet Virgil still drew nigh him, with a prayer
       That he would show the ascent; the shadowy man
       Ignored all this, demanding who we were,

70     And whence. Straightway my courteous guide began:
       "Mantua . . ." And, starting from his sullen smother,
       All self-absorbed, the shade leapt up and ran

73     From where he was to meet him, crying: "Brother!
       O brother-Mantuan! Sordello am I
       Of thine own city!" And they embraced each other.

76     O house of grief! O bond-slave Italy!
       Ship without pilot in a raging gale!
       No mistress-province, but a stews and sty!

79     That noble soul was swift; he did not fail,
       For the sweet name, his city's name – no more –
       To bid his fellow-countryman all-hail.

82     But in thy borders is no rest from war
       For living men; those whom one moat doth bound,
       One wall, destroy each other and devour.

85     Search, wretched! search thy seas and coasts around;
       Then search thy bosom; see if thou canst hit
       On any nook where pleasant peace is found.

88     What though Justinian fettled up thy bit
       If still the saddle's empty? That can do
       Nought but make worse the bitter shame of it.

91     You reverend gentlemen, who should pursue
       Your calling, and let Caesar mount and ride,
       Could you but read what God set down for you,

94     See how this brute turns vicious in her pride,
       Missing the spurred heel, since you snatched at her,
       Fumbling the rein with hands not fit to guide.

Thou, German Albert, who hast left this mare      97
   To run wild and ungoverned, thou indeed
   Shouldst now bestride her back – what dost thou care?

Let judgement fall, judgement on all thy breed      100
   From the just stars! be it strange and manifest,
   So that thine heir shall tremble and give heed;

Because thy father and thou, by greed possessed,      103
   Lingering up there, have suffered this abuse
   To lay the garden of the Empire waste.

Come, see the Capulets and Montagues;      106
   See, heedless man, Monaldi's house made poor,
   The Filippeschi shaking in their shoes.

Come, see thy nobles, persecuted sore,      109
   And bind their bleeding wounds; come, heart of stone,
   And see how safe life is in Santafior.

Come, see thy city, weeping there alone,      112
   That cries by night and day, poor widowed Rome,
   "Caesar and husband, whither art thou gone?"

Come, see how all thy people here at home      115
   Love one another. If no ruth can move,
   Then for fame's sake, for very shame's sake, come!

Nay (be the thought permitted) most high Jove,      118
   Once for our sins slain here upon the rood,
   Are Thy just eyes turned elsewhere and aloof?

Or dost Thou thus prepare, as seemeth good      121
   To Thine abysmal wisdom, some great plan,
   Dark to our eyes, not to be understood?

For every town in Italy is a den      124
   Swarming with tyrants; any churl's Marcellus,
   Who comes along to play the partisan.

Florence, my Florence, laugh! enjoy this jealous      127
   Little digression, for it galls thee not,
   Thanks to thy citizens, so wise, so zealous!

Some people's justice is heart-deep, slow-shot,      130
   Stopping to think ere loosing from the bow;
   Thy folk have justice at tongue's tip, I wot.

133   Some shun the cares of office: thy folk? No!
         "I'll sacrifice myself!" they gaily shout
         Long before anybody asks them to.

136   Be glad, with so much to be glad about,
         Thou rich, thou peaceable, thou well-advised!
         Do I speak truth? the facts will bear me out.

139   Athens and Lacedaemon, that devised
         Old laws and arts urbane in years bygone,
         Had scarcely started to be civilized

142   Compared with thee, whose planning's so well-done,
         Thou hast ere now run through by mid-November
         The store of thread that thy October spun.

145   How often, in the days thou canst remember,
         Have customs, coinage, codes been redesigned,
         Each office changed, and changed thy every member!

148   Bethink thee then, and if thou art not blind
         Thou'lt see thyself a woman sick with pain,
         Who on the softest down no rest can find,

151   Tossing and turning weary limbs in vain.


THE IMAGES. *Sordello*: Since Virgil (whether considered *literally* as an Ancient and a heathen, or *allegorically* as the Natural Man) cannot of himself know all the inhabitants of Mount Purgatory or explain its organization in detail, an interpreter is provided at each stage of the journey to supply the deficiency. Sordello performs this office in Ante-Purgatory, as does Statius later on in Purgatory Proper, and Matilda in the Earthly Paradise.

In this canto we are still in the region of the Unshriven.

NOTES. l. 1: *hazard (la zara)*: a gambling game played with three dice, the winner of the cast being the player whose pips added up to a number previously called.

ll. 13–19: *that Aretine*: Benincasa da Laterina; *he who drowned*: Guccio dei Tarlati; *the Pisan*: Farinata, son of Marzucco degli Scornigiani; for these, and for *Frederick Novello* and *Count Orso* see Glossary.

l. 22: *Pierre de la Brosse*: surgeon and afterwards chamberlain to Philip III of France. He accused Philip's wife Mary of Brabant (l. 23) of having poisoned her stepson Louis, and she in revenge started a campaign of slander against him, as the result of which he was hanged in 1278, on a charge of treason which Dante obviously thought was undeserved.

l. 24: *lest this procure her other mates, and worse*: i.e. lest after death she go to a worse place than Purgatory.

ll. 28–9: *thou didst condemn expressly once*: the reference is to *Aen*. vi. 376. Aeneas (see Glossary) on his visit to Hades meets the shade of the drowned steersman Palinurus, who begs to be conveyed across Styx, the passage of which is forbidden to those whose bodies are unburied. The Sibyl rebukes Palinurus with the words: "Cease to hope that prayer can alter the fixed decree of the gods."

ll. 37–43: *high justice does not stoop*, etc.: Virgil explains that (*a*) when one person assumes another's debt of restitution and pays it all off in one moment of burning charity, the divine Justice is not diminished, since all its demands are fulfilled: but that (*b*) in the case of Palinurus and Aeneas, who were heathens, neither the petitioner nor the mediator was qualified to utter that "prayer from a soul in grace" which alone is effective (v. *Purg*. iv. 133–5, xi. 33). The delay in Ante-Purgatory being purely penal, it can be *remitted* when satisfaction is made by another (see Introduction, pp. 63–4).

l. 56: *ere he return*: i.e. the sun, which has now passed behind the mountain: the time is therefore about 3 P.M.

l. 71: *Mantua*: Virgil is doubtless about to quote the inscription on his tomb in Naples (see iii. 25 and note) which begins: "*Mantua me genuit* – Mantua gave me birth."

l. 74: *Sordello* the troubadour was born at Goito near Mantua about 1200. After wandering from court to court of Italy, Provence, Spain, Poitou, Portugal, and various parts of France, he attached himself to Charles of Anjou (who thought highly of him) and spent most of his later life in Provence. All record of him is lost after 1269, but there is a tradition that he died a violent death. Later in the *Comedy* we are reminded of Sordello's intrigue with Cunizza (wife to Ricciardo di San Bonifazio and sister to Ezzelino III da Romano) whom Dante places in the Heaven of Venus (*Para*. ix. 25–36); the repentance of this pair of lovers seems to be of Dante's own imagining. Sordello wrote all his poems (some forty of which are preserved), not in his own language but in Provençal; incidentally there is nothing in them to support Browning's fanciful treatment of him (in *Sordello*) as a kind of fore-runner of Dante himself. One poem, the *Lament of Blacatz*, contains an impassioned and reproachful address to all the foremost princes of Europe, and it is presumably because of this that Dante chooses him, in the next canto (*q.v.*), to point out and name the various sovereigns in the Valley of the Rulers, besides echoing the *Lament* in the great passage of reproach which here follows.

ll. 79–81: *he did not fail*, etc.: Sordello in his lifetime was certainly no patriot: he was an expatriate, who had renounced even his own language and had fought against Italy under a French banner; this perhaps is why we find him so solitary and self-absorbed (ll. 58 *sqq.*). The emotion stirred in him by the mere mention of his birthplace is for that very reason the more striking, and thus provokes Dante to his diatribe against Italy.

l. 88: *Justinian fettled up thy bit*: The Roman law was codified in the sixth century by the Emperor Justinian (see Glossary), but there is now no one to enforce it. (See *Inf.* Introduction, p. 45.)

l. 91: *you reverend gentlemen*: the clergy, who ought not to meddle with the temporal power but leave it to the Emperor ("Caesar").

l. 97: *German Albert*: Albert I of Austria (1248–1308) elected Emperor in succession to his father, Rudolph of Hapsburg, in 1298.

Dante's attitude to the Hapsburg emperor is ambivalent, according as he regards him (*a*) as King of the Germans – i.e. the feudal head of an invading and usurping race, or (*b*) as Roman Emperor – i.e. the divinely ordained guardian of law and civilization (see *Inf.* Introduction, p. 45). Compare his attitude to Julius Caesar (see *Inf.* xxxiv. Images under *Judas, Brutus, Cassius*) and to Pope Boniface VIII (see *Inf.* Introduction, p. 35, and *Purg.* xx. 86–90 and note).

ll. 100–3: *let judgement fall*, etc.: a prophetic allusion to the murder of Albert by his nephew John, eight years after the supposed date of Dante's vision. *Thine heir*: i.e. Henry VII of Luxemburg, the emperor on whom Dante built such high hopes (see *Inf.* Introduction, pp. 43–7).

ll. 103–7: *thy father and thou*: Both Rudolph and Albert neglected Italy ("the garden of the Empire"), being preoccupied with their hereditary possessions.

ll. 106–11: *come, see the Capulets*, etc.: As examples of internal dissension in Italy Dante points to the feud between the Capulets and Montagues of Verona, made familiar to us by Shakespeare; to that between the Monaldi and Filippeschi in Orvieto; to the sufferings of the ancient nobility at the hands of the "new rich" middle classes; and to the precarious conditions of life in Santafiora (a county in the Sienese Maremma) where incessant warfare raged between the Aldobrandeschi family and the commune of Siena.

l. 113: *poor widowed Rome*: cf. *Lamentations* i. 1: "How doth the city sit solitary. ... How is she become as a widow!" The condition of the Empire's neglected capital was at this period impoverished, squalid, and disorderly, comparing very unfavourably with that of other Italian cities.

l. 118: *most high Jove*: the name "Jove" (possibly on account of its resemblance to "Jehovah") is used more than once by Petrarch to designate "God the Father", or "God" in general. Its use here with special reference to God the Son is more unusual: but Dante, being an accurate theologian, never hesitates to call the Second Person of the Trinity "God", without qualification, in whatever connexion.

l. 125: *Marcellus*: a Roman consul, who supported Pompey against Julius Caesar, and was a violent opponent of the Empire. Dante means that any demagogue who defies the constitution is hailed by the populace as a hero.

ll. 127–51: *Florence, my Florence*, etc.: the eulogy is, of course, ironical from start to finish (cf. the parallel passage in *Inf*. xxvi. 1–3).

l. 139: *Athens*: the cradle of Greek art and culture; *Lacedaemon*, chief city of Sparta, renowned for its laws and administration.

l. 147: *changed thy every member*: an allusion to the perpetual shift of parties, banished and recalled in turn (see *Inf*. Introduction, pp. 29–30). We need not suppose that Dante was altogether fair to Florence, whose institutions had all the qualities, as well as all the defects, of elasticity.

# CANTO VII

THE STORY. *After repeatedly embracing his fellow-Mantuan, Sordello
asks who the travellers are, and Virgil names himself. Sordello at once
drops down to clasp his knees, inquiring anxiously about Virgil's fate in
the after-life, and is answered. In reply to Virgil's question, he then ex-
plains the Rule of the Mountain, which prevents any climbing after sun-
set. He then leads the Poets to a beautiful Valley, where they see a group
of highly distinguished persons, representing the Third Class of the Late-
Repentant – the Preoccupied – many of whom Sordello points out and
names.*

When with a glad and solemn courtesy
　　Greetings had been exchanged three times or four,
　　Sordel drew back: "Who are you, though?" said he.

4　"Ere to this mount those spirits fit to soar
　　Upward to God were brought first to be shriven,
　　Octavian to my bones gave sepulture.

7　Virgil am I; and I came short of Heaven
　　For no default, save that I had not faith."
　　In such wise was my leader's answer given.

10　Like one who sees what takes away his breath,
　　Who half-believes, and then must hesitate
　　And doubt: "It is – it cannot be," he saith;

13　So seemed that shade; and then, returning straight,
　　He stooped before him, and with bended head
　　Embraced him where the humble clasp the great.

16　"O glory of the Latins! thou," he said,
　　"In whom our tongue showed powers beyond compare!
　　O deathless fame of the land where I was bred,

19　What merit or grace has let me see thee here?
　　If of thy words I am but worthy, say,
　　Art thou from Hell, and from what cloister there?"

22　The other answered: "I have made my way
　　Through every circle of the realm of woe,
　　Moved by Heaven's power, which brings me here to-day.

Not what I did, but what I did not do,                         25
  Lost me the sight of that high Sun, the prize
  Thou seekest, whom too late I learned to know.

Below there in the deep, a region lies                         28
  Made sad by darkness only, not by pain,
  And where no shrieks resound, but only sighs;

And there dwell I, with guiltless infants, ta'en              31
  By nipping fangs of death, untimely soon,
  Ere they were washed from sinful human stain;

And there dwell I, with those who ne'er put on               34
  The three celestial virtues, yet, unsinning,
  Knew all the rest and practised every one.

But now, point out how we may best be winning                37
  Our way – if thou dost know it and canst tell –
  Upward to Purgatory's true beginning."

"There's no set place," said he, "where we must dwell;       40
  I may go up and round, and at thy side
  I'll guide thee on as far as possible.

But see how it draws on to eventide;                          43
  'Twere well to think – since none can climb by night –
  Of some good lodging where we may abide.

There are some souls apart here on the right;                 46
  I'll bring thee to them, if thou wilt permit,
  For meeting them will give thee true delight."

"How's this?" was the reply; "if one thought fit             49
  To go up in the dark, would one be stopped
  By somebody? or merely fail at it?"

"Look!" said the good Sordello, and he stooped               52
  And drew upon the ground; "thou couldst not cross
  Even this line when once the sun had dropped.

Not that there's any hindrance, save the loss                55
  Of light, to going up; it is night's gloom
  Makes impotent the will and thwarts it thus.

We might indeed go down again, and roam                       58
  All round the hill, while the horizon's ring
  Seals down the day, until the morning come."

61 "Nay," said my lord, as it were marvelling,
  "Lead on then; bring us where thy speech conveys
  Such pleasant promise of fair harbouring."

64 We'd not gone far when I perceived a place
  Scooped, so to call it, from that sloping lawn,
  As valleys here scoop out a mountain's face.

67 "That's where we'll go, to yonder spot withdrawn,"
  The spirit said, "at which the ridges dip
  To make a fold, and there await the dawn."

70 A winding path, not level but not steep,
  Led us to where the rising hill-spurs lose
  Half of their height along the valley's lip.

73 Gold and fine silver, crimson and ceruse,
  Wood yellow-lustrous, clear cerulean dye,
  Indigo, fresh-cracked emerald's brilliant hues,

76 Matched with the foliage and the flowers that lie
  Heaped in that lap, would faint, as minor faints
  Beneath its major, and show dim thereby.

79 Here nature had not only plied her paints,
  But had distilled, unnameable, unknown,
  The mingled sweetness of a thousand scents.

82 *Salve Regina* singing on and on,
  Close-hid till then beneath the valley's lee,
  On flowers and grass I there saw spirits strown.

85 Our Mantuan guide began: "Ask not of me
  That I should lead you down to them before
  This last thin rim of sun nests in the sea.

88 You'll con their looks and all their actions o'er
  Far better from this terrace than among
  Their company, upon the dell's low floor.

91 He that sits yonder, highest of the throng,
  Who looks a do-naught and a task-neglecter,
  And does not move his lips to join their song,

94 Is Emperor Rudolph, Italy's protector
  By rights, who might have staunched her mortal wound;
  There's one shall come – too late to resurrect her.

And he who seems to comfort him was crowned    97
   King of that realm whose waters Moldau sends
   Down to the Elbe, and Elbe to ocean's bound;

His name was Ottocar – in swaddling bands    100
   A better man than bearded Wenceslas
   His son, who lolls at ease and folds his hands.

The snub-nose there, who's talking of some case    103
   In conclave with that lord of kindly mien,
   Fled, died, and brought the lilies to disgrace;

Behold him beat his breast, the other lean    106
   His bedded cheek upon his palm, and glance
   Mournfully down, with bitter sighs and keen;

These are the father of the Pest of France,    109
   And father-in-law; they know his crimes and vices;
   And hence the grief that stabs them like a lance.

The burly form, whose voice in concert rises    112
   With that of Hook-nose yonder, was a lord
   Girt with all praise of knightly enterprises;

And had that lad lived longer afterward    115
   Who sits behind him, he'd have shown this age
   The wine of worth from cup to cup outpoured.

Not so with the remaining lineage;    118
   Unto the realms Frederick and James are heirs,
   But none now holds the nobler heritage.

The root of human virtue seldom bears    121
   Like branches; and the Giver wills it so,
   That men may know it is His gift, not theirs.

These words hold good no less for Hook-nose, too,    124
   Than Pedro who sings near him, as lamenting
   Apulia and Provence already know;

For high as Constance, of her lord still vaunting,    127
   Can crow o'er Beatrix and Margaret,
   So far beneath his seed the plant shows wanting.

Look! there the king of simple life is set    130
   Alone – Harry of England, far more blest
   In those fair branches that he did beget.

133  And modestly below these others placed,
          And gazing up, is William the Marchese,
          Whose war with Alessandria left distressed

136  The men of Montferrat and Canavese.

THE IMAGES. *The Rule of the Mountain*: Throughout the *Purgatory*, the Sun is frequently taken as the symbol of God (e.g. in l. 26 of this canto). *Allegorically* therefore, the meaning of the Rule of the Mountain, which prevents all ascent between sunset and sunrise, is that no progress can be made in the penitent life without the illumination of Divine Grace. When this is withheld, the soul can only mark time, if it does not lose ground, while waiting patiently for the renewal of the light. Nights in Purgatory thus correspond to those periods of spiritual darkness or "dryness" which so often perplex and distress the newly-converted. (Cf. *John* xi. 9–10.)

*The Late-Repentant:* (3) *The Preoccupied.* The third class of the Late-Repentant is composed of those who neglected their spiritual duties through too much preoccupation with worldly cares. They occupy the highest and most beautiful place upon the Second Terrace, because their concern was, after all, for others rather than for themselves. As with the other inhabitants of Ante-Purgatory, the taint or habit of their former sin still clings to them: they continue to discuss and worry about the affairs of the family or the nation. As we learn from *Para.* xvii. 136–42, Dante in his vision is shown only the most striking and illustrious representatives in each category; but we need not doubt that he would place in this class not only kings and statesmen, but also humbler examples of the Pre-occupied, such as anxious parents, over-burdened housewives and breadwinners, social workers, busy organizers, and others who are so "rushed off their feet" that they forget to say their prayers. In his *Convivio* (see *Inf.* Introduction, pp. 40–2) Dante speaks with sympathy of "the domestic and civic cares by which the greater number of people are quite properly absorbed, so that they have no leisure for speculation."

NOTES. l. 3: *who are you, though?*: the "you" is here plural; but Sordello's excitement at hearing Virgil's name makes him forget to ask about Dante: and since the sun is behind the mountain (vi. 56–7), there is no betraying shadow to arouse his curiosity. Note how carefully and cunningly the poet prepares his effects over some 290 lines so that he may keep Virgil in the foreground at this point and reserve the revelation that Dante is alive (which would here be an anticlimax) for viii. 59, where he can make good dramatic use of it.

l. 4: *ere to this mount*, etc.: i.e., before Christ's Harrowing of Hell. Previous to that, "no human soul had ever seen salvation" (*Inf.* iv. 63); the souls of the elect had gone, not to Purgatory, but to Limbo, from which Christ released them.

l. 6: *Octavian*: Caesar Augustus (see Glossary). Cf. iii. 27.

l. 8: *I had not faith*: see *Inf.* iv. Images.

l. 26: *that high Sun*: i.e. God.

l. 35: *the three celestial virtues*: the theological (Christian) graces of Faith, Hope, and Charity, which the good pagans did not know, though perfect in their practice of the four cardinal (natural) virtues of Justice, Prudence, Temperance, and Fortitude (cf. i. 37–8 and note).

l. 40: *there's no set place*: an echo of *Aen.* vi. 673–5, where the Sibyl asks: "What region [of Hades], what place is the abode of Anchises?" and is answered: "*Nulli certa domus* – none has any fixed abode: we inhabit the shady groves, the river-banks are our bed, the freshly-watered meadows our dwelling."

l. 82: *Salve Regina*: the compline hymn to the Blessed Virgin, beginning: "Hail, O Queen, Mother of mercy, our life, our sweetness and our hope, hail! To thee we cry, the exiled children of Eve, to thee we sigh, weeping and lamenting in this valley of tears."

l. 94: *Emperor Rudolph*: Rudolph of Hapsburg (see Glossary) mentioned in vi. 103 in connexion with his son Albert I. He is placed in this section of Ante-Purgatory probably on account of having been so preoccupied with affairs at home that he neglected the Empire to which he had been divinely called (vi. 103–6).

l. 96: *there's one shall come*: i.e. Henry VII of Luxemburg (see *Inf.* Introduction, pp. 43–7).

ll. 100–1: *Ottocar* [II] and *Wenceslas* [IV] of Bohemia: See Glossary.

l. 103: *the snub-nose*: Philip III of France, called "the Bold", defeated and killed in 1285 when fighting against Peter III of Aragon. (See Glossary.)

l. 104: *that lord of kindly mien*: Henry the Fat of Navarre, brother of Tibbald the Good (*Inf.* xxii. 52 and note); and see Glossary.

l. 109: *The Pest of France*: Philip IV of France, called "the Fair", for whom Dante never has a good word (see *Inf.* xix. 87: *Purg.* xx. 91, xxxii. 152: *Para.* xix. 118–20). He was the son of Philip the Bold, and married Joan, the daughter of Henry the Fat. (See Glossary.)

ll. 112–13: *the burly form* is that of Peter III of Aragon, called "the Great", who married Manfred's daughter Constance (iii, 143). *Hook-nose* is Charles I of Anjou, whom Peter drove from the throne of Sicily. The two former enemies now "sing in concert". (See Glossary.)

ll. 115–20: *that lad*, etc.: Alfonso III, King of Aragon, son of Peter III, died in 1291; his brothers James II (King of Sicily and later of Aragon) and Frederick II (King of Sicily), survived to 1327 and 1337 respectively. Dante is saying that Frederick and James inherited only their father's possessions, whereas Alfonso, if he had lived, would have inherited also his "praise of knightly enterprise" ("the nobler heritage").

ll. 124–9: *These words hold good ... shows wanting*: All this is merely an involved way of saying that Charles I's offspring is as degenerate as Peter III's. Charles II, the son of Charles I ("Hook-nose") was king of Naples (Apulia) and Provence; Charles I married successively Beatrix of Provence and Margaret of Burgundy; Peter II married Constance. Consequently: "The plant (Charles II) is as *inferior* to the seed (Charles I) from which it sprang as Constance may boast her husband (Peter III) *superior* to the husband of Beatrix and Margaret (Charles I), as Apulia and Provence know only too well." (Not, perhaps, one of Dante's best efforts.)

ll. 130–1: *the king of simple life ... Harry of England*: Henry III. Dante's estimate of him seems to be derived from Villani's *Chronicle*: "Of Richard [I, Cœur-de-Lion] was born Henry his son who reigned after him, but was a simple man and of good faith and of little worth. Of the said Henry was born the good King Edward [I], still reigning at the present time, who did great things" (v. 4): and in another passage: "Henry, father of the good Edward, was a man of simple life, so that the barons held him for naught" (vii. 39). Dante can scarcely have thought that Henry neglected his soul in his care for his subjects, since he died, after 56 years of incompetent misgovernment, with a great reputation for piety: "In proportion as the king was held to be lacking in prudence in worldly actions, so he was the more distinguished for devotion to Our Lord; for it was his custom to hear three sung masses daily and, since this was not enough for him he assiduously attended private masses" (Matthew Paris). In his case, therefore, the fault which he is expiating in Ante-Purgatory may be the neglect of his kingly, through preoccupation with his religious, duties (since to pray when one ought to be working is as much a sin as to work when one ought to be praying). This may be the reason why he sits apart from the others, though the reason usually given is that England was outside the Empire. Henry is one of the rulers blamed by Sordello for sloth and cowardice in *The Lament for Blacatz*.

l. 134: *William the Marchese*: William, Marquis of Montferrat (Monferrato) and Canavese (1254–92), headed a league of important towns against Charles of Anjou. In 1290, one of these, Alessandria in

Piedmont, rebelled against him, and he was captured by the citizens and kept on show in an iron cage for seventeen months until he died. An attempt by his son to avenge him ended in the invasion of Montferrat by the Alessandrians.

# CANTO VIII

THE STORY. *Night is now falling; and after the Souls of the Preoccupied Rulers have sung their evening hymn, two Angels descend from Heaven to protect the Valley. Led by Sordello, the Poets advance, and Dante is recognized by Judge Nino Visconti, who, learning that his former friend is still alive, sends a message by him, asking for prayers. While he is speaking, Dante notices that the Four Stars which he had seen before daybreak have set, and Three Others risen in their place. A Serpent comes creeping into the Valley, but is immediately put to flight by the Angels. Dante converses with the soul of Conrad Malaspina, to whose family he will, as he learns, shortly have cause to be grateful.*

Now – in the hour that melts with homesick yearning
    The hearts of seafarers who've had to say
    Farewell to those they love, that very morning –

4    Hour when the new-made pilgrim on his way
    Feels a sweet pang go through him, if he hears
    Far chimes that seem to knell the dying day –

7    Did I suspend the office of my ears,
    And turn to watch a spirit rising there,
    And beckoning with his hand for listeners.

10    Folding his palms, he lifted them in prayer,
    With gaze set eastward, that said visibly
    To God: "For Thee and nothing else I care."

13    *Te lucis ante,* so devoutly he
    Breathed forth, so sweet the singing syllables,
    All sense of self was ravished out of me.

16    The others joined their sweet, devout appeals
    To his, and sang the whole hymn afterward,
    Fixing their eyes on the eternal wheels.

19    Sharpen thy sight now, Reader, to regard
    The truth, for so transparent grows the veil,
    To pass within will surely not be hard.

I saw that goodly host stand sentinel                                    22
   Thereafter, speechless, in expectant love
   Scanning the sky with lowly looks, all pale;

And then I saw descending from above                                     25
   Two angels, bearing fiery swords in hand,
   Broke short and bated at the points thereof.

Green as fresh leaves new-budded on a wand                               28
   Their raiment was, which billowed out and blew
   Behind, by flutter of green pinions fanned.

One lit down just above us, and one flew                                 31
   To the far bank and poised there in his place,
   So that the folk lay folded 'twixt the two.

Clearly I saw their bright heads, but the face                           34
   Dazzled the eye beneath the locks of yellow,
   As every sense is vanquished by excess.

"They're sent from Mary's bosom," said Sordello,                         37
   "To guard the vale; for any moment now
   The serpent comes." Then to my friend and fellow

I turned, not knowing whence 'twould come or how,                        40
   And to those trusty shoulders clung affrighted,
   Shuddering, an ice-cold sweat upon my brow.

"And now come down," Sordel again invited,                               43
   "Visit these noble shades in their green nook,
   And talk to them – I know they'll be delighted."

I think 'twas but three paces that I took,                               46
   Ere I was down, and saw a shadow peer
   At me, with knowledge dawning in his look.

Darkness was falling now, yet not so sheer                               49
   But that the truth it had at first made dim
   To our two pairs of eyes grew plain and clear.

So he advanced to me, and I to him;                                      52
   What joy to see thou wast not damnified,
   Worthy Judge Nino, dear to my esteem!

No welcoming word was left on either side                                55
   Unspoken; then: "How long since thou," said he,
   "Cam'st to the hill's foot o'er the waters wide?"

58   "This morn I left the abodes of misery
      And still in my first life I journey thus,
      Though journeying thus I gain the life to be."

61   I told him this: whereat, unanimous,
      He and Sordello started back anon,
      Like men astounded and incredulous.

64   Then this to Virgil turned, and that, to one
      Set near him, crying: "Conrad, up! come here,
      See this great thing God's grace hath willed and done!"

67   Then turned to me: "By that most singular
      Favour thou ow'st to Him whose primal *why*
      Lies so deep hid, no wit can wade so far,

70   When the great seas once more behind thee lie,
      Bid my Giovanna plead for me, before
      That court which hears the guiltless when they cry.

73   Her mother does not love me any more,
      I think, since she put off those weeds of white
      Which, hapless wretch, she soon will hanker for.

76   Easy it is in her to read aright
      How brief a blaze a woman's love will yield
      If not relit by frequent touch and sight.

79   The viper that Milan bears on his shield
      Will make a tomb less goodly for her rest
      Than if Gallura's cock had held the field."

82   Thus he; while all his countenance expressed
      A measured anger, such as sets its seal
      Rightly upon a warm and generous breast.

85   But my rapt gaze grew fixed in heaven, where reel
      The slowest-gyring stars, as the wheel's gyre
      Is slowest near the axle of the wheel.

88   "What is it, son," my lord began inquire,
      "That takes thine eye so?" "Those three torches there,"
      Said I, "that kindle all this pole with fire."

91   And he: "The four bright stars that shone so fair
      To greet thee in the dawn have dipped from view
      Yonder, and these have risen up where they were."

While he yet spake, Sordello seized and drew      94
  Him close and cried: "See there, the enemy!"
  Pointing the way that he should look unto.

And there, where no bank fenced beneath its lee      97
  That little vale, came sliding in the snake,
  Such as gave Eve the bitter fruit, maybe.

'Twixt grass and flowers flickered the wicked strake,      100
  With head turned ever anon to lick its back,
  As a beast licks itself for sleekness' sake.

I cannot tell – my sight could not keep track –      103
  Of how the heavenly falcons moved to stoop;
  But well I saw them in the mid-attack

Moving; and when it heard the swish and swoop      106
  Of the green wings, the serpent fled; and they
  Back to their posts wheeled equal round and up.

The shade the judge had called to, while this fray      109
  Went on, stood by and gazed upon me still,
  Nor for one moment took his eyes away.

"So may thy guiding light in thy free will      112
  Find wax enough to feed on till thou stand
  Safe on the flower-bright summit of the hill,"

Said he, "if thou have certain news at hand      115
  Of Valdimagra or the parts near by,
  Tell me, who once was mighty in that land;

Currado Malaspina then was I –      118
  Not the old man, his grandson; to mine own
  I bore that love which here we purify."

"O," I replied, "I never yet have gone      121
  Through your domain; yet who lives so remote
  But that all Europe knows it by renown?

The fame that of your noble house goes out      124
  Proclaims the rulers and the land abroad,
  Even to men who never there set foot;

And, as I hope to speed, I pledge my word,      127
  Your lineage still maintains inviolate
  The honour of the purse and of the sword.

130    So rare its blood and wont, that though the great
        Lord of Misrule wrench all the world aside,
        It shuns ill ways, and it alone goes straight."

133    Then he: "Go to; or ere the seventh tide
        Bring back the sun to rest in that bright bed
        The Ram's four feet arch over and bestride,

136    Events shall hammer home into thy head
        That courteous judgement with much stouter nails
        Than this and that that other men have said,

139    If nothing stay the hand that bears the scales."

THE IMAGES. *The Serpent and the Angels*: The intrusion of the Serpent "such as gave Eve the bitter fruit, maybe", into this Eden-like valley naturally raises the question whether, in the *literal story*, the souls in Ante-Purgatory are still liable to temptation and sin. It would appear that they are – not in the conscious will, which in the hour of death was firmly set towards God – but in the subconscious, the region of dreams, which is not yet subject to the will, so that a special intervention of Divine Grace is needed to protect it from assault. (The souls in Purgatory Proper are definitely beyond the reach of sin – see Canto xi. 22 and note.)

The green robes of the Angels are the colour of Hope – specifically the hope of salvation. Their fiery swords remind us of the flaming sword of *Gen.* iii. 24, set at the gate of Eden after the expulsion of Adam and Eve; but these are blunted at the point: "salvation, in these souls, is now working out the reversal of the Fall" (J. D. Sinclair). The blunted points are usually taken to signify Mercy as opposed to Judgement; but it is, perhaps, rather that the contest with the Serpent is now hardly more than a fencing bout: the creature needs only to be routed and not slain, for sin "has retreated to its last stronghold" (J. S. Carroll), and is reduced to a mere fantasy, which can only trouble and not corrupt.

In its *allegorical application* – i.e. to the experience of the soul in this world – the episode may perhaps be taken to mean that so long as the will *truly* intends penitence and amendment, the Christian need not, and should not, be unduly troubled about the involuntary aberrations of the unconscious, but should simply commend the matter to God, in the confident assurance that it will be taken care of.

*The Three Stars*: These typify the Theological Virtues (or Graces): Faith, Hope, and Charity.

NOTES. ll. 1–6: *Now – in the hour*, etc.: This is the famous passage imitated by Byron in *Don Juan*, iii. 108.

l. 7: *did I suspend the office of my ears*: i.e. ceased listening to Sordello.

l. 12: *for Thee and nothing else I care*: the Preoccupied turn from the worldly cares which have become their punishment to that greater care which they once neglected.

l. 13: *Te lucis ante [terminum]*: "Before the ending of the day": the compline hymn of St Ambrose, for protection against evil dreams and phantoms of the night (for an English translation see *Hymns A. & M.* 15).

l. 18: *the eternal wheels*: the courses of the planets (see Dante's Universe, *Inf.* p. 292).

ll. 19–20: *Sharpen thy sight now, Reader*: Cf. the parallel passage in *Inf.* ix. 61–3, which likewise announces the arrival of aid sent from Heaven to deal with a danger against which reason and will are powerless.

l. 36: *as every sense is vanquished by excess*: Dante is quoting from Aristotle, *De Anima*, ii. 12: "The excess of the sensibles corrupts the senses": i.e. a too strong light dazzles, a too loud noise deafens, a too concentrated scent paralyses the sense of smell, or a too pungent taste, the palate.

l. 37: *from Mary's bosom*: The help and protection of the Queen of Heaven were invoked previously in the *Salve Regina* (vii. 82).

l. 54: *worthy Judge Nino*: Nino (Ugolino) Visconti, Justiciary of Gallura in Sardinia, was on the mother's side a grandson of Count Ugolino della Gherardesca (see *Inf.* xxxiii. 13 and note), and his rival in the leadership of the Guelfs in Pisa, to which city Sardinia at that time (1288) belonged. After the Ghibellines under Ruggieri degli Ubaldini had driven him from Pisa and assumed power in the city, Nino became head of the Tuscan Guelf league against Pisa, to which he returned in 1293. Later he went to Sardinia to punish Fra Gomita, his vicar in Sardinia, for bribery and corruption (see *Inf.* xxii. 81 and note). He appears to have been personally known to Dante, whom he may have met when visiting Florence from time to time between 1288 and 1293 on business connected with the Guelf league, if he was not actually his companion in arms at Caprona (see *Inf.* xxi. 95 and note). He died in 1296 in Sardinia. The old commentators speak of him as a man of noble spirit, stout, courageous, and well-bred.

Generations of commentators have made mildly merry over Dante's joy (in which they detect a note of surprise) in finding that his friend Nino is not among the damned. But this is, surely, to forget where we are. Everybody in Ante-Purgatory has, by hypothesis, attained salvation only at the last moment and by the skin of his teeth; and Dante, knowing Nino, may be supposed to have known whether or not his friend was careless about religion. He had already been distressed by seeing in Hell many people whom he had cause to love and admire (see *Inf.* xv. xvi.), and his relief now is natural enough.

Nino's presence among the saved need not, on the other hand, mean that in Dante's eyes he is exempted from all blame in the matter of his quarrel with Ugolino. What qualifies a soul for Purgatory is not innocence, but repentance. All we are entitled to infer from Dante's placing of the two men is that he is representing the one as a penitent, the other as an impenitent, sinner.

l. 65: *Conrad*: this is Conrad, or Currado, Malaspina. See note on l. 118.

l. 71: *my Giovanna*: Nino's daughter by Beatrice d'Este. In 1300 (see ll. 73 *sqq.*), four years after Nino's death, Beatrice was remarried to Galeazzo Visconti of Milan. Nino's "measured anger", with which Dante sympathizes, at this infidelity to the dead appears to us scarcely justified; but it must be remembered that the medieval Church had no great liking for second marriages.

l. 74: *weeds of white*: the widow's dress – black robe with white veil – such as we see still used in the *"deuil blanc"* portrait of Mary Queen of Scots. The suggestion in l. 75, that Beatrice will soon repent her marriage, refers to the misfortunes which overtook the Visconti family from 1302 onwards.

ll. 79 and 81: *the viper [of] Milan ... Gallura's cock*: the arms of the Milanese and Pisan Visconti family respectively. "It would have been more to Beatrice's honour if she had died the widow of Nino than the wife of Galeazzo."

ll. 85–6: *where reel the slowest-gyring stars*: i.e. near the Pole. We may infer that neither the four stars of Canto i, nor the three stars of Canto viii, ever actually set in Purgatory, any more than the Great and Little Bears ever set in the Northern Hemisphere. But since in these latitudes the pole is only 32° above the horizon, and the mountain itself permanently shuts off half the heavens from the view of those upon its lower slopes, the four stars are now behind the mountain and beneath the pole, while the three are just emerging into sight from the eastward edge of the mountain.

l. 104: *the heavenly falcons*: i.e. the angels.

l. 109: *the shade the judge had called to*: see l. 65.

ll. 112–14: *thy guiding light*: Divine grace; *the flower-bright (lit.* enamelled) *summit*: the Earthly Paradise at the top of the mountain.

l. 116: *Valdimagra*: see Glossary and *Inf.* xxiv. 142, note.

l. 118: *Currado Malaspina*: Conrad Malaspina I ("the old man", l. 119) was grandfather to three cousins: Conrad II (now addressing Dante), who died about 1294; Moroello (see *Inf.* xxiv. 142 and note); and Franceschino (d. between 1313 and 1321) whose hospitality Dante enjoyed in Lunigiana in the autumn of 1306 – i.e. less than seven years (l. 133) from the time of this encounter in Purgatory.

l. 120: *that love which here we purify*: Conrad implies that it was absorption in family pride and family affection which placed him among the Preoccupied.

l. 122: *through your domain*: the "your" is here singular and honorific.

ll. 130–1: *the great Lord of Misrule*: (*lit.* "the evil head"): probably Satan: but possibly either Pope Boniface VIII or the Emperor.

ll. 134–5: *that bright bed the Ram's four feet arch over*: i.e. the sign of Aries, in which the sun now is.

ll. 136–8: *events ... other men have said*: Dante has said that he has never visited Conrad's domain (Lunigiana) but knows the generosity of the Malaspina family by repute. Conrad replies that he will before long know it by experience (thus prophesying Dante's coming exile and dependence on the hospitality of his patrons).

# CANTO IX

THE STORY. *Dante, waking from a dream in which he is snatched away by an Eagle, finds that he has actually been carried up, in his sleep, by St Lucy to the Gate of Purgatory itself. Here Virgil and he are challenged by the Porter, who, hearing that Lucy has sent them, invites Dante to climb the three steps that lead to the Gate, marks the sign of the Seven Capital Sins upon his forehead, and opens the Gate with the Keys of Peter. On entering Purgatory the Poets are greeted by the strains of the* Te Deum.

Now, glimmering on her eastward balcony,
 Came the white leman of Tithonus old
 Forth of her lover's arms reluctantly;

4 Her brow was starred with jewels manifold,
 Set in the likeness of the beast whose tail
 Smites on the people, and whose blood is cold.

7 Already, on the stair night has to scale,
 Two paces, in that sky of ours, were stept,
 And now the third flagged on the wing as well,

10 When I – in whom old Adam's nature kept
 Its share – began to nod, and on the lawn
 Where all we five now sat, I sank and slept.

13 About the hour when the sad swallow, drawn
 In memory back, maybe, to her old woes,
 Pipes out her mournful lay to greet the dawn,

16 And when the pilgrim soul a-roving goes
 So far from flesh and thought's entangling snare
 That half-divine her dreaming vision grows,

19 I dreamt I saw an eagle in mid-air,
 Plumed all in gold, hovering on wings outspread,
 As though to make his swoop he poised him there.

22 Meseemed me in the place whence Ganymede
 Up to the high gods' halls was snatched one day,
 Leaving his comrades all discomfited.

I thought: Perhaps this eagle strikes his prey 25
  Always just here; his proud feet would think shame
  Elsewhere to seize and carry it away.

Then, in my dream, he wheeled awhile and came 28
  Down like the lightning, terrible and fast,
  And caught me up into the sphere of flame,

Where he and I burned in one furnace-blast; 31
  The visionary fire so seared me through,
  It broke my sleep perforce, and the dream passed.

Not otherwise, I think, Achilles threw 34
  Wild eyes about him, waking with a start,
  Wondering what place he had awakened to,

When his fond mother, cradled on her heart, 37
  Brought him from Chiron unto Scyros' coast,
  Whence the Greeks caused him later to depart,

Than I so stared and started and felt lost 40
  When the dream fled and left the face of me
  Pale, as of one whom fear congeals like frost.

Beside me sat my Comfort – only he; 43
  And lo! the sun was now two hours and more
  Risen; and my eyes were turned toward the sea.

"Fear nothing," said my lord, "sit thou secure 46
  At heart; we've come into a good estate,
  Faint not, but be the more alert therefore.

Thou hast reached Purgatory; see, the great 49
  Rampart of rock that compasses it round;
  And where the cleft shows yonder, there's the gate.

In the white daybreak hour just now, when sound 52
  Thy soul slept in thee down below, thy head
  Lodged on the flowers which there adorn the ground,

A lady came: 'I am Lucy' – thus she said; 55
  'Come, let me take this sleeper; I've a mind
  To help him on the road he has to tread.'

Sordel and all those shades of princely kind 58
  Were left; but thee she took and bore thee hither
  Up with the daylight, and I came behind.

61  She set thee down; then turned her fair eyes thither
    Towards the rock, to show me where the fissure
    Opened; she went then, and thy sleep went with her."

64  Like one consoled, released from the dull pressure
    Of doubt, who changes all his former fright,
    When the glad truth is told him, into pleasure,

67  So my face changed; and when he saw me quite
    Carefree, my leader moved; and so did I,
    Up by the rampart, onward toward the height.

70  Look, Reader, how my theme would scale the sky!
    Marvel not, therefore, if with greater art
    I seek to buttress what I build so high.

73  So we drew near and came unto a part
    Whence, in what first had seemed a simple breach
    Or fissure such as rives a wall apart,

76  I saw a gate; three steps beneath it, each
    Of different hue, led upward; and thereat
    A porter, who as yet vouchsafed no speech.

79  Widening my eyes, I saw him, how he sat
    Over the topmost step, in countenance
    Such as would not abide the looking-at.

82  A naked sword was in his hand, whose dance
    Of mirrored rays so binding blazed and shot,
    I tried and tried, but could not fix my glance.

85  Then he began: "Make answer from that spot;
    What would you? Where's the escort? Take good heed
    That your ascending hither harm you not."

88  "A lady out of Heaven, well skilled indeed
    In matters such as this," my lord replied,
    "Told us: 'There stands the gate; go there with speed.'"

91  To whom, immediately: "And may she guide
    Your journey on to a good end and fair!
    Approach our steps," the courteous porter cried.

94  And when we reached the first step of the stair
    It was white marble, polished to such gloss
    That, even as I am, I saw me there;

And dyed more dark than perse the second was –    97
   A calcined stone, rugged and rough in grain,
   And it was cracked both lengthways and across;

The third step, piled above the other twain,    100
   Seemed all of porphyry that flamed and shone
   Redder than bright blood spurting from a vein,

And this, God's Angel held both feet upon,    103
   And on the threshold of the door he sate,
   And that seemed made of adamantine stone.

With great goodwill my master led me straight    106
   Up those three steps: "And now," said he, "entreat
   Most humbly of him to unlock the gate."

Devoutly falling at the holy feet    109
   I prayed him let me in for mercy's sake,
   But first upon my breast three times I beat.

Then did he write with his sword's point, and make    112
   Upon my brow the mark of seven P's;
   "Wash thou these wounds within there"; thus he spake.

Colour of ash, or earth dug dry, agrees    115
   Well with the sober vesture on him clad,
   And from beneath it he brought out two keys;

One golden and one silver key he had;    118
   With the white first, the yellow afterward,
   He wrought so with the gate that I was glad.

"Should one or other of the keys stick hard,    121
   Turning askew so that the tumblers block,"
   He said, "this wicket cannot be unbarred.

One's costlier; the other needs good stock    124
   Of wit and skill to get the bolt to stir,
   For that one grips the wards and frees the lock.

From Peter hold I these, who bade me err    127
   In opening rather than in keeping fast,
   So men but kneeled to me without demur."

That blest gate's door he pushed then, saying at last:    130
   "Enter; but I must warn you: back outside
   He goes, who looks behind him once he's passed."

133    When in their sockets now began to gride
        The turning pivots of the sacred door,
        Which are of strong and ringing bronze, they cried

136    Aloud – so loud Tarpeia did not roar,
        Nor with such dreadful discord, when she found
        The good Metellus gone, her wealth made poor.

139    Then, as I leaned, hearkening to that first sound,
        Methought a voice sang, like some chorister's,
        *Te Deum laudamus*, sweetly interwound

142    With music; and its image in my ears
        Left such impression as one often catches
        From songs sung to an organ, when one hears

145    The words sometimes and sometimes not, by snatches.

THE IMAGES. *Dante's Dream of the Eagle*: This is the first of the three dreams which Dante has, on the three nights he spends in Purgatory. All three symbolize and interpret something which is occurring or about to occur. On this occasion he dreams that he is walking, like Ganymede, upon Mount Ida, and, like Ganymede, is caught up to heaven by an eagle. The dream is induced by a reality (Dante's dream-psychology is always plausible): he has actually been carried up the face of the Mountain by St Lucy, and this movement both induces and fulfils the dream which symbolizes it.

    *Ganymede* was the son of Tros, ancestor of Aeneas and mythical founder of Troy. Enamoured of his beauty, Jove sent the divine eagle to fetch him one day as he was hunting with his friends upon Mount Ida, overlooking Troy, and Ganymede was carried away to Olympus to become cupbearer to the gods. The legend thus provides two threads of symbolism. (1) Primarily, it is a story in which God takes the initiative, moved by love for a human being, and carries the beloved away to be with Himself. (We need not let any prejudices about Olympian morality interfere with our, or Dante's, allegorizing of the myths.) (2) Secondly, throughout the *Comedy*, the Eagle always symbolizes the true Empire and, in particular, the Justice of the Empire – a concept which we shall see fully elaborated in the *Paradiso*, in the Heaven of Jupiter (*Para.* xviii. xix. xx). To this true Empire ("The Rome where Christ Himself is a Roman", *Para.* xxxii. 102) the souls of men are brought by the purgatorial path, which is the fulfilling of Justice. (See

Introduction, pp. 54 *sqq.*) Ganymede the Trojan, of the line that founded Rome, is thus the type of human society, taken up into the City of God, here and hereafter.

*Lucy*: St Lucy, it will be remembered, was the second of the "Three Blessed Ladies" who interested themselves in Dante's welfare. It was she who was sent by the Blessed Virgin to call Beatrice's attention to Dante's peril in the Dark Wood (*Inf.* ii. 97 *sqq.*). As the saint who looks after people's eyesight, she figures as a symbol of illuminating grace, and is thus fitly typified in the dream by the eagle which can, traditionally, bear to look on the sun with naked eyes.

In the *allegory*, the intervention of Lucy means, I think, that in entering actively upon the way of Penitence and Purgation the soul is dependent upon God's grace. It is too great a leap for it to make by its natural light and natural powers, though these will, of course, accompany and assist it. Thus Lucy is sent from Heaven to carry Dante up, and Virgil only "comes behind".

*The Three Steps*: These are the three parts of Penitence: (1) Confession, (2) Contrition, and (3) Satisfaction. (See Introduction, p. 56.) The first is of polished white marble: the penitent looks into his heart, sees himself as he is, recognizes his sinfulness, and so admits and confesses it. The second is black, the colour of mourning, and cracked in the figure of the cross: "A broken and contrite heart, O God, shalt thou not despise" (*Ps.* li. 17, *Vulg.* i. 19). The third is of porphyry redder than blood: the colour symbolizes not only the penitent's pouring out his own life and love in restitution for sin, but also the Blood of Christ's "oblation of Himself once offered, to be a full, perfect and sufficient sacrifice, oblation, and satisfaction for the sins of the whole world" (*Book of Common Prayer*), with which the penitent's satisfaction must unite itself in order to be complete.

*The Threshold* of adamant is the foundation on which the Church is built: in her human aspect, the Rock which is Peter; in her Divine aspect, the Cornerstone which is Christ.

*The Angel at the Gate*: He is usually taken as representing the ideal Confessor, or the ideal Priesthood, and so, in the immediate context, he is; but in a wider sense he might be called, I think, the Angel of the Church. He wears the ashen garments of penitence, not only because the good confessor must himself be a penitent, but because the Church, so long as she sojourns in Time, must sojourn in sorrow and tribulation; he bears "the sword of the Spirit, which is the Word of God"; and he is invested with the Keys of the Kingdom of Heaven, which were given to Peter as the Church's authority to bind or unloose the bonds of sin. The Gate itself is the "Peter's Gate" mentioned in *Inf.* i. 134: and we may note that the soul which is within the Gate and set on the Way of Purgation is already within "the Kingdom of Heaven".

*The Seven P's*: "P" stands for *peccatum* = sin; thus the Seven P's represent the Seven Capital Sins which must be purged successively on the Seven Cornices of Purgatory. They "are signs of the conviction of sin, the new sense that sin is a 'wound', which is wrought in [the penitent] by the sword of the word" (J. D. Sinclair).

*The Keys*: These are the two parts of absolution: The Golden Key is the Divine authority given to the Church to remit sin; it is "the costlier" because it was bought at the price of God's Passion and Death. The Silver Key is the unloosening of the hard entanglement of sin in the human heart: and this needs great skill on the part of the Church and her priesthood when administering the sacrament of Penance. Both keys must function smoothly for a valid absolution: the use of the golden key without the silver lands you exactly where it landed Guido da Montefeltro (*Inf.* xxvii. 67 *sqq.*): the silver without the golden (i.e. remorse for sin without seeking reconciliation) leads only to despair and the Gorgon at the Gates of Dis. (*Inf.* ix.)

NOTES. ll. 1–9: *now, glimmering ... on the wing as well*: The lunar Aurora, or Moon-Dawn – called "the leman" of old Tithonus (see Glossary) as distinguished from the solar Aurora, who is his wife – was standing in the eastern sky like a lady looking out from her balcony, wearing on her forehead stars set in the shape of the Scorpion, the cold-blooded creature which has a stinging tail. In other words, the moon was rising in Scorpio, and Night, in Purgatory ("in that sky of ours") had completed two steps (hours) of her journey, and the third hour was drawing to a close, so that it was now between 8 and 9 P.M. (This appears to me the best interpretation of this much disputed passage: but see Appendix, p. 342.)

l. 10: *old Adam's nature*: Dante was still wearing his earthly body, which needed sleep. Note that it is only in Purgatory, which is situated in *time*, that Dante sleeps at all; not in Hell or Heaven, which are *eternal* states.

l. 12: *we five*: i.e. Dante, Virgil, Sordello, Nino, and Conrad.

ll. 13–18: *about the hour*, etc.: the hour of (the solar) dawn (6 A.M.).

l. 13: *the sad swallow*: Tereus, King of Thrace, the husband of Procne, violated her sister Philomena and cut out her tongue, so that she should not betray his crime. Philomena, however, by means of a piece of tapestry, denounced him to Procne who, in revenge, killed her son Itys and with Philomena's help served up his flesh to Tereus. When Tereus, discovering this, tried to kill both sisters, the gods changed all three into birds – Tereus into a hoopoe, and the two sisters into a swallow and a nightingale respectively. (Ovid, *Metam.* vi. 424–

676.) Dante follows the less usual version, which makes Procne the nightingale and Philomena the swallow (*Purg.* xvii. 19).

l. 18. *half-divine her dreaming vision grows*: it was commonly held that a dream at morning was prophetic (cf. *Inf.* xxvi. 7).

l. 30: *the sphere of flame*: this was believed to surround the earth between the sphere of air and the sphere of the moon.

ll. 34–9: *Achilles*, etc.: Achilles, the Greek warrior, hero of Homer's *Iliad*, was the son of Peleus, King of the Myrmidons, and the nymph Thetis. So that he should not take part in the war against Troy, where it had been prophesied that he would be killed, his mother took him from the Centaur Chiron (see *Inf.* xii. 65 and note) by whom he had been brought up, and carried him in his sleep to the island of Scyros, where she dressed him as a girl and hid him among the queen's maidens. His astonishment on awaking in Scyros is described by Statius (*Achill.* i. 247 *sqq.*). Eventually his whereabouts was discovered by the cunning Ulysses, who came with Diomede and took him away to Troy.

l. 44: *two hours and more risen*: i.e. it was now past 8 A.M.

l. 86: *where's the escort?*: this informs us that, in the ordinary way, a soul whose time in Ante-Purgatory was finished would have been as it were officially released and accompanied to the Gate by a heavenly minister. Compare this with the entirely spontaneous departure of the purged souls from the Cornices (xxi. 58–66, and Introduction, p. 58).

l. 88: *a Lady out of Heaven*: Cf. Virgil similarly presenting their "credentials" to Cato (i. 52–4).

l. 111: *upon my breast three times I beat*: in making his confession to a priest the penitent knocks three times upon his breast, saying that he has sinned in thought, word, and deed "by my fault (*knock*), by my own fault (*knock*), by my own most grievous fault (*knock*) – *meâ culpâ, meâ culpâ, meâ maximâ culpâ.*"

l. 114: *within there*: i.e. within the Gate, in Purgatory.

l. 119: *with the white first*: the penitent's disposition must be right before the authority to pardon is exercised.

ll. 127–9: *who bade me err*, etc.: we need not make heavy weather about the possibility of the Angel's "erring". The meaning is that, provided the penitent has whole-heartedly submitted to the Church's authority (l. 29), the most merciful and generous view is to be taken of his case.

ll. 131–2: *back outside he goes*, etc.: in the *literal* sense it is not possible that a saved soul should "look behind him" (i.e. falter in his purpose of purgation): the *allegorical* sense has here taken charge of the passage. (But see Introduction, p. 60.)

l. 135: *they cried aloud*: the pivots are rusty because so few men take the way of salvation ("strait is the gate and narrow is the way that leadeth unto life, and few there be that find it." *Matt.* vii. 14: and cf. *Purg.* x. 2).

ll. 136–8: *Tarpeia*, etc.: the Roman treasury was kept in the Temple of Saturn on the Tarpeian Hill. Lucan (see *Inf.* iv. 90 and Glossary) in his *Pharsalia* tells how the tribune Metellus was prevented by a colleague from holding it against Julius Caesar, when he entered Rome in 49 B.C. (see Glossary: Caesar, Julius): "When Metellus had been led away, forthwith the temple was flung open. Then did the Tarpeian Rock re-echo, and with a loud peal bear witness to the opening of the doors" (*Phars.* iii. 153–68).

l. 141: *Te Deum laudamus*: "We praise thee, O God": the great hymn written by St Ambrose on the occasion of St Augustine's conversion. It is usually sung on Festival, not on penitential, occasions. Here it is perhaps chosen with reference to *Luke* xv. 10; though some writers suggest that it is sung, not by any angel (cf. xxvii. 58 and note) but by the spirits in Purgatory for joy that a new soul has entered on the way of purgation, just as they sing the *Gloria in excelsis* whenever a purified soul is released from his pains (*Purg.* xxi. 58–60).

# CANTO X

THE STORY. *As Peter's Gate clangs to behind them, the Poets begin climbing the steep and narrow zigzag cleft in the rock which leads to the First Cornice. This, when they get there, turns out to be a ledge some eighteen feet wide running all round the Mountain, and, at the moment of their arrival, quite empty from end to end. The face of the cliff opposite the mouth of the hollow way is adorned with sculptured examples of the Great Humilities: and while they are examining these, they see a company of the Proud approaching, each one bent double beneath the weight of an enormous stone.*

When we had crossed the threshold of that gate
 Which the soul's evil loves put out of use,
 Because they make the crooked path seem straight,

I heard its closing clang ring clamorous,       4
 And had I then turned back my eyes to it
 How could my fault have found the least excuse?

We had to climb now through a rocky slit       7
 Which ran from side to side in many a swerve,
 As runs the wave in onset and retreat.

"Now here," the master said, "we must observe    10
 Some little caution, hugging now this wall,
 Now that, upon the far side of the curve."

These labours made our steps so slow and small    13
 That the diminished moon from out the sky
 Back to her restful bed had time to fall

Before we'd threaded through that needle's eye.    16
 But when we had come up and out to where
 The hill's face was set back, there he and I

Stood still, I weary, both quite unaware      19
 Which way to turn us, on a level place
 Bare as a desert track, and lonelier.

From where the brink verges on empty space    22
 Back to the foot of the still-soaring height,
 'Twould measure thrice a man's length more or less;

143

25   And far as e'er my eye could wing its flight,
        Still just the same, throughout its whole extent,
        The Cornice seemed, whether to left or right.

28   Now, while we stood up there, and ere we went
        One step, I saw how that rock-bastion
        Which, rising sheer, showed no means of ascent,

31   Was pure white marble, and had carved thereon
        Sculptures so rare, that Polyclete – nay, more –
        Nature might blush there, being so outdone.

34   The angel that to earth came down and bore
        The edict of the age-long wept-for peace
        Which broke the long ban and unbarred Heaven's door,

37   Appeared to us, with such a lively ease
        Carved, and so gracious there in act to move,
        It seemed not one of your dumb images;

40   You'd swear an *Ave* from his lips breathed off,
        For she was shown there too, who turned the key
        To unlock the treasure of the most high love;

43   And in her mien those words stood plain to see:
        *Ecce ancilla Dei*, stamped by art
        Express as any seal on wax could be.

46   "Do not restrict thy gaze to this one part,"
        Prompted my gentle guide, who had me now
        That side of him on which men wear the heart.

49   Wherefore I turned mine eyes and witnessed how,
        At Mary's back, to right of me, where stayed
        He who thus urged me on, the mountain's brow

52   Showed a new story carven and portrayed;
        So, passing across Virgil, I drew near,
        The better to observe the scene displayed.

55   And sculptured in the living marble here
        Oxen and wain that holy Ark were bringing,
        Whence all who snatch at office should learn fear;

58   And here the folk in seven great choirs went singing
        Ahead, so that two wits of mine contended:
        One said, "No, no," the other, "Yes, they're singing."

So likewise from the thuribles ascended 61
   Such pictured smoke as brought from eyes and nose
   Their ay and no contrariously blended.

Before the sacred vessel, girded close, 64
   His dancing feet the humble Psalmist plied,
   And more than king in this and less he was.

Here Michal's image, on the other side, 67
   Looked on from a great palace window, seeming
   A scornful lady and a mortified.

I moved from where I stood, to scan this limning 70
   More close at hand, and saw another story
   Behind the back of Michal whitely gleaming.

And there in stone narrated was the glory 73
   Of the great Roman prince, whose virtues wooed
   Gregory to conquer Heaven with oratory;

I mean the Emperor Trajan; there he rode; 76
   And a poor widow to his bridle clung,
   Tears and bereavement in her attitude.

Horsemen surged round him in a trampling throng, 79
   And visibly above him in the breeze
   The golden-fielded eagles flapped and swung.

There the distressful wretch amid all these 82
   Appeared to say: "Avenge me, lord! my son
   Is slain, my heart cracked through with miseries."

"Wait now," he seemed to answer, "and anon 85
   I shall return." And, "O my lord," again
   She seemed to cry, like one whom grief goads on,

"If thou return not?" He: "My heir shall then 88
   Do all." But she: "If thou canst so forget
   Good faith, what boots thee that of other men?"

He therefore: "Be consoled; it is right meet 91
   I do my duty ere I quit this spot;
   Justice requires it, reverence stays my feet."

He unto whom no sight is strange thus wrought 94
   Visible speech, a strange thing in our eyes,
   Since in this world of ours we find it not.

97    The image of the great humilities
          Still held me thralled – a sight beyond compare
          And, for the Craftsman's sake, beyond all price,

100   When, "Look!" the poet murmured, "over there
          Comes on, but very slowly, quite a throng;
          They will direct us to the upward stair."

103   My eyes turned promptly toward him, for a strong
          Desire possessed them (it's the way I'm made)
          To see whate'er new thing might come along.

106   Reader, I would not have you turn dismayed
          From good resolves, for having heard me say
          How God ordains our debt should be repaid;

109   Heed not the form of the affliction – nay,
          Think of what follows; pray you, think, this woe
          Cannot, at worst, outlast the Judgement Day.

112   "Master," I faltered, "that which creeps so slow
          This way – it does not look to me like men;
          It's like – my sight's at fault – I just don't know."

115   And he to me: "Their heavy load of pain
          So bows them down that I was doubtful quite
          Myself at first and could not see them plain.

118   Look hard, and disentangle with thy sight
          What walks beneath those stones; they're clear to thee
          By now – thou seest them on their bosoms smite."

121   Alas, proud Christians, faint with misery,
          So warped of vision in the inward sense
          You trust in your backslidings! Don't you see

124   That we are worms, whose insignificance
          Lives but to form the angelic butterfly
          That flits to judgement naked of defence?

127   Why do you let pretension soar so high,
          Being as it were but larvae – grubs that lack
          The finished form that shall be by and by?

130   As, for a corbel, holding on its back
          Ceiling or roof, one sometimes sees a figure
          Cramped knees to chest, so that real twinges rack

146

One's joints at sight of that unreal rigour,                    133
   So did I see those spirits in distress
   When I surveyed them with my mind's full vigour.

And true it is, they were cramped more or less                  136
   As more or less upon their backs they bore;
   Even he who showed most patience in duress

Seeming to say with tears: "I can no more."                     139

THE IMAGES. (1) *Lower Purgatory: Love Perverted.* (See Introduction, pp. 66–7.)

   *Cornice 1: Pride.* Taken in its wider aspect, *Pride* (*Superbia*) is the head and root of all sin, both original and actual. It is the endeavour to be "as God", making self, instead of God, the centre about which the will and desire revolve. In its narrower and more specific aspect, pride exhibits itself as *Vainglory* (*Vana gloria*) – an egotism so overweening that it cannot bear to occupy any place but the first, and hates and despises all fellow-creatures out of sheer lust of domination. Some theologians separate these two aspects, placing Pride in a class by itself, as the generic sin of which Vainglory and the rest are the species: but Dante follows the more usual arrangement which puts Pride and Vainglory together as the first of the Seven Capital Sins.

NOTES. l. 2: *the soul's evil loves*: in this phrase Dante adumbrates the definition which Virgil will give later, of love as the root of all vice as well as of all virtue (see Introduction, p. 66).

   l. 3: *they make the crooked path seem straight*: the pursuit of a fancied good, which we take to be the true good, makes us mistake our aberrations for the *diritta via*, the road, in Bunyan's words "straight as a rule can make it".

   ll. 7–12: *we had to climb*: that the poets were scrambling up a steep, zigzag cleft or "chimney" in the rock, everybody agrees: but of the details of the performance there are as many explanations as there are translators and commentators. (See Appendix, p. 341.)

   ll. 14–16: *the diminished moon*, etc.: the moon, which had been full on the night of Good Friday, and was now three days on the wane, had set by the time they emerged from the cleft: i.e. it was after 9.30 A.M.

   l. 16: *that needle's eye*: Ref. Matt. xix. 24, Mark x. 25, Luke xvii. 25.

   l. 28: *ere we went one step*: the poets are standing with their backs to the cleft by which they have just ascended, with Dante on Virgil's left (l. 48), facing the wall of the cornice, some 15–18 feet away (l. 24). At l. 53, Dante crosses to stand on Virgil's right.

l. 32: *sculptures*: these are the "Whip of Pride" (see Introduction, pp. 67-8), exhibiting examples of Humility. *Polyclete* (Polycletus) the Greek sculptor, who *fl.* about 480 B.C., is frequently mentioned by Aristotle.

l. 34 *sqq.*: *the angel*, etc.: The first example, from the life of the B.V.M., is the Annunciation; it exhibits (*a*) God's humility in stooping to become Man, (*b*) Mary's humility in accepting her Divine burden.

l. 40: *Ave* (Hail): the opening word of the Angel's salutation: "Hail, thou that art highly favoured" (*Luke* i. 28).

l. 41: *the key*: "*The key of David opens and no man shuts* (*Rev.* iii. 7). The Son of David is the Key of David, Christ Jesus; He hath opened Heaven for us all" (John Donne: *Sermon for Easter Day*, 1629). The anthem O *clavis David* ("O Key of David") is sung at the end of Advent.

l. 44: *ecce ancilla Dei* (for *Domini*): "behold the handmaid of God" (*Luke* i. 38).

ll. 56 *sqq.*: *oxen and wain*, etc.: The next two examples, from the O.T. and classical history respectively, exhibit Humility towards man. For King David, dancing before the Ark of the Covenant, and the contempt of his wife Michal, see 2 *Sam.* vi.

l. 57: *all who snatch at office*: Uzzah, who officiously laid his hand on the sacrosanct Ark to steady it, was struck dead (2 *Sam.* vi. 6-7).

l. 64: *girded close*: "and David danced before the Lord with all his might: and David was girded with a linen ephod" (2 *Sam.* vi. 14).

ll. 74 *sqq.*: *the great Roman prince*, etc.: The legend of Trajan (see Glossary) and the poor widow exists in various medieval versions, which also relate how St Gregory brought the dead emperor back from Hell by his prayers and baptized him to salvation. In *Para.* xx. 43-5 we meet Trajan in the Heaven of the Just.

l. 81: *the golden-fielded eagles*: Dante imagined the Roman imperial standards (actually poles surmounted by bronze figures) as flags of the modern type showing a black eagle on a gold field. They are so depicted, some hundred years after Dante's death, by Piero della Francesca in his great murals of the victories of Heraclius and Constantine in the church of S. Francesca at Arezzo.

l. 93: *reverence*: Dante's word is *pietà* – not here, I think, "pity", as it is usually translated, but "piety" (Lat. *pietas*): the religious reverence which dictates a sense of duty. The line is thus an echo of Cicero's phrase, "*pietas et justitia*".

l. 95: *visible speech*: It will be observed that, whereas the modern art critic is apt to praise the art of the Middle Ages for its symbolism and stylization, the medieval critic himself tended to rejoice in an almost photographic realism. This is not merely because, with Dante, we are drawing on towards the Second Renaissance; the preference is equally marked in, say, a poem like the *Tristan* of Thomas, in the middle of the twelfth century. It is, however, not quite fair to say that Dante's artistic ideal would have been that bunch of grapes which was so deceptively lifelike that a fly came and settled on it; for he mentions expressly that the reliefs were not naturalistically coloured, but executed in white marble. The quality he admires is not so much realism as a (literally) supernatural *expressiveness*.

l. 99. *for the Craftsman's sake*: the reliefs are carved by God's own hand – or (more probably, on the analogy of the engineering works of Hell, *Inf.* xv. 11 and note) by an Intelligence under His direction.

l. 101: *a throng*: these are the Proud, whose penance will presently be described. (See Images for Canto xi.)

ll. 110–11: *this woe cannot, at worst, outlive the Judgement Day*: Purgatory is temporal, and its pains end when time ends (though for most souls they will, of course, end long before that).

ll. 124–9: *that we are worms*, etc.: "we have nothing in this world to be proud about, since we are but half-finished beings – grubs existing only to produce the butterfly (emblem of the soul), which, when it leaves the body, must fly to stand naked and defenceless before the judgement-seat."

# CANTO XI

THE STORY. *The penitent Proud draw near, saying the Lord's Prayer.*
*Virgil inquires the way, and is told by Humbert Aldobrandesco to turn*
*right and go along with them until the stair is reached. While Humbert is*
*telling his own story and asking for prayers, Dante hears another soul call-*
*ing him and recognizes the painter Oderisi, who discourses upon the vanity*
*of earthly fame. Oderisi then points out his fellow-penitent, Provenzano*
*Salvani, who by one great act of humility performed for love's sake*
*obtained release from the place of waiting and immediate admission to*
*Purgatory.*

"Our Father, dwelling in the Heavens, nowise
   As circumscribed, but as the things above,
   Thy first effects, are dearest in Thine eyes,

4   Hallowed Thy name be and the Power thereof,
   By every creature, as right meet it is
   We praise the tender effluence of Thy Love.

7   Let come to us, let come Thy Kingdom's peace;
   If it come not, we've no power of our own
   To come to it, for all our subtleties.

10   Like as with glad Hosannas at Thy throne
   Thine angels offer up their wills alway,
   So let men offer theirs, that Thine be done.

13   Our daily manna give to us this day,
   Without which he that through this desert wild
   Toils most to speed goes backward on his way.

16   As we, with all our debtors reconciled,
   Forgive, do Thou forgive us, nor regard
   Our merits, but upon our sins look mild.

19   Put not our strength, too easily ensnared
   And overcome, to proof with the old foe;
   But save us from him, for he tries it hard.

22   This last prayer is not made for us – we know,
   Dear Lord, that it is needless – but for those
   Who still remain behind us we pray so."

Even thus, for their and our good speed, arose     25
  Prayer from those souls beneath their burden curled
  And going, as in dreams one sometimes goes,

Where the First Cornice its slow length unfurled,     28
  Painfully round, diversely laden thus,
  Purging away the tarnish of the world.

If a good word's said always there for us,     31
  What should not here be done for them by prayers
  From those whose will takes root where all good does?

Truly we ought to help them cleanse the smears     34
  They carried hence, that, weightless and washed white,
  They may fare forth and seek the starry spheres.

"Now, as may mercy and justice soon make light     37
  Your load, that toward the goal you long to see
  You may find power to move your wings in flight,

Show which direction will more speedily     40
  Bring us to where the stair goes up; or show
  The gentlest rise, if more than one there be,

Because this man who's with me has to go     43
  Burdened with Adam's flesh wherein he's dressed,
  So that, with his best will, his climbing's slow."

From whom the question, thus to them addressed     46
  By him whom I still followed close at hand,
  Received its answer was not manifest;

But someone said: "Turn right, and with our band     49
  Follow the ledge, and you will find a crack
  That living feet may manage to ascend.

And if I were not hindered, my proud back     52
  Being thus subdued beneath this stony weight,
  Which makes me keep my face bent to the track,

I'd look at this live man – I didn't get     55
  His name – to see if he to me is known,
  And win his pity for my burdened state.

Latian was I; a great man called me son:     58
  Guillim Aldobrandesco of Tuscany –
  Though if you ever heard of such a one

61      I know not. Ancient blood, past chivalry,
            These puffed me up – forgetting in my pride
            The common mother of humanity –

64      To such contempt of all the world beside
            As killed me; all Siena, every child
            In Compagnatico knows why I died.

67      I am Humbert; and my arrogance beguiled
            To loss not only me, but all my kin
            It dragged down with it, ruined and reviled.

70      Therefore, till God be satisfied for sin,
            It here behoves me bear among the dead
            The load I bore not among living men."

73      I'd bowed my face, listening to what he said,
            And one of them – not he who spoke – slewed round
            Beneath the load that weighted down his head

76      And saw and knew and called me, as he wound
            Skew-wise along to keep me in his gaze
            Who paced with them, bent double toward the ground.

79      "Why, sure," I cried, "that's Oderisi's face,
            Honour of Gubbio and the art they call
            *Illuminating*, in the Paris phrase!"

82      "Brother," said he, "a touch more magical
            Smiles now from Franco of Bologna's page;
            Some honour's mine, but his is all in all.

85      I should have been less generous, I'll engage,
            While yet I lived, and ardour to outshine
            Burned in my bosom with a kind of rage.

88      For pride like that we here must pay the fine;
            Nor yet should I be here, but that contrition
            Turned me to God while power to sin was mine.

91      O empty glory of man's frail ambition,
            How soon its topmost boughs their green must yield;
            If no Dark Age succeed, what short fruition!

94      Once, Cimabue thought to hold the field
            In painting; Giotto's all the rage to-day;
            The other's fame lies in the dust concealed.

Guido from Guido wrests our native bay,       97
   And born, belike, already is that same
   Shall chase both songsters from the nest away.

A breath of wind – no more – is earthly fame,     100
   And now this way it blows and that way now,
   And as it changes quarter, changes name.

Ten centuries hence, what greater fame hast thou,   103
   Stripping the flesh off late, than if thou'dst died
   Ere thou wast done with *gee-gee* and *bow-wow*?

Ten centuries hence – and that's a briefer tide,    106
   Matched with eternity, than one eye-wink
   To that wheeled course Heaven's tardiest sphere must ride.

His name who creeps so slow along the brink    109
   Before me, once through Tuscany rang loud;
   Now in Siena even, 'tis scarce, I think,

Whispered, though he was lord there when they bowed  112
   And broke the fury of Florence, now, alas!
   As much degraded as she then was proud.

All your renown is like the hue of grass,     115
   Which comes and goes; who caused it first to start
   Green from the ground, he makes it fade and pass."

"True words," said I, "that rightly teach my heart  118
   Meekness, and prick my blown-up self-esteem;
   But of whom spak'st thou in the latter part?"

"Of Provenzan Salvani; his extreme     121
   Presumption brought him here," said he; "he sought
   To tread down all Siena under him.

Thus hath he gone, and goes, and resteth not   124
   Ever since he died, for those who yonder were
   O'erweening bold, in this coin pay the scot."

"But if," said I, "the soul who takes no care   127
   For his repentance till his latter end
   Must wait below, and thence, if no good prayer

Aid him, is not permitted to ascend     130
   Till he have passed his life's length there perforce –
   Then by what means was his admittance gained?"

133    And he: "In full mid-splendour of his course
       He in Siena's market went and stood,
       Of his free-will, all shame thrown out of doors;

136    And, to redeem his friend from servitude
       In Charles's dungeon, there he bore to do
       A thing he winced at in his very blood.

139    I've said enough; my speech is dark, 'tis true,
       But soon thy neighbours shall do so to thee
       That thou shalt learn to write the gloss thereto.

142    That deed undid the ban and set him free."

THE IMAGES. *The Penance of the Proud: the Heavy Stones.* On this Cornice the penance consists in submission to the opposite virtue. The heads that were held high are now bowed in a necessary humility beneath the weight of sinfulness externalized as cold and heavy stone; and the eyes that looked down upon their neighbours are now unable to look up. (That, incidentally, is why the "Whip" of Pride is placed opposite the Mouth of the hollow way, so as to be seen by the soul on its arrival and before it assumes its burden.)

The Proud: (1) *Pride of Race*: Humbert Aldobrandesco the aristocrat; (2) *Pride of Achievement*: Oderisi the artist; (3) *Pride of Domination*: Provenzano Salvani the despot.

NOTES. ll. 1–24: *Our Father*, etc.: this is the Prayer of the Proud: the *Paternoster*, expanded by a brief meditation upon each clause, directed throughout to the virtue of Humility.

*Clause 1.* (ll. 1–3): *in the heavens* (both the Gk. and the Vulgate have the plural here) *nowise as circumscribed*: i.e. not as implying that God is either confined spatially to the spheres or excluded from converse with any part of His creation, but acknowledging that the Angels (Intelligences) which were His first works ("effects") are nearest and dearest to Him, because most like Himself. (This clause, a reminder to the Proud that Man is by no means the noblest of the creatures, might also serve to remind some modern writers that "the medievals" did *not* believe the entire universe to have been created for Man's sole benefit.) There is a very illuminating passage on the meaning of "heaven" in this connexion in Charles William's *He Came Down from Heaven* (opening paragraph).

(ll. 4–6): *Thy Name ... Power ... Love*: allusion to the Trinity.

*Clause 2.* (ll. 7–9): *let come ... Thy Kingdom's peace*: the peace of the Kingdom comes by God's initiative, not ours (cf. *John* xiv. 27).

*Clause 3.* (ll. 10–12): *Thine angels offer up their wills*: as the joy of the blessed Angels is the perpetual sacrifice of their own wills to God, so should man's be.

*Clause 4.* (ll. 13–15): *our daily manna*: the spiritual bread which is Christ (*John* vi. 31–3 and cf. the "supersubstantial bread" of *Vulg. Matt.* vi. 11), without which our own efforts are self-defeating. (A petition for material bread would be meaningless in Purgatory.)

*Clause 5.* (ll. 16–18): *nor regard our merits*: an echo from the Canon of the Mass (*non aestimator meriti*) at the prayer for fellowship in the communion of saints ("not weighing our merits, but pardoning our offences" – *Book of Common Prayer*).

*Clauses 6 and 7.* (ll. 19–21): *the old foe*: Satan ("that old serpent, which is the devil", *Rev.* xx. 2); translating "deliver us from the Evil One", as in R.V. margin. For this task Man's strength is insufficient.

ll. 22–4: *this last prayer*, etc.: the petition against temptation and the assaults of the devil is unnecessary for those in Purgatory, who are no longer able to sin; but the Proud, who in their lifetime cared for nobody but themselves, now learn to pray for those they have left behind on earth (and possibly also in Ante-Purgatory, see Canto viii and Images).

ll. 31 *sqq.*: *if a good word*, etc.: The bond of prayer and charity between the Church on earth and the Church Expectant should be mutual; the souls in Purgatory pray for us and we for them, as the Saints in Heaven pray for all and further the petitions of all.

l. 47: *him whom I still followed*: i.e. Virgil.

l. 48: *was not manifest*: the speaker was so bent beneath his burden that his face was not visible.

ll. 58–9: *a great man called me son, Guillim Aldobrandesco*: the speaker is Humbert (Omberto) of the great Ghibelline family of the Aldobrandeschi, counts of Santafiora, whose perpetual strife with Siena is mentioned in vi. 11. In 1259, the Sienese, exasperated by his arrogance, stormed the stronghold of Campagnatico and killed him. The habit of pride which still clings to him makes him begin by boasting of his father's greatness; his new-learned humility makes him quickly correct himself – "I do not know if you ever heard of him."

l. 63: *the common mother of humanity*: prince or peasant, we are alike sons of Eve; moreover, our First Parents fell by pride; hence Humbert had doubly "forgotten Eve".

l. 68: *all my kin*: the whole Aldobrandeschi family shortly became extinct, and their possessions passed into Sienese hands.

l. 70: *till God be satisfied for sin*: see Introduction, p. 58.

l. 79: *Oderisi*: of Gubbio (or Agobbio) in Umbria: a celebrated illuminator of manuscripts. He is said to have been summoned to Rome by Boniface VIII in 1295 to paint a number of books in the Papal library.

l. 81: *"Illuminating", in the Paris phrase*: the usual Italian expression was not *illuminare* but *miniare* = to paint with *minium* (red lead), whence the word "miniature". Paris was in the fourteenth century the leading school and centre of the art of illumination, and Dante indulges in a little display of his knowledge of the right technical phrase.

l. 83: *Franco of Bologna*: little of this painter's work remains, but he is said to have been an excellent artist, and to have been employed in the Papal library at the same time as Oderisi, who now hastens to pay to his rival the honour which he would have scorned to pay in his lifetime.

l. 90: *while power to sin was mine*: i.e. "while I was still alive and well". Had he delayed repentance till his death-bed, he "would not yet be here", but would have been detained in Ante-Purgatory.

l. 93: *if no Dark Age succeed*: an artist's reputation is quickly eclipsed in the next generation unless, indeed, he is followed by a barbarous age which produces no artists at all.

ll. 94–5: *Cimabue ... Giotto*: Giovanni Cimabue (1240–1308) was a Florentine painter, highly celebrated in his time, whose art was the first to free itself from the hieratic stiffness of the Byzantine tradition. His pupil and fellow-Florentine, Giotto di Bondone (1266–1337) surpassed him in fluency of line and truth to nature, and has been called "the father of modern painting". Giotto was a personal friend of Dante, whose portrait in the Bargello at Florence is said to be by his hand.

l. 97: *Guido from Guido*: The two poets who are thus said to contest the glory of the Italian tongue are usually thought to be Guido Guinicelli of Bologna (*c.* 1230–*c.* 1276), whom we shall presently meet on the 7th Cornice (*Purg.* xxvi. 16 *sqq.*), and Dante's friend, Guido Cavalcanti (mentioned in *Inf.* x. 63 and Glossary) of Florence (*c.* 1256–1300). Some, however, identify the first Guido with Guittone d'Arezzo (see Canto xxvi. 124 and note) and the second with Guinicelli.

l. 98: *and born, belike, already is that same*: Most commentators suppose (without the smallest evidence) that Oderisi is here alluding to Dante himself – which would make "born, perchance, already" a highly ironical meiosis, seeing that Dante was 35 at the date he assigns to his vision. But it is more becoming to acquit the poet of paying himself this compliment, and allow him to be speaking generally.

l. 105: *ere thou wast done with "gee-gee" and "bow-wow"*: (lit. "with *pappo* and *dindi*" – baby-talk for "food" and "money"): "while you were still in the nursery".

l. 108: *Heaven's tardiest sphere*: the outermost sphere, that of the Fixed Stars; "the almost imperceptible movement which it makes from west to east, at the rate of a degree in a hundred years" – Dante, *Convivio*, ii. 15. (Note that in its *daily* motion from *east to west* the outermost sphere is, of course, the swiftest; but in its *proper* motion from *west to east*, the slowest. The motion of the Primum Mobile is incalculable, and the Empyrean, being beyond space, cannot be said to have motion at all.) (See Dante's Universe, *Inf.* p. 292.)

ll. 112–13: *when they bowed and broke the fury of Florence*: i.e. at the Battle of Montaperti (see *Inf.* Introduction, p. 30; *Inf.* x. 85; xxxii. 81 and note).

l. 121: *Provenzan (o) Salvani*: a powerful Sienese nobleman, leader of the Tuscan Ghibellines after Montaperti, when he was one of those who urged the destruction of Florence (see *Inf.* x. 92 and note). He was killed in 1269, when the Sienese were defeated at Colle di Valterra (see Canto xiii. 115–19).

l. 127: *the soul who takes no care:* Dante, knowing (no doubt from public report) that Provenzan had remained arrogant to the day of his death, asks how it is that he has been in Purgatory, "ever since he died", and was not detained with the other Late Repentant on the Terrace below. Oderisi tells him how one heroic act of humility done for a friend's sake availed to "undo the ban". This is Dante's only instance of a sinner's being released from the "place of waiting" as a consequence of his *own* conduct – in every other case he has to depend upon the charity of others. Charity is the operative word: the time is redeemed only by charity, bestowed or received (cf. vi. 37 and note).

ll. 133–8: *in full mid-splendour ... his very blood*: In order to procure the ransom of a friend (probably Mino dei Mini) who had been taken prisoner (? at Tagliacozzo) by Charles of Anjou, Provenzan took his stand in the public square at Siena and begged from the passers-by.

l. 140: *thy neighbours shall do so to thee*: Oderisi hints that Dante himself will soon experience, in the days of his exile and ruin, the humiliation of having to ask for money.

# CANTO XII

THE STORY. *As he goes along, Dante sees graven upon the floor of the Cornice images representing the sin and fall of Pride. The Poets are met by the Angel of Humility, who erases the first P from Dante's forehead and, pronouncing the appropriate Beatitude, guides them up by the Pass of Pardon. Already, with the purging of Pride, the penitent's feet move more lightly.*

So, step for step, like oxen in the yoke,
    Beside that burdened soul I held my way
    So long as my kind schoolmaster would brook;

4    But when he said: "Now leave him; come, I say,
    Press on; for here must each with sail and oar
    Urge the ship forward strongly as he may,"

7    I raised me, as good walkers should, and bore
    My body upright, though the thoughts in me
    Remained bowed down and shrunken as before.

10    I'd put on speed and was most willingly
    Following my master's footsteps, he and I
    Showing how fleet of foot we both could be,

13    When he addressed me: "Downward cast thine eye;
    For solace of the way, 'twere good thou fall
    To scanning what beneath thy feet may lie."

16    And as, to give the dead memorial,
    We trace on many an earthly sepulchre
    Figures that may their living forms recall,

19    The sight of which will very often stir
    Men to lament them, memory being still
    Piety's sharpest, or its only, spur:

22    So there, with livelier likeness, due to skill
    Of craftsmanship, I saw the whole ledge graven
    Where, for a road, it juts out from the hill.

25    Mine eyes beheld there him to whom was given
    The noblest form of any creature made
    On one side fall like lightning down from heaven.

Mine eyes beheld Briareus, breast and blade 28
  Riven by the bolt divine, on the other side
  Lie on the earth, heavy and cold and dead.

Mine eyes beheld Thymbraeus, they espied 31
  Pallas and Mars in arms about their sire
  Viewing the Giants' limbs flung far and wide.

Mine eyes beheld Nimrod, beneath his dire 34
  High handiwork, look stunned upon the men
  That shared in Shinar his proud heart's desire.

Ah, Niobe, with eyes how full of pain 37
  I saw thine image on the roadway scored
  Set between seven and seven thy children slain!

Ah, Saul, how fallen, and by thine own sword, 40
  Didst thou appear, dead on Gilboa, where
  Nor rain nor dew fell ever afterward!

Ah, mad Arachne! I beheld thee there, 43
  Already half turned spider, on the shreds
  Of that sad web thou wov'st to thy despair.

Ah, Rehoboam! now there's none that dreads 46
  Thy face; it threats no more; the chariot flies
  Though none pursue; terror behind thee treads.

Now showed the stubborn pavement in what wise 49
  Alcmaeon made his hapless mother pay
  For that curst gaud, and at how dear a price.

Now showed it how his sons rushed in to slay 52
  Sennacherib in the temple where he stood,
  And slew, and left him there, and went their way.

Now showed it how with carnage all imbrued 55
  Queen Tomyris made mock of Cyrus, saying:
  "Blood hast thou craved – I'll fill thee full with blood."

Now showed it the Assyrian host's dismaying 58
  And rout, when Holofernes was undone,
  And showed the grisly relics of his slaying.

Mine eyes beheld Troy Town in ashes strown; 61
  Ah, sacred Ilium, how vile and mean
  Now showed thine image in the carven stone!

64    What master of the graver or the pen
      Such lines as these, such shading could contrive
      For subtle minds to find amazement in?

67    The dead seemed dead, the living seemed alive;
      Who saw the fact saw not more clear than I
      Those scenes I trod, leaned down contemplative.

70    Be proud, then, march with haughty heads held high,
      Children of Eve, nor bend them toward the ground
      To see the evil road you travel by!

73    Farther about the mount our way had wound,
      And more of the sun's course by now was spent
      Than one could judge with faculties thus bound,

76    When he who all the time alertly went
      In front of me began: "Lift up thy brow,
      The time is past to go thus ruminant.

79    Look at the angel over there, and how
      He moves to come to us; look how the day's
      Sixth handmaiden resigns her office now.

82    Adorn with reverence both thy mien and face,
      That he may joy to speed us up the mount;
      Think that it dawns but once, this day of grace."

85    So oft he'd urged me – well I knew his wont –
      Never to waste a moment, that I might
      Scarcely mistake his meaning on that count.

88    On came the beauteous creature, clothed in white,
      And seeming as he came in countenance
      A star of dawn all tremulous with light.

91    He spread his arms abroad, and spread his vans,
      And, "Come," said he, "the stairs are nigh; henceforth
      An easier climb is yours and every man's."

94    Glad summons – but with few to prize its worth!
      O human race, born to take flight and soar,
      Why fall ye, for one breath of wind, to earth?

97    He brought us to the rock's cleft aperture,
      And there he brushed my forehead with his wings;
      Then promised me a journey safe and sure.

As, where the road over Rubaconte swings     100
  Up to the height and the church whose walls command
  The city that so discreetly orders things,

The steep grade's eased by steps on the dexter hand,     103
  Hewn out in times that kept inviolate
  The bushel-stave, and let the audit stand,

So is the cliff, which drops precipitate     106
  Here from the upper cornice, made less sheer,
  Though either side the high rock-walls are strait.

As we turned thither, voices in our ear     109
  Sang out *Beati pauperes spiritu*:
  No tongue could tell how sweet they were to hear.

What different passes these from those we knew     112
  In Hell! for there with hideous howls of pain,
  But here with singing, we are ushered through.

When by the sacred stair we now again     115
  Were climbing, lighter far meseemed I trod
  Than I had done upon the level plain;

Wherefore I said: "Master, what heavy load     118
  Has slipped from me, so that I walk with ease,
  And scarcely feel fatigue upon the road?"

And he: "When from thy forehead all the P's     121
  Which, half-effaced and dim, remain there yet
  Are rubbed clean out, as one already is,

Then shall good-will so over-rule thy feet,     124
  That they will climb, and not be merely strong
  And uncomplaining, but delight in it."

Then I behaved like one who goes along     127
  Quite unaware of something on his head,
  Till winks and smiles make him suspect what's wrong;

And, to make sure, the hand must lend its aid,     130
  And feels, and finds, for when the doors are shut
  On sight, the touch does duty there instead;

So, with my right-hand fingers all spread out,     133
  I found those letters only six, which he
  Who bare the keys had on my temples cut;

And, as he watched, my leader smiled at me.     136

THE IMAGES. *The Pass of Pardon and the P of Pride*: The passage from one Cornice to the next is by way of a staircase cut in the rock. Dante particularly emphasizes that by these steps "the steep grade's eased" and "the cliff made less sheer", by contrast with the painful scramble up the Terraces and, particularly with the zigzag and difficult "needle's eye" leading to the First Cornice. This is because when Pride, the root of all sin, is overcome, the conquest of the rest is easier. For the same reason he emphasizes the freedom and lightness which the pilgrim feels when the P of Pride has been rased out.

NOTES. l. 1: *so, step for step*: In xi. 78 Dante mentions that in order to converse with the burdened spirits he "paced with them, bent double toward the ground", and he continues to share their stooping posture until summoned by Virgil to desist (l. 7). Only on three of the Cornices does Dante thus associate himself with the punishment of the spirits, viz. on those of Pride, Wrath, and Lust. Since these are precisely the three failings of which Dante has always been accused, one may perhaps infer that he knew his own weaknesses as well as anybody. He says himself (xiii. 133–8) that though he dreads the punishment of Pride, he believes himself fairly free from the sin of Envy; we know from Boccaccio that he was an abstemious man and not given to Gluttony; Avarice he particularly hates, and nothing in his history suggests that he was either a hoarder or a spendthrift; and the last sin anybody would lay to his charge is Sloth; on these four Cornices he remains, therefore, merely a spectator.

ll. 25–63: *Mine eyes beheld*, etc.: The images carved upon the pavement constitute the "Bridle" of Pride (see Introduction, pp. 67–8) and, like the "Whip", are drawn partly from sacred and partly from classical sources. They are divided into three groups of four examples (each group providing a contrast to the corresponding image in the "Whip"), followed by a concluding example.

Each example occupies one terzain; each terzain of the first group begins with the word *Vedea* = I saw; each terzain of the second group begins with the word: O; and each terzain of the third group begins with the word *Mostrava* = showed; while the three lines of the final terzain begin with *Vedea, O, Mostrava* respectively. Thus the initial letters of the three groups, as also of the concluding terzain, if read as an acrostic, display the word VOM or (since V and U in medieval script are the same letter) UOM, which is the Italian for MAN. This may, of course, be an accident; but such an acrostic would be entirely in the taste of the period, and the probability is that the poet did it deliberately. I have accordingly reproduced the acrostic in the translation, and the operative letters have been printed in larger type so as to make it clear.

This is by far the most elaborate set of "examples" in the *Purgatory*.

ll. 25–36: *Mine eyes beheld*: This first group, which contrasts with the humility of God Himself in being made Man of the Blessed Virgin, shows the Creature thrusting himself into the place of God.

ll. 25–7: *him to whom was given the noblest form*: Satan ("fairest once of the sons of light" *Inf.* xxxiv. 18) who led the rebel angels in their attempt against God's throne. "I beheld Satan fall as lightning from Heaven," *Luke* x. 18.

ll. 28–30: *Briareus*: a giant who attempted to overthrow the Gods of Olympus (see *Inf.* xxxi. 99 and note); a profane parallel to Lucifer.

ll. 31–3: *the Giants*: these also attempted to scale Olympus, but upon a different occasion; they were overthrown by Apollo (Thymbraeus, so called from his temple at Thymbra). The picture of Apollo, Pallas (Minerva), and Mars standing in triumph beside their father Jove is borrowed from Statius *Theb.* ii. 597–9, where, however, it is related to the victory over Briareus.

ll. 34–6: *Nimrod*, who endeavoured to scale heaven by building the Tower of Babel in the plain of Shinar (*Gen.* x. 8, xi. 1–9; and cf. *Inf.* xxxi. 46–81), is the sacred parallel to the Giants.

ll. 37–48: *Ah!*: The second group, which contrasts with David's joyful humility in the presence of the Ark of God, shows that arrogance in the face of Heaven which in Greek is called *hubris*, and in English presumption or over-weening.

ll. 37–9: *Niobe*: wife of Amphion (see *Inf.* xxxii. 16 and note) King of Thebes, had fourteen children, and boasted herself superior to Latona, who had borne to Jove only Apollo and Diana. The archer god and goddess in revenge killed all fourteen children with their arrows, and Niobe was turned to an ever-weeping stone statue.

ll. 40–2: *Saul*: The presumption of Saul, first king of Israel, and the gradual deterioration of his character is told in the *First Book of Samuel* (v. esp. 1 *Sam.* xiii. 13, 1 *Sam.* xv. 11, 35 in their context). He was defeated by the Philistines on Mount Gilboa and fell upon his own sword (1 *Sam.* xxxi. 1–4). *Nor rain nor dew*: (see 2 *Sam.* i. 21).

ll. 43–5: *Arachne* of Lydia boastfully challenged Minerva to a contest in weaving, and was changed into a spider (*Ovid: Metam.* vi. 1–145).

ll. 46–8: *Rehoboam*: king of Israel, despising the advice of his old counsellors, boasted that he would prove a greater tyrant even than his father Solomon; the people rebelled against him and he "made speed to get him up to his chariot to flee to Jerusalem." His story is told in 1 *Kings* xii.

ll. 49–60: *Now showed*: the third group, which contrasts with Trajan's humility before the poor widow, shows examples of pride in the face of man.

ll. 49–51: *Alcmaeon*: The "curst gaud" is the necklace with which

Eriphyle, the wife of Amphiaraus, was bribed to betray his hiding-place so that he went to his death in the Theban war (see *Inf.* xx. 34 and note). Alcmaeon his son slew Eriphyle by his father's instructions. This example displays that particular type of Vainglory which is called Vanity.

ll. 52–4: *Sennacherib*, king of Assyria, was a proud tyrant who, after his defeat by Hezekiah, was slain by his own sons (2 *Kings* xix. 37).

ll. 55–7: *Cyrus* the Persian tyrant (560–529 B.C.) murdered the son of Tomyris Queen of Scythia; she defeated and slew him, and throwing his head into a vessel of blood said mockingly: "Drink thy fill of the blood for which thou hast insatiably thirsted these thirty years."

ll. 58–60: *Holofernes*, captain of the army of Nebuchadnezzar, was contemptuous of the Jews and of their God, and, disregarding the advice of Achior, went up to besiege them at Bethulia. But he was outwitted and slain by the beautiful widow Judith, who cut off his head and had it displayed on the walls of the town ("the grisly relics of his slaying": *Judith* vi, viii–xiv).

ll. 61–3: *Troy Town*: the series is summed up in the image of Troy ("proud Ilium" *Aen.* iii. 2–3), whose ruin was the great classical example of the fall of pride.

l. 79: *the angel*: this is the Angel of Humility. This virtue is so little prized to-day, and interpreted in so negative a sense, that to understand the shimmering radiance of its angel one needs to study all the contexts in which Dante uses the words *umile, umiltà*, especially, perhaps, in the *Vita Nuova*. "[When I beheld Beatrice] there smote into me a flame of charity [so that] if anyone had asked me about anything whatsoever, my reply would have been simply, *Love*, with a countenance clothed in *umiltà*" (*V.N.* xi). "She bore about her so true an *umiltà*, that she seemed to say, *I am in peace*" (*V.N.* xxiii). "She goes upon her way, hearing herself praised, benignly clothed with *umiltà*, and seems a thing come from heaven to earth to show forth a miracle" (*V.N.* xxvi). "Therefore, when [love] so deprives me of power that my spirits seem to desert me, my frail soul tastes such sweetness that my cheeks grow pale. Then [my sighs beseech] my lady to grant me yet further *salute* (salutation, salvation). This happens every time she looks upon me, and is a thing so *umil* that it passes belief" (*V.N.* xxviii). The connotation is always of peace, sweetness, and a kind of suspension of the heart in a delighted tranquillity.

ll. 80–1: *the day's sixth handmaiden*: the sixth hour of the day: i.e. it is just past noon.

l. 91: *he ... spread his vans*: the gesture of salutation: his angelic humility receives them as honoured guests.

l. 98: *he brushed my forehead with his wings*: with this gesture (as we see a few lines later) he erases the P of Pride.

ll. 100–3: *the road over Rubaconte*, etc.: the church of San Miniato commands Florence from the far side of the Arno, and is approached from the city by way of the Rubaconte Bridge (now called the Ponte alle Grazie). A flight of shallow stone steps, each about six feet wide, leads up the side of the hill for the convenience of worshippers. The commendation in l. 103 is, of course, an irony on a par with the conclusion of Canto vi.

l. 105: *the bushel-stave and ... the audit*: the allusion is to two public frauds committed in Florence in Dante's time: one official, at the head of the Salt Import Department, reduced the size of the bushel-measure by one stave, and appropriated the balance of the salt; another pair of rogues tore a leaf out of the public ledger to conceal their pilferings. (These delinquents are referred to again in *Para.* xvi.)

l. 110: *Beati pauperes spiritu*: "Blessed are the poor in spirit": This, taken from the Beatitudes, *Matt.* v. 3, is the Benediction of the First Cornice.

l. 116: *lighter far meseemed I trod*: see Images.

# CANTO XIII

THE STORY. *The Poets reach the Second Cornice, where the sin of Envy is purged, and hear voices crying through the air examples of the virtue of Generosity. Presently they come to where the Envious sit like blind beggars, dressed in sackcloth, and having their eyes stitched up with wire. Dante talks with Sapìa of Siena, who tells him her story.*

We'd gained the stair-head, where, the second time,
    A cutting comes to break that mountain-flank
    Which sets us free from evil as we climb;

4   Here once again, winding all round the bank,
    A level cornice, like the former one,
    Though curved more sharply, stretches bare and blank;

7   No figures to be seen, no image, none;
    Barren the cliff seems, barren seems the way,
    Barren the livid colour of the stone.

10  "Now," so the poet argued, "if we stay
    Till some one comes from whom to ask advice
    I fear our choice may make too long delay."

13  Then on the sun he fixed his steady eyes
    And made a pivot of his right-hand side,
    Turning his left upon it swivel-wise.

16  "Blest fire," said he, "in whom my feet confide
    Entering on this new way untrodden quite,
    As we would fain be guided, do thou guide.

19  'Tis thou dost warm the earth and give it light;
    If reason good dissuade not, let us still
    Trust to thy beams to lead our steps aright."

22  We'd gone already yonder what our skill
    In reckoning here would call a mile, maybe,
    And quickly, too, we walked with such good will,

25  When borne towards us came – we could not see
    But heard them – spirits on the wing, and crying
    Their summons to love's table courteously.

166

And loud above our heads the first voice flying 28
   *"Vinum non habent"* cried, and passed, and sent
   The call reiterate behind us dying.

And ere the echo of the first was spent 31
   With distance, came a second cry likewise:
   "I am Orestes"; and stayed not, but went.

"Father," said I, "what is it that so cries?" 34
   And even while I questioned him thereof,
   Lo! the third voice, saying: "Love your enemies."

Then my good lord: "This circle doth reprove 37
   And scourge the sin of Envy; that is why
   Its whip is fashioned from the cords of love;

Doubtless the bridle sounds the counter-cry; 40
   Thou wilt, I think, most likely hear it, ere
   Thou reach the Pass of Pardon by and by.

But fix a steady gaze now through the air 43
   Before us; thou wilt see folk sitting down,
   Huddled against the cliff-side over there."

I looked attentively and, further on, 46
   Beheld some shades wrapped up in cloaks, whose grey
   Could scarcely be distinguished from the stone;

And when we had advanced a little way 49
   I heard them crying: "Mary, pray for us!"
   And, "Michael, Peter, and All Hallows, pray!"

I think there's no man so dispiteous 52
   Walking the earth, whose heart would not be stung
   By what I saw, could he but see them thus;

For when I'd travelled far enough along 55
   To make their features plainly visible,
   The heavy sorrow from my eyes was wrung.

It seemed coarse hair-cloth clothed them one and all, 58
   And each one's shoulder propped his neighbour's head,
   And all of them were propped against the wall.

In just that way the blind who lack for bread 61
   Sit at the pardons, begging for their need,
   Pillowing each other, all their suffering spread

64    Before the passer-by, that he may heed
          More quickly, moved not only by their speech
          But by their piteous looks, which likewise plead.

67    And as no profit of the sun can reach
          Blind men, so with the aforesaid shades: the fire
          Of heaven is niggard of his light to each;

70    For all their eyelids with an iron wire
          Are stitched and sealed, as to a wild young hawk
          That won't be still, men do to quiet her.

73    It seemed a kind of outrage thus to walk
          Staring at them when they could not see me;
          I turned to my wise mentor, but of talk

76    There was no need, for he right easily
          Guessed what the dumb would say, nor stayed for it:
          "Speak – to the point and briefly, please," said he.

79    Virgil was now abreast of me, to wit
          That side the cornice whence, if you mis-stept,
          You'd fall, since there's no girding parapet.

82    My other side, the praying shadows kept
          Their places still, and through the ghastly seam
          Squeezing slow drops to bathe their cheeks, they wept.

85    "O people," I began, being turned to them,
          "Assured of looking on that one great good
          Your hearts desire, the heavenly Light supreme,

88    So may grace quickly scour away the mud
          Of conscience, that through channels clean and clear
          Remembrance' stream may pour its crystal flood,

91    Tell me – 'twill be most kind to me and dear –
          Is any Latian with you? If there be,
          It may be good for him that I should hear."

94    "O brother mine, citizens all are we
          Of one true city; any, thou wouldst say,
          That lived a sojourner in Italy."

97    This answer seemed to come from one who lay
          Somewhat ahead of where I was; I threw
          My own voice, therefore, rather more that way;

And there a spirit came within my view           100
  Who looked expectant. "How?" did you exclaim?
  She tilted up her chin as blind folk do.

"Spirit, learning to soar, that here dost tame     103
  Thy wings," said I, "if 'twas thy voice that spake,
  Make thyself known to me by place or name."

She answered: "I was Sienese; I make         106
  My foul life clean, weeping with these amain
  To Him, to lend Him to us for love's sake.

That I was sapient, no one could maintain,      109
  Though I was called Sapìa; my heart conceived
  More joy from others' loss than my own gain.

Does that sound too absurd to be believed?     112
  Nay, hear and judge if I o'erstate my folly.
  My life's arch was declining – I'd achieved

Ripe age – the day my countrymen, near Colle,   115
  Joined with their foes; and I prayed God for what
  His will already had determined wholly.

Beaten they were, and fled in bitter rout;     118
  And there thrilled through me, when I saw the chase,
  Such glee as till that hour I'd tasted not;

So that I lifted up my impudent face,       121
  Shrilling to God: 'I fear Thee now no more,'
  As doth the blackbird for a few fine days.

Right on the brink of death, and not before,   124
  I made my peace with God; nor could have won me
  Penance as yet for paying off my score,

Had not a wealth of charity been shown me   127
  By Peter Combseller, who was distressed
  For me, and showered his holy prayers upon me.

But who art thou, so urgent to request      130
  News of our state, who go'st, I think, with sight
  Unsealed, and speakest from a breathing breast?"

"Mine eyes have yet to be deprived of light   133
  Up here, though not for long; their sin," I said,
  "In casting looks of envy has been slight;

136     Much more – immensely more – my soul must dread
            The torment down beneath; I'll not dispute
            Feeling that load already crush my head."

139     But she: "Who led thee up, then, to set foot
            Here, if thou thinkest to return below?"
            And I: "He who is with me, and stands mute.

142     And I am living; tell me then, pray do,
            Spirit elect, if thou have, over there,
            Some errand that my mortal feet can go."

145     "O, but this is so strange a thing to hear,"
            Said she, "it shows that God must love thee dearly;
            Help me, then, sometimes, with a little prayer.

148     And, by the wish that touches thee most nearly,
            Shouldst thou tread Tuscan soil, report good news
            Of me, and tell it to my kinsfolk clearly.

151     Seek them among those harebrains who will lose
            More hopes in Talamone than they lost
            Digging to set the alleged Diana loose;

154     Though there the admirals stand to lose the most."

THE IMAGES. *The Penance of the Envious: the Sealed Eyes.* The sin of
    Envy (*Invidia*) differs from that of Pride in that it contains always
    an element of fear. The proud man is self-sufficient, rejecting with
    contempt the notion that anybody can be his equal or superior.
    The envious man is afraid of losing something by the admission of
    superiority in others, and therefore looks with grudging hatred
    upon other men's gifts and good fortune, taking every oppor-
    tunity to run them down or deprive them of their happiness. On
    the Second Cornice, therefore, the eyes which could not endure
    to look upon joy are sealed from the glad light of the sun, and
    from the sight of other men. Clad in the garments of poverty and
    reduced to the status of blind beggars who live on alms, the Envi-
    ous sit amid the barren and stony wilderness imploring the charity
    of the saints, their fellow-men. Because they are blind, the Whip
    and Bridle of Envy are brought to them by the voices of passing
    spirits.

*Sapìa*, the spirit who converses with Dante in this canto, is the image
    of Envy's malicious delight in the misfortune of others.

NOTES. ll. 13–21: *then on the sun*, etc.: the sun being in all religions a natural symbol of the divine, Virgil here takes it for his guide, supposing (rightly) that in Purgatory the direction to take will always be with the sun (right-handed), as in Hell it was always widdershins (left-handed). Cf. *Inf. passim.*

ll. 22–3: *what our skill … would call a mile*: this is another of Dante's reminders that the realms of the dead are not enclosed in our familiar time–space continuum.

ll. 25–36: *when borne towards us … love your enemies*: these voices in the air are the Whip of Envy. The first example of the opposing virtue of *Generosity* is taken, as always, from the life of the Blessed Virgin; the second is from a classical source. The third is taken from Our Lord Himself, and stands in isolated honour, not having any counterpart in the Bridle.

l. 29: *Vinum non habent* = they have no wine. See *John* ii. 3.

l. 33: *I am Orestes*: When Orestes, the son of Agamemnon, was condemned to death, his devoted friend Pylades wished to give himself to die in his stead, saying that he himself was Orestes. The story is told by Cicero (*De Amicitia*).

l. 36: *love your enemies*: See *Matt.* v. 44; *Luke* vi. 27–8. Note that the words of Christ are not "cried" but quietly "said", as though the poet wished to surround them with an atmosphere of especial reverence.

ll. 50–1: *Mary, pray for us*, etc.: This is the Prayer of the Envious, taken from the Litany of the Saints.

l. 58: *coarse hair-cloth*: the garments of penitence as well as of poverty.

l. 62: *the pardons*: Dante uses the word to mean the churches at which pardons, or indulgences, could be obtained, and whose porches were always thronged with beggars.

ll. 70–2: *with an iron wire*: To tame a hawk that has been caught wild it is necessary to blindfold her. In the west this is usually done with the hood, but the method of sealing the eyes was also known in Dante's time, being perhaps imported from the east, where it is still used. It is effected "with a sharp needle and waxed silk. Carefully, the … falconer threads the silk through the edge of the lower eyelids, drawing them closed by twisting the thread and tying it across the bird's head. This method does not hurt the falcon, and as she sheds her … fear … the thread is gradually untwisted, letting her see a little more light, until finally the eyes are wide open and the thread can be removed" – Frank Illingworth: *Falcons and Falconry*, p. 81. The "iron wire" and the "ghastly seam" belong to the Cornice of Envy, not to falconry.

l. 92: *Latian*: i.e. Italian; see *Inf.* xxii. 65 and note.

ll. 103–4: *that here dost tame thy wings*: this line carries on the simile of the hawk.

l. 110: *Sapìa*: a lady of the Bigozzi family of Siena, who married Ghinibaldo dei Saracini, lord of Castiglioncello. It appears that she had been banished from Siena, on some grounds of suspicion, and bore a jealous grudge against her countrymen in consequence. Her account of herself, which begins with a wry pun on her own name (meaning "Sapience" or "Prudence"), is tinged throughout with a lively self-mockery. This, since few sins take themselves with such savage seriousness as jealousy, is in itself a sign of her change of heart.

l. 115: *near Colle*: In 1269 the Sienese, together with other Ghibelline forces, under Provenzano Salvani (see Canto xi. 121 and note) were totally defeated by the Florentines at Colle near Volterra. Sapìa, who was living at Colle, watched the battle from a tower overlooking the field.

l. 123: *as doth the blackbird*: In Lombardy the occasional fine, spring-like days which sometimes occur in January are popularly called *giorni di merla*, "blackbird's days", the fable being that the foolish bird, seeing the sun, cried out: "Lord, I fear Thee no more, spring has come!"

ll. 124–5: *on the brink of death*: In 1269, after the death of her husband, Sapìa apparently became reconciled to the Sienese and made them a grant of his castle, presumably dying herself soon after.

ll. 125–6: *nor could have won me penance as yet*: her late repentance would have caused her to be detained on the Second Terrace of Ante-Purgatory, had she not been assisted by "prayers from a heart in grace".

l. 128: *Peter Combseller* (Piero Pettignagno or Pettinaio): a celebrated hermit, who had been a comb-seller in Siena, and is said to have been of so scrupulous an honesty that if he found a defective comb in his stock he would throw it into the Arno, saying that he did not wish anyone to buy bad merchandise from him, even at a reduced price. He was popularly reputed a saint even in his lifetime, and in 1328, 39 years after his death, a tomb and altar were dedicated to him in the church of St Francis at Siena.

ll. 133–8: *mine eyes have yet*, etc.: see xii. 1, note.

ll. 151–4: *those harebrains*, etc.: The reference is to two Sienese projects which had been notorious failures. One was an attempt to tap the supposed underground river which supplied the city fountains, and which was provisionally referred to as the Diana. (This scheme eventually succeeded, but not until after Dante's time.) The other was the purchase (for 8000 gold florins) of the small port of Talamone in the Maremma, near Orbetello, in the hope of converting it into a fine harbour and so making Siena a great commercial power, like Genoa. The port filled up with sand as fast as it was dredged, and the place was found to be malarial and uninhabitable. These projects were thus the contemporary equivalents of a South Sea Bubble, or a Ground-Nuts Scheme. Dante seldom loses an opportunity of twitting the Sienese for their vanity (cf. *Inf.* xxix. 122 *sqq.*).

l. 154: *the admirals*: either this is an ironical allusion to the shipping which the Sienese hoped to base upon the elusive harbour (as who should speak of "the Swiss Navy"), or, as others think, the word means the contractors or workers on the dredging scheme (cf. our "navvies" – navigators), who stand to lose not only money and hope, but also their lives through sickness.

# CANTO XIV

THE STORY. *Dante converses with the spirits of two Romagnol noble-men, one of whom – Guido del Duca – speaks bitterly of the various towns upon the banks of the Arno, and recounts the degeneracy that has over-taken the noble families of Romagna. Passing on, the Poets hear voices crying out examples of the sin of Envy.*

     "Who's this, that makes the circuit of our hill
       Or ever death has freed his flight to go,
       And shuts his eyes or opens them at will?"

4   "I don't know who; he's not alone, I know;
       Thou'rt nearer to him – ask him; greet him fair,
       With words he will be glad to answer to."

7   Thus, on my right, discussing me, a pair
       Of spirits talked, leaning their heads together;
       Then raised their chins and spoke for me to hear:

10  "O soul," said one, "still in the body's tether,
       Yet journeying on to Heaven, pray comfort us,
       And be so charitable altogether

13  As tell us whence and who thou art, because
       Thy meed of grace such wonder doth instil
       As such a thing well may as never was."

16  I said: "In Falterona springs a rill
       That flows on through the heart of Tuscany,
       Nor in a hundred miles has flowed its fill.

19  I've brought this body from its banks; let be
       The rest – to tell you who I am were vain;
       Not much is known yet of my name or me."

22  "If rightly," the first speaker said again,
       "Seizing the sense my wits have pierced the cloud,
       Who says the Arno speaks thy meaning plain."

25  The other asked him: "Wherefore did he shroud
       That river's name as men do with a thing
       Too horrid to be spoken of out loud?"

Whereon the shade whom he was questioning      28
  Gave judgement thus: "I know not; yet 'twere fit
  The name should perish past remembering;

For in that valley, from the head of it      31
  (A massy part, scarce rivalled on that score,
  Of the high range from which Pelorus split)

To where it yields its increase to restore      34
  What from the sea is sucked up by the skies
  And rolled back with the rivers to the shore,

Virtue's an enemy in all men's eyes,      37
  And chased out like a snake; the spot's accurst,
  Or all its folk a prey to ingrained vice.

They've altered so from what they were at first,      40
  You'd think, to see the men of this vile valley,
  Circe had pastured them and done her worst.

It starts to drive its puny little alley      43
  Past brutes who eat like men but are such hogs,
  Acorns, you'd think, would come more naturally.

Then down it goes and meets with snarling dogs      46
  More fierce than formidable, gives a twitch
  And turns a scornful snout on them; then jogs

Down, always down; the more, with steepening pitch,      49
  It swells, the more it finds the dogs there growing
  To wolves, this ill-starred, god-forsaken ditch.

Through many a deep-cut gorge it plunges, going      52
  Still down, and comes to foxes last, who fear
  No trap that skill can set, they are so knowing.

Nor will I cease to speak, though this man hear;      55
  'Twere well indeed he mind the things I'm saying
  Which a true spirit in my mouth makes clear.

I see thy grandson hunting out and slaying      58
  The wolves upon the banks of the fierce stream,
  Striking them all with horrible dismaying.

He sells their living flesh, then slaughters them      61
  Like worn-out cattle; wrecks a multitude
  Of lives and wrecks himself in men's esteem.

64     He comes blood-boltered from the dreadful wood,
       Which in a thousand years shall not re-leaf
       To its first growth nor make the damage good."

67     As at the news of some appalling sheaf
       Of troubles, trouble clouds the hearer's face,
       From whence soever or whate'er the grief,

70     So when the other soul, that in its place
       Had turned to listen, let these tidings reach
       Its mind, I saw it moved with sad amaze.

73     This one's appearance and the other's speech
       Made me so long to know their names, I pressed
       My question, mingling it with prayers, on each.

76     "Nay," said the shade by whom I'd been addressed
       At first, "must I oblige thee? wilt thou claim
       From me what thou deniest to my request?

79     Yet, since God wills to shine with such a flame
       Of grace in thee, I'll not be niggard – learn,
       Guido del Duca am I called by name;

82     And in my heart such envy used to burn,
       If I'd caught some one looking pleased with life,
       Thou wouldst have seen how livid I could turn.

85     I reap the straw whose seed I sowed so rife;
       Why, why set heart on things which must forbid
       All partnership, O human race at strife?

88     And this is Rinier, honour of his breed
       And glory of the House of Calboli,
       Since whom, his worth finds no heir to succeed.

91     'Twixt Po and peak, 'twixt Reno and the sea,
       Lost to his blood, nor to his blood alone,
       Is all that makes true men live merrily;

94     For all within these marches is o'ergrown
       With poisonous weeds, and hardly shall the share
       Uproot them, or the sour land be resown.

97     Guy of Carpigna, Harry Mainard, Pier
       Of Traversaro, Lizio great of note,
       Where are they now, bastard Romagnols, where?

When in Bologna shall a Fabbro root          100
   Again, Faenza breed a Bernardine
   Of Fosco, lowly plant but lordly shoot?

Marvel not, Tuscan, if I now begin          103
   To weep, remembering well how once with us
   Lived Guy of Prata, Azzo's Ugolin,

Frederick Tignoso's goodly court, the House      106
   Of Traversaro, Anastagi's line
   (Both heirless now) and all those numerous

Ladies and knights; and how we joyed to shine   109
   In deeds and sports, when courtesy and love
   Called us, where now men's hearts grow so malign.

Why, Brettinoro, wilt thou not remove        112
   And flee? Thy lords and many more have fled,
   Shunning the crimes that thou art guilty of.

Well done, Bagnacaval, thou barren bed!       115
   Right ill doth Castrocaro, and Conio worse,
   Troubling to breed more counts like those they've bred.

When the Pagani rid them of their curse,       118
   Their Demon, they'll do well; but on their fame
   A stain will rest that nothing can disperse.

O Ugolin de' Fantolin, thy name           121
   Is safe; it cannot look for heirs again
   To grow debased and blacken it with shame.

But go thy ways now, Tuscan; I am fain      124
   Rather to weep than to find more to say;
   Our talk has wrung my heart with so much pain."

We knew those dear souls heard us move away,   127
   And in their silence we could well confide
   For good assurance we were not astray.

As by ourselves we journeyed side by side,    130
   There came a voice, like lightning suddenly
   Cleaving the air, that smote on us and cried:

"Behold now, every one that findeth me       133
   Shall slay me!" and passed us like the crackling lash
   Of thunder when the cloud-burst sets it free.

136    Our ears had truce, when lo! with such a crash
       And peal the second followed hard upon,
       As when quick thunders chase down flash on flash:

139    "I am Aglauros that was turned to stone!"
       And huddling to the poet in alarm
       I took a step backward instead of on.

142    Then, when on every side the air was calm,
       He said to me: "That was the iron bit,
       Meant to keep man in bounds and out of harm;

145    But you gulp down the bait, the hook's in it,
       The old foe winds you in upon the reel,
       And lure nor bridle profits you one whit.

148    The high heavens call you and about you wheel,
       Showing eternal beauties to invite you;
       But all you see's the earth beneath your heel,

151    And therefore doth the All-discerning smite you."

THE IMAGES. *Guido del Duca* is the image of the grudging type of Envy, which resents joy in other people (ll. 82–4). To the penitent Guido, looking back upon his life, the gay companionship which in the old days filled him with envy and uncharitableness now appears a thing full of happiness, to be wistfully regretted.

NOTES. ll. 7–8: *a pair of spirits*: The first speaker is Guido del Duca of Brettinoro (now Bertinoro), belonging to the Onesti family of Ravenna. He was, from about 1202, a follower of the Ghibelline leader, Pier Traversaro (l. 97), who in 1218, with the help of the Mainardi (l. 97), drove out the Guelfs from Ravenna. They in turn attacked Brettinoro and expelled Guido with the rest of Pier's adherents. Guido is last heard of in 1229 at Ravenna.

The second speaker is Rinieri de' Paolucci da Calboli, a very distinguished member of a Guelf family of Forlì. He was podestà of Faenza (1247 and 1292), Parma (1252), and Ravenna (1265). In 1276 he, with other Guelfs including Lizio da Valbona (l. 98), attacked Forlì, but was driven back to his own castle, where he surrendered to Guido da Montefeltro (whom we met in *Inf.* xxvii.). Guido spared his life, but burned the castle of Calbolito to the ground. In 1292, Rinier, together with Mainardo Pagano da Susinana, captain of Forlì, marched against the Counts of Romagna (the three brothers mentioned in *Inf.* xxx. 77) and drove them out of Forlì. The victorious

Guelfs were expelled again in 1294, returned in 1296, and shortly after were finally driven out, Rinier being killed in this action.

l. 16: *in Falterona springs a rill*: the Arno takes its rise in Monte Falterona, on the borders of Romagna, flowing thence through the steep valleys of the Casentino; increased by the water of other streams, it runs past Arezzo into the plain of Florence, and so through Pisa, and finally into the Mediterranean.

l. 22: *if rightly*: The Tiber also rises in Mount Falterona; Guido seems to ponder which stream is meant, and then (guided partly perhaps by Dante's accent and partly by his own knowledge) decides for the Arno.

l. 33: *the high range from which Pelorus split*: the Apennines, of which Mount Pelorus (now Capo del Faro) in Sicily geologically forms part.

l. 42: *Circe*: the sorceress who turned men into swine (v. *Inf.* xxvi. 91 and note). The "hogs" are the inhabitants of the Casentino.

l. 46: *dogs*: these are the Aretines.

l. 48: *turns a scornful snout*: just above Arezzo the Arno makes a bend eastward, passing 3 miles to the N. of the city.

l. 51: *wolves*: the Florentines. Arezzo was a Ghibelline, Florence a Guelf, city: here as elsewhere (e.g. *Inf.* xxxiii. 28–33) Dante symbolizes the Ghibellines by dogs, the Guelfs by wolves.

l. 53: *foxes*: the Pisans; cf. *Inf.* xxvii. 74–5, where the Pisan captain, Guido da Montefeltro, calls his own behaviour "foxy".

l. 58: *thy grandson*: Fulcieri da Calboli, podestà of Florence in 1302. He was in the pay of the Black party, and committed many atrocities against both the Ghibellines and the White Guelfs remaining in the city.

l. 64: *the dreadful wood*: Florence.

l. 91: *'twixt Po and peak, 'twixt Reno and the sea*: the line defines the limits of Romagna (see map, *Inf.* p. 173); the *peak* denotes the Apennines; the *sea*, the Adriatic.

ll. 97–107: *Guy of Carpigna*, etc.: for these various Romagnol notables, see Glossary.

l. 115: *Bagnacaval*: Bagnacavallo is a town in the neighbourhood of Ravenna and Faenza; the line of its native nobility, having greatly degenerated, had recently become extinct.

l. 116: *Castrocaro and Conio*: the one near Forlì and the other near Imola.

l. 118: *the Pagani*: Ghibellines of Faenza; their "Demon" is Mainardo Pagano (mentioned in *Inf.* xxvii. 50, as perpetually changing sides), so-called because of his cunning and cruelty.

l. 121: *Ugolin de' Fantolin(i)* of Faenza: called by the chroniclers a "brave, virtuous, and noble person". He died in 1282, leaving no surviving issue.

ll. 131–9: *a voice*, etc.: these examples are the "bridle" of Envy; the one taken from the O.T., and the other from classical mythology.

ll. 133–4: *every one that findeth me shall slay me*: this is the cry of Cain who for envy murdered his brother Abel (*Gen.* iv. 14).

l. 139: *I am Aglauros*: Cecrops, king of Athens, had three daughters, Pandrace, Aglauros, and Herse. Mercury bribed Aglauros to admit him to the presence of Herse, of whom he was enamoured; but she, seized with jealousy of her sister, denied him entrance and was turned to stone (*Ovid: Metam.* ii. 708–832).

# CANTO XV

THE STORY. *The Poets are met by the shining Angel of Generosity, who erases the second P from Dante's forehead and directs them to the Pass leading to the Third Cornice. While they are climbing the stair, Virgil delivers his First Discourse on Love. At the entrance to the Cornice, Dante is shown in a vision examples of the Virtue of Meekness; and after walking a little further they are met and enveloped by a cloud of thick Smoke rolling along the Cornice.*

As much as, 'twixt beginning of the day
   And third hour's end, shows of the restless sphere
   That see-saws ever like a child at play,

So much by this time of the sun's career      4
   Seemed left to run towards his evening rest:
   'Twas vesper-tide out yonder, midnight here.

And as we circled round the mountain's breast,      7
   Right on our noses' bridge we caught the rays,
   Being turned so far, that now we faced due west;

When lo! I felt the splendour and the blaze      10
   With twofold weight my forehead overbear,
   And this new portent filled me with amaze;

So, lifting up my hands, I held them square      13
   Across my eyebrows, as one does to gain
   A kind of awning when there's too much glare.

And as from water or the mirror's plane      16
   The beam reflected leaps away, to go
   In the opposed direction up again,

Just as it first descended, making so      19
   An equal angle with the plummet-line,
   As theory and experiment will show,

So, from before me, on these eyes of mine      22
   Such a reflected brilliance seemed to smite
   That they shrank promptly from the blinding shine.

25    "O my dear father, what is this, so bright,
          No effort serves to screen it off," said I,
          "And moving toward us, if I guess aright?"

28    "No marvel if the household of the sky
          Are dazzling to thee still," said he: "it is
          A herald sent to summon us on high.

31    Full soon, to look on beings such as this
          Shall be to thee no burden, but a cause
          Of all thy nature can endure of bliss."

34    And when we came where that blest angel was:
          "Enter," his glad voice cried, "to an ascent
          Less steep by far than any former pass."

37    Parting, we climbed, and heard the while we went
          "*Beati misericordes*" sung behind,
          And, "Thou that hast prevailed, be jubilant."

40    Now, when my guide and I were left to wind
          Our upward way alone, I thought to glean
          Some wayside discourse to improve my mind,

43    So, turning toward him, thus did I begin:
          "That spirit from Romagna – 'partnership'
          He mentioned, and 'forbid' – what did he mean?"

46    "He knows," said he, "his own sin's sore eats deep;
          No wonder he rebukes it, being zealous
          That it should give the world less cause to weep.

49    You set desire where sharing with one's fellows
          Means that each partner gets a smaller share,
          Wherefore you sigh, and envy works the bellows.

52    Did but the love of the most lofty sphere
          Turn your desires to take the upward way,
          Your hearts were quit of all this fearful care;

55    Because the more there are who there can say
          'Ours', the more goods each has, and charity
          Burns in that cloister with a larger ray."

58    "So far," said I, "is this from filling me,
          I famish more than if I'd held my tongue,
          And in my mind pile up perplexity.

How can it be that when a greater throng 61
  Divides the goods, there is more wealth for each
  Than if a few possessed them all along?"

And he: "Because once more thy mental reach 64
  Stops short at earthly things, thy dullard mood
  From truth's own light draws darkness black as pitch.

Than infinite and unexpressive Good 67
  Up there, so speeds to love as the ray speeds
  To bodies with clear lucency endued;

Lavish of self, all fires it finds it feeds; 70
  And thus, as charity yet rifer runs,
  Rifer thereby the immortal vigour breeds.

The more enamoured souls dwell there at once, 73
  Ever the better and the more they love,
  Each glassing each, all mirrors and all suns.

Now, should my words thy hunger not remove, 76
  Beatrice shalt thou see, and she'll speak plain,
  This and all cravings else to rid thee of.

Do thou but strive that those five wounds which pain 79
  Alone can heal, still marked upon thy head,
  Be rased out quickly, like the other twain."

'Twas on my lips to say: "I'm now well fed," 82
  When, see! the cornice! We were up, I found,
  So that my eager eyes struck all speech dead.

Then of a sudden I was caught and drowned 85
  Deep in a trance of ecstasy; and lo!
  A temple there, with people thronging round;

And through its gates I saw a Lady go, 88
  Saying, with a mother's tender gesture, "Why,
  My dearest Son, hast thou dealt with us so?

Nay – for behold now how thy father and I 91
  Have sought thee sorrowing." As she ceased to speak,
  This vision that I first beheld fled by,

And next, such hot tears streaming down her cheek 94
  As grief distils from rage, before me came
  Another woman, and she seemed to speak:

97     "If lord thou art of that high city whose name
         Sowed strife among the gods – if lord declared
         Of that great hearth whence learning spreads its flame,

100    Avenge thee on the insolent arms which dared
         Embrace our daughter, O Pisistratus!"
         And with unruffled mien that lord appeared

103    Thus to make answer mild and generous:
         "What shall we do to those who wish us ill,
         If those who love us are condemned by us?"

106    Then I beheld a mob, who'd set their will,
         Inflamed with wrath, to stone a lad to death,
         And each to each cried out aloud, "Kill! Kill!"

109    Him too I saw already crushed beneath
         The death-stroke, sink to earth; but of his eyes
         He still made gates to Heaven, and prayed forthwith

112    To the high Lord, 'mid all these agonies,
         And with such looks as mercy opens to,
         Imploring pardon for his enemies.

115    Now when at length my soul returned to view
         Those facts which have their truth outside the soul,
         I saw my error – error not untrue;

118    And seeing me act like one who seeks to roll
         Slumber away, my lord exclaimed: "What's wrong?
         What's robbed thee of all power of self-control?

121    Here hast thou come a good half-league along
         With thine eyes glazing and thy legs a-sprawl,
         Like one who sleeps, or finds the wine too strong."

124    "O my dear father, I will tell thee all,
         Wilt thou but listen – all the things," I cried,
         "Shown me while thus my legs were held in thrall."

127    And he: "Although a thousand masks were tied
         Upon thy face, for me 'twould all amount
         To nothing – no, nor could thy least thought hide.

130    Those signs were shown thee that on no account
         Thou find excuse to shut thy heart to peace
         Whose waters well from the eternal fount.

I did not ask 'what's wrong', as he who sees                     133
   Only with eyes so ignorant and dim
   That when the body's senseless their powers cease;

I asked to strengthen thee in heart and limb,                    136
   As one must prod the sluggard idling on
   After his waking hour returns to him."

So we pressed forward as the day sank down,                      139
   Peering ahead as far as eyes could look
   Through the slant shining of the level sun,

When lo! by slow degrees a cloud of smoke                        142
   Came rolling toward us, all as black as night;
   No room to dodge it – on it came, and took

At once from us the fresh air and our sight.                     145

THE IMAGES. For the *Penance of the Wrathful (the Smoke)* see Images
to Canto xvi.

NOTES. ll. 1–6: *As much as*, etc.: the general sense of the paragraph is
quite clear: the sun had as much of his course left to run as he runs
between his rising and the third hour of the day: i.e. it was three hours
to sunset. Opinion differs much about the sphere that "plays like a
child", some thinking that the reference is simply to the diurnal motion
of the heavens, playing "ring-a-ring-of-roses" about the earth, as it
were: others that it is to the ecliptic which plays up and down with a
see-saw motion, between summer and winter. I have adopted the
latter interpretation, though with no great confidence.

   l. 6: *vesper-tide out yonder, midnight here*: i.e. it was 3 P.M. in Purgatory
(and consequently 3 A.M. at Jerusalem), and midnight in Italy where
the poet was subsequently recording his vision.

   l. 9: *that now we faced due west*: the poets have now almost reached
the northernmost point of the mountain, and have the setting sun in
their faces (see diagram, p. 340).

   ll. 10–11: *the blaze with twofold weight*: the Angel of the Cornice is
coming towards them from the west, so that his brilliance is added to
the brilliance of the sun.

   ll. 16–24: *and as from water ... blinding shine*: Dante, having screened
his eyes from the sun, finds himself still dazzled by the yet greater bril-
liance of the angel which seems to beat up towards him like light re-
flected from water or a mirror (the angel is below the sun and sheds
his brilliance all along the path); *theory* (i.e. the science of optics) and

*experiment* show the angle of reflection to be equal to the angle of incidence. Some think that the simile of *reflected* light refers to the fact that the light of the angel is a reflection of the light of God; but this latter phenomenon is scarcely subject to the laws of optics.

l. 34: *that blest angel*: the Angel of the Second Cornice is often referred to (in accordance with his Benediction) as the Angel of Mercy; but since the showing of mercy (in the narrow sense) is the fruit of a generous spirit, it is perhaps preferable to call him the Angel of Generosity, and this name seems to accord better with the examples shown in the "Whip". See also below l. 38, note.

l. 36: *less steep by far*: once the root sin of Pride is purged, the way becomes easier.

l. 38: *beati misericordes*: "blessed are the merciful": *Matt.* v. 7: this is the Benediction of the Second Cornice. "Envy is the direct opposite of mercy ... for the envious man is saddened by his neighbour's prosperity, whereas the merciful man is saddened by his neighbour's misfortune; hence the envious are not merciful, and conversely" (Th. Aquinas: *S.T.* II.II$^{ae}$, q. 36, a. 3). *Misericordes*, translated in the A.V. and R.V. as "merciful", is wider in its meaning than the English word, and might be better rendered "tender-hearted", "sympathetic", or "generous-minded".

l. 39: *thou that hast prevailed, be jubilant*: probably a paraphrase of *Matt.* v. 12: "Rejoice and be exceeding glad, for great is your reward in heaven"; possibly an allusion to *Rev.* ii. 7: "To him that overcometh will I give to eat of the tree of life."

ll. 44–5: "*partnership*" ... "*forbid*": the ref. is to Guido del Duca's words in xiv. 86–7.

l. 49: *you*: i.e. the living.

l. 52: *the most lofty sphere*: the Empyrean, where God is.

l. 67: *than infinite and unexpressive Good*: i.e. God.

ll. 68–9: *as the ray speeds to bodies with clear lucency endued*: the love of God is received and reflected by love as light by a shining surface.

l. 79: *those five wounds*: we are to understand that the second P has been effaced by the angel as Dante enters the Pass.

l. 82: *'twas on my lips to say*, etc.: Virgil has expounded, "so far as his school goes", the doctrine of the increase of spiritual goods by sharing them, and of the reciprocity of love. It is probably not by accident that before Dante can express himself content with this he is shown a vision of a still more universal and Christian conception of love, extended so as to conform to the Dominical precept: "Love your enemies ... and pray for them which despitefully use you and persecute you." (*Matt.* v. 44.)

l. 86: *a trance of ecstasy*: this is the "Whip" of the Third Cornice, exhibiting examples of Meekness, drawn, one from the life of the Blessed Virgin, one from classical history, and one from the *Acts*.

ll. 87–93: *a temple there*, etc.: the first vision, of the finding of Christ in the Temple (*Luke* ii. 41–50) is an example of meekness towards God.

ll. 94–105: *and next*, etc.: the second vision is an example of meekness towards human friends. A young man who loved and wished to wed the daughter of Pisistratus, tyrant of Athens (560–527 B.C.), unceremoniously embraced her in public. For this insult her mother would have had him executed, but was rebuked by Pisistratus in the words quoted. The story is told by Valerius Maximus.

ll. 97–9: *that high city*, etc.: Athens, the centre of ancient Greek culture and civilization. Neptune and Minerva (*Gk.* Poseidon and Athene) competed as to which of them should give the city its name. Neptune produced a salt spring out of the earth, and Minerva an olive tree; the tree was adjudged by the gods to be the better gift, and the city was named for Athene.

ll. 106–14: *then I beheld a mob*, etc.: the third vision, of the stoning of Stephen (*Acts* vii. 54–60), is an example of meekness towards human foes.

l. 117: *error not untrue*: i.e. Dante realized that the things he had seen were only visions, but nevertheless visions of real events.

l. 129: *nor could thy least thought hide*: we are meant, I think, to understand that Virgil has not seen the visions directly, but read Dante's mind (as he did, for example, in *Inf.* xvi. 118–20). He explains that he asked Dante about them, not for information, but to remind him of the purpose of such visions, i.e. that a man should not lose himself in dreaming but be stimulated to fresh endeavour.

# CANTO XVI

THE STORY. *As they stagger blindly through the Smoke, the Poets hear the prayer of the penitent Wrathful rising about them on all sides. Dante is addressed by the spirit of Marco Lombardo, who discourses with him on Determinism and Free Will, and on the misdirection of the Temporal Power. A thinning of the Smoke announces the imminent approach of the Angel of the Third Cornice.*

Darkness of hell, or midnight disendowed
 Of every planet, under a poor shred
 Of starveling sky hung thick as thick with cloud,

4 Never had wrapped a veil about my head
 So gross in grain and gritty to the touch
 As was that smoke which held us blanketed;

7 One's eyes could not keep open, insomuch
 That my good escort came up close beside,
 Offering a trusty shoulder to my clutch.

10 Even as a blind man goes behind his guide,
 Lest he should stray or, to the jeopardy
 Of life and limb, should stumble or collide,

13 So through that foul and acrid air went I,
 Hearkening to him who led me: "Take good care
 We don't get parted!" was his constant cry.

16 Then I heard voices speak, entreating there
 The Lamb of God who takes our sins away
 For peace and mercy; this was all their prayer,

19 For *Agnus Dei* did they still begin,
 So that one speech, one measure kept they all,
 And perfect concord seemed to fold them in.

22 "Master," said I, "these voices I hear call
 Are spirits?" "Thou art right," said he, "they go
 Loosening the knot of wrath that held them thrall."

25 "Say, who and what art thou that cleavest through
 Our smoke, and speak'st like one who reckons still
 The time by kalends as the living do?"

Thus from their midst a voice was audible:        28
  "Answer," my master said, "then ask, and see
  If this is the right way to mount the hill."

"Creature of God," said I, "now cleansing thee     31
  To come home beauteous to thy Maker's house,
  Wouldst thou hear wonders, walk along with me."

"As far," he answered, "as our rule allows      34
  I'll follow; though the smoke has made us blind,
  Hearing instead of sight shall neighbour us."

Then: "In those bands death shall at last unbind,"  37
  Thus I began, "I scale the heavenly ways;
  Hell and its woes I've passed and left behind.

Now, as God deigns admit me to His grace     40
  Thus far, and bids me to behold His court
  After this fashion, strange in modern days,

Hide not whose life it was thy death cut short,   43
  But tell me; and tell if a true course I frame
  Stairward; thy words shall guide us to our port."

"Lombard was I and Marco was my name;     46
  I knew the world and loved that worth upright
  Whereat no man will now bend bow to aim;

Rightly thou steerest for the stairs' next flight."  49
  Thus he replied, and added: "Pray consent
  To pray for me when thou hast gained the height."

"Now by my faith I bind me to content      52
  Thy will," said I; "but all my mind's so vext
  With doubt, I'll burst if I don't give it vent.

Singly at first, now doubly I'm perplext     55
  By these thy words, confirming, as they do,
  Here and elsewhere, my problem's theme and text.

The world indeed is barren through and through,  58
  As thou hast said, of virtue and of worth,
  Sin-laden and sin-clouded – that's most true;

But show me, pray, the cause of all this dearth,  61
  That I may see it and make others see,
  For some in heaven locate it, some on earth."

64   A deep sigh, wrung by grief to an *Ay me!*
     Came first, and then: "Brother, the world is blind,
     And thou art of it, sure enough," said he.

67   "By you who live, causation's all assigned
     To the sole stars, as though they could compel
     Into their own fixt paths all things combined.

70   If that were so, it would destroy free will
     Within you, and it were unjust indeed
     You should have joy for good or grief for ill.

73   Promptings of motion from your stars proceed –
     I say not all, but if I did, what then?
     Light's given you to know right from wrong at need.

76   And free will, so its stuff can stand the strain
     Of its first tussles with the stars, will fight,
     If nourished well, to win the whole campaign;

79   For of a nobler nature, mightier might,
     You're the free subjects – might which doth create
     A mind in you that's no star's perquisite.

82   So, if the world now goes with crooked gait
     The cause is in yourselves for you to trace;
     I'll be thy scout therein to set thee straight.

85   Forth of His hands whose brooding tenderness
     Loves her or ere she comes to be, is brought,
     Laughing and weeping, like a babe that plays,

88   The simple, infant soul, that, all untaught,
     But moved by a glad Maker, turns with pleasure
     To this or that by which her fancy's caught.

91   First she's attracted by some trifling treasure,
     Then runs, beguiled, in hot pursuit to scour,
     Save manage sway her love with the curb's pressure.

94   Hence did we need the curb of legal power,
     And need a ruler, one that could, and should,
     Glimpse the true city, or at least the tower.

97   The laws are there, but what hand makes them good?
     None; for the shepherd that goes on before
     Parts not the hoof, though he can chew the cud.

Therefore the flock, seeing their guide set store 100
  By such goods only as themselves have craved,
  Batten on these, and look for nothing more.

Clear cause, then, why the world's so ill-behaved 103
  Is that it's governed after an ill mode,
  Not that the nature in you is depraved.

Of old, when Rome reformed the world, she showed 106
  Two suns to lighten the twin ways that went
  One with the other: world's road and God's road;

But one has quenched the other; the sword's blent 109
  Now with the crook; when one and other meet
  Their fusion must produce bad government;

For one fears not the other when one seat 112
  Holds both; believ'st thou not that this is so?
  The plant's known by its fruit – look to the wheat!

On soil that's fed by Adige and Po 115
  Once, ere the strife with Frederick's rule began,
  Worth and high courtesy were wont to grow;

Now there's free travel; every ruffian 118
  Goes safe there that for shame hath long forsook
  Commerce or speech with any decent man.

Three greybeards still, in whom old times rebuke 121
  The new, live on and find time tedious
  Till on a better world God bid them look:

Conrad Palazzo, the good Gerard – those, 124
  And Guy Castel, whom fitter 'twere to call
  'The simple Lombard' as the French phrase goes.

Henceforth say this: the Church of Rome doth fall 127
  Into the mire, and striving to combine
  Two powers in one, fouls self and load and all."

"O," then said I, "well argued, Marco mine! 130
  Clearly I see now why the heritage
  Was barred to all the sons of Levi's line.

But who's this sample of a lineage 133
  Now lost, this Gerard who is left awhile,
  Thou sayest, to reprove a barbarous age?"

136 "Is this a test?" said he, "or is it guile?
  Not know Good Gerard? That sounds strange, if true,
  Upon a Tuscan tongue! How else to style

139 The man I know not, unless this.will do —
  The style his daughter Gaia still displays.
  God keep you both! I can't go on with you.

142 See how beyond the smoke the gathering rays
  Brighten to whiteness now! The angel's near,
  And ere he sees me I must go on my ways."

145 Then he turned back, and more he would not hear.

THE IMAGES. *The Penance of the Wrathful: the Smoke*: the effect of Wrath is to blind the judgement and to suffocate the natural feelings and responses, so that a man does not know what he is doing. The penance of the Wrathful is therefore, once again, the endurance of the sin itself. Dante habitually connects Wrath with images of smoke and suffocation – cf. the Sullen Wrathful in the fifth circle of Hell (*Inf.* vii. 118–26), whose "hearts smouldered with a sulky smoke", and whose punishment is to lie gurgling and choking in the muddy bed of Styx.

*Marco Lombardo*: Dante here shows us only one image of the Wrathful – probably because he has already given sufficient space in the ferocious and sullen types in the *Inferno*. In Marco he offers a third, and more pleasing, variation: the open-hearted, generous man with a hot temper.

NOTES. l. 16: *voices*: these are the voices of the Wrathful.

 l. 19: *Agnus Dei* [*qui tollis peccata mundi, miserere nobis, dona nobis pacem*]: "O Lamb of God, that takest away the sins of the world, have mercy upon us; grant us Thy peace": this is the Prayer of the Third Cornice. It is taken from the Canon of the Mass, and derives from *John* i. 29.

 ll. 25–6: *that cleavest through our smoke and speak'st*: the spirit cannot see Dante, but he notices the disturbance of the smoke by the passage of Dante's solid body, and the wheezing and choking of his mortal lungs when speaking in this Purgatorial "London Particular".

 ll. 26–7: *who reckons still the time by kalends*: This is another of Dante's indications that the time and space of Purgatory do not correspond with ours (cf. ii. 68 and note); *Kalends*: the first day of any Roman month: hence, the system of reckoning time by the *calendar*.

 l. 42: *strange in modern days*: cf. *Inf.* ii. 13–30.

 l. 46: *Marco*: of Marco Lombardo (i.e. of Lombardy, or of the Lombard family) not much is certainly known. Most of the old commentators agree that he lived at Venice in the thirteenth century, and was a man of great courtesy, generosity, and nobility of mind, though of a peppery temper.

l. 55: *singly at first, now doubly*: Dante has been worrying all this time over Guido del Ducas's words (in Canto xiv) about the wickedness and degeneracy of the world. Marco's remarks, confirming Guido's opinion, encourage him to ask whether this wickedness is determined by destiny (the influence of the stars) or due to the corruption of man's will.

l. 63: *in heaven*: i.e. in astral influences.

ll. 67 sqq.: *by you who live*, etc.: Here begins the first great Discourse on Free Will – a subject with which Dante is always deeply concerned. It may not be immediately obvious why the discussion is initiated on the Cornice of Wrath and occupies the whole of the time spent there; but there is in fact a quite rational connexion of ideas. If everything that happens is the result of a rigid determinism, Wrath can no longer be called either sinful or righteous – it becomes simply meaningless. It is useless, on the one hand, to be angry with anyone for doing what he could not help doing; and on the other, the anger itself is merely a mechanical gesture, as much determined as the behaviour which appears to provoke it.

ll. 67–8: *causation's all assigned to the sole stars*: Here and elsewhere it has to be borne in mind that Dante's talk about the stars should not be summarily dismissed as "mere astrology" or "medieval superstition". When he speaks of the stars as the sole origin of causation he means by that exactly what the modern determinist means by saying that all events in the universe, including human behaviour, follow each other in inevitable sequence as the result of the physical interaction of the atoms composing it. A man is what he is and does what he does because the course of nature threw him up at such and such a time and under such and such conditions; in this context the "disposition of the heavens" is simply a shorthand way of indicating "environment". We shall see that Dante rejects mechanical determinism. The idea that the heavens themselves, by means of their movers the Intelligences, are partially responsible for creating or modifying these conditions is a different matter, and in this hypothesis Dante is disposed to believe. The further idea that by observing and calculating the positions and movements of the planets one can predict and control the future is yet a third thing – astrology in its more debased manifestations; Dante consigns the practitioners of this art to the Bowge of the Sorcerers (see *Inf.* xx).

ll. 73–8: *promptings of motion*, etc.: i.e. every man is born with certain tendencies, due to inheritance, environment, and so forth. Even if his disposition were thus wholly determined by exterior causes (which Marco says he does not assert), even so he has judgement ("light to know right from wrong") and free will, which can be strengthened

by exercise to make him victorious over his "conditions". The whole
argument is taken up again in more detail in Canto xviii.

l. 80: *free subjects*: the will that is truly free seeks God, the natural
object of its desire; therefore true freedom consists in willing subjec-
tion to God, "whose service is perfect freedom" (cf. *Book of Common
Prayer*, 2nd Collect for Morning Prayer).

ll. 82 *sqq.*: *so, if the world*, etc.: Having rejected determinism,
Marco now goes on to show the political reasons for the present social
disorders, viz. that the world is ill-governed, owing to the Emperor's
failure to do his duty, and the Church's usurpation of the temporal
power. (For Dante's political theory, see *Inf.* Introduction, pp. 42–7,
*Purg.* Introduction, pp. 46 *sqq.*)

l. 85: *forth of His hands*: the rational soul is the direct creation of
God, breathed into the embryo when the body is sufficiently formed
to receive it. (See below, Canto xxv.)

l. 95: *a ruler*: i.e. an active and virtuous Emperor.

l. 97: *the laws are there, but what hand makes them good?*: cf. vi. 88–90
and note.

l. 98: *the shepherd*: the Pope.

l. 99: *parts not the hoof, though he can chew the cud*: "as the camel,
because he cheweth the cud but divideth not the hoof; he is unclean
unto you" – *Lev.* xi. 4. As this passage is allegorically interpreted by
Aquinas and others, the chewing of the cud signifies meditation; the
parting of the hoof, the power of discrimination (as e.g. between the
Old and New Covenants or between the two natures of Christ, or
between good and evil). Dante here means discrimination between
the spiritual and temporal powers.

The picture of a "shepherd" with these odd physical characteristics
is either one of Dante's wildest mixed metaphors, or an intentional
grotesque (quite in contemporary satirical taste) which would grace
any carved capital or miserere seat.

l. 106: *of old, when Rome reformed the world*: Dante is probably think-
ing chiefly of the great days of the Byzantine Empire, particularly,
perhaps, under Justinian. The empire envisaged by Dante in his politi-
cal writings "is not the Holy Roman Empire of Western feudalism,
nor is it the pagan empire of Augustus or Trajan. It is the empire of
Constantine, Theodosius, and Justinian, whose splendours were re-
corded at San Vitale and Sant' Apollinare in Classe [in Ravenna]."
Geo. Every: in *An Essay on Charles Williams*.

l. 115: *soil that's fed by Adige and Po*: i.e. Lombardy, or N. Italy in
general, plunged into continual strife by the struggle between Pope
and Emperor that broke out under Frederick II (for whom see *Inf.*
Introduction, p. 25).

l. 124: *Conrad Palazzo* (Currado di Palazzo): a Guelf from Bres-
cia who held various offices in Tuscany towards the end of the thir-

teenth century; *the good Gerard*: Gherardo da Cammino (*d.* 1306), captain-general of Treviso from 1283. Dante uses him as an example of nobility in *Conv.* IV. xiv: his son Riccardo, who is mentioned in *Para.* ix. 49–50, was the husband of Judge Nino's daughter Giovanna (*Purg.* viii. 71).

l. 125: *Guy Castel* (Guido da Castello): a Trevisan gentleman of the Roberti family, much honoured for his prudence, virtue, and liberality. He was from time to time a guest of Can Grande della Scala, and dined at his table, where he may have met Dante. The expression "the Simple Lombard" is variously interpreted. The French tended to call all Italians "Lombards"; but since Guido actually *was* a Lombard, there would seem little point in calling him so *à la française*. The best explanation seems to be that the French also used the word "Lombard" to designate a usurer, and that Guido was jestingly called "the Simple Lombard" in the sense of the "honest" or "guileless" usurer, because of his generous readiness to lend money without interest. (The charging of interest was, in fact, forbidden by the Church, although by this time the prohibition was largely a dead letter.)

l. 132: *the sons of Levi's line*: the Levites, the priestly house, were debarred from inheriting property, because of their spiritual calling: "the Lord is their inheritance" (*Deut.* xviii. 2); they were to be supported by the offerings of the people. Marco, by showing Dante the evils resulting from a rich and worldly church, has shown him the reason for this prohibition. (Cf. *Inf.* xix. 88–117; and also *De Mon.* III. xiii, last paragraph.)

ll. 133–40: *who's this sample ... still displays*: since Marco has not mentioned Gerard's family name, Dante asks for more precision. Marco thinks Dante must be joking: everybody in Tuscany surely knows "the Good Gerard" without further definition; but if not, the family name has been made notorious by Gerard's daughter Gaia, a lady, apparently of more beauty than virtue, who still bears that name, having married another member of the da Cammino family.

l. 143: *the angel's near*: the brightness of the approaching Angel indicates that they are nearing the end of the smoke-cloud, from which Marco must not emerge until his purgation is complete.

# CANTO XVII

THE STORY. *On issuing from the Smoke-cloud, Dante sees in a vision examples of the sin of Wrath. The Angel of the Cornice meets the Poets, erases the third P from Dante's forehead, and, having pronounced the Benediction, directs them to the next stairway. Night falls as they reach the top step, and, since the Law of the Mountain prevents them from ascending further, Virgil beguiles the time by explaining the arrangement of the Cornices and the nature of the sins purged on each of them.*

Remember, Reader, if you've ever been
    Caught in the mountains when a mist came on
    Through which you peered as moles peer through the skin,

4    How, when the thick damp vapours have begun
    To lift, there steals upon you, faintly winking
    Through thin-drawn veils, the pale disc of the sun;

7    And little trouble then you'll have in thinking
    Just how things looked to me when first I spied
    The sun again, which now was near to sinking.

10    Thus with my leader, stride for trusty stride,
    Forth from such clouds I came to the bright ray,
    Though from the shore below all light had died.

13    O fantasy, that reav'st us oft away
    So from ourselves that we remain distraught,
    Deaf though a thousand trumpets round us bray,

16    What moves thee when the senses show thee naught?
    Light moves thee, formed in Heaven, by will maybe
    Of Him who sends it down, or else self-wrought.

19    The impress of her impious cruelty
    Who turned into the bird that most doth dote
    On song, was shown me in a fantasy,

22    Which seized my mind and caged it so remote
    Within itself that outside things passed by,
    And it received them not and took no note.

And then a man hanged on a gallows high          25
   Came to me in this visionary mood,
   And even in death his look was fierce and high;

There great Ahasuerus, there the good          28
   Esther his queen, there he that was in word
   And deed most true, just Mordecai stood.

And when the image of its own accord          31
   Burst as a bubble formed within a stream
   Bursts on the water's surface, afterward

A girl rose wailing up into my dream          34
   Who cried: "Why didst thou let wrath lay thee low,
   Most royal lady? Better didst thou deem

To slay thyself than lose Lavinia – lo!          37
   Now hast thou lost me; I am she, who cries,
   Mother, for thee and for none else cries so."

As, when new light smites sudden on closed eyes,          40
   Sleep breaks and flutters broken a brief spell
   Before it wholly drops away and dies,

So my imaginations broke and fell          43
   Soon as a brilliance smote mine eyes, which shined
   Beyond all wont of ours and nonpareil.

Where had I got to? I looked round to find;          46
   But then a voice which said: "Here is the place
   Where one ascends," drove all else from my mind

And filled me with a mighty eagerness          49
   To see the speaker, such as knows no rest
   Till it beholds its object face to face;

But as sight shrinks from the sun's fiery vest          52
   That shrouds his form in its excessive bright,
   So here my powers shrank fainting and oppressed.

"This is a spirit of God that toward the height          55
   Directs us on our way, and this he does
   Unasked, and he goes veiled in his own light.

As a man treats himself, so he treats us;          58
   Who waits the asking when he sees the need,
   In his mean heart goes half-way to refuse.

61 Let's move our feet to follow this good lead,
  And ere night falls climb briskly as we can,
  Else, till the sun return, we'll make no speed."

64 Thus far my leader; wherefore, as one man,
  We hastened toward the stair; and when my tread
  Touched the first step where the ascent began

67 I felt as 'twere a wing-beat, felt my head
  Fanned, and "*Beati*", then, "*pacifici*,
  Who know not evil wrath," I heard it said.

70 Soon, overhead, went slanting up so high
  Those last bright beams whereon night follows fast
  That on all sides the stars peeped from the sky.

73 "Alack, my strength! O why hast thou thus passed
  Away from me?" so ran my inward speech –
  It seemed that gyves about my legs were cast.

76 We'd come now to the stairway's topmost reach,
  And there we were, powerless to lift a limb,
  Stuck like a vessel grounding on a beach.

79 I bent my ear to the new circuit's rim
  To see if any sound would issue thence;
  Then, turning to my master, said to him:

82 "My gracious father, tell me what offence
  Is purged here on this cornice where we bide;
  Let feet be stayed, but not thy eloquence."

85 "Love of the Good," said he, "that once let slide
  Its proper duties, is restored up there;
  There once again the slackened oar is plied.

88 But now, to make this matter fully clear,
  Give me thy full attention; thus we'll get
  Some useful fruit of our forced tarrying here."

91 So he began: "Never, my son, was yet
  Creator, no, nor creature, without love
  Natural or rational – and thou knowest it.

94 The natural cannot make an erring move;
  The other may, either by faulty aim
  Or else by too much zeal or lack thereof.

When to the great prime goods it makes full claim,    97
   Or to the lesser goods in measure due,
   No sin can come of its delight in them;

But if it swerve to evil, or pursue    100
   Good ends too hot of foot or slack of speed,
   Then would the Workman's work His work undo.

Bethink thee then how love must be the seed    103
   In you, not only of each virtuous action,
   But also of each punishable deed.

Now, to the object of its predilection    106
   Love cannot but wish well; this means, of course,
   That from self-hatred no one needs protection;

And self-sufficient being, in divorce    109
   From primal Being, is not thinkable:
   Hence, no effect can hate its own First Source;

*Restat* (if I decide and judge with skill)    112
   That love of hurt means love of neighbours' hurt,
   Which love springs in your clay from three roots still.

Some hope their neighbour's ruin may divert    115
   His glory to themselves, and this sole hope
   Prompts them to drag his greatness in the dirt;

Some, in their fear to lose fame, favour, scope,    118
   And honour, should another rise to power,
   Wishing the worst, sit glumly there and mope;

And some there are whose wrongs have turned them sour,    121
   So that they thirst for vengeance, and this passion
   Fits them to plot some mischief any hour.

This threefold love below us finds purgation;    124
   Next, I would have thee know that other kind,
   Which seeks the good, though in disordered fashion.

Everyone vaguely pictures in his mind    127
   A good the heart may rest on, and is driven
   By his desire to seek it and to find.

If to the vision and the quest you've given    130
   But lukewarm love, and then repent of this,
   Upon this cornice you're chastised and shriven.

133     There is another good which brings not bliss:
           Bliss it is not, nor that essential Good
           The fruit and root of all the good there is;

136     Love which sets too much store on that is rued
           Above us on the mountain's triple shelf,
           Being triple too – I'll not say how; I would

139     Thou shouldst work out the answer for thyself."

NOTES. l. 3: *as moles peer through the skin*: the extreme smallness of the mole's eyes gave rise to a belief that it had none, or could not see (cf. Shakespeare: "the blind mole", *Tempest*: IV. i, *Pericles*: I. i). Dante, however, knows that it has eyes, and can see, though (as he supposes) dimly, through a protective membrane. Pliny held that a mole died at once if exposed to the full light of day, and this view was common in the Middle Ages.

l. 9: *the sun ... which now was near to sinking*: it is close on 6 P.M.

ll. 19–39: *the impress*, etc.: The three visions which follow are the Bridle of Wrath: one is taken from classical myth, one from the O.T., and one from the *Aeneid*. They correspond, though not very exactly, nor in the same order, to the examples of Meekness.

l. 19: *her impious cruelty*: "She" is Procne, for whose story see Canto ix. 13, note. (Wrath against kindred and friends.)

ll. 25–30: *a man hanged*, etc.: Because Mordecai refused to do reverence to him, Haman in his rage ordered all the Jews in Persia to be destroyed. Esther intervened with King Ahasuerus, and Haman was hanged. The story is told in the *Book of Esther*. (Wrath against God's Chosen.)

ll. 34–9: *a girl rose wailing*, etc.: Lavinia, daughter of King Latinus, was betrothed to Turnus. Her mother Amata, thinking (mistakenly) that Turnus had been killed in battle, hanged herself for rage and despair; *and for none else*: i.e. not for Turnus, who was then still alive, though he was later killed by Aeneas. (*Aen.* xii. 595–607.) (Wrath provoked by foes.)

l. 47: *a voice*: this is the voice of the Angel of Meekness. He is, in Charles Williams's phrase, "unseen and unbesought", as is fitting to his nature.

ll. 67–8: *I felt as 'twere a wing-beat, felt my head fanned*: the Angel's wing erases the third P from Dante's forehead.

l. 68: *beati pacifici*: "blessed are the peacemakers": this is the Benediction of the Third Cornice (*Matt.* v. 9).

l. 69: *evil wrath*: Dante here distinguishes the sin of Wrath from righteous anger.

l. 73: *alack, my strength!*: the sun has set, and the poets feel the effect of the Law of the Mountains, which inhibits all ascent after nightfall (see vii. 44–60, and Images).

ll. 85–7: *love of the Good*: Virgil explains that they are now approaching the Cornice of Sloth, where Love Defective is purged (see Introduction, p. 67). The *Good* is the true Good (which is, ultimately, God), love of which can never be excessive (see below, l. 97), but may err by defect.

ll. 91–139: *so he began*, etc.: This is Virgil's exposition of the arrangement of Purgatory, forming the prologue to his Second Discourse on Love, which follows in the next canto. The gist of his exposition is set out in the Introduction, pp. 66–7 *q.v.*

l. 93: *natural or rational*: the *natural* love is the unselfconscious instinct, which in itself is wholly free from blame; the *rational* is that which has the conscious assent of the will, and may err by "faulty aim" (love perverted), "too much zeal" (love excessive) or "lack thereof" (love defective).

l. 97: *the great prime goods*: i.e. God, and the virtues which spring from the love of God. To these love must "make full claim" (i.e. desire them in the highest degree), since love for those objects can err only by defect.

l. 98: *to the lesser goods in measure due*: the "lesser goods" are all those legitimate objects of love which are not God. If any one of them is preferred before God, then the love errs by excess; further, a right order must be observed among them; e.g. to put love of money before love of one's neighbour would also be an error by excess. But provided that "due measure" is kept there is no sin in loving pleasant things. Throughout this passage Dante explicitly and emphatically repudiates the Gnostic heresy that natural desires and their objects are, or can be, evil in themselves.

ll. 103–5: *how love must be the seed*, etc.: Virgil sums up his argument so far: love is the root of every action, whether good or bad.

ll. 106–23: *now to the object*, etc.: Virgil now proceeds to show (*a*) what is the object of Love perverted, (*b*) which are its three main kinds, and (*c*) where they are purged.

(*a*) (ll. 106–13):

(1) He dismisses *self*; everybody naturally loves himself, and therefore cannot really wish to harm himself.

(2) He dismisses *God*: since every creature is wholly dependent on God, no one can really hate the source of his own existence.

(Any appearance of hatred against God or the self is one of the delusions of Hell. "It is the rational choice of which [Virgil] is speaking, and in Hell the rational choice no longer exists; there are 'the people who have lost the good of intellect' " – Charles Williams, *The Figure of Beatrice*, p. 163.)

| | | | CIRCLE | SINNERS | | PENANCE |
|---|---|---|---|---|---|---|
| ANTE-PURGATORY | Salvation in articulo mortis | | Terrace 1 | The Excommunicate | | Detention for 30 times period of contumacy |
| | | | Terrace 2 | The Late-Repen-tant | (a) The Indolent | Detention for period equal to that of earthly life |
| | | | | | (b) The Unshriven | |
| | | | | | (c) The Preoccupied | |

PETER'S GATE:   Step 1: Confession   Step 2: Contrition   Step 3: Satis-

| | | | | CIRCLE | SINNERS | PENANCE |
|---|---|---|---|---|---|---|
| THE SEVEN ROOTS OF SIN | LOWER PURGATORY | Love of Neighbours' Harm (Love Perverted) | | Cornice 1 | The Proud (Superbia or Vana Gloria – Pride or Vainglory) | Heavy Stones |
| | | | | Cornice 2 | The Envious (Invidia – Envy) | Sealed Eyes |
| | | | | Cornice 3 | The Wrathful (Ira – Wrath) | Smoke |
| | MIDDLE PURGATORY | Dis-ordered Love of Good | Love Defective | Cornice 4 | The Slothful (Acedia – Sloth or Accidie) | Running |
| | UPPER PURGATORY | | Ex-cessive Love of Second-ary Goods | Cornice 5 | The Covetous (Avaritia – Avarice) | Prostration |
| | | | | Cornice 6 | The Gluttonous (Gula – Greed) | Starvation |
| | | | | Cornice 7 | The Lustful (Luxuria – Lust) | Fire |

THE EARTHLY PARADISE:   Pageant of the Sacrament   ] BEATRICE [

*This Table is arranged in 'reading order', from top to bottom.*

| MEDITATION (a) Whip (b) Bridle | PRAYER | GUARDIAN | BENEDICTION | NUMERICAL SCHEME |
|---|---|---|---|---|
| — | — | Cato (General Guardian of the Mountain) | — | 2 |
| | (a) — | | | |
| ⁓ | (b) Miserere | | — | |
| | (c) Salve Regina Te lucis ante | [Guardian Angels of the Valley] | | |
| faction (The Seven P's) | | Angel of the Church | [Te Deum] | |
| Examples of (a) Humility (b) Pride (Sculptures in the rock) | Paternoster | Angel of Humility | Beati pauperes spiritu | 9 |
| Examples of (a) Generosity (b) Envy (Voices in the air) | Litany of the Saints | Angel of Generosity or Mercy | Beati misericordes | 3 |
| Examples of (a) Meekness (b) Wrath (Visions in the mind) | Agnus Dei | Angel of Peace | Beati pacifici | 10 |
| Examples of (a) Zeal (b) Sloth (Voices of penitents) | [Their labour is their prayer] | Angel of Zeal | Beati qui lugent | 1 / 7 |
| Examples of (a) Liberality (b) Avarice (Voices of penitents) | Adhaesit pavimento | Angel of Liberality | Beati qui esuriunt justitiam | |
| Examples of (a) Temperance (b) Greed (Voices in trees) | Labia mea, Domine | Angel of Temperance | Beati qui sitiunt | 3 / 4 |
| Examples of (a) Chastity (b) Lust (Voices of penitents) | Summae Deus clementiae | Angel of Chastity | Beati mundo corde | |
| Pageant of Church and Empire | [Delectasti] | Matilda | [Lilia date manibus plenis / Veni sponsa de Libano, or Benedictus qui venis] | [Lethe and Eunoë] 1 |

*For the geographical arrangement of the Ascent of the Mountain, see Diagram on page 62.*

    (3) There remains (*restat*) only the love of harm to one's neigh-
        bour. This is the object of Love Perverted, and the only means
        by which "the work can seek to work against the Workman"
        – i.e. by "the harming of an image or images given to one for
        due love" (Charles Williams, *op. cit.* p. 164).

  (*b*) (ll. 114–23) the three kinds are:

    (1) *Pride*: the intolerance of any rivalry.

    (2) *Envy*: the fear of loss through competition.

    (3) *Wrath*: the love of revenge for injury.

  (*c*) (l. 124) those sins in that order are purged on the Cornices of
    Lower Purgatory.

ll. 125–39: Virgil now comes to the objects and purgations of legiti-
mate love which errs by (*a*) defect, (*b*) excess.

  (*a*) (ll. 127–32): *Defect*: There is a true and satisfying Good (which
    "the heart may rest on"), of which everybody has at least some
    kind of nostalgic glimmering. This is the love of God; failure to
    pursue it with one's whole will is called Sloth (*Accidia*), and is
    purged on the fourth Cornice (Mid-Purgatory).

  (*b*) (ll. 133–9): *Excess*: There is a love which though good as far as
    it goes, cannot of itself bring one to Heaven (it "is not bliss")
    because it is not the love of God (the essential Good and source
    of all contingent goods). This love is threefold, and purged on
    the three Cornices of Upper Purgatory.

For all this arrangement see diagram, p. 62, and table, pp. 202–3.

# CANTO XVIII

THE STORY. *In answer to a question from Dante, Virgil proceeds to his Second Discourse on Love and on Free Will. By the time he has finished, the gibbous Moon is high in the sky and putting out the stars. Dante is just dozing off when he is roused by the noisy approach of the spirits of the Slothful, who run continually around the Cornice crying aloud the examples of Zeal and Sloth which form the Whip and Bridle for their meditation. The spirit of the Abbot of San Zeno, as he rushes by, calls out directions for the Poets' journey and tells them about his convent. Presently, Dante falls asleep.*

Thus the great teacher closed his argument,
    And earnestly perused my face, to see
    Whether I now appeared to be content:

While I, though a new thirst tormented me,     4
    Kept outward silence, and within me said:
    "My endless questions worry him, maybe."

But he, true father that he was, had read     7
    My timid, unvoiced wish, and now by speech
    Nerved me to speech; and so I went ahead:

"Master," said I, "thy light so well doth reach     10
    And quicken my dim vision, that it sees
    Clearly whate'er thy words describe or teach;

Wherefore, my kindest, dearest Father, please     13
    Define me love, to which thou dost reduce
    All virtuous actions and their contraries."

And he: "Fix then on me the luminous     16
    Eyes of the intellect, and plain I'll prove
    How, when the blind would guide, their way they lose.

The soul, which is created apt for love,     19
    The moment pleasure wakes it into act,
    To any pleasant thing is swift to move.

Your apprehension draws from some real fact     22
    An inward image, which it shows to you,
    And by that image doth the soul attract:

25 And if the soul, attracted, yearns thereto,
   That yearning's love; 'tis nature doth secure
   Her bond in you, which pleasure knits anew.

28 And as fire mounts, urged upward by the pure
   Impulsion of its form, which must aspire
   Toward its own matter, where 'twill best endure,

31 So the enamoured soul falls to desire –
   A motion spiritual – nor rest can find
   Till its loved object it enjoy entire.

34 Now canst thou see how wholly those are blind
   To truth, who think all love is laudable
   Just in itself, no matter of what kind,

37 Since (they would argue) its material
   Seems always good; yet, though the wax be good,
   The imprint is not always good as well."

40 "That's love," said I, "and well I've understood,
   Thanks to thy words and my attendant wit;
   But now I teem with fresh incertitude.

43 If from without love beckons us to it,
   And with no choice the soul's foot followeth,
   Go right, go wrong, we merit not a whit."

46 "So much as reason here distinguisheth
   I can unfold," said he; "thereafter, sound
   Beatrice's mind alone, for that needs faith.

49 To each substantial form that doth compound
   With matter, though distinct from it, there cleaves
   Specific virtue, integral, inbound,

52 Which, save in operation, none perceives;
   It's known by its effects, as, in the plant,
   Life manifests itself by the green leaves.

55 So how his intellect's made cognizant
   Of the prime concepts, or what guides his aim
   Toward the first appetibles, man's ignorant;

58 Such things are instincts in you, much the same
   As is in bees the honey-making bent;
   This prime volition earns nor praise nor blame.

Now, to keep all volitions else well blent     61
  With this, you have a counsellor-power innate
  Set there to guard the threshold of assent:

That is the principle to which relate     64
  All your deserts, according as its fan
  Is strict to purge right loves from reprobate.

They who by reasoning probed creation's plan     67
  Root-deep, perceived this inborn liberty
  And bequeathed ethics to the race of man.

Grant, then, all loves that wake in you to be     70
  Born of necessity, you still possess
  Within yourselves the power of mastery;

And this same noble faculty it is     73
  Beatrice calls Free Will; if she thereon
  Should speak with thee, look thou remember this."

Retarded near to midnight now, the moon,     76
  Shaped like a mazer fiery-new and bright,
  Was making the stars appear but dimly strewn,

As counter-heaven she ran by the road whose light     79
  Flares red at night when the sun, beheld from Rome,
  'Twixt Corsica and Sardinia sinks from sight.

That shade who gives to Pietola, his home,     82
  More fame than even Mantua city knows,
  Disburdened of my problems, now sat dumb;

So I, who'd reaped succinct and luminous     85
  Replies to all my questions, could relax
  In rambling thoughts, half dropped into a doze.

When, all at once, and close behind our backs     88
  Startling me up, a throng came roundabout,
  Wheeling towards us in their circling tracks.

As on their banks by night a rush and rout     91
  Of old Ismenus and Asopus spied,
  When Thebans to their aid called Bacchus out,

So round that circle sweeping, stride on stride,     94
  I saw them come whom love, devoutly vowed,
  And glad good will, like horsemen, spur and ride.

97     Soon they were on us, for the whole great crowd
        Were running at top speed; and there were twain
        Who went before and, weeping, cried aloud:

100    "Mary ran to the hills in haste!" and then:
        "Caesar, to subjugate Ilerda, thrust
        Hard at Marseilles and raced on into Spain!"

103    "Quick, quick! let not the precious time be lost
        For lack of love!" the others cried, pursuing;
        "In good work strive, till grace revive from dust!"

106    "O people, now with eager haste renewing
        The time, belike, that slipped in dalliance by,
        Or sloth, through lukewarm fervour for well-doing,

109    This living man – indeed I speak no lie –
        Would fain ascend when day brings back the sun;
        So tell us, please, where there's an opening nigh."

112    Such were my leader's words. Then answered one
        Among those spirits, hallooing; "Come this way –
        Thou'lt find the pass if thou behind us run.

115    Zeal to be moving goads us so, that stay
        We cannot; if our duty seem at first
        Too like discourtesy, forgive us, pray.

118    San Zeno's abbot in Verona erst
        Was I, 'neath good King Barbarossa brave,
        Who in Milan's still talked about and cursed.

121    A man there is with one foot in the grave,
        Shall for that convent soon have tears to shed,
        Ruing his influence and the powers it gave,

124    Because he's set his own son – bastard-bred,
        Deficient of his body, worse in wit –
        To rule there in its rightful pastor's stead."

127    If more he spake, or ceased there, never a whit
        Know I – he'd fled so far beyond us both;
        Thus much I heard, and gladly noted it.

130    Then he who in my need was never loth
        To aid me, said: "Turn hither, see where come
        Two others, pulling on the curb of sloth."

These, running last, cried out: "The folk for whom    133
  The Red Sea opened died ere Jordan river
  Beheld their heirs pass over and win home";

And then again: "The folk whose faint endeavour    136
  Failed good Anchises' son, and did not last,
  Sank to a slothful life, disfamed for ever."

Then, when these shades so far from us had passed    139
  That nothing could be seen of them, there rose
  New fancies in my mind, whence thick and fast

Sprang others, countless, various; and from those    142
  To these I drifted, down so long a stream
  Of rambling thought, my lids began to close,

And meditation melted into dream.    145

THE IMAGES. *The Penance of Sloth: Ceaseless Activity*: The sin which in English is commonly called *Sloth*, and in Latin *accidia* (or more correctly *acedia*), is insidious, and assumes such Protean shapes that it is rather difficult to define. It is not merely idleness of mind and laziness of body: it is that whole poisoning of the will which, beginning with indifference and an attitude of "I couldn't care less", extends to the deliberate refusal of joy and culminates in morbid introspection and despair. One form of it which appeals very strongly to some modern minds is that acquiescence in evil and error which readily disguises itself as "Tolerance"; another is that refusal to be moved by the contemplation of the good and beautiful which is known as "Disillusionment", and sometimes as "knowledge of the world"; yet another is that withdrawal into an "ivory tower" of Isolation which is the peculiar temptation of the artist and the contemplative, and is popularly called "Escapism".

The penance assigned to it takes the form of the practice of the opposite virtue: an active Zeal. Note that on this Cornice alone no verbal Prayer is provided for the penitents: for them, "to labour is to pray".

NOTES. ll. 4–15: *while I*, etc.: A comparison of the tone of these lines with the corresponding passage in *Inf.* xi. 67–79 shows how subtly Dante conveys the development of the intimacy and affection between himself and Virgil during the course of their journey. Dante is no longer importunate, and Virgil no longer sharp with him.

l. 18: *when the blind would guide*: an allusion to *Matt.* xv. 14.

ll. 19–75: *the soul, which is created apt for love*, etc.: This opens Virgil's second great Discourse on Love: the first (xv. 49–81) turned on the operation of love; this, on its origin and nature.

l. 20: *pleasure*: the origin of love is our instinctive attraction to what pleases us; an attraction in itself natural (ll. 26–7) and blameless (ll. 58–61, *subt.*).

ll. 22–6: *your apprehension*, etc.: an exterior object is presented (by means of the senses) to the apprehensive faculty, which forms it into a comprehensible impression or image, to which the mind, or soul, directs its attention; *some real fact*: the image must be of something really existing outside the self; i.e. love must be directed to a *real other*. (The implications of this will be taken up in the next canto.)

ll. 26–7: *nature doth secure her bond in you*: the natural tie of affection which knits all creation is reinforced by pleasure in an attractive object.

ll. 28–30: *as fire mounts,* etc.: Medieval philosophers for the most part followed Aristotle in supposing that fire mounted, earthy bodies sank, etc., because each element tended towards its "natural place", where it was most at home (i.e. in the case of fire towards the "sphere of fire") (ix. 30, note). The theory (since proved correct) that these movements were due to a difference in weight was put forward in the eleventh century, but was unfortunately rejected by Avicenna, whose authority influenced all subsequent scientific speculation until the seventeenth century; *its form*: the *form* is that essential principle of structure which, when united to the component matter, makes a thing what it is (v. *subt.* l. 49, note).

l. 32: *a motion spiritual*: "motion", in the Aristotelian vocabulary, signifies any kind of change, or action. At this point the conscious will comes into play, reaching out toward the beloved object and desiring complete union with it; this is a spiritual action (not a local movement).

ll. 35–9: *that all love is laudable*, etc.: It is interesting to see that this prevalent sentimental heresy was not unknown even in Dante's day. "People argue that because love is, generally (i.e. as regards its *matter*), directed to the good, therefore each and every love must itself be good; but that is not true, for it is the *form* which specifically determines what kind of love it is; just as if a seal is clumsily impressed the print is a bad print however good the wax may be."

ll. 43–9: *If from without*, etc.: Dante here voices a fresh perplexity, which brings up the problem of determinism versus free will in a new form. Granted that (as Marco Lombardo showed in Canto xvi) our actions are not determined by the material "course of the heavens", are they not determined from within by the fact that we are inevitably bound to pursue that which we happen to fall in love with? Are we not, that is, the helpless victims of our own temperamental urges? Virgil proceeds to deal with the problem of free will in love, so far as reason can; beyond that point it becomes a matter of faith (i.e. depends upon the Christian revelation) and must be left to Beatrice.

l. 49: *substantial form*: in scholastic terminology, a *substance* is an *individual existing being*. Most of the beings we meet with are *material* substances, consisting of *matter* and *form*; the form being the organization of the substance, and the matter being that which is organized. At the lowest end of the scale of creation we have *inanimate* substances, in which the form is merely the shape or arrangement of the matter. Thus, a glass button is a lump of matter (glass) formed into a certain (button-) shape. Such "individuality" as it has is purely numerical and derives from its matter: out of a card of similar buttons, it is the particular quantum of glass used in its manufacture which gives Button A its "thisness" and distinguishes it from Button B. On the other hand, the form gives the matter its "thusness", in virtue of which it is one *kind* of thing and not another – a button, and not, for example, a wine-glass or a test-tube.

At the highest end of the scale there are the *spiritual* or *immaterial* substances, such as angels. These are *pure forms*, subsisting as individual beings in their own right, and not needing matter either for their self-expression, or for communication among themselves.

Between these two extremes we have an ascending order of *animate* substances, extending from the lowest forms of plant-life to man. In these, it is the *soul* which is the form of the matter and makes the being the kind of being it is. Thus a cat, for example, is not merely a lump of cat-matter organized into a cat-shape: such a being exists, but it is a dead cat. The living cat has an "animal" or "sensitive" soul (*anima sensitiva*) which, animating and *informing* the cat-matter-shape, confers being upon it – makes it, that is, *substantially* the cat we know, which eats and runs and purrs and catches mice and has kittens; and this is its *substantial form*. When the animal soul is withdrawn at death, all that is left is the material shape; and this, in the absence of the substantial form, quickly loses both its cathood and its individual identity, corrupting away into mere disorganized matter.

The substantial form of a *man* is the *rational soul*. This so far partakes of the nature of the lower forms that it needs a body by means of which it may express and communicate itself and develop into a complete personality. But it also partakes of the nature of spiritual forms in that it is self-subsistent, containing within itself its own principle of individuation; so that after the death of the body it survives and retains unimpaired the fullness of the personality it has built up.

Note, once and for all, that in the technical vocabulary of the schools, "substance" and "substantial" are *never* used, as they are today, to mean "matter" and "material" (or "solid" or "thick" or "firm" or "considerable" – a "substantial oak table"; a "substantial fortune"). We remain nearer to the scholastic use when we say: "Give me the *substance* of that document" – meaning by that, neither the material ink and paper, nor yet the "accidental" form of the words, but the underlying (*sub-stantial*) sense which makes the document what it essentially *is* – a greeting, a transfer of property, a proposal of marriage, a dog-licence, or what-not.

ll. 49–50: *that doth compound with matter, though distinct from it*: the rational soul, although, as we have seen, essentially distinct from the material body, is in life inextricably welded with it: i.e. man is not (as Plato thought) a soul *imprisoned* in a body, like brandy in a bottle. The body-soul is a compound, in which the matter nourishes the soul and the soul "informs" the matter – rather as, in a poem, the sound expresses the sense and the sense "informs" the sound, though the two are distinguishable for the purpose of analysis.

l. 51: *specific virtue*: a "specific virtue" is a power belonging to all the members of a *species* and to them only. In the human species, this characteristic power is the *discursive intellect* (sometimes called the "possible" or "potential" intellect) which builds up knowledge by arguing from the known to the unknown. (Animals know by instinct, appetite, or acquired habit; angels, by intuition; only man *argues*.)

ll. 52–4: *save in operation*, etc.: We cannot directly observe this power, any more than we can *see* life; but, just as, if the leaves of a plant are green, we know that life is in it, so we infer the presence of the discursive intellect from the fact that we observe the process of argument going on.

ll. 55–7: *the prime concepts ... the first appetibles*: Observation of the process cannot tell us how the intellect gets the original data from which to start its argument. We can only say that certain things seem to be self-evidently true, and these we call the "first cognitions" or "prime concepts". Other things appear to be obviously desirable, and these we call the "prime appetibles" or "first objects of desire"; and from these implanted or instinctive perceptions the process of reasoning starts. If we whittle the content of these perceptions down to the minimum, we may say that, in the natural order, the first intelligible is *being* (we are aware that we exist), and the first appetible is our own *good* (we are aware of preference). Taken absolutely, God is both the First Intelligible and the Prime Appetible (since He *is* all the *Being* there is and all the *Good* there is); but Virgil is here speaking of the natural order.

l. 60: *prime volition*: this ground of inquiry and desire is neutral and innocent, and the volition which it involves is simply the mainspring of action, in itself neither laudable nor blameworthy.

ll. 61–2: *all volitions else*, etc.: these are the exertions of the conscious will, which it is our business to keep as innocent as our instincts.

ll. 62–3: *a counsellor-power ... the threshold of assent*: it will be seen that this famous image of the Censor and the Threshold is not the invention of the nineteenth-century psychologists. Dante is not, of course, concerned here with those "volitions" so shocking to the self that harbours them that the Censor will not even allow them to pass the "threshold of consciousness". The whole allegory of the *Inferno* may, if one likes, be regarded as an exploration "into the hidden things" (*Inf.* viii. 12) beneath that threshold and the dragging into consciousness of the unfathomable mystery of iniquity. But here we have to do with desires which, impelled by the "prime volition", arise in the consciousness and present themselves at the "threshold of *assent*". We can either (1) whole-heartedly accept them; (2) whole-heartedly repudiate them; or (3), in the useful modern phrase, sublimate them – (the *Commedia* itself is, from one point of view, the story of the successful sublimation of a natural desire). The Censor is Free Will (see below, l. 74).

ll. 64–6: *that is the principle*, etc.: Merit or blame depends upon the discrimination of the will in distinguishing good from evil desires and giving or withholding assent accordingly (this answers Dante's question in ll. 43–5).

ll. 67–9: *they who by reasoning*, etc.: the philosophers who first perceived the freedom of the will found in it their justification for drawing up a code of *ethics*, which in a determinist world would be quite meaningless.

ll. 70–2: *grant then*, etc.: "although the first motions of love are prompted by an inner necessity, you have a corresponding inner power of control." (Cf. Marco's words in xvi. 73–81, which give to free will the power of control over *exterior* necessity.)

l. 74: *Free Will*: the Latin is *liberum arbitrium* (lit. "free choice" or "free judgement"). Actually, two freedoms are involved: (1) right choice; (2) power to implement the choice. When the judgement is enslaved one cannot discriminate; when the will is enslaved one may "know and approve the better, but follow the worse." To this gulf between will and power, Virgil's philosophy can find no bridge; it is for Beatrice to show how, through the Incarnation, human nature is taken up by Grace into the Divine Nature ("where will and power are one"), so that the will can freely perform what the judgement freely chooses.

ll. 76–7: *retarded near to midnight now, the moon, shaped like a mazer*: the moon, which was full on Maundy Thursday when Dante's journey began (v. *Inf.* xx. 127) is now gibbous, or bowl-shaped, and rising some four hours later. She would actually have risen about 10 or 10.30 P.M., a little south of east, so that she is now ("near to midnight") already high enough in the sky to quench the starlight and just coming into view from behind the mountain.

ll. 79–81: *as counter-heaven she ran*, etc.: the moon in her proper monthly motion from W. to E. (*against* the daily motion of the heavens) is backing through the constellations, and has reached that part of the Zodiac in which the Sun is when people in Rome see him setting between Corsica and Sardinia. This by modern calculations would bring the Moon into *Libra* (the Scales); but we know that she cannot be there, because on the previous night she rose in *Scorpio* (the Scorpion) – cf. ix. 4–6. Dante must therefore be mistaken about the latitude of Sardinia – which is quite likely, since medieval geography was very inaccurate. The Moon would actually be in the last degrees of *Scorpio* or the first of *Sagittarius* (the Archer).

l. 82: *Pietola* (anciently called Andes): a small village near Mantua, the traditional birthplace of Virgil.

l. 89: *a throng*: these are the spirits of the Slothful.

l. 92: *Ismenus and Asopus*: rivers of Boeotia, along whose banks the Thebans ran at night with lighted torches calling Bacchus, the patron of the city, to send rain for the vines.

ll. 100–3: *Mary ... Caesar*: these are the examples of Zeal, or Energy, which form the Whip of Sloth. The first (from the life of the Blessed Virgin) is taken from *Luke* i. 39: the second (from Classical History) is related in Lucan's *Pharsalia* (Bks. iii and iv). Caesar, on his way to encounter Pompey in Spain, laid vigorous siege to Marseilles, and then, leaving part of his army to complete the operation, hastened on to defeat the enemy at Ilerda (now Lerida) in Catalonia.

l. 118: *San Zeno's abbot in Verona*: perhaps Gherardo II, who died in 1187. Nothing is now known of him or his sins of sloth.

l. 119: *Barbarossa*: Frederick Barbarossa, emperor 1152–90; he destroyed Milan in 1162.

ll. 121–6: *a man there is*, etc.: Alberto della Scala (*d.* 1301), lord of Verona, father of Dante's friends Bartolommeo and Can Grande (for whom see Glossary) and of the deformed and depraved bastard Giuseppe who by his appointment held the Abbacy of San Zeno from 1291 to 1314.

l. 129: *and gladly noted it*: In view of the benefits Dante had received from the della Scala family, Dante's severe treatment of Alberto may appear unbecoming; but the legitimate sons may well have resented the family scandal, so that he could represent himself as being "glad", on their account as well as his own, to know that this shocking piece of nepotism would be repented (whether in life or in Purgatory).

ll. 132–8: *the curb of sloth*: The examples which form the Bridle of Sloth are taken, the first from the Israelites who, after the crossing of the Red Sea, "murmured", and, refusing to follow Moses over Jordan to the Promised Land, perished in the desert (*Ex.* xiv. 10–20; *Num.* xiv. 1–39; *Deut.* i. 26–36); the second from the *Aeneid* (v. 604 *sqq.*), where Aeneas ("Anchises' son") left behind in Sicily those of his companions who, having "no desire of high renown", were unwilling to follow him to Latium.

# CANTO XIX

THE STORY. *Shortly before dawn, Danté dreams of the Siren and her song, and sees her unmasked by Virgil at the bidding of a Discreet Lady. He wakes at Virgil's call to find that it is broad daylight, and as they proceed on their way they are met by the Angel of Zeal, who pronounces the Benediction and directs them to the next stairway. Coming to the Fifth Cornice, they encounter the spirits of the Covetous, fettered face downwards, and Dante talks with the shade of Pope Adrian V.*

What hour the heat of day can warm no longer
    The chill moon's influence, because the cold
    Of earth, or sometimes Saturn's power, is stronger;

4    When geomancers, looking east, behold
    Their Greater Fortune rising through a reach
    Of sky that darkness cannot long enfold;

7    In dream a woman sought me, halt of speech,
    Squint-eyed, on maimed feet lurching as she stept,
    With crippled hands, and skin of sallowy bleach.

10    I gazed; and as to cold limbs that have crept
    Heavy with night, the sun gives life anew,
    Even so my look unloosed the string that kept

13    Her utterance captive, and right quickly drew
    Upright her form that all misshapen hung,
    And stained her withered cheek to love's own hue.

16    Then she began to sing, when thus her tongue
    Was freed – and such a spell she held me by
    As had been hard to break; and so she sung:

19    "Lo, the sweet Siren! yea, 'tis I, 'tis I
    Who lead the mariners in mid-sea astray,
    Such pleasures in my melting measures lie.

22    I turned Ulysses from his wandering way
    With music; few, I trow, to me who grow
    Know how to go, longing I so allay."

Her lips yet moved to that melodious flow 25
    When hard at hand a lady I espied,
    Holy, alert, her guiles to overthrow.

"O Virgil, Virgil, who is this?" she cried 28
    Indignant; and he came, with heedful eyes
    On that discreet one, and on naught beside.

The first he seized, and, rending her disguise 31
    In front, showed me her belly, which released
    So foul a stench, I woke with that surprise.

I looked about for my good lord: "At least 34
    Three times," said he, "I've called thee; rise and come;
    Let's find the breach whereby thou enterest."

I rose; we went. Broad day had masterdom 37
    Now of the holy mountain's every ledge,
    And on our backs the new sun's rays smote plumb.

So, following on along the circle's edge, 40
    With bended brow, like one who, bowed in thought,
    Makes of himself the half-arch of a bridge,

"Come, here's the pass," I heard, in accents fraught 43
    With so benign a tenderness of tone
    As never ear in mortal precinct caught.

He who thus spake, wide-winged as 'twere a swan, 46
    Signed our steps upward to our destination
    Between the two unyielding walls of stone;

Then fluttering, fanned us with his wings' vibration, 49
    And told us, blessed should *qui lugent* be,
    Having their souls made queens of consolation.

Now, when we'd climbed a little, I and he, 52
    Above the angel, thus my guide began:
    "Still gazing on the ground? what aileth thee?"

"A strange, disturbing dream, I cannot ban 55
    From out my mind, has set me in a scare,"
    Said I, "and makes me only half a man."

"Saw'st thou that ancient witch, for whose sole snare 58
    The mount above us weeps? and how one deals
    With her," he answered, "and is rid of her?

61      Suffice it thee! spurn earth beneath thy heels;
           Look only to the lure the eternal King
           Whirls yonder with the great celestial wheels."

64      Like to a hawk, that sits with folded wing,
           Eyeing its feet, and at the call turns swift,
           Eager for food, wings spread to soar and swing,

67      Such I became; and so, right through the rift
           One climbs by, up to where the shelf runs round
           Once more, did I my cheerful flight uplift.

70      Emerging on the open ledge, I found,
           On the Fifth Cornice, people stretched out here
           Weeping, their faces turned towards the ground.

73      "*Adhaesit pavimento anima mea*"
           I heard, though such deep sighs clothed their laments
           That the faint words well-nigh escaped the ear.

76      "Spirits elect of God, whose punishments
           Both hope and justice help you to endure,
           Pray you, direct us toward the high ascents."

79      "If needing no prostration for your cure
           You come, and seek swift passage undeferred,
           Turn right-hand to the brink, and go secure."

82      Thus did the poet ask, and thus I heard,
           A little way ahead, the answer made,
           And grasped the implications of that word.

85      I looked towards my master, who conveyed
           At once, by a pleased gesture, his consent
           To the request my eager looks portrayed.

88      Then I, set free to follow my intent,
           Advanced to where I saw that being lie
           Whose words I'd marked, and over him I bent.

91      "Spirit, whose flowing tears mature," said I,
           "Man's only means to God, awhile repress
           Thy greater care; tell me thy name, and why

94      You're laid backs up, and whether, in that place
           From which, still loaded with their mortal bias,
           My feet have brought me, I can do thee grace."

"Why Heaven has turned our backs to Heaven, to lie as    97
    Up here we do, I'll tell," said he, "but first,
    *Quod ego Petri fui successor scias.*

'Twixt Chiaveri and Sestri drops dispersed    100
    A noble river; thence derives our blood,
    And thence its proudest title is rehearsed.

One month, scarce more, I learned how every load    103
    Is gossamer to the Great Mantle's weight
    Pressing on him who keeps it from the mud.

My change of heart, alas for me! was late;    106
    But when I stood upon ambition's crest
    Pastor of Rome, I learned how life can cheat.

I saw how there the heart can find no rest,    109
    And higher in that life no man could climb;
    So love for this life kindled in my breast.

A wretched soul was I until that time,    112
    Cut off from God, consumed with avarice;
    Here, as thou see'st, I'm punished for my crime.

What avarice works is known here as it is,    115
    In the purgation of the souls contrite;
    The mount has no more bitter pain than this.

For as our eyes would never seek the height,    118
    Being bent on earthly matters, earthward thus
    Justice here bends them in their own despite.

As love of all true good was quenched in us    121
    By avarice, and our works were left undone,
    So justice here doth hold us prisoners close,

Fettered and tied by hands and feet each one;    124
    And for so long as the just Lord shall please,
    Outstretched and motionless we must lie prone."

Here I, who'd promptly fallen on my knees,    127
    Started to speak; but my first word betrayed
    My reverent posture to those ears of his.

"What's bowed thee down like that?" said he. I said:    130
    "My standing upright wronged your dignity;
    I felt my conscience, as it were, upbraid."

133    "Brother, make straight thy knees," he answered me;
        "Rise up; err not; a fellow-servant I
        To one sole power, with others and with thee.

136    If e'er thou'st understood that holy and high
        Word of the Gospel, *Neque nubent*, thou
        Wilt well perceive wherefore I thus reply.

139    Now go; I am reluctant to allow
        Thy longer stay; thy presence keeps confined
        The tears which ripen what thou saidst just now.

142    I've one niece, named Alagia, left behind
        Yon side, who in herself is virtuous, save
        Our house's bad ways should corrupt her mind;

145    And over younder, she is all I have."

THE IMAGES. *Dante's Dream of the Siren*: This, the second of Dante's
dreams in Purgatory, is the subtlest and most difficult of the three.
It has often been imitated since his time, but never with his wealth
of implication.

Virgil (ll. 58–9) calls the *Siren* that "ancient witch" because of
whose beguilements the souls do penance in Upper Purgatory.
Obviously, she does not represent the "Secondary Goods" them-
selves, for whom love (in due measure) is right and proper. More-
over, she is at first sight unattractive; she only acquires strength and
beauty from Dante's own gaze. She is, therefore, the projection
upon the outer world of something in the mind: the soul, falling
in love with itself, perceives other people and things, not as they
are, but as wish-fulfilments of its own: i.e. its love for them is not
love for a "true other" (cf. xviii. 22–6 and note), but a devouring
egotistical fantasy, by absorption in which the personality rots
away into illusion. The Siren is, in fact, the "ancient witch" Lilith,
the fabled first wife of Adam, who was not a real woman of flesh
and blood, but a magical imago, begotten of Samael, the Evil One,
to be a fantasm of Adam's own desires. (According to Rabbinical
legend, God, seeing that "it was not good for man to be alone"
with himself in this fashion, created Eve to be his true other, and
to be loved and respected by him as a real person.) In later legend,
the magical fantasm of man's own desire is the demon-lover called
the *succubus* (or in the case of a woman, the *incubus*), intercourse
with which saps the strength and destroys the life.

*The Lady* who intervenes to thwart the Siren is not to be identified
with Beatrice, Lucy, or any other of the poem's *dramatis personae*.

It will be noticed that she acts more promptly than Virgil (reason); but she cannot herself unmask the Siren; she calls upon Virgil to do so. She symbolizes something immediate, instinctive, and almost automatic: one might call her an intuition, or perhaps the reflex action of a virtuous habit, whose instant warning puts the soul on the alert and prompts it to think rationally about what it is doing.

[Charles Williams's novel, *Descent into Hell*, is a brilliant expansion and interpretation of the theme of Dante's dream of the Siren. Those who do not care for commentary in the form of fiction may find illumination in a phrase of Fr Gerald Vann's: "If you exalt the objects of your love until your picture is a false one; if you idealize them; *if you project upon them your own ideal self*; then you are loving not a real person but a dream" (*The Seven Swords* – italics mine).]

*The Penance of the Covetous: Binding in fetters face downwards*: Covetousness (*Avaritia*) is the inordinate love of wealth, and the power that wealth gives, whether it is manifested by miserly hoarding or by lavish spending. It is a peculiarly earth-bound sin, looking to nothing beyond the rewards of this life (cf. Bunyan's "man with the muck-rake"); it is expiated here by the endurance of its effects; the souls are so fettered that they can see nothing but the earth on which they once set store.

*Pope Adrian* is the image of Covetousness in the form of Ambition – the concentration upon worldly place and power – an ambition no less earth-bound for being centred upon ecclesiastical preferment.

NOTES. ll. 2–3: *the chill moon's influence ... or sometimes Saturn's power*: The Moon (no doubt because of her heatless light) and Saturn (on account of his distance from the Sun) were from ancient times regarded as cold planets, both in themselves and in their influence. Virgil (*Georg.* i. 336) calls Saturn "*frigida stella*", and Dante (*Canz.* Io son venuto) "the planet that strengthens the cold". *Sometimes*: Dante is here careful not to suggest that Saturn is exerting his influence at the time he is describing, for Saturn is in Leo (*Para.* xxi. 14), and will only rise two signs after the Sun.

l. 5: *their Greater Fortune*: the *Fortuna Major* of the Geomancers, who predicted the future from the random dispositions of points on the earth, paper, or elsewhere (as certain of their successors from the random disposition of tea-leaves), was a group of stars in the last degrees of *Aquarius* (the Water-Carrier) and the first of *Pisces* (the Fishes), forming the figure ‡ ‡ ‡ * *. The time is therefore some two hours before dawn (about 4 A.M.).

The mention here of the forbidden art of divination has its sinister appropriateness as an introduction to the dream of the "ancient witch".

ll. 7–33: *in dream a woman sought me*: See Images.

l. 22: *I turned Ulysses*: in the *Odyssey* (which Dante had not read, knowing no Greek) Ulysses stops his ears with wax and so escapes the lure of the Sirens. Moore suggests that the source here may be Cicero, *De Finibus*, v. 18.

l. 35: *"three times"*, *said he*, *"I've called thee"*: Dante's dream-psychology is excellent as usual: the voice of Virgil introduces the speaker as a character into the dream and, at the same time, breaks the dream and wakes the sleeper.

ll. 37–9: *broad day ... smote plumb*: the sun has risen due east, and the poets continue their journey due west.

l. 46: *he who thus spake*: this is the Angel of Zeal, guardian of the Fourth Cornice. The wide sweep of his wings indicates his celerity in doing his task.

l. 49: *fanned us*: here the fourth P is erased from Dante's forehead.

l. 50: *qui lugent*: this is the Benediction of the Fourth Cornice, from the Beatitude: *Benedicti qui lugent, quoniam ipsi consolabuntur*: "blessed are they that mourn, for they shall be comforted" (*Matt.* v. 5). The benediction refers, not merely to the "healing tears" of the penitents, but to the fact that depression of spirits accompanies the sin of Accidie (see Images to Canto xviii) and has now been purged away.

ll. 58–9: *that ancient witch*, etc.: See Images.

ll. 62–3: *look only to the lure*: God is compared to a falconer, whirling his lure to recall the hawk to the fist. The following terzain carries on the simile of the hawk.

l. 71: *the Fifth Cornice*: here the sin of Covetousness is purged.

l. 73: *adhaesit pavimento anima mea*: "my soul cleaveth to the dust": This is the Prayer of the Covetous, taken from *Ps.* cxix. 25 (*Vulg.* cxviii. 25).

ll. 79–80: *needing no prostration*, etc.: the speaker (who, being face downwards, cannot see the questioner) takes Dante and Virgil to be spirits in Purgatory.

l. 84: *the implications*: Dante grasps that (as we see later) any soul that has already (in life) made full satisfaction, both as to guilt and stain, for the sin purged on any particular Cornice, is not detained on that Cornice, but passes straight on to the next.

l. 89: *that being*: this is the spirit of Pope Adrian V (Ottobuono dei Fieschi); elected Pope July 1276; died in August of the same year (l. 103). He was papal legate to England in 1268.

l. 99: *Quod ego Petri fui successor scias*: "Thou must know that I was the successor of Peter": i.e. that I was Pope. Adrian uses Latin as the official language of the Church.

l. 100: *'twixt Chiaveri and Sestri*: the Fieschi, who were Counts of Lavagne, derived their title from a little river of that name, which enters the Gulf of Genoa between these two towns.

l. 104: *the Great Mantle*: i.e. of the Pope.

l. 134: *a fellow-servant I*: cf. *Rev.* xxii. 9.

l. 137: *Neque nubent* = "They neither marry [nor are given in marriage"] (*Matt.* xxii. 23–30; *Mark* xii. 18–25; *Luke* xx. 27–35): Every bishop, including the Pope, is ceremonially wedded to his see (which is why he wears a ring and changes his name to that of his diocese). But this marriage, like any earthly marriage, is dissolved in Heaven, together with all legal and official ties and all earthly rank and privilege (cf. v. 88 and note). This holds good, despite the sacramental nature of the ties of marriage, orders, and unction: for in Heaven there is no longer any need of sacraments.

l. 142: *Alagia*: she was the wife of Moroello Malaspina II (see Canto vii. 118, note).

# CANTO XX

THE STORY. *As they pass along the Fifth Cornice, the Poets hear the spirit of Hugh Capet proclaiming the Whip of Covetousness. Hugh utters a great lamentation over the crimes of the Capetian House and recites to Dante the examples of the Bridle. Proceeding on their way, the travellers are startled by feeling the whole Mountain shake from top to bottom, while all the prostrate penitents join in a great shout of* Gloria in excelsis Deo. *Dante is consumed with curiosity.*

       Ill fares the will that fights a better will;
          So, to content him, I, though discontent,
          Withdrew the sponge ere it had drunk its fill.

4    I moved; my guide moved too, and on he went
          Where space allowed, hugging the rock, like him
          Who, on a rampart, hugs the battlement;

7    For those who, drop by drop from eyes a-brim,
          Distil the drug that sets the whole world raving,
          Lie, on the outer side, too near the rim.

10   Cursèd be thou, thou ancient wolf, that having
          More victims than all other beasts of prey,
          Canst find no bottom to thine endless craving!

13   O Heaven, whose circling motions, some folk say,
          Govern the fortunes of this world below,
          When shall he come who'll hunt the brute away?

16   Thus we proceeded with few steps and slow,
          Nor could I give my mind to anything
          Except those shades who wept and sorrowed so.

19   Then, just ahead, by hap I heard one fling
          A cry out: "Ah, sweet Mary!" – such a moan
          As of a woman in her travailing.

22   "How poor thou wast we know," the voice went on,
          "Seeing to what hostel thou didst bring thy precious
          And blissful burden, there to lay it down."

And after that I heard: "O good Fabricius!       25
   Thou didst prefer to live thy whole life long
   Virtuous and poor, rather than rich and vicious!"

These words so pleased me that I sped along,      28
   Eager to make acquaintance with the shade
   Who, as it seemed to me, had given them tongue;

While he, continuing, praised the bounty paid     31
   To the poor girls by Nicholas, whereby
   To lead to honour their young maidenhead.

"Spirit that speakest such good things," said I,     34
   "Tell me, who wast thou, and why none with thee
   Reiterate lifts these noble lauds on high.

Not without recompense thy words shall be,     37
   If I return to walk the dwindling ways
   Of life that fleets to death so rapidly."

And he: "I'll tell thee – not as toward yon place   40
   Looking for succour, but as to salute
   One, not yet dead, in whom shines such great grace.

Of that malignant tree was I the root     43
   Whose shade so blights all Christian lands that small
   Their harvest is of any wholesome fruit;

But if Douay, Lille, Ghent, and Bruges could call  46
   Power enough up, vengeance should smite it – yea,
   I pray it may, to Him that judgeth all.

On yonder side they called me Hugh Capet;    49
   Of me those Philips and those Lewises
   Were born, that have ruled France this many a day.

A Paris butcher sired me. When the lease     52
   Of all the ancient kings ran out, except
   For one, who'd donned the habit of grey frieze,

I found I held within my hand fast-gripped     55
   The reins that sway the realm, and was at once
   So strong in new possessions, so equipped

With friends, that to the widowed crown my son's  58
   Head was promoted; and from him first came
   The dynasty of their anointed bones.

61     So long as till from every sense of shame
        The great dower of Provence had set them free,
        My race, though not worth much, earned little blame;

64     Then they began their course of robbery
        By force and fraud; and next, to make amends,
        Seized Normandy, Ponthieu, and Gascony.

67     Charles came to Italy; to make amends
        He slaughtered Conradin; and after this
        Packed Thomas off to Heaven, to make amends.

70     I see the day, and not long hence it is,
        Another Charles shall out of France appear
        To give the world more news of him and his.

73     Alone he comes, unarmed but for the spear
        That Judas jousted with, and smites it clean
        Through Florence, till the guts burst out of her.

76     No land he'll get of it, but shame and sin –
        Ay, and for him the evil's the more grave
        That he can work such harm and care no pin.

79     Another, once shipped captive o'er the wave,
        I see sell his own daughter, haggling, too,
        Like any corsair with a woman-slave.

82     What more to us, O Avarice, canst thou do,
        Having so thralled our blood that it's mislaid
        Even the kindness to its own flesh due?

85     To put crimes past and future in the shade,
        I see the Lily storm Alagna's paling,
        And in Christ's Vicar, Christ a captive made.

88     I see once more the mockery and the railing,
        I see renewed the vinegar and gall,
        'Twixt two live thieves I see his deadly nailing,

91     See the new Pilate so tyrannical
        That, all unchartered and insatiate still,
        He flaunts his plundering sails into Temple and all.

94     When shall I thrill, my God, when shall I thrill
        To see the vengeance that, unseen, makes sweet
        Thy wrath, within the secret of Thy will?

What of the sole Bride of the Paraclete    97
    I said but now – the cry which turned thy course
    Hither to me, to seek a gloss on it –

That's the response to every prayer of ours    100
    While daylight lasts, but when night's curtains fold,
    We use instead a contrary discourse;

Then we proclaim Pygmalion, that of old    103
    Turned traitor, thief, and parricide, possessed
    Wholly by his insatiate lust for gold;

Then avaricious Midas, whose request    106
    Brought by its greed a retribution grim,
    Fitly provides us with an endless jest;

Next, Achan's frenzy is our common theme,    109
    Who stole the spoils; when here we tell the news
    Joshua's wrath seems still to bite at him;

Sapphira and her spouse we then accuse,    112
    And praise the hoofs that battered Heliodorus,
    And all around the mountain rings abuse

Of Polymnestor murdering Polydorus;    115
    And lastly: 'Tell us, Crassus – thou dost know –
    What is the taste of gold?' we cry in chorus.

One will at times cry loud, another low,    118
    For as the impulse moves us, shrill or soft
    To make our utterance, we rehearse it so;

Nor was I lonely in that praise we waft    121
    By daylight; but just then no urge was driving
    Any one near to raise his voice aloft."

We had already left him, and were striving    124
    To pick our arduous way along the rock
    As best we might with all our powers' contriving,

When sudden I felt the whole mount shake with shock,    127
    Like as to fall, and chillness gripped me, even
    As it grips one who's going to the block.

No more stupendous thrust, for sure, was given    130
    To Delos, ere Latona nested there
    For to give birth to the twin eyes of heaven.

133    Then all around a shout went through the air,
         Such that my master drew him to my side
         And said, "Fear nothing; thou art in my care."

136    "*Gloria in excelsis*," far and wide –
         As I perceived by hearing those near me –
         All "*in excelsis Deo!*" called and cried.

139    Quite motionless and stupefied stood we,
         Just like the shepherds who first heard that strain,
         Till the strain closed and earthquake ceased to be.

142    Then we took up our holy way again,
         Our eyes upon the prostrate shades, returning
         Already to their wonted sad refrain.

145    Never with such a frantic lust for learning
         Did any ignorance in my life assail me
         As now, perpending mysteries past discerning –

148    Never in my life, if memory does not fail me.
         I dared not waste time asking what this meant,
         And my own eyes saw nothing there to tell me,

151    So I trudged on, perplexed and diffident.

THE IMAGES. *Hugh Capet*: after the lust of spiritual power, the lust
   of temporal power: Pope and Emperor are alike victims of the
   "ancient wolf". Worldly ambition is accompanied by a more
   literal covetousness for wealth and possessions, with the inevitable
   manifestations of cruelty, callousness, and meanness, as exempli-
   fied in the history of the House of Capet.

NOTES. l. 10: *thou ancient wolf*: avarice (cf. *Inf.* i. 94–111 and Images
*Inf.* vii. 8; and note to *Inf.* vi. 115).
   l. 15: *when shall he come*: i.e. the "Greyhound" (cf. *Inf.* i. 101 *sqq.* and
Images).
   ll. 20–33: "*Ah, sweet Mary!*" etc.: the spirits themselves cry out the
"Whip" of the Covetous – examples of holy poverty and generosity.
The first exemplar is, as always, the Blessed Virgin (ll. 19–24), with
reference to the birth of Our Lord in the humble inn at Bethlehem.
The second, from classical history, is Caius Fabricius, Roman Consul
(282 B.C.) and Censor (275), who refused bribes when negotiating
with the Samnites and with Pyrrhus, King of Epirus. He is mentioned
by Virgil (*Aen.* vi. 844) as a man "great with little means", and by
Lucan (*Phars.* x. 151) as an example of simplicity of life. The third,

from Christian history, is Nicholas, the fourth-century Bishop of Myra in Lycia (better known to many of us as "Santa Claus"). In order to save the three daughters of a poverty-stricken neighbour from having to go on the streets for their livelihood, he secretly threw into their window at night bags of gold, as dowries to enable them to marry respectably. (Hence his connexion with the nocturnal filling of stockings; his sledge and reindeer are the adventitious results of his being the patron saint of Russia; and the popular form of the name "Claus" comes from America by way of the old Dutch settlers who kept a holiday on his feast-day, 6 December).

l. 43: *of that malignant tree was I the root*: The speaker is Hugh Capet (l. 49), founder of the Capetian dynasty of the kings of France, which, by alliance, inheritance, or conquest, exercised a dominating influence throughout Europe for some two and a half centuries. Many of Dante's most virulent hatreds attach to members of this family, though one of them (Charles Martel) was his personal friend, and is placed by him in the Heaven of Venus (*Para.* viii. 31 *sqq.*).

l. 46: *Douai, Lille, Ghent, and Bruges*: the four chief cities of Flanders. The allusion is to the Flemish wars of Philip the Fair, and in particular to the treachery of Charles of Valois in 1299, when, having by a promise of liberal terms and honourable treatment of his person induced Count Guy of Flanders to surrender Ghent, he subjected Flanders to all the indignities of a conquered country, and sent the Count and his sons as prisoners to Paris, "the which", says Villani (*Chron.* viii. 32), "was held throughout the universal world as a great disloyalty to so noble a gentleman." The looked-for vengeance (ll. 47–8) was executed in 1302, when – the Flemings having made a great rally under Pierre König and Jean Beide – the French were beaten at the Battle of Courtrai, losing 6000 horse, including the Constable of France and the flower of their chivalry.

l. 49: *Hugh Capet*: This is certainly Hugh Capet the Great, Duke of France, Burgundy, and Acquitaine, and Count of Paris and Orléans (*d.* 956), and not his son Hugh Capet, King of France 987–96; but Dante has so "telescoped" dates and events as to appear to have confused the two. The Carolingian line did not in fact dwindle away to one representative in Duke Hugh's time – nor even in that of his son. When Louis IV died in 954, he was succeeded by his 14-year-old son, Lothair, who was, however, king only in name, the reins of government being actually held by the powerful Duke Hugh (ll. 55–7), and, after the latter's death in 956, by Hugh Capet the Younger. In 986 Lothair was succeeded by his son Louis V, surnamed *le Fainéant* (Do-nothing), who died fifteen months later without issue. With him, the direct Carolingian line came to an end; there remained his uncle, Charles of Lorraine, who was so highly unpopular that Hugh Capet the Younger was able to secure his own election to the throne, and was consecrated in 987, thus becoming founder of the "dynasty of their [the Capets'] anointed bones" (l. 60). Charles of Lorraine spent the rest of his days as King Hugh's prisoner, and, after an attempt by his son Otto to claim the crown, his branch of the family fled to Germany and extinguished itself in obscurity at the beginning of the eleventh century.

l. 50: *those Philips and those Lewises*: From 1060 to 1322, when the Capetian line became extinct with Philip V, every king of France was called either Philip or Louis.

l. 52: *a Paris butcher sired me*: Hugh Capet the Elder derived in fact from the noble line of the Counts of Paris, but legends accumulated about his name. He was said to be descended (*a*) from St Arnoul; (*b*) from Charlemagne; (*c*) from a butcher or other plebeian stock. This last was the popular tradition, widely current in Italy in Dante's time.

l. 54: *one who'd donned the habit*: This is the fundamental error which has given rise to all the confusion. No member of the Carolingian royal house took the habit; Dante is probably mixing up the Carolingians with the Merovingians, whose last member, Chilperic III, did become a monk after his deposition in 752. Or he may have been following (regardless of chronology) a legend which had popularly attached itself to Charles of Lorraine (Godfrey of Viterbo, *Memoria Saeculorum*, xii–xiii).

l. 62: *the great dower of Provence*: the wealth brought to the House of Capet through the marriages of Louis IX (St Louis) and his brother Charles of Anjou respectively with Margaret and Beatrice, the two daughters of Raymond Bérenger, Count of Provence (cf. *Purg.* vii. 124–9 and note).

l. 66: *Normandy, Ponthieu, and Gascony*: Normandy had actually been taken from King John of England in 1202, but the title remained in dispute. In 1259, by a treaty with Louis IX, Henry III renounced his claims to Normandy, Anjou, Touraine, and Poitou, and did homage for Acquitaine, in return for the recognition of his rights in Périgord, Limousin, and other provinces. Gascony was ceded by Edward I to Philip the Fair in 1295, but (it was claimed) only as a formality, his rights being secured by a secret clause which was later repudiated.

l. 67: *Charles came to Italy*: this was the expedition of Charles I of Anjou (son of Louis VIII) against Manfred (cf. Canto ii. 112 and note), which culminated in the Battle of Benevento (1266); later, in 1268, Charles defeated Conradin at Tagliacozzo (cf. *Inf.* xxviii. 17 and note) and had him beheaded. (See Glossary.)

l. 69: *packed Thomas off to heaven*: according to a popular legend, St Thomas Aquinas was poisoned by the orders of Charles of Anjou while on his way to the Council of Lyons in 1274. There is no reason to believe that his death was not in fact perfectly natural.

l. 69: *to make amends (per ammenda)*: this ironic phrase is given savage emphasis by its repetition at each rhyme of the terzain. Some MSS. and editors, however, read *per vicenda* ("for a change") at the end of l. 67.

ll. 71–5: *another Charles*, etc.: Charles of Valois, brother of Philip the Fair. His "peace-making" intervention in Florence (1301) delivered the city over to the Black party, and brought about the expulsion of all the Whites, including Dante himself (see *Inf.* Introduction, pp. 34–6). *No land he'll get of it* – an allusion to his nickname "Lackland" (*Sansterre*).

l. 73: *the spear that Judas jousted with*: i.e. treachery.

l. 79: *another [Charles]*: this is Charles II of Anjou ("the Lame"), son of Charles I, and father of Dante's friend Charles Martel. He was taken prisoner by the Spanish Admiral in a naval action against Pedro of Aragon (1284). He accepted a large sum of money from the elderly and disreputable Azzo d'Este as payment for his daughter's hand in marriage.

ll. 86–90: *I see the Lily*, etc.: In 1303 the long struggle between Pope Boniface VIII and Philip the Fair ("the Lily" of France) terminated in a notorious scandal and tragedy. Philip, who found the Papal claims thwarting to his own ambitions, had demanded a general council to examine charges of heresy and profligacy against Boniface; the Pope retorted by excommunicating Philip and releasing his subjects from their allegiance. On the eve of the publication of the Bull of Excommunication in the Cathedral of Alagna (now Anagni) where Boniface was residing, Sciarra di Colonna – whose family had many grievances to avenge – aided by William de Nogaret, the emissary of the King of France, broke in upon the Pope, laid violent hands upon him, and held him prisoner for three days, sacking his palace, and subjecting him to many indignities. The old man (he was then about 86) was eventually rescued by the people of Alagna, but died at Rome within a month, of shock and mortification.

Nothing in Dante is more paradoxical or more magnificent than his treatment of Boniface VIII. Of all his enemies, personal and political, none is so hateful to him as Boniface. Yet, stained with simony, with murder, with treason, with the rape and robbery of the Church and the ruin of the Empire, his see usurped, so that it now stands "vacant in God's Son's sight" (*Para.* xxvii. 23–4); the tomb of Peter made by his means a sewer of filth and blood, a scandal to all Heaven, and a delight to the Great Apostate (*ibid.*), nevertheless, Christ's Vicar is Christ's Vicar still, identified with Him in the sacrament of his anointing; and to lay hand on him is to crucify Christ afresh. This balance of two equal and opposed indignations, both blazing, and mutually unmitigated, is a triumph of the passionate intellect unsurpassed in literature and scarcely paralleled.

ll. 88–90: *I see once more ... I see*, etc.: The distinction between the man and his function which lies at the base of all Dante's ambivalences (see *Inf.* xxxiv. Images: *Judas, Brutus, and Cassius*), is here not quite clear-cut. This terzain, with its repeated "I saw ... I saw ..." echoes verses written by Boniface himself upon the Blessed Virgin standing at the foot of the cross and seeing the sufferings of her Son, and the "vinegar mingled with gall". It is Dante's tribute to the personal qualities of his enemy. And indeed the old man met his persecutors with great courage and dignity. "Seeing himself abandoned by all his cardinals ... even by most of his own household, he ... said valiantly: 'Since like Jesus Christ I am to be taken by treachery and needs must die, at least I will die as Pope.' And immediately he caused himself to be arrayed in the mantle of St Peter, with the crown of Constantine on his head, and the Keys in his hand, and set himself in the Papal Chair." (Villani, *Chron.* viii. 63.)

l. 90: *two live thieves*: Colonna and Nogaret, "living robbers", as contrasted with the dying robbers between whom Christ was nailed.

l. 91: *the new Pilate*: Philip the Fair.

l. 93: *into Temple and all*: The rich and powerful order of the Knights Templars was suppressed in 1312 by Pope Clement V at Philip's instigation. The pretext was an accusation of heresy, which may or may not have been founded on fact.

l. 95: *the vengeance that makes sweet Thy wrath*: God's wrath, being pure of fear or passion or impatience, is without the haste, bitterness, and violence which we associate with human anger.

l. 97: *the sole Bride of the Paraclete*: the Blessed Virgin (*Luke* i. 35). Hugh, having answered the first part of Dante's question ("who wast thou?"), now proceeds to the second (ll. 35-6) showing in what manner the penitents of the Fifth Cornice pursue their allotted Meditation.

ll. 103-17: *then we proclaim*: Having explained that the Whip is recited by day, Hugh now enumerates the examples composing the Bridle. The first, taken from the *Aeneid* (i. 350 *sqq.*), is Dido's brother Pygmalion, who for love of gold murdered her husband Sichaeus before the very altar of the gods. The second, from classical Mythology, is Midas, king of Phrygia, who, being granted one wish by Bacchus, whom he had obliged, avariciously desired that everything he touched might be turned to gold. Finding that as a result all his food became uneatable, he was obliged to ask to have the gift taken away again (Ovid, *Metam.* xi. 100 *sqq.*). The third, from the O.T., is Achan. At the capture of Jericho, Joshua ordered all the captured treasure to be consecrated to the Lord; but Achan seized part of it for himself, and he and his family were stoned to death by Joshua's orders and their bodies burned (*Josh.* vi. and vii). The fourth, from the N.T., is Ananias and his wife Sapphira, who, when the first Christian converts had all their possessions in common, sold some property for the use of the community, but brought the Apostles only part of the price, saying that it was the whole. Peter rebuked them for this gratuitous hypocrisy, and they fell dead at his feet. (*Acts* iv. 32–7, v. 1–11.) The fifth, from the O.T. Apocrypha, is Heliodorus, chancellor to King Seleucus, who went in arms to rob the Temple treasury at Jerusalem so that the king might get the money. But "the Sovereign of spirits and of all authority caused a great apparition ... a horse with a terrible rider upon him and adorned with beautiful trappings, and he ran fiercely and smote at Heliodorus with his forefeet, and it seemed that he that sat upon the horse had complete harness of gold" (2 *Macc.* iii. 1–40). The sixth, from the *Aeneid* (iii. 49 *sqq.*) is Polymnestor, King of Thrace, to whom Priam of Troy had entrusted a great reserve of gold by the hands of his son Polydorus. When Troy fell, Polymnestor killed Polydorus and took the gold for himself (cf. *Inf.* xxx. 13–21). The seventh, from classical history, is Marcus Licinius Crassus, surnamed "the Rich", triumvir with Caesar and Pompey, 60 B.C. He was killed in battle against the Parthians, whose king, Hyrodes, knowing his notorious cupidity, had molten gold poured down his throat.

l. 131: *Delos, ere Latona nested there*: Delos, in the Greek Archipelago, was originally a floating island; but when Latona came to it, fleeing from the jealousy of Juno, Jupiter made it fast; and there Latona gave birth to the divine twins Apollo and Diana.

ll. 136–8: *Gloria in excelsis ... Deo*: "Glory to God in the highest": the angels' hymn when announcing the birth of Christ to the shepherds. (*Luke* ii. 8–14.)

# CANTO XXI

THE STORY. *While passing along the Fifth Cornice, Dante and Virgil
are overtaken by the shade of the poet Statius, who tells them that the
shouts and the shaking of the Mountain celebrate the release of a soul from
Purgatory, and explains how that release is effected. It is he himself who
has just risen up from over 500 years of prostration among the Covetous.
In answer to Virgil's question, he names himself, saying how much he
wishes he could have seen the author of the Aeneid, to whose example his
own poetry owes so much. Despite Virgil's warning, Dante betrays him-
self by an irrepressible smile and, on being desired to explain this apparent
breach of good manners, has to admit that his companion is Virgil himself.
Only Virgil's own earnest dissuasions prevent Statius from falling at his
feet.*

    The natural thirst which nothing quenches, bar
        That water which was begged, a bounty free,
        By the poor woman of Samaria,

4    Distressed me still, while haste was urging me
        Behind my guide along the cluttered way,
        Where the just vengeance moved my sympathy;

7    When lo, now! like the tale in Luke – how they,
        Those two wayfaring men, saw Christ appear,
        New-risen from the rocky tomb that day –

10    A shade appeared to us, who from the rear
        O'ertook us, while, with eyes downcast to view
        The prostrate throngs, we knew not he was near

13    Till he spoke first: "God give His peace to you,
        My brothers!" Then we turned as quick as thought,
        And, having made the countersign thereto,

16    Virgil began: "So may that one true court
        Which has doomed me to exile without ending
        Bring thee in peace where all the blest consort –"

19    "How now!" said he – we pressed on notwithstanding –
        "If you are souls shut out from God's high grace,
        Who brought you by His stair thus far ascending?"

To whom my Doctor: "Look on this man's face,    22
  Which bears the marks the angel set therein,
  And know him bound to reign in that good place.

But because she who night and day doth spin    25
  Hath not for him spun all the flax to twine
  Which Clotho loads and binds for each man's skein,

His soul, which is our sister, thine and mine,    28
  Could not come up this mountain path alone,
  Not having eyes which see like mine and thine;

Therefore from Hell's wide throat was I withdrawn    31
  To be his showman, and – so far, that is,
  As my school goes – I'll show and guide him on.

But tell us, if thou canst, why, just ere this,    34
  The mount so quaked, and rang, as 'twere one cry,
  Down to its marshy base with jubilees."

Thus did his question thread the needle's eye    37
  Of my desire, and hope to be fed full
  Sufficed at once to make my thirst less dry.

The shade replied: "This mountain's holy rule    40
  Admits no breach of order; nothing strange
  Troubles or makes its custom mutable;

These slopes are free from every natural change;    43
  What of its own Heaven for its own doth take,
  Nought else, can act as cause within their range.

Wherefore nor rain nor hail nor snowy flake    46
  No frost nor dew falls higher than that spot
  Where the three steps their little stairway make;

Clouds dense or rare, the flashing thunder-shot,    49
  And Thaumas' daughter, yonder side so fleet
  To shift her lodging, this place knows them not.

No dry and gusty vapours can o'erbeat    52
  The top step of the three I've spoken of,
  The step where Peter's vicar sets his feet.

Below that point the hill belike may move    55
  Little or much, but winds pent underground –
  I know not how – shake nothing here above;

58    But when some spirit, feeling purged and sound,
        Leaps up or moves to seek a loftier station,
        The whole mount quakes and the great shouts resound.

61    The will itself attests its own purgation;
        Amazed, the soul that's free to change its inn
        Finds its mere will suffice for liberation;

64    True, it wills always, but can nothing win
        So long as heavenly justice keeps desire
        Set toward the pain as once 'twas toward the sin;

67    Thus I, who've languished in this torment dire
        Five hundred years and more, felt only now
        The enfranchised will urge me to thresholds higher;

70    Then didst thou feel the shock, then heardest how –
        God send them happy – the kind souls to speed me
        Gave praise from mountain-foot to mountain-brow."

73    Thus said the shade; and since, as you'll concede me,
        There's nought so fine as drinking when you're dry,
        I cannot tell you how much good he did me.

76    "Ah! now I see," my wise guide made reply,
        "The net that holds you here, and how 'tis broken,
        Why the mount quakes, and why your joint glad cry.

79    Next, I beseech thee, let a word be spoken
        Of who thou wast; and fain would I be told
        What all those centuries of tears betoken."

82    "When the good Titus was avenging bold –
        Having the High King's aid to reckon on –
        The wounds whence gushed the blood that Judas sold,

85    I, with that title honour waits upon
        Longest and best, lived yonder," said the spirit;
        "Great fame had I, but faith as yet had none.

88    So sweet a gift of song did I inherit
        That from Toulouse Rome called me 'neath her sway,
        And crowned my brows with myrtle for my merit.

91    Statius men call me yonder to this day;
        I sang of Thebes and great Achilles' fame,
        But with that second load fell by the way.

The sparks that lit the music in me came          94
   From that great fire divine whence many another,
   Thousand by thousand, fetched their light and flame;

I mean the *Aeneid*, which to me was mother,          97
   To me was nurse of song; if plucked asunder
   From that rich fount, I'd ne'er have weighed a feather.

And to have had the joy of living yonder          100
   When Virgil lived, I'd lie a whole sun more
   Beyond my term, in exile and face under."

These words turned Virgil's face to me, which wore          103
   A look that silent said: "Be silent still,"
   But will with us is not made one with power;

Tears, laughter, tread so hard upon the heel          106
   Of their evoking passions, that in those
   Who're most sincere they least obey the will.

I did but smile – a hint beneath the rose          109
   As 'twere. The shade cut short what he was saying,
   And looked me in the eyes, where truth most shows.

"Tell me," said he, "so may a glad repaying          112
   Crown thy long toil, why, as I spoke to you,
   That flickering smile across thy lips went playing."

So now I'm fairly caught between the two;          115
   One signals silence, one entreats me speak;
   I heave a sigh – what else is there to do?

And to interpret me my guide is quick:          118
   "Don't be afraid to say – say on," said he,
   "Give to his anxious doubts the clue they seek."

Then I: "Thou wonderest at my smile, maybe,          121
   Spirit of old; but now I want to bring
   A greater wonder yet to seize on thee.

He who gives eyes to me for journeying          124
   Stands here, and he is Virgil, whose high theme
   Put power in thee of men and gods to sing.

If other cause for laughter thou didst deem          127
   I had, 'tis false – dismiss it; nothing weighed
   With me, except those words thou saidst of him."

130        Already stooping to my lord, he made
               To kiss his feet; but: "Brother, do not so,
               For shade thou art and look'st upon a shade."

133        Thus he; and the other, rising: "Now thou'lt know
               How large and warm my love about thee clings,
               When I forget our nothingness, and go

136        Treating these shadows like material things."

THE IMAGES. *Statius*: Publius Papinius Statius (*c.* A.D. 45–96) was the author of the *Thebaid* (an epic on the history of Eteocles and Polynices – v. *Inf.* xxvi. 54 and note) and part of an *Achilleid*, together with a volume (the *Silvae*) of occasional poems, the libretto of a pantomime, the *Agave* (now lost, but mentioned by Juvenal), and a poem on the German wars of Domitian (also lost).

Dante's evident admiration for this poet of the "Silver Age" was a standing puzzle to the older and severer school of classical criticism, but modern scholarship tends to take a more favourable view (see *Oxf. Class. Dict.*, art. *Statius*), and his poems were highly popular both in the Middle Ages and in his own day. C. S. Lewis (*Allegory of Love*, pp. 49–56) finds in his work the first beginnings of allegory as a literary form, and this may help to account for Dante's interest in him.

The significance of Statius in the imagery of the *Comedy* has been much disputed; but it seems likely that Dante wished to show the soul as being accompanied and helped on its journey, not only by Old Rome (natural Humanism) but also by the New (Christian) Rome (redeemed Humanism). The story of Statius's conversion, if it does not derive from ecclesiastical legend, may have been invented by Dante for this purpose.

NOTES. l. 3: *the poor woman of Samaria*: See John iv. 15.

l. 6: *the just vengeance (la giusta vendetta)*: i.e. the divine retribution for sin. This is Dante's first use of this famous phrase, which is given a profounder significance in *Para.* vi. 88–93 and vii. 20 *sqq.*

l. 7: *the tale in Luke*: Luke xxiv. 13 *sqq.*

l. 15: *the countersign thereto*: i.e. the ritual response. The shade greets them with "*Pax vobiscum* – peace be unto you," and Virgil replies – "*Et cum spiritu tuo* – and with thy spirit."

l. 25: *she who night and day doth spin*: Lachesis, the Fate who spins the thread of every man's destiny, which Clotho has arranged upon the distaff, and which is cut at death by the shears of Atropos.

l. 30: *not having eyes*, etc.: another of the poet's indications that the Three Kingdoms of Death are not located in the world of sense. Virgil is Dante's "contact", by whom he is able to perceive what takes place in the world of spirits.

l. 44: *what of its own Heaven for its own doth take*: i.e. the human soul, which belongs to the supernatural order. Changes in the *natural* order (l. 43) do not affect the Mountain above Peter's Gate, the point at which it emerges from the Earth's atmosphere (ll. 46 *sqq.*).

l. 50: *Thaumas' daughter*: Iris, the rainbow. Thaumas was the son of Pontus (the Sea) and Ge (the Earth), and father by the Ocean-nymph Electra of Iris and the Harpies.

l. 61: *the will itself*, etc.: (See *Purgatory: the Doctrine*, p. 58.)

l. 82: *the good Titus*: Roman Emperor A.D. 79–81. The son of Vespasian, he served under his father in the Jewish wars, and in 70 besieged and captured Jerusalem, thus avenging upon the Jews the death of Christ (l. 84). During his brief reign he was immensely popular for his generosity and clemency; Suetonius calls him "the darling of the human race".

l. 85: *that title*, etc.: the title of poet.

l. 89: *from Toulouse*: Dante follows a common error of his period in confusing the poet P. Papinius Statius, who was born at Naples, with the rhetorician Lucius Statius, who was born at Toulouse *c.* A.D. 58. He is correct in saying that the greater part of Statius's life was passed in Rome, where he enjoyed the protection of Domitian, to whom his father had been tutor.

l. 91: *Statius*: See Images; *yonder*: in the N. hemisphere.

l. 93: *fell by the way*: the *Achilleid* was left unfinished at Statius's death.

l. 131: *Brother, do not so*: Cf. Canto xix. 127 *sqq.* Virgil, who had allowed Sordello to do him honour (vii. 13–15), appears to have profited by Pope Adrian's instruction to Dante.

# CANTO XXII

THE STORY. *The three Poets ascend by the Pass of Pardon, where the Angel of Liberality pronounces the Benediction of the Fifth Cornice and erases the P of Covetousness from Dante's forehead. Statius explains that he has been doing penance, not for Avarice, but for Prodigality, and that opposing sins are purged together on the same Cornice. He tells how a study of Virgil's writings led him to become a Christian, though secretly, for fear of persecution, and how his cowardice has had to be expiated by a long detention on the Cornice of Sloth. After Virgil has given him news of various Greeks and Romans now dwelling in Limbo, they reach the top of the stair and turn right-handed along the Sixth Cornice. Presently they come to a tall Fruit-tree, watered by a sparkling Cascade. A voice from the braches forbids the eating of the Fruit, and rehearses the examples of Temperance which constitute the Whip of Gluttony.*

> By now the angel was behind us – he
>    Who toward the sixth of the round cornices
>    Had turned us, and brushed one more scar from me,
>
> 4   Pronouncing those who crave for righteousness
>    *Beati*; and with *sitiunt* and no more
>    To end the phrase, his words accomplished this.
>
> 7   And lighter-footed than I'd felt before
>    At any pass, following with ease complete
>    Those two swift spirits, on and up I bore.
>
> 10   Virgil meanwhile began: "The love that's lit
>    By virtue must, when once its flame is shown,
>    Kindle a love reciprocal to it;
>
> 13   So, since the day when Juvenal came down
>    To join us in Hell's Limbo there, and brought
>    News of thy love for me, and made it known,
>
> 16   I've felt goodwill for thee of such a sort
>    As ne'er to one unseen held heart enchained,
>    So that this stair will now seem all too short.
>
> 19   But say – and if I run on two slack-reined
>    Through over-boldness, then in friendly wise
>    Forgive me, and speak now as friend to friend –

How could thy heart find room for covetise,                    22
   When thou hadst filled it with such treasure-trove
   Of wisdom, by thy pains and exercise?"

These words did Statius first a little move                    25
   To laughter; then: "Thine every word," said he,
   "Is a dear token to me of thy love.

Yes, many things there are, which seem to be                   28
   Perplexing, though quite falsely so, because
   They have good reasons which we cannot see.

Thou dost conceive me, as thy question shows,                  31
   In yonder life a hoarder – thus, I guess,
   Concluding from that circle where I was.

Now know that avaricious stinginess                            34
   Was all too far from me, so that since then
   Thousands of moons have punished this excess;

And had I not made straight my paths again,                    37
   Pondering thee where, in anger and disgust,
   Thou seem'st to cry against the race of men:

'With what constraint constrain'st thou not the lust           40
   Of mortals, thou devoted greed of gold!'
   I'd now be trundling in the dismal joust.

But then, perceiving hands might well unfold                   43
   Their spendthrift wings too wide, I cleansed me straight
   Of that, with all my evil ways of old.

How many shall be raised with shaven pate                      46
   Through ignorance, which forbids this fault to win
   Repentance, both in life and in death's gate!

And know, all sin that seeks to drive out sin                  49
   By its immediate opposite, must here
   At that sin's side dry up its sappy green;

So, if I was constrained to purge me there                     52
   With those who weep their avarice away,
   'Twas that I held its contrary too dear."

To whom the poet of the Eclogues: "Nay,                        55
   But when, methinks, Jocasta's twin-born bale
   Thou sangest, and the fierce, unnatural fray,

58     Seeing how thou and Clio tell the tale,
       Thy fealty to that faith had not begun
       For lack of which, good works may not avail.

61     If this be so, what candle or what sun,
       Scattering the dark, made thee set sail to scud
       Behind the Fisherman from that time on?"

64     Then he: "Thou first didst guide me when I trod
       Parnassus' caves to drink the waters bright,
       And thou wast first to lamp me up to God.

67     Thou wast as one who, travelling, bears by night
       A lantern at his back, which cannot leaven
       His darkness, yet he gives his followers light.

70     'To us,' thou saidst, 'a new-born world is given,
       Justice returns, and the first age of man,
       And a new progeny descends from Heaven.'

73     Poet through thee, through thee a Christian –
       That's my bare sketch; but now I'll take to limning,
       And make a clearer page for thee to scan.

76     The whole wide world was then already teeming
       With the true faith, sown by the messengers
       Of the eternal realm; I, therefore, deeming

79     That the new preachers made with that same verse
       Of thine I quoted wondrous harmony,
       Became a frequent visitor of theirs.

82     So good and holy they appeared to be
       That when Domitian's persecution came
       No groan of theirs but had its tear from me;

85     And while I lived yon side I succoured them,
       And thought all other cults contemptible,
       These innocent lives so put the rest to shame.

88     And ere I'd brought, by my poetic skill,
       The Greeks to Theban streams, I was baptized;
       Yet fear kept me a secret Christian still

91     For many years, in pagan shows disguised;
       Which slackness, more than four long centuries, spent
       Speeding round the fourth cornice, have chastised.

But tell me, thou by whom the veil was rent     94
  Which hid that great boon from me, canst thou say –
  Since we've yet time to spare on this ascent –

Where is our ancient Terence? where to-day     97
  Are Plautus, Varius, and Caecilius?
  Are they condemned, and in which ward are they?"

"These," said my guide, "and I and Persius     100
  And many more beside, are with that Greek
  Whom most the Muses suckled – all of us

In the dark jail's first circle; there we speak     103
  Oft of the mount which houses evermore
  Our nursing-mothers on its sacred peak.

Other great Grecians, laurel-crowned of yore,     106
  Are there: Euripides, Simonides,
  Antiphon, Agathon, and many more.

Of thine own people also there one sees     109
  Antigone, Deipyle, Argeia,
  Ismene sorrowing still; there dwells with these

She who led down the troops to the Langeia;     112
  There is the daughter of Tiresias, there
  Thetis, and, with her sisters, Deidamia."

Both poets here fell silent, all their care     115
  Being to look round them with a zest reborn
  The moment they'd got free from walls and stair;

Already now four handmaids of the morn     118
  Were left behind, and at the chariot-pole
  The fifth urged upward still its flaming horn.

My leader said, "I think, upon the whole,     121
  We should go round the hill as we've begun,
  Right-handed to the brink, to gain our goal."

So custom was our guide, and we went on     124
  With less misgiving now of any kind
  Since that pure soul agreed this should be done.

They walked in front, and all alone behind     127
  I followed, listening to their words, which shed
  Much light on poetry to aid my mind.

130    But soon, to break their talk's delightful thread,
        Right in mid-road we found a tree, whose crop
        Of tempting fruit ambrosial odours spread;

133    And as a fir-tree tapers to the top
        From branch to branch, so this one tapered down –
        Doubtless to hinder folk from climbing up;

136    While on the closed side of the way, where frown
        The lofty rocks, a clear and crystal flood
        Cascaded, sprinkling all its verdant crown.

139    As the two poets neared the tree and stood
        Beneath, a voice there from some leafy bough
        Cried out: "Ye shall be famished of this food!"

142    And then again: "More thought had Mary, how
        To make the marriage worthy and complete
        Than for her mouth, which answers for you now.

145    In ancient Rome, dames asked no better treat
        Than water for their drink; Daniel of old
        Chose wisdom, and despised the body's meat.

148    The primal age was beautiful as gold;
        Hunger made acorns savoury to its need,
        Streams for its thirst like rills of nectar rolled.

151    Locusts and honey were enough to feed
        The Baptist in the desert; whence his glory
        Is such, and such his greatness, as ye read

154    Revealed for ever in the Gospel story."

THE IMAGES. (*See next Canto.*)

NOTES. l. 1: *the angel*: this is the Angel of Liberality; he is not described, but his action of erasing the fifth P from Dante's forehead is noted.

    l. 5: "*Beati*"; *and with* "*sitiunt*" *and no more*: the Benediction of the Fifth Cornice is taken from the Beatitude "*Beati qui [esuriunt et] sitiunt justitiam* – blessed are they who [hunger and] thirst after righteousness" (*Matt.* v. 6), but the Angel omits the words about hunger, which are reserved for the Cornice of Gluttony.

    l. 7: *lighter-footed*: Cf. iv. 88–96; xii. 116–26 and Images.

    l. 13: *Juvenal* (Decius Junius Juvenalis): the Roman satirist, *b.* under Nero (A.D. 54–68), *d.* under Antoninus Pius (A.D. 138–61), aged over

80. Dante several times quotes and refers to Juvenal in his prose works: his mention of him here is doubtless due to the fact that Statius is alluded to in Juvenal's *Seventh Satire*.

ll. 34–5: *avaricious stinginess was all too far from me*: Here, as in the corresponding circle of Hell (*Inf.* vii *passim*) Dante shows hoarders and spendthrifts punished together, as offending, though in opposite ways, against the golden mean of a prudent liberality. In ll. 49–51 he explains that the same rule holds good in the other Cornices of Purgatory, though he gives no examples of this.

ll. 40–1: *With what constraint*, etc.: These lines purport to represent *Aen.* iii. 56–7: *quid non mortalia pectora cogis, Auris acra fames?* But Dante's translation is such a very odd one as to suggest that he either completely misunderstood the Latin, or for his own ends deliberately twisted its meaning to the precise opposite of what Virgil intended. There are cogent objections to both theories, and I have, though with some misgiving, adopted a half-way position. See Appendix, p. 343.

l. 46: *with shaven pate*: Cf. *Inf.* vii. 57.

l. 55: *the poet of the Eclogues*: Virgil.

ll. 56–7: *Jocasta's twin-born bale*: Jocasta, widow of Laius king of Thebes, unwittingly married her own son Oedipus, by whom she became mother of the twins, Eteocles and Polynices, whose fraternal contest for the Theban crown is the subject of Statius's *Thebaid* (see also *Inf.* xxvi. 52–4 and note).

l. 58: *Clio*: the Muse of History. Virgil means that the theme and treatment of the *Thebaid* are still entirely pagan.

l. 63: *the Fisherman*: St. Peter.

l. 65: *Parnassus' caves*, etc.: Mount Parnassus, a few miles above Delphi, was the abode of Apollo and of the Muses, who had there a sacred cave, and a sacred spring, the Castalian fountain, in which they bathed.

ll. 70–2: "*To us*," thou saidst, "*a new-born world is given*," etc.: An almost literal translation of the famous lines from Virgil's Fourth Eclogue: *Magnus ab integro saeclorum nascitur ordo; Jam redit et virgo* (the virgin = *justice*), *redeunt Saturnia regna* (the Saturnian reign; cf. *Inf.* xiv. 95–6 and note), *Jam nova progenies caelo demittitur alto* (*Ecl.* iv. 5–7). Written apparently to celebrate the expected birth of a son to Octavian (or perhaps to Antony), the lines were not unnaturally received by the early Church as an inspired, though unconscious, prophecy of Christ; and for many years, during the Middle Ages, Virgil was commemorated at the Christmas mass in Rouen and elsewhere as "Maro, Prophet of the Gentiles."

l. 83: *Domitian's persecution*: Domitian (Titus Flavius Domitianus Augustus), son of Vespasian, was born in A.D. 51, and succeeded his brother Titus (xxi. 82) as Emperor in 81. He was the patron of Statius, whose *Thebaid* compliments him in the extravagant style of the period. His persecution of the Christians is mentioned by Tertullian and Eusebius, and also by St Augustine, though by no contemporary writer. He was murdered in 96.

ll. 88–9: *ere I'd brought ... Theban streams*: i.e. before I had reached the eighth Book of the *Thebaid*, in which Adrastus, bringing Greek forces to the aid of Polynices, reaches the rivers Ismenus and Asopus (*Purg.* xviii. 91 and note).

l. 92: *more than four long centuries*: this period, added to the "five centuries and more" spent on the Cornice of Covetousness, account for some 950 of the 1200 years or so between the death of Statius and the alleged date of Dante's vision. This leaves about 250 years, which were presumably spent on one or all of the three Lower Cornices.

ll. 97–100: *Terence .. Plautus, Varius, Caecilius ... Persius*: for these Latin poets, see Glossary.

l. 103: *the dark jail's first circle*: Limbo.

l. 104: *The mount*: Parnassus;

l. 105: *Our nursing-mothers*: The Muses.

ll. 107–8: *Euripides*, etc.: for these Greek poets, see Glossary.

l. 109: *thine own people*: the characters mentioned in Statius's works, for whom see Glossary.

l. 117: *free from walls and stair*: they have now reached the Sixth Cornice, where Gluttony is purged.

ll. 118–20: *four handmaids ... horn*: the first four hours of the day are past, and the fifth hour is guiding the chariot of the Sun as it continues its upward journey to the zenith; i.e. it is between 10 and 11 A.M.

l. 126: *that pure soul*: Statius, who has finished his purgation, and whose opinion is therefore the more authoritative.

ll. 140–54: this is the "Whip" of the Sixth Cornice, comprising examples of Temperance. The first, that of the Blessed Virgin, refers to the marriage at Cana (*John* ii. 1–12); the second, that of the women of Ancient Rome, is probably taken, by way of St Thomas Aquinas, from Valerius Maximus, who says: "The use of wine was in olden days unknown to Roman women" (II. i. 3); the third, that of Daniel, is from *Dan.* i. 8, 17; the fourth, that of the fabled Age of Gold, from Ovid: *Metam.* i. 103 *sqq.* and/or Boethius, *Cons. Phil.* II. v. 1 *sqq.*; the fifth, that of John the Baptist, from *Matt.* iii. 4, *Mark* i. 6.

ll. 153–4: *Such his greatness, as ye read*, etc.: v. *Matt.* xi. 11, *Luke* vii. 28.

# CANTO XXIII

THE STORY. *The Poets are overtaken by the emaciated shades of the Gluttonous, one of whom recognizes Dante. This turns out to be his former boon companion Forese Donati. The two friends exchange news.*

While thus I stood and peered the green leaves through,
  Like one who wastes his life from day to day
  Idling after a little bird or two,

"Son," said my more than father, "don't delay        4
  But come; our time, which has its limit set,
  Ought to be spent in a more useful way."

So to my sages turning eyes and feet        7
  I went, the readier that their talk conferred
  Such pleasure, I could go without regret.

And lo! a sobbing and a song was heard:        10
  "*Labia mea Domine,*" till the ear
  Felt joy and grief twin-born in every word.

"O dearest father, what is this I hear?"        13
  Thus I began; he answered: "Shades who go
  Loosening the knot of debt, belike, draw near."

Like men who walk preoccupied, and throw        16
  A quick look back, not stopping, but move fast
  When overtaking people they don't know,

So, from behind, with wondering glances cast        19
  On us, outstripping us, now come, now gone,
  Silent, devout, a band of shadows passed.

Hollow and dark of eye was every one,        22
  With pallid face so wasted that the skin
  Had all its contours moulded on the bone;

Not Erysichthon ever grew so thin,        25
  I'll swear, though withered to the very hide,
  In the worst fear that hunger put him in.

28      Behold indeed, my heart within me cried,
            The very folk who lost Jerusalem
            When Miriam's teeth gnawed at her own son's side!

31      Each socket seemed a ring without a gem;
            He who reads OMO in man's countenance
            Right plain in these might recognize the M.

34      Who would believe that the mere redolence
            Of fruit and water (if he knew not how)
            Rousing desire, could breed this consequence?

37      I viewed their famished forms with puzzled brow,
            The cause that made them lean and scurvy-rid,
            Poor souls, not being apparent up to now;

40      When lo! from the deep caverns of his head
            One shade turned eyes on me; a stare – a shout:
            "What's this? what grace is shown me here!" he said.

43      Ne'er by his looks should I have found him out,
            But what his altered countenance disguised
            His voice revealed to me beyond a doubt;

46      That spark lit up remembrance, advertised
            Beneath the features changed a face I knew:
            Forese's self I clearly recognized.

49      "Ah! do not gaze," he begged me, "on my hue
            Discoloured so by this dry leprosy;
            Heed not the shrivelled husk I've dwindled to;

52      But tell me truly, what's the news with thee,
            And who are these two souls that with thee go?
            O do not stand there dumb, but speak to me!"

55      "Thy face," said I, "once made me weep for woe,
            Seeing it dead, and now mine eyelids swell
            With tears again to see it ravaged so.

58      What has thus withered thee? o' God's name, tell!
            Bid me not speak while wonder fills my mind;
            When thoughts are elsewhere, how can lips speak well?"

61      And he: "By subtle virtue I'm refined
            That from the eternal counsel whence it springs
            Falls on the tree and water there behind;

And all this multitude that weeps and sings 64
  By dearth and drouth is here resanctified
  From an excessive greed of life's good things.

Craving for food and drink's intensified 67
  By the sweet smell of fruit and of the spray
  Which from above sprinkles the foliage wide;

And not once only, as we make our way 70
  Around this path, our pain is thus renewed –
  I call it pain: solace, I ought to say;

For that which draws us to the tree's green wood 73
  Is that desire which gladdened Christ to cry
  'Eli' when He redeemed us with His blood."

"Nay, but Forese, from that day," said I, 76
  "That changed thy worldly for a better life,
  Up to this time, not five years have rolled by.

If power to sin did not in thee survive 79
  The coming of that hour when holy sorrow
  Reweds the soul to God as His true wife,

How didst thou get up here? Full many a morrow 82
  I'd think to find thee lingering still down there
  Where souls repay with time the time they borrow."

And he: "It was my Nella whose kind care 85
  Brought me so quickly here, to drink the sweet
  Wormwood of torment; she by instant prayer

And streaming tears and sighs did so entreat, 88
  That from the waiting-place she drew me soon,
  And from the other circles loosed my feet.

And God looks the more kind and loving on 91
  My poor young widow, whom I held so dear,
  That in good works she is so much alone.

Barbagia in Sardinia can't come near 94
  That worse Barbagia where I've left her – yea,
  Indeed the women there are decenter.

Brother of mine, what wilt thou have me say? 97
  This hour shall not be very old perhaps
  Ere time shall bring what I foresee to-day:

249

100    A pulpit interdict, no less, which claps
          Down on our brazen jades of Florentines
          Flaunting unveiled the bosom and the paps.

103    What female Turk or Berber e'er showed signs
          Of needing to be covered up by force
          Of spiritual or other disciplines?

106    But could these wantons know what Heaven's swift course
          Prepare for them, they'd have their mouths ajar
          Already, fit to bellow themselves hoarse;

109    For, if my foresight's not misled me far,
          They'll need to weep ere down shall clothe the lips
          Of him that's soothed now with *lulli, lulla.*

112    But come, explain thyself! thou dost eclipse
          The sunlight, brother, to our wondering gaze –
          Look! not mine only – all this fellowship's."

115    Then I: "If thou recall'st our former ways,
          What thou wast like with me, and I with thee,
          Fresh grief will wring thee still for those past days.

118    From that life he who goes ahead of me
          Saved me the other day, when round of rim
          Yon fellow's sister showed for you to see –"

121    (I pointed to the sun); "so through the dim
          Deep night, where dwell the truly dead, came I,
          Clothed on with this true flesh which follows him.

124    Thence he's sustained and brought me up thus high
          Still climbing and still circling round the hill
          Which rights in you what the world bent awry.

127    He says he'll bear me company until
          I shall be where Beatrice also is,
          And after that he needs must say farewell.

130    Yon shade" (I pointed) "who has told me this
          Is Virgil, and that other's he who took
          His full discharge when, speeding him to bliss

133    Just now, your whole realm's every cornice shook."

THE IMAGES. *The Penance of the Gluttonous: Starvation*: The sin of
Gluttony (*Gula*) is – specifically – an undue attention to the pleas-
ures of the palate, whether by sheer excess in eating and drinking,
or by the opposite fault of fastidiousness. More generally, it in-
cludes all over-indulgence in bodily comforts – the concentration,
whether jovial or fretful, on a "high standard of living". It is ac-
cordingly purged by starvation within sight of plenty.

Since Gluttony tends to be, on the whole, a warm-hearted and
companionable sin, often resulting from, and in, a mistaken notion
of good-fellowship, it is placed higher than the egotistical and
cold-hearted sins. (Compare the corresponding classification in
Hell.)

NOTES. l. 11: *Labia mea Domine [aperies, et os meum annuntiabit laudem
tuam]* (O Lord [open thou] my lips [and my mouth shall show forth
Thy praise]): this is the Prayer of the Gluttonous, from *Ps.* li. 15
(*Vulg.* l. 17); it appropriately reminds the penitent that the mouth was
made for other things besides eating and drinking.

l. 25: *Erysichthon*: a Thessalian who, for cutting down an oak in her
sacred grove, was punished by Ceres with such pangs of hunger that
he gnawed his own flesh – reduced by that time to mere skin and bone
(Ovid: *Metam.* viii. 738–878).

l. 30: *Miriam*: When Titus was besieging Jerusalem (see Canto xxi.
82–4 and note) the famine in the city was so great that a Jewess called
Miriam killed and ate her own child (Josephus, *Jewish War*, vi. 3).

l. 32: *he who reads OMO in man's countenance*: according to a pious
medieval conceit, the words "[H] OMO DEI" (man [is] of God)
were plainly written in the human countenance, the eyes representing
the two O's, the line of the cheeks, eyebrows, and nose forming a
script M, while the D, E, I are shown in the ears, nostrils, and mouth.
On these wasted faces the bony outline of the M stood out with start-
ling clearness.

l. 48: *Forese's self*: Forese Donati, brother of Corso Donati (see *Inf.*
Introduction, p. 36, and *Purg.* xxiv. 79–90) and of Piccarda (*Purg.* xxiv.
10–15), was a close friend of Dante's and probably a distant connexion
of his wife, Gemma Donati. From what Dante says in this canto (ll.
115–17), it would seem that the two friends had led a somewhat

dissipated life together. In support of this, we have a series of abusive sonnets exchanged between them, of whose meaning nobody can be certain – except that, whatever it is, it is rude, vulgar, and obscene. The exchange of this kind of scurrility was popular in the Middle Ages – its tradition surviving to this day in the Fourth Form – and was dignified with the title of *tenzon* or "dispute".

l. 50: *dry leprosy*: the scabby disfigurement caused by starvation.

ll. 61 *sqq.*: *by subtle virtue*, etc.: "The tree and the water derive from God (the Eternal Counsel) a peculiar virtue which causes me and my companions to waste away thus."

l. 74: *which gladdened Christ to cry Eli*: by a beautiful oxymoron Christ is said to have been *glad* when He uttered from the Cross His great cry of dereliction, *Eli, Eli, lama sabachthani* (My God, my God, why hast thou forsaken me?); because it sprang from His desire, or thirst, for man's salvation. (The "I thirst" is the next Word from the Cross, and is followed by the cry of accomplishment, "It is finished.")

ll. 76–84: *from that day ... time they borrow*: Forese died in July 1296. Dante apparently knows that he had continued in sin to the day of his death. If, therefore, his was a repentance *in articulo mortis* (when all power to sin further was already lost, ll. 80–2) how is it that he has not been detained in Ante-Purgatory among the Indolent for a term equal to that of his natural life?

l. 85: *my Nella*: Forese's wife, concerning whom, and her husband's neglect of her, Dante had said some scurrilous things in the *tenzon*.

ll. 85–90: *whose kind care ... loosed my feet*: Nella's devoted prayers obtained for Forese *remission* of the waiting-time, and enabled him to make such good speed with his purgation that he soon *found himself freed* from the Lower Cornice (for the distinction, see Introduction, pp. 58, 64). Forese's tribute (which follows) to his ill-used wife is evidence of his amendment of heart.

l. 95: *Barbagia*: a hilly district in central Sardinia, of whose inhabitants St Gregory (third century) said that they lived like brute beasts. Their ill reputation continued into Dante's time.

l. 100: *a pulpit interdict*: the reference is apparently not merely to sermons, but to an official decree, by either the spiritual or civil authorities, published from the pulpit. No such interdict during this period has been traced, though Villani (*Chron.* ix. 245) mentions one directed against the sumptuary extravagance of the Florentine women, which was promulgated in 1324, three years after Dante's death.

ll. 110–11: *ere down shall clothe the lips*, etc.: i.e. within 16 years or so of the vision. This prophecy can be taken to cover the various misfortunes of the Florentines from the internecine feuds of the Blacks and Whites in 1300 (see *Inf.* Introduction, p. 33 *sqq.*) to their disastrous defeat in 1315 at Monte Catini by the forces of Lucca and Pisa under Uguccione della Faggiuola.

l. 120: *yon fellow's sister*: i.e. the moon, which had been full on the night of Maundy Thursday when Dante was in the Dark Wood. Apollo and Diana (the Sun and the Moon) were the twin children of Leto or Latona (see xx. 130 and note).

# CANTO XXIV

THE STORY. *Forese Donati speaks of his sister Piccarda, now in Heaven, and names a number of his fellow penitents. Among them is Bongiunta of Lucca, who, recognizing Dante as a fellow poet, asks him about the "sweet new style" of the Florentine school of lyricists. Forese then hastens on his way, after prophesying the terrible death of his brother, Corso Donati. The Poets come to a second Tree, surrounded by other starved and tantalized shades; from the boughs a voice bids the travellers pass on without eating, and rehearses the examples which form the Bridle of Gluttony. Presently the Angel of Temperance makes his appearance; after brushing the sixth P from Dante's forehead, he pronounces the Benediction of the Cornice and speeds them upward by the Pass of Pardon.*

Nor speed made speech nor speech our speeding slow,
　　But walking hard and talking hard we sped
　　Even as a ship when favouring breezes blow;

4　And all those shades, who looked like things twice dead,
　　Drank in amazement through their hollow eyes,
　　When in my face the signs of life they read;

7　While I went on to say: "Perhaps he plies
　　His step less briskly, out of kindliness
　　To those he's with, than he would otherwise.

10　But, if thou know'st it, tell me now, where is
　　Piccarda; and what notables there are
　　Amid these folk who stare at me like this."

13　"My sister – if more virtuous or more fair
　　She was, I know not – on Olympus high
　　Rejoices her triumphal crown to wear."

16　This he said first, and then: "No reason why
　　I should not here name each at thy demand,
　　Since our starved features are so shrunk and dry.

19　That one's Bongiunta" (pointing with his hand)
　　"Bongiunta of Lucca; next him in the line
　　That, the most puckered face in all the band,

Once in his arms did Holy Church entwine;　　　　22
　　He came from Tours, and fasts to purge the famed
　　Bolsena eels and sweet Vernaccia wine."

Thus many another first and last he named,　　　　25
　　And all seemed quite content with this, nor took
　　Offence – I saw no angry glances aimed.

Ubaldin dalla Pila met my look,　　　　28
　　Chewing the air for hunger: Boniface,
　　Who pastured such great numbers with his crook;

And Lord Marchese, who found means to chase　　　　31
　　Once, at Forlì, less drought with far more drink,
　　But was for ever thirsty none the less.

And, as one may see many things, but think　　　　34
　　Chiefly of one, I picked out him of Lucca,
　　Who seemed most anxious to contrive some link

With me; he muttered and at length he shook a　　　　37
　　Something from where they feel the fret and fray
　　Of justice most – it sounded like "Gentucca".

"Thou who, it seems, wouldst fain address me, pray,　　　　40
　　Spirit," said I, "speak so that I can hear,
　　And please us both with what thou hast to say."

"A woman's born," said he, "nor yet doth wear　　　　43
　　The wimple, who shall make my town seem kind
　　To thee, let men reproach it howsoe'er.

Go, take this forecast with thee; if thy mind　　　　46
　　Have misconstrued my mutterings, time shall prove
　　By the event the truth that lies behind.

But say, do I see here the man who wove　　　　49
　　The strands of those new verses which begin
　　*Ladies, who have intelligence in love?*"

I said: "I am one who when Love breathes within　　　　52
　　Give ear, and as he prompts take mode and pitch
　　From him, and go and sing his mind to men."

And he: "O brother, now I see the hitch　　　　55
　　That kept back me, the Notary, and Guitton',
　　And put this sweet new style beyond our reach;

58    I see how your pens follow hard upon
       His voice who thus dictates the argument;
       So did not ours, as I must freely own;

61    And further search, however far it went,
       Would find no other difference in the style
       'Twixt old and new." He ceased, and seemed content.

64    Now, as the birds that winter by the Nile
       First form an aery squadron in close flight,
       Then put on speed and stream away in file,

67    So on a sudden all the folk in sight
       Spun round and fled away from us in haste,
       Being by leanness and desire made light.

70    And, as a weary runner lets the rest
       Go by, and walks awhile to ease the strain
       Of panting lungs that labour in his chest,

73    So did Forese let the holy train
       Of souls sweep past, and went along with me,
       Asking: "And when shall we two meet again?"

76    I said: "I know not what my span shall be
       Till my return, but come I ne'er so swift,
       Still to the shore my heart shall outrun me;

79    For every day the place I must make shift
       To live in, more and more – as though resolved
       On rueful wrack – casts rectitude away."

82    "Too true; and him whose guilt is most involved
       I see," he said, "at a beast's tail dragged dying
       Toward the dark vale where sin is not absolved.

85    With every plunge the maddened brute goes flying
       Faster and faster, till the battering heels
       Smash down, and leave the mangled horror lying.

88    Nor have they far to turn, those rolling wheels,"
       (He looked to heaven) "ere thou see clear the fate
       Which, by command, my tongue but half reveals.

91    Now drop behind; in this our realm and state
       Time's precious, and I make too long delay,
       Pacing thee step for step at this slow rate."

As from a troop that rides upon its way     94
  Sometimes a rider gallops forth to win
  The signal honour of the first affray,

So he strode swifter on and left me then     97
  Upon my way beside those two that were
  Such mighty captains in the world of men.

And when he'd shot ahead of us so far     100
  That eyes and mind alike were at a loss
  To catch him or his meaning howsoe'er,

Another tree with green and laden boughs     103
  Appeared to me, and no great distance off,
  For as we turned the corner, there it was.

And I saw folk that toward the leaves thereof     106
  Stretched hands below, crying I knew not what,
  As eager children, bootlessly enough,

Beg and beseech, while he who is besought     109
  Won't answer, but, on teasing still intent,
  Holds high the tempting prize and hides it not.

Then as though disabused, away they went;     112
  And now that stately tree which makes a mock
  Of all those tears and prayers loomed imminent.

"Pass on; avoid it; farther up the rock     115
  Stands yet the tree which fed that greed of Eve's;
  This is a scion of the self-same stock."

Thus some one spoke amid the spreading leaves;     118
  So Virgil, I, and Statius, closely pressed,
  Passed, on that side which runs beneath the cliffs.

"Think," said the voice, "upon that brood unblest,     121
  Cloud-formed, who having gorged their fill began
  To war on Theseus, double-breast to breast;

Think on the stream where many a Hebrew man     124
  Drinking at ease might not with Gideon go
  When he marched down the hills on Midian."

So on we filed, hugging one verge, and so     127
  The tale of ancient gluttonies we heard
  Recited, and how all their gain was woe.

130 And then, strung out along the road where stirred
   Never a soul, we all went thoughtful on
   A thousand paces quite, without one word.

133 "What ponder you, ye three who walk alone?"
   The voice rang out so sudden just ahead,
   It made me jump like any startled fawn.

136 I looked to see by whom the words were said,
   And ne'er was seen in any furnaces
   Metal or glass so glowing or so red

139 As I saw one who spake: "And if you please
   Ascend, turn here and you will walk aright,
   For by this path go those who seek for peace."

142 His countenance had deprived mine eyes of light,
   And as behind my guides I turned away
   I had to move by hearing, not by sight.

145 And lo! as, ushering in the dawn of day,
   Impregned with fragrance of the flowers and grass
   Rustles and stirs the scented breeze of May,

148 Even so I felt across my forehead pass
   A wind, and felt the wafting of the plumes
   With such an odour as ambrosia has.

151 "Blessed are they whom so great grace illumes,"
   I heard it said, "that in their bosom's core
   The palate's lust kindles no craving fumes,

154 And righteousness is all they hunger for."

THE IMAGES. *The Trees and the Water*: The punishment of the Gluttonous closely resembles the torment allotted in the Classical Tartarus to Tantalus, who stole the food of the gods. In Homer (*Od.* xi. 582 *sqq.*) he stands in water up to the chin beneath a laden fruittree; but when he tries to drink, the water sinks from his lips, and when he tries to reach the fruit, it is carried away by the wind. This punishment by hunger and thirst captured the imagination of the Middle Ages; it nearly always figures in popular pictures of Hell, and even in illustrations to the *Inferno*, in which it has no place, Dante having substituted for it the wallowing in mud and the cold rain of the Third Circle, under the teeth and claws of Cerberus (*Inf.* vi *passim*).

On the Sixth Cornice, Dante has retained the image of the water and the tree, turning the former into a sparkling cascade (doubtless emanating from the twin-spring of Lethe and Eunoë, cf. Canto xxxiii. 112–14), and ingeniously making the latter a scion of the Tree of Knowledge, thus linking up the Sin of Gluttony with the sin of Eve and the Fall of Man ("all for an apple, an apple which he took").

By another dexterous economy, he uses this Penance as a springboard for Statius's discourse (in the next Canto) on the nature of the soul.

NOTES. l. 7: *perhaps he plies*: i.e. Statius, of whom Dante has been speaking.

l. 11: *Piccarda*: Forese's sister was a nun of the order of St Clare, but was forcibly abducted by her brother Corso Donati and married to Rossellino della Tosa, to whom she had been previously betrothed. We shall meet her again in the Heaven of the Moon (*Para.* iii. 34 *sqq.*).

l. 14: *on Olympus high*: i.e. in Heaven.

l. 16: *no reason why*, etc.: this hesitation about naming other spirits does not appear elsewhere in Purgatory. Perhaps, with the courtesy of the place, Forese feels that the contrast between the former appearance of the shades and their present disfigurement makes the matter a delicate one. But since Dante could not possibly recognize them (cf. xxiii. 43–8) in their present condition he feels justified; and in fact (ll. 26–7) none of the shades is at all offended.

l. 20: *Bongiunta of Lucca*: Bongiunta Orbicciani degli Overardi, a poet of the second half of the thirteenth century. He had a reputation as a hard drinker.

ll. 21–4: *the most puckered face*, etc.: This is Simon de Brie, a native of Tours in France, who, as Martin IV, was Pope ("held Holy Church in his arms") from 1281 to 1285. He died of a surfeit of eels from the Lake of Bolsena, stewed in Vernaccia wine. Contemporary wit devised this epitaph for him: *Gaudent anguillae, Quia mortuus hic jacet ille Qui quasi morte reas Excoriabat eas* (There was joy among the eels When death laid him by the heels For he skinned 'em and sorted 'em As though death had county-courted 'em).

l. 28: *Ubaldin dalla Pila*: of the Ubaldini family, of Florence; brother of Cardinal Ottaviano ("the Magnificent") whom Dante places in Hell among the Epicureans (*Inf.* x. 120 and Glossary) and father of Roger (Rùggieri) degli Ubaldino, archbishop of Pisa (see *Inf.* xxxiii. 13 and note). He is said to have been a liberal and cultivated man, with a great knack for inventing new culinary recipes.

l. 29: *Boniface*: Archbishop of Ravenna, of the Genoese family of Fieschi, a man of immense wealth, who, as Dante insinuates, not only used his pastoral crook to "pasture" his spiritual flock, but fed an enormous train of attendants and hangers-on out of the emoluments of his benefice.

l. 31: *Lord Marchese*: a renowned drinker from Forlì, of the Arguglioso family. He is said to have asked his secretary: "What do they say of me in the city?" – "My lord, that you are always drinking" – "They might add" (said the Marchese, laughing) "that it is because I am always thirsty." (Ben. da Imola.)

l. 39: *Gentucca*: This would appear to be the name of the Lady mentioned in ll. 43–5; she has been identified, though with no great certainty, as Gentucca Morla, wife of Bonaccorse Fondora of Lucca. Speculation has run rife about her relations with Dante; but since a blessed soul in Purgatory is scarcely likely to have approved beforehand of anything improper, and since for Dante to divulge a lady's name in such a connexion would have been a most scandalous breach of all the rules of courtesy, we may assume that Monna Gentucca merely showed kindness to him during his stay in Lucca (probably about 1307–9). In 1300 she would have been young and unmarried, and not entitled to wear the *benda* (wimple) which was the head-dress of married women.

l. 51: "*Ladies, who have intelligence in love*": This is the opening line of one of the most famous odes in *The New Life* (*Vita Nuova*).

l. 56: *me, the Notary, and Guitton'*: Bongiunta, Giacomo da Lentino (known as "the Notary"), and Guittone d'Arezzo belonged to the so-called "Sicilian" school of poetry, whose influence extended throughout Central Italy during the latter half of the thirteenth century. Italian vernacular poetry derived its method and inspiration from that of the Provençal troubadours, and for some time found a focus in the Imperial court in Sicily. After the death of Frederick II in 1250, and the extinction of the House of Hohenstauffen at the Battle of Tagliacozzo (see *Inf.* Introduction, p. 25), Italy was left without a Court, and the "gay science" of courtly love, which depended for its vitality upon the existence of a courtly life, declined into an artificial convention. From the aristocratic subtleties of the "amorous debate" and the chivalrous romance popularized by the French *trouvères* and German *minnesinger*, the "Sicilian School" turned to a more scientific philosophy of love. Their doctrine, which owed much to classical sources such as Ovid's *Art of Love* (*Ars Amatoria*), and coincided to some degree with that of the Schoolmen, tended to define Love as an irresistible and largely malignant passion, originating in the pleasure of the eyes, nourished by the imagination, and overthrowing the reason. Their analysis, frigid and cerebral as it may appear in modern eyes, marks an advance towards a serious psychological study, and forms a necessary transition between two important periods of poetic development.

l. 57: *this sweet new style* (*il dolce stil nuovo*) is the name used to designate the work of the Florentine school of poets, who founded their theory and practice upon the example of Guido Guinicelli of Bologna. (We shall meet Guinicelli on the Cornice of Love, Canto xxvi. 91 *sqq.*) In his famous Ode, *Al gentil cor ripara sempre Amore* (Love shelters ever in the gentle heart), we find the first authentic expression of the new doctrine, which conceives Love, purified of its sensual elements, as a power of divine origin inseparable from true nobility of soul, and (in the modern phrase) "sublimating" the passions. To this poem Dante pays tribute in his early sonnet *Amor e gentil cor son una cosa* (Love and the gentle heart are one same thing – *V.N.* xx). Other poets of the *dolce stil nuovo* are Lapo Gianni de' Ricevati and Cino da Pistoja, together with Dante's friend, Guido Cavalcanti (see *Inf.* x. 63 and note, and Glossary), in whom the doctrine finds tragic expression, owing to his inability to reconcile the tension between "Sweet desire" and the frustration which attends all earthly achievement. It was left for Dante to arrive at a completely successful resolution of the antinomy always implicit in the "courtly" doctrine, by accepting sexual love at its most exalted as one symbol and manifestation among many of the Divine Love which moves the universe, and into whose beatitude all lesser loves are taken up and there fulfilled. This conception, first adumbrated in *The New Life* and further developed in *The Banquet*, reaches its final expression in the *Paradiso*.

l. 82: *him whose guilt is most involved*: Forese is speaking of his own brother, Corso Donati, who was the leader of the Black party in Florence, and was to be chiefly responsible for the massacre and expulsion of the Whites in 1301 (see *Inf.* Introduction, p. 34). Corso fell into bad odour with his own party, and officers were sent to arrest him. After strenuous resistance, he fled from pursuit and, falling from his horse, was either, as Dante tells the story, dragged and battered to death or (according to Villani's account) killed by the troopers (6 Oct. 1308).

l. 115: *farther up the rock*: i.e. in the Earthly Paradise at the summit, where the Tree of Knowledge still stands.

ll. 121–6: This is the Bridle of Gluttony, the examples being: (1) (from class. myth.) the Centaurs who were invited to the wedding of Pirithous, King of the Lapithae, with Hippodamia. Getting very drunk, they attempted to violate the bride and the other women present. Theseus, the King's friend, rescued Hippodamia, and a fight took place between the Lapithae and the Centaurs, in which the Centaurs were beaten. The fight is depicted in the metopes of the Parthenon frieze, and the story is told by Ovid (*Metam.* xii. 210–535). (2) (from the O.T.) the Jewish soldiers rejected by Gideon when he was preparing to march from Mount Gileàd against the Midianites. By divine command, Gideon led his troops to drink at the river and observed which of them, remaining at the alert, merely scooped up water and lapped from the palms of their hands, and which, abandoning all precautions, kneeled down and swilled their fill from the stream. With the 300 who displayed their soldierly quality by lapping, he advanced upon the hosts of Midian and destroyed them (*Judges* vii. 1–7 *et sqq.*).

l. 136: *by whom these words were said*: this is the Angel of Temperance. His description is perhaps taken from that of the Angel who appeared to Daniel after his three weeks' fast: "His body also was like the chrysolite and his face as the appearance of lightning, and his eyes as lamps of fire, and his arms and his feet like in colour to polished brass" (*Dan.* x. 6).

l. 149: *a wind, and felt the wafting of the plumes*: Here the Angel erases the P of Gluttony.

ll. 151–4: *Blessed are they*, etc.: This is the Benediction of the Sixth Cornice, which consists of the remainder of the verse: "*Beati qui esuriunt ... justitiam*" – "Blessed are they that hunger after righteousness" (*Matt.* v. 6), omitting the [et] *sitiunt* – [and] thirst – which was used on Cornice Five (Canto xxii. 4–6). On this Cornice Dante does not give the Latin, but translates and expands in the vernacular.

# CANTO XXV

THE STORY. *As the three Poets are climbing the Sixth Stair, Dante asks a question about the apparent bodies of the Shades. Statius, in a long Discourse, expounds the nature of the Rational Soul, and its connexion with the material body before, and the aery body after, death. They now all emerge upon the Seventh Cornice, where the souls of the Lustful are purged by fire.*

Now was the hour to climb without delay,
    For lo! the Sun had to the Bull transferred,
    Night to the Scorpion, their meridian sway;

And like a man who's not to be deterred,         4
    No matter what turns up, but drives ahead,
    When go he must, by pressing business spurred,

So did we enter through the gap, to thread     7
    In single file the stair that mounts on high
    And parts the climbers by its narrow tread.

And like a baby stork, that longs to fly     10
    And flaps its wings, and then, afraid to quit
    The nest, flops down again, just so was I –

On fire to ask, but quenched as soon as lit;     13
    I got as far as making sounds like one
    About to speak, and then thought better of it.

My gentle father failed not thereupon     16
    To say, although the pace was brisk: "Release
    Thy bow of speech that to the head is drawn."

So I, now opening up my lips at ease,     19
    Began: "How can such leanness come to pass
    Where meat and drink are superfluities?"

"Wouldst thou recall how Meleager was     22
    Wasted," said he, "by wasting of a brand,
    Thou'dst find it easier to discern the cause;

Or wouldst thou ponder how thou movest, and     25
    Behold! thy mirrored image moves with thee,
    This seeming-hard were plain to understand.

28      But that thy heart may rest contentedly,
            Here's Statius, whom I beg and pray also
            To heal the wound of thy perplexity,"

31      "If in thy presence," Statius said, "I throw
            External vistas open to his sight,
            My excuse is that to thee I can't say no."

34      Then he began: "Do thou receive and write
            My words upon the tablet of thy brains,
            And on that 'how' of thine they will shed light.

37      Blood perfect and undrunk by thirsty veins,
            Which – like a dish that's sent away from table
            Untouched – in full perfection still remains,

40      Takes in the heart informing virtue, able
            To build – as vein-streams build the limbs they flood –
            Man's members all, in manner comparable.

43      Thence, redistilled, it sinks where names are rude
            And silence seemlier, till at length it sprays,
            In nature's vessel, on another's blood;

46      There the two mingle, one to passive ways
            Adapted, but the other formed to act,
            Because deriving from that perfect place.

49      This, joined to that, starts work; to clot, compact,
            And then to vivify the solid whole
            It moulds as matter for its artefact.

52      The active virtue, now become a soul –
            Plantlike, but differing in that this has still
            To journey, while the plant has reached its goal –

55      Works till it can, like some sea-fungus, feel
            And move; then starts on organs for those powers
            Of which it is the seed and principle.

58      Now swells and spreads that virtue, son, which showers
            From the begetter's heart, where nature plans
            Animal members for a frame like ours.

61      But how its being grows from beast's to man's
            Thou seest not yet; 'twas at this point a mind
            Wiser than thine was tripped by ignorance,

So that from soul his teaching quite disjoined 64
   Possible intellect, for which, although
   He sought with care, no organ could he find.

Open thy mind, the truth is coming; know, 67
   When the articulation of the brain
   Has been perfected in the embryo,

Then the First Mover turns to it, full fain 70
   Of nature's triumph, and inbreathes a rare
   New spirit, filled with virtue to constrain

To its own substance whatso active there 73
   It finds, and make one single soul complete,
   Alive, and sensitive, and self-aware.

And, lest this seem too wondrous to thy wit, 76
   Think how the sun's warmth mingles in the vine
   With its moist sap, and turns to wine in it.

When Lachesis has no more flax to twine, 79
   It quits the flesh, but bears essentially
   Away with it the human and divine –

Each lower power in dumb passivity, 82
   But memory, intelligence, and will
   Active, and keener than they used to be.

All of itself, as by a miracle, 85
   Instant it lights on one or other shore;
   Then first it knows its ways, for good or ill.

When place has circumscribed it there once more, 88
   The informing virtue radiates round, retaining
   The shape and size the living members wore;

And as the air, soaked through with heavy raining, 91
   Refracts the rays that strike it from outside
   And is adorned and shot with rainbow staining,

Even so the neighbouring air is modified, 94
   And takes the imprint of the form it owes
   To the soul's virtue which doth there abide.

Then, even as the flame which follows close 97
   On fire, and, as the fire moves, moves withall,
   The new form follows where the spirit goes;

100    And thence its semblance, which we therefore call
          A *shade*, derives henceforward; thence 'twill make
          For every sense an organ – sight and all;

103    Thence do we speak and thence we laugh, thence take
          Wherewith to fashion forth the tears and sighs
          Thou'st heard, belike, from all the mountain break.

106    Even as desires and other feelings rise
          To vex us, so the shade takes form, and there's
          The reason of what caused thee such surprise."

109    By now we'd reached the last turn of the stairs,
          And, to the right hand wheeling as we came,
          Suddenly were absorbed by other cares.

112    Here the bank belches forth great sheets of flame,
          While upward from the cornice edge doth blow
          A blast that shields it, backward bending them,

115    So that in single file we had to go,
          Where space allowed; and I was sore afraid,
          On this side, fire – on that, the depths below.

118    "This is a place," my leader therefore said,
          "Where wandering eyes a strict control require,
          Since a false step were all too easy made."

121    And now from that great heat and heart of fire
          *"Summae Deus clementiae"* I heard sung,
          Which drew my gaze with but the more desire;

124    And I saw spirits pass the flames among,
          So that I watched them and my footsteps too,
          With looks this way and that alternate flung.

127    And they, when they had sung that hymn all through,
          Cried, *"Virum non cognosco"* loud and plain;
          Then softly they began the hymn anew,

130    And soon as it was done they cried again:
          "Dian within the forest dwelt, and chased
          Helice forth, who'd drunk of Venus' bane."

133    Then they resumed their singing; then they praised
          Husbands and wives who, faithful to the code
          Of virtue in the marriage-bond, were chaste.

> And they persist, I think, in this same mode,          136
> So long as by those fires they are annealed,
> For it is by such treatment and such food
>
> That the last wound of all must needs be healed.          139

THE IMAGES. *The Penance of the Lustful: the Fire.* By contrast with the common run of eschatological writers, Dante is strangely economical in his use of fire. Even in Hell, the naked flame makes only four appearances (in the Sixth Circle, Ring ii of the Seventh, and Bowges iii and viii of the Eighth), and is never unaccompanied by some touch of greatness amid the squalor: Farinata, Capaneus and the Three Noble Florentines, Ulysses, the outraged majesty of the Most High Keys. On the Blissful Mountain, the traditional "Purgatory Fire" is conspicuous by its absence: only on its last and highest and most triumphant Cornice does this great Scriptural image blaze out with a sudden splendid lucidity.

"For He is like a refiner's fire"; "the fining-pot is for silver and the furnace for gold"; "the words of the Lord are pure words, even as the silver, which from the earth is tried, and purified seven times in the fire." Fire, which is an image of Lust, is also an image of Purity. The burning of the sin, and the burning charity which is its opposing virtue, here coalesce into a single image and a single experience; here, where the souls of great poets go singing and weeping through the flame, the noblest of earthly lovers is purged and set in order.

NOTES. ll. 2–3: *the Sun ... to the Bull, Night to the Scorpion*: in Purgatory the sign of Aries (the Ram), in which the Sun stood, was going down the sky and the next sign, Taurus (the Bull), had come to the Zenith; while in the other hemisphere Libra (the Scales), the midnight sign, had yielded the zenith to Scorpio (the Scorpion). Since the signs follow one another at two-hourly intervals, it was now 2 P.M. in Purgatory (and consequently 2 A.M. at Jerusalem). See clock diagram between pages 350 and 351.

l. 22: *Meleager* was the son of Oeneus, King of Calydon. When he was newly born, his mother Althaea saw the Fates spinning the thread of his life. They threw a log upon the fire and prophesied: "An equal span of life we give, O babe, to you and to this wood." Then they vanished, and Althaea snatched the log from the fire and carefully preserved it. Meleager grew up to win the love of the swift-footed maiden Atalanta, and when he had slain the Caledonian boar, he gave the skin to her. But his brothers, who were jealous, took the skin from her; whereupon Meleager killed them. Althaea, in her anger, threw the log upon the fire, and as it burned, Meleager was consumed with an inward fire, and, as it fell into ashes, his soul fled into air (Ovid, *Metam.* viii. 451 *sqq.*). The theme of the "external soul" is common in folk-tale; Virgil seems to suggest that, as a correspondence may be established between soul and extraneous matter by sympathetic magic, so that life wastes with the wasting of the matter, so (conversely) divine power can establish a similar connexion, so that the sufferings of the soul are communicated to a material envelope.

ll. 26–7: *thy mirrored image,* etc.: Virgil's second example is directed to show how a movement may be projected upon an exterior substance without altering that substance, and without material contact between that which moves and that upon which the movement is projected.

l. 29: *here's Statius*: Virgil has already (iii. 31–3) told Dante that the apparent bodies of the shades are "ordained" to them by Providence as a means for the endurance of suffering. He has suggested illustrations which may shed some light upon *how* this is brought about; but for a complete exposition of the subject, he refers Dante to Statius the Christian, because it involves (as we shall see) questions which only a revealed theology can answer.

ll. 34–108: *Then he began,* etc.: The modern reader who finds Statius's long Discourse a little boring may be helped to endure it by (*a*) considering how full of interest it must have been to Dante's contemporaries; (*b*) studying the remarkable skill with which the poet has fitted together his scientific and theological jig-saw. Purporting at the outset to be simply a plain answer to a plain question about the apparent bodies of the shades, the discourse leads up naturally to its real subject, which is the origin of the rational soul and the nature of the human body-soul complex. On the way it contrives to provide the curious inquirer with a handy guide to embryology, an explanation of what it is we see when we see ghosts, and the solution of various problems which may have presented themselves in the course of the poem – e.g. how the dismembered Profligates (*Inf.* xiii) and Schismatics (*Inf.* xxviii) are able to reunite their seeming substance, and so on. We may also admire Dante's tact in timing and placing his discourses, which he never permits to dislocate the action of the story. He does not, like Milton, interrupt a battle to assure us that none of the combatants can be permanently damaged, or keep a celestial from his dinner while he discusses the process of angelic digestion; he allows each incident to produce its own dramatic effects, reserving comment for such linking passages as the ascent of stairways, etc., to which they lend a welcome variety.

l. 37: *blood perfect and undrunk by thirsty veins*: the semen is considered to be blood in perfect condition, without the impurities which give venous blood its colour. (The physiology of this whole passage is founded on Aristotle.)

l. 40: *informing virtue*: the heart is the organ which imparts formative power to the blood: whether in the veins, to build up the limbs through which they run, or in the semen, to make the body of the embryo.

ll. 43-5: *thence redistilled*, etc.: "after undergoing a second process of purification, it descends to the male genitals and is sprinkled in the vulva (or perhaps the uterus) upon the blood of the female."

l. 46: *one to passive ways adapted*: the theory that the female's part in generation was purely passive (the womb being merely as it were the soil that receives the "seed") was almost universally accepted until very recent times, when it became possible to distinguish microscopically the action of the genes in sperm and ovum. (Popular psychology and popular moral standards still remain surprisingly faithful to the scientific theory of the third century B.C.)

l. 48: *that perfect place*: the heart.

l. 52: *now become a soul*: this is the *nutritive* or *vegetative soul* (*anima nutritiva* or *vegetativa*), such as is found in plants, which live and grow and feed but are without consciousness. (Medieval scientists were quite aware of the recapitulation of the race-history in the embryo, though they did not deduce from it a doctrine of evolution. They would look upon it, rather, as a recapitulation of the Days of Creation.)

ll. 56 *sqq.*: *organs*, etc.: with the appearance of the bodily organs, the embryo acquires the *animal soul* (*anima sensitiva*), which is not only alive but also conscious, though not self-conscious or reflective.

ll. 62-3: *a mind wiser than thine*: Averroes, who, finding no special organ for the discursive or "possible" intellect (cf. Canto xviii. 51 and note) which distinguishes man from the beasts (the brain, which is common to beasts and men, being regarded as the organ of the *anima sensitiva*), concluded that man's rational soul was not individuated but one, universal, and transcendent. This intellect, in which the individual participated during his lifetime, was withdrawn from him at death; so that for Averroes there was no such thing as a rational and immortal *individual* human soul. This doctrine was vigorously combated by St Thomas. (See Canto xviii. 49 *sqq.*, notes.)

l. 72: *new spirit*: this is the "substantial form" of man – the *rational human soul*, with its "possible intellect". It is created individually and directly by God and implanted in the embryo as soon as the brain is sufficiently formed to receive and sustain it.

ll. 74-5: *one single soul complete*, etc.: the new soul combines with and into itself all the active powers of the vegetative and sensitive souls, so that we have not "soul kindled above soul in us" (cf. Canto iv. 6) nor yet a divine soul imprisoned in an animal organism, but a single complete body-soul complex: "alive and sensitive and self-aware" (lit. "which lives and feels and *turns round upon itself*": i.e. is *self*-conscious, and able to reflect upon itself).

ll. 77–8: *the sun's warmth*, etc.: Statius illustrates his point with a simile of chemical action, by which two things combine to make a third thing, different from either separately.

l. 79: *Lachesis*: the Fate who spins the thread of human life.

ll. 80–4: *but bears essentially away*, etc.: As we saw earlier (xviii. 49 and note) the human soul does not lose at death either its individuality or the faculties which it has taken up from the vegetative and animal souls with which it has compounded. It is still "alive and sensitive and self-aware"; but the lower faculties, which need a body for their expression, are left passive or "in potentiality"; the higher (those which share the nature of spiritual forms) remain active, and all the keener for being no longer obliged to express themselves through a material medium.

l. 86: *on one or other shore*: i.e. on the shore of Acheron or of Tiber.

l. 87: *then first it knows its ways*: in the moment of death, the soul undergoes the "Particular Judgement" (see Introduction, p. 59), and for the first time clearly realizes its own choice between Hell and Heaven.

ll. 88 *sqq.*: *when place has circumscribed it*: unlike Heaven and Hell, Purgatory is, in a manner "in space and time", though its space and time do not altogether correspond to ours. The soul now exercises its formative power ("informing virtue") to make for itself an apparent body, formed by air (the "aery body"), somewhat as the appearance of a rainbow is formed in the cloud. This is the body "ordained to it" by Providence, by means of which it can exercise those lower faculties to the degree required by its penance ("to bear pain, cold, and heat", iii. 31–3), the aery body reproducing all the motions of the spirit as the flame moves with the heat. This is what we call a "shade" (or what, when it appears on earth, we call a "ghost"). Note that the aery body will do exactly what is required of it, no less and no more. Consequently, if it is desirable that it should be palpable it can be palpable, as a violent wind is palpable; if not, not: it is wholly subordinate to its function; thus Virgil, but not Casella, is palpable to Dante.

*N.B.*, the aery body, which is only an interim appearance, must not, of course, be confused with the Body of Glory which will be assumed at the Resurrection, and which is a real, although (in St Paul's words) a "spiritual" body, with powers transcending those of the "natural" body.

ll. 109–14: *we'd reached the last turn of the stairs*: the poets emerge and turn to the right along the Seventh and last Cornice, where the Lustful are purged.

l. 122: *Summae Deus clementiae*: "God of supreme clemency": This is the Prayer of the Lustful, taken from the old version of the Hymn sung at Matins on Saturday (the modern version begins: *Summae parens clementiae*). One verse appropriately runs: "Burn with meet fires our reins and our sick heart [lit. "liver" – the seat of the passions] that having put off evil lusts we may keep watch with loins girded."

ll. 128–35: *Virum non cognosco*: "I know not a man", etc.: These are the examples composing the "Whip" of Lust. The first, from the Life of the Blessed Virgin, is taken from the story of the Annunciation (*Luke* i. 34). The second example, from class. myth., is Diana, the virgin hunter-goddess, who expelled the nymph Helice from her train because she had borne a son to Jupiter (Ovid, *Metam.* ii. 401–530). These examples of virgin chastity are followed by other examples (unspecified) of chastity within the bond of marriage.

l. 139: *the last wound*: the brand of the seventh and last P.

# CANTO XXVI

THE STORY. *Along the Seventh Cornice the Penitents of Natural and Unnatural Lust run in opposite directions, exchanging swift embraces as they pass one another, and each troop crying the Bridle of its own sin. Dante talks with the spirits of two Poets: Guido Guinicelli and Arnaut Daniel.*


While thus along the brink we made our way
    Singly – my kind lord heedful to recite
    From time to time: "Take care! mind what I say!" –

4    The sun smote on my shoulder from the right,
    For now his beams were blanching out the blue
    And turning all the western sky to white;

7    And where my shadow fell, the fire changed hue,
    Reddening; and I saw several spirits take
    Note, as they passed, even of this slender clue.

10    It prompted them to canvas me, and make
    Debate together, muttering, "That one's frame
    Appears no aery body, but opaque."

13    Then some among them, with great caution, came
    Approaching me, till they could come no nigher,
    Being scrupulous not to o'erstep the flame.

16    "Thou walking last of all – through no desire
    To loiter, but through reverence as I deem –
    Answer to me, who burn with thirst and fire;

19    Nor I alone – all these, with thirst extreme,
    Pant for an answer more than ever yet
    Indian or Ethiop for a cooling stream.

22    Tell us, what art thou? Wherefore dost thou set
    Thy body like a wall against the sun
    As though not yet entangled in death's net?"

25    Thus one addressed me; I'd have made me known
    Forthwith, but now another grand surprise
    Arrived, to fix my whole attention on.

Lo! through the highway's heart of fire there flies,     28
    But in the opposite direction bent,
    A quite new throng, which halts me in surmise.

I see each shade, on swiftness all intent,     31
    Kiss one from out the other troop, and go,
    Not pausing, with this brief salute content.

(Thus, as their black bands scurry to and fro,     34
    Ant nuzzles ant, belike to verify
    The route, or swap the news – I do not know.)

This friendly greeting done, and ere they fly     37
    One foot, each party shouts as though it must
    Shout down the other; loud the new folk cry:

"Sodom! Gomorrah!" and their rivals, just     40
    As loud: "Into the cow Pasiphaë
    Leaps, that the bull may hasten to her lust!"

Then like two flocks of cranes, that severally     43
    Wing towards Rhipean heights or desert sands,
    Whether from frost or from the sun to flee,

So those go off and these come on, both bands     46
    With tears reverting to their former strain
    And such fit outcry as their case demands;

And those who'd first addressed me now again     49
    Drew closer to my side, all eagerness
    To listen to me, as their looks made plain.

Then I, who twice had seen them thus express     52
    Fervent desire, began: "O souls secure
    Of peaceful state, be the time more or less,

The harvest of my limbs, green or mature,     55
    Yonder was never reaped – I have them here,
    Complete with blood and bone and ligature,

And hence ascend to have my sight made clear;     58
    There is on high a Lady wins me grace
    This mortal burden through your world to bear.

But, so may you in shortest time embrace     61
    Your hearts' great wish, and reach that heavenly house
    Which brims with love and fills the ends of space,

64　　Tell me – that I on paper may engross
　　　　These matters – who you are, and who the band
　　　　That now behind you speeds away from us."

67　　No more amazed does the rough hillsman stand
　　　　When, rude and wild, he comes into the town
　　　　And dumbly stares at this new wonderland,.

70　　Than all those shades stood then; but when they'd grown
　　　　Free from these perturbations of the sense –
　　　　Which, in a noble mind, are soon calmed down –

73　　"Thrice blest," I heard the first shade recommence,
　　　　"Thou, that in hopes a better death to die
　　　　Upon our shores dost ship experience!

76　　Those who go not beside us went awry
　　　　In that for which Caesar of old heard 'Queen!'
　　　　Flung at him as he passed in triumph by;

79　　Therefore they call, as thou hast heard and seen,
　　　　'Sodom!' in self-reproach when they take flight,
　　　　That shame may aid the fire to burn them clean.

82　　As for our sin, it was hermaphrodite;
　　　　But since we did the human law despise,
　　　　And like brute beasts were slaves to appetite,

85　　We pour opprobrium on ourselves likewise,
　　　　And cry her name who did in bestial mime
　　　　Imbrute her in the wicker brute's disguise.

88　　I've now explained our actions and our crime;
　　　　If chance thou wouldst have all our names supplied,
　　　　I cannot do it, nor would there be time.

91　　Of mine, indeed, thou shalt be satisfied:
　　　　I'm Guido Guinicelli, thus straightway
　　　　Purged, because fully contrite ere I died."

94　　Like twain who in Lycurgus' tragic day
　　　　Beheld their mother after so long loss,
　　　　Such (though I rose not to such heights as they)

97　　Grew I, to hear him name himself who was
　　　　Father to me and to my betters – all
　　　　Who use love's own sweet style and chivalrous.

Long did I pace on pondering, held in thrall,       100
  Deaf, dumb, my gaze devouring him – yet drew
  No nearer, for I feared that flaming wall.

And when I'd feasted eyes on him, I threw       103
  My whole self at his service, pledging him
  Such vows as hearers must give credence to.

"So sharp and deep an impress of esteem       106
  Thou mak'st on me," said he, "by what I hear,
  As Lethe shall not wash away or dim;

But if these oaths are valid, pray make clear       109
  What cause thou hast to hold me – as I think
  Thy words and looks attest – thus lief and dear."

Then I: "Your verse, forged sweetly link by link,       112
  Which while our modern use shall last in song,
  Must render precious even the very ink."

And he: "O brother, I can show among       115
  Our band" (he pointed out a spirit in front)
  "A better craftsman of his mother-tongue.

Love-rhyme or prose in language of Romaunt       118
  He topped them all; and let the fools proclaim
  Him of Limoges to be of more account!

They, caring less for truth than common fame,       121
  Pronounce off-hand, not waiting to be told
  What art and reason have to say to them.

Thus with Guittone many did of old,       124
  From mouth to mouth cracking him up sole best –
  Till truth taught most of them what views to hold.

Now, if high favour do thee so invest       127
  That to the cloister thou shalt enter in
  Where Christ is abbot of the college blest,

Speak Him a paternoster there within       130
  For me, so far as our state calls for one
  Who in this world have no more power to sin."

Then, to make room for neighbours pressing on       133
  Perhaps, he vanished through the flame, even as
  Through a deep pool a fish slips and is gone.

136     I to that soul he'd shown advanced a pace,
            Begging he would vouchsafe his name to me
            Who hoped to write it in an honoured place;

139     And he at once made answer frank and free:
            "Sae weel me likes your couthie kind entreatin',
            I canna nor I winna hide fra' ye;

142     I'm Arnaut, wha gae singin' aye and greetin';
            Waefu' I mind my fulish deeds lang syne,
            Lauchin' luik forrit tae the bricht morn's meetin'.

145     Pray ye the noo, by yonder micht that fine
            Sall guide ye till the top step o' the stair,
            Tak' timely thocht for a' my mickle pine" –

148     Then veiled him in the fires that fine them there.

THE IMAGES. *The Embrace*: As with the fire, so with the exchanged embrace: the image of the sin is also the image and means of the remedy. More clearly here than on any other Cornice, we are *shown* what Virgil has already *told* us – that love is the root of virtue and vice alike: the purging fires burn off the dross, and the good that remains is the good that lay always at the heart of the sin. The swift exchange of kisses, reflected in the speed of the verse, contrasts with the exchanged kiss of Paolo and Francesca – the heedless dallying with temptation, and the relaxed abandonment to indulgence: "we read no more that day". Between these two kisses, damnation and salvation swing balanced.

NOTES. ll. 4–8: *the sun smote on my shoulder*, etc.: it is now somewhere between 4 and 5 P.M. The poets are approaching the most westerly point of the mountain, and the sun, half-way down the northern sky and radiating incandescence over the whole west, is striking over Dante's right shoulder and throwing his shadow upon the wall of fire.

l. 13: *some among them*: these spirits, whom Dante saw (xxv. 124) passing through the flames, were moving according to the usual rule of the mountain, from east to west, so that, pacing alongside the poets, they could keep Dante under observation.

l. 15: *scrupulous not to o'erstep the flame*: Dante once more makes it plain that it is by their own will that the souls persevere in their penance.

l. 30: *a quite new throng*: these spirits are those of the Sodomites, and they, alone among the souls in Purgatory, circle the mountain from west to east (against the sun). This doubtless because they had sinned against the rule of nature. The two sets of spirits thus meet and exchange kisses as they pass each other.

l. 40: "*Sodom! Gomorrah!*": This is the Bridle of unnatural Lust; the example is taken from the O.T. Sodom and Gomorrah were those "cities of the plain" which were destroyed by fire from heaven because of the homosexual vice with which they were riddled.

ll. 41–2: *Into the cow Pasiphaë leaps*: This is the Bridle of natural Lust, the example being taken from class. myth. (for the story of Pasiphaë see *Inf.* xii. 13 and note).

l. 44: *Rhipean heights*: a name given in classical times to a range of mountains in Scythia, but used in the Middle Ages as a general term for mountains in the N. of Europe or Asia.

l. 44: *desert sands*: i.e. the hot deserts of Africa.

l. 59: *a Lady*: probably Beatrice; possibly the Blessed Virgin (see *Inf.* ii. 52 *sqq.*, 94 *sqq.*).

ll. 62–3: *that heavenly house*: the Empyrean.

l. 73: *the first shade*: i.e. the one who had originally addressed Dante in ll. 16–24. As we see later (l. 92) this is the poet Guido Guinicelli.

l. 76: *those who go not beside us*: i.e. the Sodomites, who had by now passed them and disappeared in an east-bound direction.

l. 77: *Caesar of old heard "Queen" flung at him*: Suetonius records in his *Life of Julius Caesar* that this epithet was bestowed on Caesar on account of his relations with Nicomedes, King of Bithynia; and that scurrilous songs to the same effect were sung by the soldiers during the triumph which celebrated his conquest of Gaul. (Vulgar and offensive songs formed part of the usual accompaniments of a triumph, licence being given to the troops to let off their high spirits in this way, lest the conqueror should begin to think himself too big for his boots.)

l. 82: *hermaphrodite*: i.e. hetero-sexual: involving intercourse between a man and a woman. The mythical Hermaphroditus was beloved by the naiad Salmace, at whose prayer the gods welded their two bodies together, so as to form one being with the attributes of both sexes (Ovid, *Metam.* iv. 288–388).

ll. 83–7: *the human law*, etc.: Various kinds of "law" are defined by St Thomas. The ultimate source of all law is the Eternal Law (*Lex Aeterna*), which is the will of God, binding upon the whole created universe; it includes both the principles of morality and what we nowadays mean by the "laws of nature". The Eternal Law is made known to Man in two forms: (*a*) the Divine Law (*Lex Divina*), by the special revelation of Scripture; (*b*) the Natural Law (*Lex Naturalis*) imprinted on every human soul by general revelation; this is "the participation by the rational creature in the Eternal Law." [*N.B.* The popular mis-use of the phrase "Natural Law" to connote the "laws of Nature" is inaccurate and misleading and should be strongly discouraged.] In obedience to the Natural Law the rational creature accepts that part of the Eternal Law which assigns to the sexes their proper functional relations, and to which the animals likewise conform instinctively under the "laws of nature". Sodomy is thus a sin against the *Natural* Law.

The Human Law (*Lex Humana*) derives, in so far as it is just, from the Natural Law, and comprises those principles of morality which are proper for the regulation of specifically human conduct, though not necessarily applicable to animals. Thus theft, for example, and (in the sphere of sexual morality) fornication, adultery, and incest are actions innocent in animals, though forbidden to Man not only by the Divine Law but also (though with varying codes of behaviour) by the Human Law.

Guinicelli explains that he and his companions, while innocent of offence against the Natural Law, sinned by indulging, as though they were brute beasts, in lusts which contravene the Human Law. Their Bridle is accordingly taken from the evil example of Pasiphaë who – though in a sense more literal than theirs – "made a beast of herself" by mating with the bull.

For a table showing the derivation of the various kinds of Law, see Appendix, p. 346.

l. 92: *Guido Guinicelli (b. ca.* 1230, *d.* ? 1276): was a member of the Principi family of Bologna. In 1274 he was expelled from his native city with other members of the Ghibelline party, and is thought to have died in exile. He was the most illustrious poet of Italy prior to Dante, and became the founder of that *dolce stil nuovo* (see Canto xxiv. 57, note) of which Lapo Gianni, Cino da Pistoia, Guido Cavalcanti, and Dante himself were exponents. Dante quotes and speaks of him with admiration, both here and in the *De Vulg. Eloq.* A number of his works (odes, sonnets, *ballate*, etc.) are extant – a few satirical, but for the most part love-poems.

l. 94: *twain who in Lycurgus' tragic day*: Hypsipyle, former Queen of Lemnos (cf. *Inf.* xviii. 91–5), was captured by pirates and sold into slavery to Lycurgus King of Nemea, who entrusted his infant son to her care. The child unfortunately was killed by a serpent and Lycurgus condemned Hypsipyle to death. On her way to execution the twin sons she had borne to Jason, and from whom she had long been parted, recognized her, rushed to embrace her, rescued her from the executioners, and prevailed on Lycurgus to pardon her (Statius: *Theb.* v. 720 *sqq.*).

l. 96: *I rose not to such heights*: Dante was not so devoted and cour-ageous as actually to rush into danger to embrace Guinicelli – any more than he had done in Hell with the Noble Florentines (*Inf.* xvi. 46–51): he was afraid of the fire.

l. 108: *Lethe*: the river of forgetfulness (cf. *Inf.* xiv. 136 and *Purg.* xxviii. 130, etc.).

l. 116: *a spirit in front*: this, as we learn from l. 142, is Arnaut Daniel, the famous Provençal troubadour who flourished towards the end of the twelfth century. He came from the Ribeyrac family in Perigord and is known to have been attached for some time to the court of King Richard I of England, and to have visited France, Spain, and possibly also Italy. His poems, of which some eighteen have been preserved, are written in his native Provençal. Modern taste does not greatly relish his highly artificial, elaborate, and enigmatic style; but Petrarch agrees with Dante's estimate, and calls him "the great master of love".

l. 118: *love-rhyme or prose in language of Romaunt*: Dante does not mean that Arnaut himself wrote prose-romances but that in writing the vernacular he surpassed all other writers (whether of prose or verse) of the so-called "Romance (i.e. Latin-derived) Languages".

l. 120: *him of Limoges*: Guiraut de Bornelh (or Borneil), *fl.* 1175–*c.* 1220, another famous Provençal poet, with a much simpler and more popular style, called by his contemporaries "master of the troubadours".

l. 124: *Guittone*: Guido d'Arezzo, called "Guittone" (cf. xxiv. 56), was born (*c.* 1250) of a noble Aretine family. He was a fine scholar and linguist and a distinguished poet, who perfected the form of the sonnet. He eventually entered the military religious order of the Jovial Friars (*Frati gaudenti* – v. *Inf.* xxiii. 103 and note) and devoted himself to preaching religion and peace, and denouncing the corruptions of the times. Guido Guinicelli at first imitated his method, but soon surpassed his model and struck out his own line. Guittone's verse is somewhat laboured and clumsy; "he expressed beautiful thoughts, but his style was not happy" (Warren Vernon).

ll. 128–9: *the cloister ... where Christ is abbot of the college*: Heaven.

ll. 131–2: *so far as our state calls for one*, etc.: i.e. omitting the clauses "lead us not into temptation but deliver us from evil" which (as we know from xi. 22–4) are not needed by the spirits in Purgatory.

l. 136: *that soul he'd shown*: i.e. Arnaut Daniel.

ll. 140–7: *sae weel me likes*, etc.: Dante has made the poet reply in his native Provençal: partly, no doubt, in compliment to Arnaut's "mastery of his mother-tongue"; partly, one may guess, in order to display his own facility in the "*langue d'oc*"; but chiefly, I am sure, because the light French vowels and monosyllabic rhymes impart a peculiar tripping gaiety to the verse and because the unexpected change of language lends an engaging sense of *difference* to this, the last exchange of speech with the souls in Purgatory. In order to preserve something of this lightness and contrast, I have translated the speech into Border Scots – a dialect which bears something of the same relation to English as Provençal does to Italian.

# CANTO XXVII

THE STORY. *Shortly before sunset the Poets reach the Westernmost point of the Mountain. Beyond the fire they see the Angel of Chastity standing at the entrance to the Pass of Pardon and hear him singing the Benediction of the Cornice. In order to gain the Pass they must needs go through the fire. Dante is terrified; but Virgil encourages him with the name of Beatrice, and at length he is persuaded to pass through the flames between his two guides. The sun sinks as they are beginning the ascent, so that they have to pass the night on the steps, and here for the last time Dante dreams – of Leah and Rachel. At dawn they swiftly climb the Seventh Stair, at the top of which Virgil resigns his office of mentor, pronouncing Dante to be now lord over himself. Before them stretch the flowery meadows which surround the Earthly Paradise.*

> As when his earliest shaft of light assails
>     The city where his Maker shed His blood,
>     When Ebro lies beneath the lifted Scales
>
> And noontide scorches down on Ganges' flood,　　　　4
>     So rode the sun; thus day was nightward winging
>     When there before us God's glad angel stood.
>
> He on the bank, across the flames, stood singing　　　7
>     *Beati mundo corde*, with a sound
>     More than all earthly music sweet and ringing.
>
> Then: "Holy souls, there's no way on or round　　　10
>     But through the bite of fire; in, then, and come!
>     Nor be you deaf to what is sung beyond."
>
> As we approached him, thus his words struck home;　　13
>     And it was so with me when this I heard
>     Even as with one who's carried to the tomb.
>
> I leaned across my clasped hands, staring hard　　　16
>     Into the fire, picturing vividly
>     Sights I had seen, of bodies burned and charred.
>
> Then both my friendly escorts turned to me,　　　　19
>     And Virgil spoke and said: "My son, though here
>     There may be torment, death there cannot be.

22    Remember, O remember! and if clear
       From harm I brought thee, even on Geryon's back,
       What shall I now, with God so much more near?

25    Rest thou assured that though this fiery track
       Should lap thee while a thousand years went by
       Thy head should not be singed nor one hair lack;

28    And if thou think that I deceive thee, why,
       Prove it – go close, hold out a little bit
       Of thy skirt's hem in thine own hand, and try.

31    Have done with fear henceforth, have done with it –
       Turn and go safe." And there was I, for all
       My conscience smote me, budging ne'er a whit.

34    Then, somewhat troubled seeing me thus fall
       Stubborn and stupid: "Look, my son," he said,
       "'Twixt Beatrice and thee there is this wall."

37    As Pyramus, when he was well-nigh dead,
       At Thisbe's name heaved up his heavy eyes
       To her, the day that dyed the mulberry red,

40    So did I turn me to my leader wise,
       My hardness melting at the name which aye
       Like a fresh well-spring in my heart doth rise.

43    He shook his head: "What! do we mean to stay
       This side?" said he; then smiled at me, as who
       Should with an apple coax a child away.

46    Then he went on before me, stepping through
       The flame, and he asked Statius now to go
       Behind, who long had walked betwixt us two;

49    And I, being in, would have been glad to throw
       Myself for coolness into molten glass,
       With such unmeasured heat did that fire glow.

52    My gentle father talked to cheer me – 'twas
       Beatrice all the way; "Methinks even now
       Her eyes," he'd say, "shine to me through the pass;"

55    While from yon side sweet singing showed us how
       To go, and led us, by the listening held,
       Forth where the road lifts to the mountain's brow.

"*Venite benedicti patris*" welled       58
  In song there from a core of blinding light;
  But look I could not, for my sight was quelled.

"The sun is sinking, soon it will be night,"     61
  The voice went on to warn us; "do not stop,
  Press on, ere darkness hide the west from sight."

Sheer through the rock the road climbed to the top,   64
  So facing, that I saw my shadow run
  Ahead, cast by a sun at point to drop.

Some steps we tried, but when we'd scarce begun   67
  I and my sages knew the sun had set
  Behind us, for the shadow now was gone;

So, ere the vast horizon's bound had yet     70
  Become one hue, and night o'er all the air
  Fully extended her protectorate,

Each for his bed chose one step of the stair,   73
  For the mount's law had robbed us, not of will
  But of all power to rise from where we were.

Like goats that have been skipping on the hill   76
  Wanton and wild, but, being fed, grow tame
  And lay them down to ruminate, quite still

Beneath the shade, when summer's all aflame;   79
  While, leaned upon his crook, their herd doth keep
  Watch, and, so leaning, takes good care of them;

And like the shepherd who beside his sheep   82
  Holds silent vigil under the night sky
  Lest the wolf scatter them from out their sleep,

Such were we then all three; the goat was I   85
  And they the herdsmen, and to fold us in
  This side and that the rocky wall rose high.

Narrow the view of any outward scene,     88
  But through those narrows I saw star on star,
  Bigger and brighter than they'd ever been.

Ruminant thus I gazed on them afar     91
  Until sleep took me – sleep that oft in dreams
  Can give us news of things before they are.

94    Such time, methinks, as Cytheraea, who seems
          Ever to burn the flames of love among,
          First on the mount shot forth her orient beams,

97    I in a vision saw a lady, young
          And beautiful, through level meadows go,
          Gathering flowers, by whom these words were sung:

100   "Whoso would ask my name, I'd have him know
          That I am Leah, who for my array
          Twine garlands, weaving white hands to and fro.

103   To please me at the glass I deck me gay;
          The while my sister Rachel never stirs,
          But sits before her mirror all the day,

106   For on her own bright eyes she still prefers
          To gaze, as I to deck me with my hands;
          Action is my delight, reflection hers."

109   Now from that gleam which, ere day breaks, expands
          Daily more dear to pilgrims homeward bound
          Still as they lodge nearer their native lands,

112   The shades of darkness fled away all round,
          And with them fled my sleep; so I arose,
          Seeing the great masters risen from the ground.

115   "That most sweet fruit which mortal hunger goes
          Seeking with so much care from many a tree
          This day shall give thy craving full repose."

118   Such were the words that Virgil used to me;
          And no glad gift of rich and precious things
          So glad a gift as that could ever be.

121   Longing on longing with such pulsing springs
          Came o'er me then to soar up to the height,
          At every step I felt my feet grow wings.

124   So when the stair had dropped, long flight on flight,
          Away beneath us, then did Virgil turn
          On the top step and fix me with his eyes,

127   Saying: "The temporal fire and the eterne
          Thou hast beheld, my son, and reached a place
          Where, of myself, no further I discern.

I've brought thee here by wit and by address;                    130
  Make pleasure now thy guide – thou art well sped
  Forth of the steep, forth of the narrow ways.

See how the sun shines here upon thy head;                       133
  See the green sward, the flowers, the boskages
  That from the soil's own virtue here are bred.

While those fair eyes are coming, bright with bliss,             136
  Whose tears sent me to thee, thou may'st prospect
  At large, or sit at ease to view all this.

No word from me, no further sign expect;                         139
  Free, upright, whole, thy will henceforth lays down
  Guidance that it were error to neglect,

Whence o'er thyself I mitre thee and crown."                     142

THE IMAGES. *The Wall of Fire*: It is the peculiarity of the Seventh
Cornice that *all* souls, whether or not they are detained there to
purge the sin of Lust, are compelled to pass through and suffer its
torment of fire before ascending the Pass. From the point of view
of the *story*, Dante has here very skilfully and economically com-
bined several themes in one. The fire in fact exercises a triple func-
tion: (*a*) it forms the Penance of the Cornice; (*b*) it represents the
flaming sword of the Cherubim who guard the entrance to the
Garden of Eden (*Gen.* iii. 24); (*c*) it provides that "Pass of Peril"
which, in so many folk-tales of other-world journeys, the hero has
to leap through in order to attain the Lady, or other object of his
search. *Allegorically*, since every sin is a sin of love, the purgation
of love itself is a part of every man's penitence.

*Dante's Dream of Leah and Rachel*: Jacob served Laban seven years for
the hand of Rachel his younger daughter. At the end of that time,
Laban gave him Leah, saying that it was not fitting for the younger
sister to be married before the elder. When Jacob had accepted
Leah and promised to serve for another seven years, Laban gave
him Rachel also. And Leah was dim of sight but fruitful; Rachel,
beautiful but barren (*Gen.* xxix. 10–31).

  In mystical writings, particularly those of Richard of St Victor
(*d.* 1173), whom Dante places in the Heaven of the Sun (*Para.* x.
131), the two wives of Jacob are frequently interpreted as alle-
gories respectively of the Active and the Contemplative Life; and
this is the function they fulfil in Dante's third dream.

  The Active Life is the Christian life lived in the world; it is abun-
dantly fruitful in good works, but those who pursue it cannot see
very far into the things of the spirit because, like Martha (another

type of the Active Life) they are "cumbered with much serving". The Contemplative Life is that which is wholly devoted to prayer and the practice of the Presence of God; it is less prolific in good works than the Active Life, but the fruit it bears is the most precious of all (Leah bore Jacob ten sons; but the two sons eventually born of Rachel were Joseph and Benjamin, the best beloved). The Active Life is in no way to be condemned; it is indeed necessary to the existence of the Contemplative Life (Leah must be wedded before Rachel), for if there were no Marthas to do the work of the world, Mary could not be nourished, nor find leisure for contemplation. Nevertheless, Mary's is the "better part", and the Active Life exists, in a manner, for the sake of the Contemplative. The complete Christian life is a blend of action and contemplation, the former leading to the latter, and being subdued to it as the means to the end.

*N.B.* The perfection of the Active and Contemplative lives must not be severally equated with the perfection of the Natural and Spiritual lives; although in *The Banquet* (*Il Convivio*) Dante sometimes uses expressions which suggest that he himself was, in his early "philosophic" days, a little confused about this. By the time he comes to writing the *Comedy* he is, however, quite clear that the Active and Contemplative lives are the two component parts of the Christian life, whose differing but complementary perfections are both displayed in the *Paradiso*. (Both Actives and Contemplatives may, of course, also be found within the framework of a natural religion, though not in their full Christian perfection.)

NOTES. ll. 1–5: *as when his earliest shaft*, etc.: it is dawn in Jerusalem (l. 2); midnight (l. 3) in Spain – i.e. on the far western horizon; and noon (l. 4) on the Ganges – i.e. on the far eastern horizon; and consequently sunset (l. 5) in Purgatory – i.e. nearly 6 P.M. See clock diagram between pages 350 and 351.

l. 6: *God's glad angel*: this is the Angel of Chastity, the guardian of the Seventh Cornice.

l. 8: *Beati mundo corde*: "Blessed are the pure in heart": This is the Beatitude (*Matt.* v. 8) which forms the Benediction of the Cornice. The verse concludes "for they shall see God"; the penitents who have passed through the refining fire have completed their purgation and are now ready to stand in God's presence.

ll. 10–11: *there's no way ... but through the bite of fire* (see Images): Twice already Dante has flinched from the fire, but this time he has to face it.

l. 18: *sights I had seen*: Dante does not, I think, refer only to accidental deaths by fire: he had probably seen men publicly burned at the stake, and it adds poignancy to his vivid apprehensions on this Cornice to remember that he and his sons had been banished from Florence on pain of being burned alive.

l. 23: *even on Geryon's back*: Cf. *Inf.* xvii; it was, incidentally, from Geryon's back that Dante had looked down upon the fires and the "grand woes" of Malbowges (*ibid.* 122–6).

ll. 37–9: *as Pyramus*, etc.: Pyramus, thinking that his lover Thisbe had been killed by a lioness, stabbed himself; and his blood, spurting from the wound, dyed red the berries of the mulberry tree beneath which the lovers had made their tryst. Thisbe, who had only fled to safety, returned and, finding him dying, "cried to him: 'Pyramus, answer! It is thine own dear Thisbe that calls thee – O listen and lift thy drooping head.' At the name Thisbe, Pyramus raised his eyes, already heavy with death, and having looked upon her, closed them again." Thisbe then killed herself upon his body, and in answer to her prayer the fruit of the mulberry has been red ever since (Ovid, *Metam.* iv. 55–166). (Shakespeare's "mechanicals", who have made it perhaps a little difficult for us to take this story tragically, seem to have found their scenic resources unequal to the transformation of the mulberries.)

l. 58: *Venite benedicti patris* [*mei*]: "Come ye blessed of My Father": This song is also sung by the Angel of the Cornice, and corresponds to the *Te Deum* which welcomed the Penitents at their entrance to the Cornices (ix. 141). The words are taken from *Matt.* xxv. 34. (It is no doubt at this point that the last P is erased from Dante's forehead.)

ll. 65–6: *I saw my shadow run ahead*: they have now traversed the whole northern face of the Mountain, from due east to due west by compass. (It will be remembered that on its sunless southern side they never set foot. See diagram, p. 340.) As they face inward to climb the seventh and last stair, the sun is setting directly behind them, and before they have ascended more than a few steps darkness falls and the Rule of the Mountain comes into operation.

l. 87: *the rocky wall*: i.e. on either side of the stair.

l. 94: *Cytheraea*: the planet Venus (the name is given to the goddess from the island of Cythera, near which she was fabled to have risen from the sea, and which was peculiarly sacred to her cult). Venus, as we know, was in Pisces (the Fishes), the sign rising next before Aries where the Sun was; this is therefore, once again, the hour before dawn in which "men dream true".

l. 109: *that gleam*: the white dawnlight which precedes sunrise.

l. 115: *that most sweet fruit*: Cf. *Inf.* xvi. 62.

l. 123: *I felt my feet grow wings*: Cf. Cantos iv. 91–5; xii. 121–6.

l. 127: *the temporal fire and the eterne*: i.e. the fires of Purgatory and of Hell.

ll. 130–1: *by wit and by address; make pleasure now thy guide*: when the stain of sin is purged, and love set in order, the wisdom and skill

of human reason are no longer needed for right conduct, because love
is then the fulfilling of the law (*Rom.* xiii. 10). In St Augustine's words:
"Love, and do as you like" – because what you *ought* to do and what
you *want* to do are now the same thing.

ll. 136–7: *those fair eyes ... whose tears sent me to thee*: Cf. *Inf.* ii. 115–16.

l. 142: *I mitre thee and crown*: the soul, its will made free and perfectly
attuned to the Divine will, has now achieved mastery over itself, and
therefore Virgil pronounces it to be invested with the symbols of
earthly authority both spiritual and temporal: the papal mitre and the
imperial crown. In the *literal* sense, the blessed dead have of course no
need of external authority: in Heaven, God is the only ruler; neither
is there any visible temple or church, "for the Lord God Almighty
and the Lamb are the temple of it" (*Rev.* xxi. 22). In the *allegorical*
sense (which concerns the present life) Dante clearly cannot mean
that Church and State are unnecessary and that it is sufficient for every
man to follow the "inner light". This would render a great deal of his
poem meaningless; moreover, all men do not attain perfection in this
life, and where there is sin, there is always need of external authority.
What he certainly does mean, at the "political" level of interpretation,
is that only when Church and State are freely conformed to the will of
God is the authority of either perfect: hence his abiding and bitter
indignation at that corruption of both powers of which he was so
acutely conscious.

# CANTO XXVIII

**THE STORY.** *Dante, followed by his companions, enters the Sacred Wood, and presently comes to a brook, on the farther bank of which is a Lady, singing and gathering flowers. She answers his questions about the Earthly Paradise, and intimates that the Golden Age of which poets have dreamed is a lingering memory of this place where Man was once innocent and happy.*

Eager to search, in and throughout its ways
    The sacred wood, whose thick and leafy tent,
    Spread in my sight, tempered the new sun's rays,

I made no pause, but left the cliff and went          4
    With lingering steps across the level leas
    Where all the soil breathed out a fragrant scent.

A delicate air, that no inconstancies          7
    Knows in its motion, on my forehead played,
    With force no greater than a gentle breeze,

And quivering at its touch the branches swayed,      10
    All toward that quarter where the holy hill
    With the first daylight stretches out its shade;

Yet ne'er swayed from the upright so, but still      13
    The little birds the topmost twigs among
    Spared not to practise all their tiny skill;

Rather they welcomed with rejoicing song         16
    The dawn-wind to the leaves, which constantly
    To their sweet chant the burden bore along.

So, in Chiassi's pinewood by the sea,           19
    From bough to bough the gathering murmurs swell
    When Aeolus has set Scirocco free.

Now, when my footsteps, slowly as they fell,       22
    So far within the ancient wood were set
    That where I'd first come in I could not tell,

Lo! they were halted by a rivulet            25
    Which ran from right to left, its ripples small
    Bending the grasses on the edge of it;

28    And whatso waters over here we call
          Clearest, were cloudy by comparison
          With this, which hides not anything at all,

31    Though darkly, darkly it goes flowing on
          Beneath the everlasting shade, which never
          Lets any ray strike there of sun or moon.

34    I stayed my feet, but let my eyes pass over
          To see the fresh and various profusion
          Of flowery branches on yon side the river;

37    And there appeared to me – as when the intrusion
          Of some new wonder takes one unaware
          And throws all one's ideas into confusion –

40    A lady all alone, who wandered there
          Singing and plucking flower on floweret gay,
          With which her path was painted everywhere.

43    "Prithee, fair lady, that in love's warm ray
          Dost sun thyself – if looks, that wont to be
          The index of the heart, mean what they say –

46    Advance," said I, "if it seem good to thee,
          So near the river that, when thou dost sing,
          The words thou singest may be clear to me.

49    O thou dost put me to remembering
          Of who and what were lost, that day her mother
          Lost Proserpine, and she the flowers of spring."

52    As a dancing lady turns with her toes together,
          Foot by foot set close and close to the ground,
          And scarcely putting the one before the other,

55    So she to me, as moves a maiden bound
          By sweet decorum, modest eyes downbent,
          Among the red and yellow flowers turned round;

58    And of my prayer she gave me full content,
          Coming so close that I could well divine
          Not only the sweet sounds but what they meant.

61    So, when she'd come to where the crystalline
          Clear water bathes the grasses, she at once
          Did me the grace to lift her eyes to mine.

Never, for sure, did such bright radiance glance      64
    From Venus' eyelids, when her wayward child
    Had pierced her with his dart by strange mischance.

So, upright on the other bank, she smiled,      67
    Still twining in her hands the blossoms pied,
    Which without seed on that high land grow wild.

Between us ran the stream, three paces wide;      70
    But Hellespont where Xerxes crossed – whose lot
    Still to this day rebukes man's foolish pride –

Earned less hate from Leander, though it shot      73
    'Twixt Sestos and Abydos in full race,
    Than this from me for straightway opening not.

"You are newcomers here, and, as I guess,"      76
    Said she, "my smiling in this spot elect
    To be the cradle of the human race

May make you wonder, and perchance suspect;      79
    But the psalm *Delectasti* gives you light
    To illuminate your clouded intellect.

And thou in front, who didst my approach invite,      82
    Wouldst thou know more, ask on; I came prepared
    To answer questions and content thee quite."

I said: "The water, and the forest stirred      85
    To music, seem to contradict what I
    Had come to think, from what I lately heard."

She therefore: "I will tell the reason why      88
    These things are so, which cause perplexities,
    And thus I'll make the offending mists to fly.

The most high Good, that His sole self doth please,      91
    Making man good, and for good, set him in
    This place as earnest of eternal peace.

Short time did he stay here, because of sin;      94
    Because of sin he changed his harmless mirth
    And joyous play for labour and chagrin.

Lest turmoil such as vapours of the earth      97
    And water make beneath them, when they flock
    Upward to reach the heat that draws them forth,

100    Should war against mankind, this mountain rock
        Was raised thus high to heaven, and lifted clear
        Above all this, from where it's under lock.

103    Now, since in circle the whole aery sphere
        Turns with the primal motion in one sense,
        Save in its circuit something interfere,

106    That motion strikes upon this eminence
        Which in the living air stands free throughout,
        And makes the wood resound, because 'tis dense.

109    And every tree is potent to give out
        Virtue when smitten, which impregns the airs,
        And these, in circling, waft it all about;

112    Thus all the earth elsewhere conceives and bears –
        As in itself 'tis apt, or to its skies
        Adapted – divers trees of kind diverse.

115    This being known, there need be no surprise
        Should some plant over yonder now and then
        Without apparent seed from earth arise.

118    Thou must know further that this holy plain
        Beneath thee teems with seeds of everything,
        And in its womb breeds fruits ne'er plucked of men.

121    This water that thou see'st wells from no spring
        By condensation of cold cloud supplied,
        Like streams that have their spate and slackening,

124    But from a fount whose sure and constant tide
        Ever by God's good will regains at source
        Whate'er it freely spends on either side.

127    With twofold powers it runs a twofold course:
        This side blots all man's sins from memory;
        That side to memory all good deeds restores;

130    Lethe this side, and that side Eunoë
        We name it; and to make its work complete
        This must be tasted first; that, secondly;

133    Lo there a taste beyond all savours sweet!
        Now, though perchance thy thirst has drunk full measure,
        Even should I now reveal no more to it,

I'll add a rider just at my good pleasure;                              136
   That words should outrun promise is no crime,
   And no less dear, I think, thou'lt prize the treasure.

Those men of yore who sang the golden time                             139
   And all its happy state – maybe indeed
   They on Parnassus dreamed of this fair clime.

Here was the innocent root of all man's seed;                          142
   Here spring is endless, here all fruits are, here
   The nectar is, which runs in all their rede."

Then to my poets standing in the rear                                  145
   I wheeled right round, and by their smiles saw plain
   That this last gloss had not escaped their ear,

So turned to face that lady bright again.                              148

THE IMAGES. *The Earthly Paradise*: The scenery of Dante's Earthly
Paradise is said to have been taken from the *Pineta* (pine-wood) of
Classe (Chiassi), near Ravenna on the Adriatic, where the last
cantos of the *Purgatory* were written. In so far as poets "take" their
ideal scenery from any actual place, this is doubtless true; but it
does not fully explain Dante's insistence on speaking always of
"the sacred *Forest*", "the ancient *Forest*", and never employing the
more usual and traditional image of a garden. We can scarcely
doubt that he is deliberately making a parallel and contrast with
the "dark Wood", the "rough and stubborn Forest", from which
he set out upon his journey (*Inf.* i. 1 *sqq.*).

In the *allegory*, the Earthly Paradise is the state of *innocence*. It is
from here that Man, if he had never fallen, would have set out
upon his journey to the Celestial Paradise which is his ultimate
destination; but because of sin, his setting-out is from that other
Forest which is the degraded and horrifying parody of this one.
His whole journey through Hell and Purgatory is thus a *return*
journey in search of his true starting-place – the return to original
innocence. Natural innocence is not an end in itself, but the neces-
sary condition of beginning: it was never intended that unfallen
Adam should remain static, but that he should progress from
natural to supernatural perfection. I think it is therefore a mistake
to suppose, as many have done, that Dante's Earthly Paradise
stands for the perfect Empire, the perfection of the Active Life, the
"felicity of this life", or even for the perfection of the Natural Life,

except in the sense that it represents the recovery of that original perfection of human nature which was impaired by the Fall. Once we remember that Eden is, and was always meant to be, a starting-place and not a stopping-place, we shall have little difficulty in finding a consistent and intelligible significance for the allegory.

*The Lady*: The *literal* and *allegorical* identity of this delightful Lady is perhaps the most tantalizing problem in the *Comedy*. Her name – as we are casually informed in the final canto – is Matilda; and from the fact that she has a name we are entitled to infer that she is no abstraction, but a personality as real and human as Beatrice herself. Beyond this, so far as her literal identity is concerned, all is conjecture. (See Appendix, p. 347.)

Much more important is her allegorical significance. The fact that she is "discovered" picking flowers, like the Leah of Dante's dream (xxvii. 97–9), assures us that she is in some way a type of the Active Life; and some commentators have seen in her the "one permanent resident" of the Earthly Paradise, and supposed her to be the image of Empire, Philosophy, or Natural Perfection. There is, however, no reason to assume that her presence in the place is permanent: what is certain is that she forms part of Beatrice's retinue; and her obvious function is to prepare Dante for his meeting with Beatrice. Accepting this for the moment, we will consider her again in the Images to Canto xxxiii.

NOTES. ll. 11–12: *all toward that quarter*, etc.: the breeze (for whose explanation see l. 103 *sqq.*) had a gentle and steady motion from east to west.

ll. 19–21: *Chiassi's pinewood*: the Pineta at Classe, which in Dante's time was still the seaport of Ravenna, but from which the sea has now withdrawn, leaving the great sixth-century church of S. Apollinare in Classe standing alone in the marshy plain. Until recent years the famous Pineta itself retained much of its beauty, but it has now been almost completely denuded by the depredations of two world wars. *Scirocco*: the S.E. wind. *Aeolus* was the god who controlled the winds (*Aen.* i. 52 *sqq.*). C. Ricci, writing in 1891, describes this murmuring of the Pineta when Scirocco blows, and also the long rides of the forest, sheltered from the dazzling sunlight and perfumed by a thick under-growth of blossoms and flowering shrubs.

l. 40: *a lady all alone*: this is Matilda.

l. 50: *of who and what were lost*: When Proserpine (Gk. Persephone, also worshipped under the title of Koré = the Daughter) was carried off by Dis to Hades, while gathering flowers in the fields of Enna, she let fall her flowers from her lap. Her mother Ceres (Gk. Demeter =

the Earth-Mother) sought her many days in vain, and in her anger forbade the earth to produce any fruits. Eventually, Proserpine was restored to her mother by the intervention of Jove; but because she had eaten in Hades the seeds of a pomegranate, she was obliged to return and pass the third part of every year underground. This classical fertility-myth is used by Dante as an image of the Fall of Man and the loss of Eden.

l. 65: *her wayward child*: Cupid. When playing one day with Venus, he accidentally scratched her breast with one of his darts, and she fell in love with the beautiful mortal, Adonis. (Ovid, *Metam.* x. 525 *sqq.*)

l. 71: *Hellespont*: the strait, now known as the Dardanelles, separating Europe from Asia Minor. It is about 40 miles long, varying in width from 1 to 4 miles. In 480 B.C., Xerxes the Persian threw a bridge of boats across it at its narrowest point, between Abydos on the Asiatic side, and Sestos on the other, in order to bring his armies into Europe. The campaign, though successful by land, ended in the appalling naval disaster of Phalerum, off Salamis.

l. 73: *Leander*: a youth of Abydos, who was in love with Hero the priestess of Aphrodite in Sestos. He swam the Hellespont every night to visit her; but one stormy night he was drowned, whereupon Hero threw herself into the sea. The current at this point is very strong (l. 74); Byron, however, showed that Leander's fabled feat was not impossible by swimming the Hellespont in 1810.

l. 80: *the psalm Delectasti*: This is not the actual opening or title of the psalm itself, but is taken from the 4th verse of *Ps.* xcii (*Vulg.* xci. 5): *Quia delectasti me, Domine, in factura tua*, etc.: "For thou, Lord, hast made me glad through thy works: and I will rejoice in giving praise for the operations of thy hands." We may suppose that these are the words which the Lady has been singing; and now that Dante and his companions have (ll. 58–9) heard them distinctly they will know better than to suppose that smiles and cheerful behaviour are inappropriate in (ll. 76–7) holy places. (Many people, however, to this day continue to suppose it.)

l. 82: *thou in front*: Dante; he, for the first time, is walking at the head of the party.

ll. 85–7: *the water and the forest stirred*, etc.: Having been told by Statius (xxi. 40–57) that above Peter's Gate the Mountain knows neither rain nor wind nor any other atmospheric disturbance, Dante is now puzzled to account for the river and for the breeze which stirs the trees. (Compare his similar interest in the meteorology of Hell, *Inf.* xxxiii. 100–5.)

ll. 91 *sqq.*: *the most high Good*, etc.: Matilda explains that, had it not been for the Fall, mankind would have continued to live in Eden, which – since it was intended (l. 93) as foretaste and pledge of the peace of eternity – was set high above the disturbances of the lower atmosphere.

ll. 97–9: *lest turmoil*, etc.: i.e. "storms due to disturbances caused in the atmosphere by evaporation under the influence of heat."

l. 102: *from where it's under lock*: i.e. above Peter's Gate.

ll. 103–8: *since in circle*, etc.: The Lady now explains that the breeze of Paradise is not caused by any "turmoil" in the atmosphere itself. It is not like an earthly wind, which may change its force or direction at any moment. For what Dante now feels is the daily movement of the whole globe of the ninefold heavens, turning steadily with the Primum Mobile in the one (east-to-west) direction about the earth. Since the earth itself is deemed to be fixed in relation to the heavens, objects upon it intercept this motion, which thus produces the swaying and rustling of the leaves, and fans Dante's forehead (l. 8) like a gentle breeze.

ll. 109–20: *and every tree*, etc.: The Lady further explains that this universal wind carries with it from the trees and other plants in Paradise a generating virtue which it distributes about the earth as it goes. This explains the sporadic appearances of new and exotic species, in places where no seed has been sown.

ll. 118–20: *this holy plain*, etc.: The earth of Paradise still retains the virtue given to it on the Third Day of Creation, when it spontaneously brought forth plants and trees of every species (*Gen.* i. 11–12).

ll. 121–6: *This water*, etc.: Finally, the Lady explains the presence of the water, which is not fed by rain, but wells perpetually from the twin fountains of Lethe and Eunoë (which Dante will presently see, xxxiii. 122 *sqq.*). Lethe, the river of Oblivion, we have met before; it is the stream whose windings Dante and Virgil followed when climbing up out of Hell (*Inf.* xxxiv. 130–2); and it also turns out to be the very rivulet on whose bank he is now standing. (We remember that in *Inf.* xiv Virgil told him he would see it "far from this Pit".) Eunoë, the river of Good Remembrance, restores the memory of good but not of evil; and "to make its work complete" (i.e. to restore perfection) the water of the two rivers must both be drunk, and in the right order. (See Introduction, p. 68.)

l. 136: *I'll add a rider*: The Lady has now fully answered Dante's questions, but, as a kind of bonus, she throws in the hint that those dreams of the Golden Age which have haunted the minds of poets (and indeed of all men) from time immemorial are a dim "racial memory" of Paradise before the Fall. This memory belongs to Man's *nature*; it is not the gift of revelation, but common to heathen and Christian alike. (It follows that when we to-day contemptuously call such dreams "nostalgic", which means "homesick", we are unwittingly calling them by their right name, for they quite literally arise from Man's longing for his true and original home.)

l. 145: *my poets*: the Lady's enchanting courtesy, aimed as it obviously is at Virgil, is also Dante's courtesy to all the pagan poets his forebears.

# CANTO XXIX

**THE STORY.** *As Dante and the Lady, one on either bank, follow the winding course of the River upstream, they see light and hear music advancing towards them through the Forest from the East; and soon the Pageant of the Sacrament comes into view, and halts before Dante on the Lady's side of the River.*

> As sings an amorous lady to elate her,
>     The music of her voice went singing on:
>     *"Beati quorum tecta sunt peccata."*

4    And even as nymphs that wont to stray alone
>     Through woodland shadows in the olden days,
>     Each seeking or to see or flee the sun,

7    So on the river-bank she went her ways
>     Upstream, and I moved on with her abreast,
>     Matching small steps to small, and so kept pace.

10    And not a hundred yards had we progressed
>     Thus, she and I, when both banks made a bend
>     And eastward now I found my face addressed;

13    Nor far in this direction did we wend
>     Ere the fair lady turned and said to me:
>     "Look now, my brother – hearken and attend."

16    And lo! a flood of brilliance suddenly
>     Through the great forest spread on every side,
>     Such that I thought it lightened there, maybe;

19    But lightning comes and goes and doth not bide,
>     While this remained and bright and brighter grew;
>     So in my mind, "What can it be?" I cried.

22    And a most dulcet melody ran through
>     The luminous air; some righteous zeal I spent,
>     Therefore, in chiding Eve's presumption, who,

25    When heaven and earth were all obedient,
>     She but one woman, then just newly made,
>     Brooked not 'neath any veil to rest content;

Beneath which veil had she devoutly stayed,      28
  These joys past speech would have been mine to treasure
  A longer time, and not so long delayed.

'Mid all these first-fruits of eternal pleasure      31
  As I was walking rapt, filled with desire
  To taste delight in even fuller measure,

We saw the air ahead shine bright as fire      34
  'Neath the green boughs, and knew beyond mistake
  The sweet sound for the chanting of a choir.

O holy, holy Maids, if for your sake      37
  Cold, hunger, vigil ever I endured,
  Now is my time my just reward to take.

All Helicon for me be here outpoured,      40
  And let Urania aid me with her chorus
  To tell in verse what even to think is hard.

Seven golden trees a little way before us      43
  We seemed to see, though, truly, the long tract
  'Twixt us and them cast this delusion o'er us;

But when so nigh that that which doth distract      46
  Our sense – the common object – could not hide
  In distance the revealing detailed fact,

That power which reason's discourse doth provide      49
  As candlesticks defined them, and the cry
  "Hosanna" in the chant identified.

The beauteous pageantry flamed forth on high      52
  Far brighter than the brightest moon could shine
  At her mid-month in a clear midnight sky.

I turned, all wonder, looking for a sign      55
  From my good Virgil, but his answering glance
  Showed a bewilderment not less than mine;

So I once more addressed my countenance      58
  To those high things, which any new-made bride
  Would have outsped, so slow was their advance.

Wherefore to me: "How now!" the lady cried;      61
  "Why ardent but to watch these torches bright,
  Heedless of all that follows on beside?"

64  Then I beheld a company clad in white
        Following as though led on, whose garments' gleam
        Candescent shone beyond all mortal sight.

67  The water on my left flashed back the beam,
        And, like a mirror, when I looked that way,
        Showed my left side reflected in the stream.

70  Now, when I'd paced my bank until there lay
        Only the brook between, I halted there
        To get a better view of this display,

73  And saw the flames advance, leaving the air
        Behind them as it had been painted on;
        They looked like pictured pennants, as it were,

76  Whose seven great bands of colour lodged and shone,
        Till the sky stood with all those hues engrossed
        That streak the Sun's bright bow and Delia's zone.

79  Backward the streamers flew till sight was lost;
        And, by my judgement, there might be a spread
        Ten paces wide between the outermost.

82  Under a sky adorned as I have said
        Came four-and-twenty elders, twain by twain,
        Each with a crown of lilies on his head:

85  "Blest among daughters born of Adam's strain
        Art thou, and blest thy beauties," was their song,
        "And to eternity shall so remain."

88  When all the flowers and tender herbs along
        The far bank opposite to me had found
        Relief from all that chosen people's throng,

91  As star succeeds to star within the round
        Of heaven, even so there followed them behind
        Four living creatures with green foliage crowned;

94  Each with six wings was plumed, their plumage lined
        All full of eyes; and were he living now
        The eyes of Argus would be of that kind.

97  Reader, no further rhymes will I bestow
        To paint their shape; so many matters claim
        My space that largesse here we must forgo,

But read Ezekiel, who's depicted them      100
   Even as he saw them from the point of cold
   Coming in cloud, in whirlwind, and in flame.

As thou shalt find them in his page enscrolled,      103
   Such were they here, save for the wings, where John,
   Differing from him, bears out what I have told.

And in the space betwixt the four came on      106
   A triumph-car, on two wheels travelling,
   And at the shoulders of a Gryphon drawn;

And he stretched up the one and other wing      109
   Between the mid band and the three and three,
   Nor cleaving them nor marring anything.

The wings rose higher than my sight could see;      112
   Golden of limb so far as he was bird,
   The rest all dappled red-and-white was he.

Rome upon Africanus ne'er conferred      115
   Nor on Augustus' self, a car so brave –
   Nay, but the sun's own car were poor, compared:

The chariot of the sun, that when it drave      118
   Awry was burned at Earth's most instant prayer,
   When Jove in secret court just judgement gave.

Three ladies dancing in a ring there were      121
   By the right wheel; the first so red of hue
   She'd scarce be noted in the furnace-flare;

The next appeared of emerald through and through,      124
   Both flesh and bone; the third of them did seem
   As she were formed of snowflakes fallen new;

Now white, now red was leader to the team,      127
   And as she sang the other two likewise
   Or quick or slow kept measure to her theme.

Four by the left wheel, clad in purple guise,      130
   Made festival; and she who led the ball
   Among them, in her forehead had three eyes.

After this group I've sketched, behind them all,      133
   I saw two aged men, diversely dressed
   But like in bearing, grave and venerable;

136  One seemed a member of the craft professed
      By great Hippocrates, whom Nature made
      To help those creatures whom she loves the best;

139  One, of its contrary: he bore a blade
      Glittering and sharp, such that this side the brook
      The very sight of it made me afraid.

142  Next, four I saw of humble mien, who took
      Their way; then, last and lone, an ancient man
      Moved in a trance, with visionary look.

145  And like that company who led the van
      These seven were dressed, save that they wore no tire
      Upon their heads of the white lilies wan,

148  But flowers all red as any rose on briar;
      And from a distance – yea, not very far –
      You'd swear that all above their brows was fire.

151  When they stood right against me with the car,
      Thunder was heard; then, as though word were passed
      To those high beings, their further march to bar,

154  They, with the forward ensigns, there stood fast.


THE IMAGES. *The Beatrician Pageants*: Readers who have followed with interest Dante's use (which was discussed in *Inf*. Introduction, pp. 11 *sqq*.) of *natural*, as opposed to *conventional*, symbols for the purpose of his allegory, now have an opportunity to see what he could, if he thought fit, do with the other method, and how he uses the one as a contrast and foil to the other. For the great focal point of the *Commedia* – the reunion of Dante with Beatrice – is deliberately set, as though upon a stage, between two great pageants or masques, in which the characters are not *symbolic personages* but *allegorical personifications* in the traditional manner, embodying abstract ideas. When I say "masques", I mean exactly that. I do not mean that Dante has suddenly changed his convention and introduced into his narrative a whole collection of abstractions who mingle with his "real" people on equal terms. I mean that the Angels and Intelligences whom he mentions in the course of these concluding cantos are, in the most literal sense, *masquers*, who represent before him a contrived pageant, in the contemporary fashion, for his personal instruction and to the honour of Beatrice and all she stands for. The persons are still actual existent beings, as all actors are existent beings; but they are actors, and they are presenting a show.

Those who complain of the "frigid allegorical conceits" of these masques have not, I think, fully grasped Dante's intention. The contrast of style is carefully contrived for its purpose; just as, in *Hamlet*, the style of the "play-within-the-play" is made quite different from that of the play itself, and much more rigidly conventional. The poet's design is to frame between these two formal spectacles the moving and intensely personal interview between Beatrice and her lover, and so give it enhanced emphasis and relief.

Between them, the two Masques display the history of the Church (1) up to and including the Incarnation, and (2) from the days of the Apostles to the time of writing. The first is primarily doctrinal; the second, historical and political.

*The First Masque: The Pageant of the Sacrament*: I have called it so because this description agrees best with its formal presentation, but what it shows is something still greater: the whole revelation of the indwelling of Christ in His creation through the union of His two natures, Divine and Human (technically known as the "Hypostatic Union"). Of this union, the Sacrament of the Altar is at once the divinely ordained symbol, and the means by which Christians participate in that union; and in the Masque, Beatrice – Dante's own particular "God-bearing Image" – plays the part of the Sacrament. It is at this point that masque and reality become inextricably welded into a single dominating Image; for the historical Beatrice *is*, for Dante, what she represents, just as, after a higher and universal manner, the Sacrament *is* what it represents, and – after a manner more absolute still – Christ *is* what He represents.

The detailed images of the Masque will be best considered in the Notes, as they occur.

NOTES. l. 3: *Beati quorum tecta sunt peccata*: "Blessed are they [whose transgressions are forgiven and] whose sins are covered": *Ps.* xxxii. 1. (*Vulg.* xxxi. 1.)

l. 27: *brooked not 'neath any veil to rest content*: Had not Eve been in such presumptuous haste to know good and evil "like the gods", this knowledge would have been revealed to Man in due course, when his nature was sufficiently developed to know evil, as God knows it – i.e. by understanding and not by participation. But her disobedience to the divine warning meant that she and Adam fell into that knowledge while their nature was still such that they could know it only by experience (cf. Chas. Williams: *He Came Down from Heaven*, chap. 2).

ll. 37–42: *O holy, holy Maids*: this is the second Invocation of the *Purgatory* (cf. i. 7–12), addressed to the Muses, and in especial to

Urania, the Muse of Astronomy, and hence of the knowledge of heavenly things and of sacred song. *Helicon*: see Glossary.

l. 47: *the common object*: each sense has its "proper object" which is perceived by that sense alone; e.g. colour by sight, sound by hearing, etc.: with regard to these (according to Aristotle) the senses are to be trusted. But with regard to those objects – motion, rest, number, shape, size, etc. – which are "common" to more senses than one, the senses are liable to err, and the judgement has to come to their assistance. So, when all these phenomena had come near enough for the apprehensive faculty to grasp them in detail and submit them to "discourse of reason", Dante perceived that the apparent golden trees were in fact candlesticks, and the indefinable sweet sound the voices of a choir singing "Hosanna".

l. 50: *candlesticks*: The form in which the Masque is presented is, in general outline, that of a Corpus Christi procession. (The feast of Corpus Christi, in honour of the Blessed Sacrament, had been promulgated for the whole Church by Pope Urban IV in 1264, and re-authorized by Clement V some 45 years later.) The seven processional torches were widely used in the West at the Bishop's Mass (now, only at a Papal Mass), their number being no doubt connected with the seven golden candlesticks of *Rev.* i. 12–13, and signifying the seven gifts of the Spirit (wisdom, understanding, counsel, might, knowledge, piety, and the fear of the Lord).

l. 56: *Virgil*: his bewilderment indicates that we are now entering upon that realm of revealed truth which is beyond Virgil's understanding and belongs to Beatrice.

l. 78: *the Sun's bright bow and Delia's zone*: the image of the rainbow is found both in *Ezek.* i. 28 and *Rev.* iv. 3, the two visions upon which the imagery of the Masque is based; *Delia's zone*: the lunar halo; Diana (the moon-goddess) was born upon the island of Delos.

ll. 83–7: *four-and-twenty elders*, etc.: these figures, taken from *Rev.* iv. 4, represent the Books of the Old Testament as grouped by St Jerome (the twelve Minor Prophets counting as one book, *Samuel*, *Kings*, and *Chronicles* as one each, and *Ezra* and *Nehemiah* being grouped together as one). They are crowned with the lilies of pure righteousness, and their song, adapted from the Angel's salutation of Mary (*Luke* i. 28), reminds us that the whole of the Old Dispensation is prophetic of, and a preparation for, the Incarnation.

ll. 93 *sqq.*: *four living creatures*, etc.: these are the four Beasts of the Apocalypse (*Rev.* iv. 6–8), the traditional emblems of the Four Evangelists, but they are also identified with the four living creatures or Cherubim of *Ezek.* i. 4–14; x. 8–14. In *Ezekiel*, each cherub has four faces and four wings; in the *Apocalypse*, each beast has one face and six wings. Dante says that, as he saw them, they were like the vision seen by Ezekiel (i.e. four-faced) but that each had six wings, as seen by St John. It is not clear why he should insist on this detail; but I think he is trying to emphasize, by conflating the two descriptions into one, that the O.T. and the N.T. are in fact one and the same Revelation.

l. 96: *Argus*: a monster with a hundred eyes. After he was killed by Mercury (*Gk*. Hermes), Juno (*Gk*. Hera) transferred his eyes to the tail of her peacock. For the eyes of the Apocalyptic Beasts, see *Rev*. iv. 8 and *Ezek*. x. 12.

l. 101: *from the point of cold*: "And I looked, and, behold, a whirlwind came out of the north ... and out of the midst thereof came the likeness of four living creatures" (*Ezek*. i. 4–5).

l. 107: *a triumph-car*: this is the centre-piece of the Masque, on which, supported by the testimony of the Evangelists, the mystery of the Incarnation will be displayed. At this central point, in the Corpus Christi procession, the Holy Host would normally be carried under a canopy; but for the canopy Dante has substituted a *carroccio*, or war-chariot, such as then belonged to every Italian city (cf. *Inf*. xxii. 8 and note). This is the triumph-car of the Church, the City of God.

ll. 108–14: *a Gryphon*, etc.: The Gryphon, a classical and heraldic monster which combines the fore-part of an eagle with the hinder part of a lion, appears in the Masque as a symbol of the Hypostatic Union of the two natures in Christ. So far as he is bird (divine) he is of gold incorruptible; so far as he is animal (human) he is mingled of red and white. White and red are the colours which Dante assigns to the Old and New Testaments respectively; so that here again he emphasizes the meeting of the two Dispensations in the Incarnation. They are also the colours of righteousness and love. But they are most especially the colours of the Sacrament itself – the Flesh and the Blood, the Bread and the Wine.

ll. 115–16: *Rome upon Africanus ... nor on Augustus' self*: Referring to the triumphs accorded to Scipio Africanus (see Glossary) and Caesar Augustus after their victories.

ll. 118–19: *the chariot ... prayer*: For the story of Phaeton who tried in vain to drive the chariot of the Sun, see *Inf*. xvii. 107, note.

ll. 121–9: *three ladies*, etc.: these are the Theological Virtues of Faith (in white), Hope (in green), and Charity (in red): cf. Pope Urban's bull on Corpus Christi: "Let faith sing psalms, let hope dance, let charity exult."

l. 130: *four ... in purple*: these are the Four Cardinal Virtues, Prudence, Justice, Temperance, and Fortitude.

l. 132: *in her forehead had three eyes*: this is Prudence. The conventional mark upon the forehead, symbolizing the "third eye" of wisdom, is to be found on statues of Buddha as early as the fourth century, and becomes later a commonplace of western allegorical iconography, being often depicted with a disquieting realism.

ll. 133 *sqq.*: *after this group*, etc.: behind the chariot and the figures of the Evangelists come the remaining books of the New Testament.

ll. 136–7: *a member of the craft … Hippocrates*: i.e. of the medical profession (see Glossary, Hippocrates); the Book of *Acts*, represented by its writer St Luke "the beloved physician" (*Col.* iv. 14).

l. 139: *of its contrary*: i.e. of the profession that takes, instead of saving, life. This figure represents the *Epistles of St Paul*, under the semblance of their author, whose traditional emblem is a sword.

l. 142: *four … of humble mien*: these are the shorter "catholic" epistles (i.e. those addressed generally to the churches) of Peter, James, John, and Jude.

l. 143: *an ancient man*: this is the Book of the *Revelation* of St John. The fact that Luke is represented twice (as Evangelist and as author of the *Acts*) and John three times (as Evangelist, author of an *Epistle*, and author of the *Apocalypse*) shows that it is the books, and not the men, who figure in the procession.

l. 148: *flowers all red as any rose*: as the white lilies of the O.T. characters represent the righteousness of the Law, so the red roses of the N.T. characters represent the love of the Gospel.

l. 154: *the forward ensigns*: the seven candlesticks.

# CANTO XXX

THE STORY. *Acclaimed by the voices and the strewn flowers of the Angels, Beatrice appears on the car. Dante, overcome by the power of his lifelong love, turns to Virgil for reassurance; but Virgil is no longer with him. Beatrice reproaches Dante.*

When the First Heaven's Septentrion stood still,
   Which rise nor setting never knew, nor aught
   To cloud its light, save fogs of sinful will;

Which there to each his proper duty taught,       4
   As ours below teaches the mariner
   To turn the helm and bring his ship to port;

Those ranks veridical whose stations were       7
   Between it and the Gryphon, first in train,
   Turned to the car, as though their peace were there;

And one, like Heaven's own herald, cried amain:       10
   "*Veni, sponsa de Libano*"; thus thrice
   He sang, and all the rest took up the strain.

As the blest dead at the last trump shall rise       13
   Swift from their graves, with glad melodious strife
   Of new-found tongues and hallelujah-cries,

So on the chariot divine rose rife       16
   By hundreds there, *ad vocem tanti senis,*
   The court and couriers of eternal life.

All these proclaimed: "*Benedictus qui venis,*"       19
   And, tossing flowers about them low and high,
   Cried: "*Manibus O date lilia plenis.*"

Oft have I seen, when break of day was nigh,       22
   The orient flushing with a rose-red gleam,
   The rest of heaven adorned with calm blue sky,

Seen the sun's face rise shadowy and dim       25
   Through veils of mist, so tempering his powers,
   The eye might long endure to look on him;

28      So, even so, through cloud on cloud of flowers
            Flung from angelic hands and falling down
            Over the car and all around in showers,

31      In a white veil beneath an olive-crown
            Appeared to me a lady cloaked in green,
            And living flame the colour of her gown;

34      And instantly, for all the years between
            Since her mere presence with a kind of fright
            Could awe me and make my spirit faint within,

37      There came on me, needing no further sight,
            Just by that strange, outflowing power of hers,
            The old, old love in all its mastering might.

40      And, smitten through the eyesight unawares
            By that high power which pierced me, heart and reins,
            Long since, when I was but a child in years,

43      I turned to leftward - full of confidence
            As any little boy who ever came
            Running to mother with his fears and pains -

46      To say to Virgil: "There is scarce a dram
            That does not hammer and throb in all my blood;
            I know the embers of the ancient flame."

49      But Virgil - O he had left us, and we stood
            Orphaned of him; Virgil, dear father, most
            Kind Virgil I gave me to for my soul's good;

52      And not for all that our first mother lost
            Could I forbid the smutching tears to steep
            My cheeks, once washed with dew from all their dust.

55      "Dante, weep not for Virgil's going - keep
            As yet from weeping, weep not yet, for soon
            Another sword shall give thee cause to weep."

58      Like to an admiral, who comes anon
            To poop or prow, to watch the crews aboard
            The other ships, and cheer their valours on,

61      So, at the car's left rail, when thitherward
            At sound of my own name I turned to look
            (Name that at this point I must needs record),

I saw the lady whose appearance shook      64
  Me first amid the angelic festival
  Gazing upon me now across the brook;

Although the veil beneath the coronal      67
  Twined of Minerva's leaves, from head descending
  O'er face and form, did not reveal her all,

Regal of aspect and withal unbending,      70
  Thus she resumed, as who, to hold the ear,
  Keeps the most telling words back for the ending:

"Look on us well; we are indeed, we are      73
  Beatrice. How hast thou deigned to climb the hill?
  Didst thou not know that man is happy here?"

I dropped my eyes down to the glassy rill,      76
  Saw myself there, and quickly to the brink
  Withdrew them, bowed with shame unspeakable;

And even as a little boy may think      79
  His mother formidable, I thought her so:
  Stern pity is a bitter-tasting drink.

She ceased: straightway broke forth the angelic flow:      82
  "*In te, Domine, speravi,*" but no line
  Further than "*pedes meos*" did they go.

As in the living rafters on the chine      85
  Of Italy the curdled snow lies close,
  Caked by Slavonian winds that whip and whine,

But slides into itself, all trickling loose,      88
  When breathe the lands where shadow disappears
  At noon – like as in fire a candle does:

So I was impotent for sighs or tears      91
  Until they sang who tune their melodies
  Still to the song of the eternal spheres.

But when I heard them in sweet harmonies      94
  More pity me than if they did protest:
  "Lady, why put him to a shame like this?"

The icy bonds which held my heart compressed      97
  Melted to breath and water, and through eyes
  And mouth burst forth in anguish from my breast.

100    Then she, still standing in the self-same wise
            The same side of the chariot, that array
            Of pitying substances did thus advise:

103    "You keep your watch in the eternal day,
            So that nor sleep nor darkness steals from you
            One step which the world takes upon its way;

106    Hence my reply has this chief aim in view:
            That he who yonder weeps should comprehend,
            And grief with guilt maintain the balance true.

109    Not the great wheels alone, whose workings tend,
            As in their aspects all their stars congress,
            To guide each seed to its appropriate end,

112    But graces also of divine largesse,
            Which have their rains from clouds too high to see,
            They so transcend our eyesight's littleness,

115    Had so endowed this man, potentially,
            In his new life, that from such gifts as those
            A wondrous harvest should have come to be.

118    But so much ranker, weedier, and more gross
            Runs the untended field where wild tares seed,
            As the good soil is rich and vigorous.

121    I with my countenance some time indeed
            Upheld him; my young eyes his beacons were
            To turn him right and in my steps to lead;

124    But when I'd reached my second age, and there,
            E'en on the threshold, life for life exchanged,
            Then he forsook me and made friends elsewhere.

127    When, risen from flesh to spirit, free I ranged,
            In beauty greater and in virtue more,
            His mind was turned from me, his heart estranged;

130    And by wild ways he wandered, seeking for
            False phantoms of the good, which promise make
            Of joy, but never fully pay the score.

133    With inspirations, prayer-wrung for his sake,
            Vainly in dreams and other ways as well
            I called him home; so little did he reck.

And, in the end, to such a depth he fell    136
 That every means to save his soul came short
 Except to let him see the lost in hell.

For this the gateway of the dead I sought,   139
 And weeping, made request of him by whom
 He has been raised thus far and hither brought.

It would do violence to God's high doom   142
 If Lethe could be passed, and ill-doers
 To taste this blessed fare could straightway come

Without some forfeit of repentant tears."   145

THE IMAGES. *The Figure of Beatrice*: If, throughout the whole course of the poem, our minds had not been insistently prepared for the coming of Beatrice, the whole symbolism of the Masque, and particularly the chanting of the *Benedictus*, would lead us to expect the appearance upon the car of the Holy Host Itself. And both expectations are quite right. What appears is indeed Beatrice, as we had been led to suppose: the unmistakable Beatrice whom Dante had loved in Florence. But she is also, in the allegory of the Masque, the Image of the Host. In this august and moving moment, Dante brings together all the "significations" of Beatrice, showing her as the particular type and figure of that whole sacramental principle of which the Host Itself is the greater Image. Bearing in mind the four levels (see *Inf.* Introduction, pp. 14–15) at which Dante meant his poem to be interpreted, we see that she is here:

 (1) *literally*: the Florentine woman whom Dante loved.
 (2) *morally* (i.e. as regards the way of salvation of the individual
  soul): the type of whatever is, for each of us, the "God-
  bearing image" which manifests the glory of God in His
  creation, and becomes a personal sacramental experience.
 (3) *historically* (i.e. in the world of human society): the Sacra-
  ment of the Altar. (And those who say that Beatrice here
  represents the Church are not wrong: for Dante has in mind
  that ancient and apostolic conception of the Eucharist which
  looks upon it, not only as the commemoration of God's single
  act in time, but as the perpetual presentation to God in Christ
  of Christ's true Body the Church – the *verum corpus* – which is
  made in the offertory of the bread and wine; so that, as St
  Augustine says, "being joined to His Body and made His
  members, we may *be* what we receive".)

(4) *mystically* (i.e. as regards the way of the soul's union with God): the whole principle of Affirmation, whereby that union is effected in and through all the images.

Having said thus much, we may admire the poetic tact with which Dante leaves the whole weight of this allegorical structure to be carried on the framework of the Masque, so that he is free to conduct the interview between Dante and Beatrice throughout in those human and personal terms which make the story dramatically effective.

NOTES. l. 1: *the First Heaven's Septentrion*: i.e. the seven candlesticks. The Septentrion is the Wain (*Ursa Major*) whose pointers show the Pole Star. The "First Heaven" is that which is governed by the Angels.

l. 7: *those ranks veridical*: the truth-telling prophecies of the O.T.

l. 10: *one, like Heaven's own herald*: the Book of *Canticles* (*Song of Songs*).

l. 11: *Veni, sponsa de Libano*: "Come, bride of Lebanon": *Cant.* iv. 8. Mystically, the Bride of the *Canticles* is the image of the soul espoused to God, and, prophetically, of Mary, the Bride of the Holy Ghost.

l. 17: *ad vocem tanti senis*: "at the voice of so great an elder": the industry of scholars has failed to discover any source for this apparent quotation: Dante probably wrote the phrase in Latin for the sake of the rhyme. The "elder" is, of course, the one who cried "*Veni, sponsa*".

l. 19: *Benedictus qui venis*: "blessed art thou that comest": (*Matt.* xxi. 9, *Mark* xi. 9, *Luke* xix. 38, *John* xii. 13) this, here transferred from the 3rd person to the 2nd, is the hymn sung immediately before the Sacring of the Mass; and it is particularly noteworthy that, although that which "comes" is Beatrice, Dante has retained unaltered the masculine ending in – *us*, which refers it definitely to Christ. He could scarcely give clearer proof of his symbolic intention.

l. 21: *Manibus [O] date lilia plenis*: "[O] with full hands give lilies": this (slightly adapted for the sake of the metre) is a line from Virgil (*Aen.* vi. 883); it is used by Anchises (see Glossary) when in the Elysian Fields he points out to Aeneas the form of him who will be born into the world as the young Marcellus (the nephew and adopted son of Augustus), and who is doomed to die in the flower of his youth. Translated here from an occasion of pagan mourning to one of Christian rejoicing, it is at once Dante's tribute to Virgil as a prophet of Christ and a gesture of tender regret for his imminent departure.

ll. 31–3: *in a white veil ... a lady*: it is not said how, or whence,

Beatrice appears; like the presence of Christ in the Eucharist, she "is here, we know not how". She is first seen veiled, like the Host covered by the corporal; and the colours of her dress are those of the three Theological Virtues. The crown of olive (Minerva's tree) signifies wisdom.

l. 48: *I know the embers of the ancient flame*: this is a translation of a line (once more) from Virgil: "*Agnosco veteris vestigia flammae*" (*Aen.* iv. 23); it is spoken by Dido of her passion which she had thought extinct.

l. 52: *all that our first mother lost*: i.e. the Earthly Paradise.

l. 54: *once washed with dew*: Cf. i. 127–9.

l. 63: *name that ... I must needs record*: to name one's self in a work of literature was, by the standards of the time, considered egotistical and unbecoming. Dante names himself only this once in the *Comedy*, and not at all in his other works (apart from the *Epistles*); in his book on *Vernacular Poetry* he always designates himself by some periphrasis, such as "the friend of Cino", or "another Florentine".

l. 83: *in te, Domine, speravi*: "in Thee, O Lord, have I put my trust": (*Ps.* xxxi. 1; *Vulg.* xxx. 2). The angels do not go beyond verse 9 – "thou hast set my feet (*pedes meos*) in a large room" – because at this point the psalm changes its character and ceases to be appropriate.

ll. 85–6: *the living rafters on the chine of Italy*: the pine-trees on the ridge of the Apennines, which are caked with snow when the N. wind blows from Russia (Slavonia).

ll. 89–90: *the lands where shadow disappears at noon*: Equatorial Africa, where at noonday an upright object casts no shadow under the vertical sun.

l. 102: *substances*: i.e. the angels: intelligences who possess substantial form in themselves, independent of matter (cf. xviii. 49, note).

ll. 103–6: *you keep your watch*, etc.: the angels, who partake of God's eternal vision, do not need that she should inform them; therefore her reply (to their appeal on Dante's behalf), though addressed to them, is intended for his benefit.

l. 109: *the great wheels*: the courses of the heavens. Dante was not only born with great natural advantages but favoured also by especial gifts of grace.

l. 116: *in his new life*: possibly merely "his early life"; but in view of the title of the *Vita Nuova*, Beatrice probably means that "new life" on which he entered when, through her means, he first knew himself to be in a state of grace (cf. *Inf.* Introduction, p. 28).

l. 124: *my second age*: In the *Convivio*, Dante divides the natural life of men into four ages: (1) adolescence (from birth to 25); (2) manhood (25–45); (3) age (45–70); (4) decrepitude (from 70 to 80 and over). Beatrice died at the age of 25, when just entering (l. 125) upon her "second age".

l. 125: *life for life exchanged*: exchanged this life for the life of eternity.

l. 131: *false phantoms of the good*: Cf. xvii. 133–5 and note.

l. 139: *the gateway of the dead*, etc.: Cf. *Inf.* ii. 52 *sqq.*

# CANTO XXXI

THE STORY. *Under the weight of Beatrice's reproaches, Dante breaks down and confesses his guilt, and is so overcome that he faints away. He recovers consciousness to find that he is being drawn across Lethe by the Lady (Matilda), who plunges his head into the stream so that he drinks the water. The Cardinal Virtues bring him to Beatrice; and gazing into her unveiled eyes he sees reflected in them the Gryphon, now wholly eagle and now wholly lion, though the Gryphon itself remains unaltered in its double nature. At the prayer of the Theological Virtues, Beatrice turns her eyes upon Dante himself, and unveils her smiling mouth.*

"O thou, yon side the sacred stream," said she,
    Turning the sharp point of her speech my way –
    Though even the edge seemed sharp enough to me –

And thus continuing without delay;         4
    "Say, say if this is true; so grave a charge
    Requires thine own confession; therefore say."

Alas! my wits were scattered so at large       7
    That the voice stirred, but faded and was gone
    Ere from its organs it could find discharge.

She waited; then: "What think'st thou?" she went on;   10
    "Answer me; thy sad memories are not yet
    Drowned by this water of oblivion."

Terror and shame inextricably knit       13
    Forced from my miserable lips a "Yes"
    Such that the sight must needs interpret it.

As a cross-bow, bended with too great stress,     16
    Snaps, string and bow together, and the bolt
    Flies to the mark, not with more power but less,

I broke beneath the weight of this assault,     19
    Choking out sighs and sobs still more and more
    Till in my throat my voice died by default.

Then she: "In that desire of me which bore     22
    Thy love along with it to seek the Good
    Past which there's nothing to be eager for,

25  What didst thou find? what pitfalls in the road?
      What chains? that thou shouldst cast all hope away
      Of pressing onward as a traveller should?

28  And what allurement, what advantage, pray,
      Seemed in those rival favours so to lie
      That thou must bow and scrape to such as they?"

31  After the heaving of a bitter sigh
      I scarce found voice; but with what pains they might
      My lips contrived to fashion a reply:

34  "Things transitory, with their false delight,"
      Weeping I said, "enticed my steps aside,
      Soon as your face was hidden from my sight."

37  She said: "Hadst thou kept silence, or denied
      What thou hast now confessed, thy crime would still
      Be known; He knows, by whom the cause is tried;

40  But when the prisoner's mouth is quick to spill
      His own sin forth, then, in our court up there,
      Backward against the edge we turn the wheel.

43  Nevertheless, that thou may'st learn to bear
      The shame of guilt, and make a better show
      Next time the sirens' song assails thine ear,

46  Stop sowing tears, and listen; thou must know
      How by a way quite other and reversed
      My buried flesh ought to have made thee go.

49  Nothing in art or nature, last and first,
      Gave thee such joy as those fair members, wrought
      To clothe me once, now in the earth dispersed;

52  And when my death brought that best joy to naught,
      What mortal thing should there have been, whose clutch
      Could draw thee to it in thy hankering thought?

55  Rather shouldst thou, at the first tingling touch
      Of these delusions, have made haste to spring
      Up after me, who was no longer such.

58  'Twas not for thee to sit with folded wing,
      Waiting the next shaft of I know not what –
      Some girl, or other brief and passing thing;

316

The fledgling waits it twice or thrice, but not          61
  The fully feathered bird, in sight of whom
  Vainly is the net spread or arrow shot."

As children, when they are rebuked, stand dumb,          64
  With downcast eyes and penitential sniff
  Listening, by consciousness of guilt o'ercome,

Just so stood I; and she proceeded: "If                  67
  The hearing grieves thee so, hold up thy beard,
  And thou by looking shalt have greater grief."

With less resistance might strong winds, careered        70
  From home or Iarbas' land, uproot and rid
  The soil of some strong oak and leave it cleared,

Than I heaved up my chin when I was bid;                 73
  And when she used my beard to mean my face
  I felt the venom the allusion hid.

When I had stretched my head erect, my gaze              76
  Lit first upon those primal creatures, who
  Had left their strewing and stood motionless;

And, scarcely steady yet, mine eyes saw too              79
  Beatrice, turned now to the Beast – to him
  That is one person sole in natures two;

And there, beneath her veil, beyond the stream,          82
  Her former self, methought, she more outshone
  Than here, with others, she once outshone them.

Such nettles of remorse stung me thereon                 85
  That of all other objects of my love
  I hated most what I'd most doted on;

And gnawing self-reproach my heart so clove,             88
  I swooned and sank; what happened to me, she
  Knows best of all who was the cause thereof.

When my heart set my outward sense free,                 91
  I saw my first-met, lone-met lady bent
  Above me, saying: "Hold on, hold on to me."

Into the stream she'd drawn me in my faint,              94
  Throat-high, and now, towing me after her,
  Light as a shuttle o'er the water went.

97      "*Asperges me*" I heard, as I drew near
          The blissful brink, so sweetly as to drown
          Power to recall, far more to write it here.

100     She stretched both hands, she seized me by the crown,
          Did that fair lady, and she plunged me in,
          So that I needs must drink the water down;

103     Then drew me forth and led me, washed and clean,
          Within the dance where those fair four paced even,
          Who lent me each her arm for shield and screen.

106     "Here are we nymphs, and stars we are in heaven;
          Ere she came down to dwell on mortal ground
          Were we to Beatrice as handmaids given;

109     We'll lead thee to her eyes; the threefold round,
           Yon side, must sharpen thine in the glad light
          Which beams there, for their gaze is more profound."

112     Thus did they chant, and thus they led me, right
          Up to the Gryphon's breast, where watchfully
          Beatrice gazed, and we stood opposite.

115     "Take heed," said they, "spare not thine eyes, for we
          Have set thee afore the orbs of emerald
          Whence Love let fly his former shafts at thee."

118     Myriad desires, hotter than fire or scald
          Fastened mine eyes upon the shining eyes
          That from the Gryphon never loosed their hold.

121     Like sun in looking-glass, no otherwise,
          I saw the Twyform mirrored in their range,
          Now in the one, now in the other guise.

124     Think, Reader, think how marvellous and strange
          It seemed to me when I beheld the thing
          Itself stand changeless and the image change.

127     So, while my soul, awe-struck and wondering,
          Fed of that food which of itself doth fill,
          And for itself sets full men hungering,

130     Those other three, of rank more notable,
          As their mien showed, moved in their roundelay
          Forward, with weaving steps angelical:

"Turn, Beatrice, O turn," thus carolled they,                    133
   "Thy holy eyes upon thy liegeman leal
   Who, seeking thee, has toiled this long, long way.

Do us more grace, and of thy grace reveal                       136
   Thy mouth to him, so that he may discern
   The second beauty which thou dost conceal."

O splendour of the living light eterne,                         139
   What man that e'er beneath Parnassus' shade
   Grew pale, or from its fountain filled his urn,

Were not o'ertasked of wit if he essayed                        142
   To show thee as thou showedst thyself to be,
   Unveiling thee in the free air displayed,

There where all heaven harmonious shadows thee?                 145

THE IMAGES. *Dante's conviction of Sin*: It may seem strange that Dante's overwhelming conviction of sin, and his abject confession, should be placed at this point, *after* his (symbolical) purgation by the ascent of the Mountain. He has already "seen himself as he is" and made his act of contrition at Peter's Gate (ix. 94 and Images), without any such violent psychological disturbance. What is meant, I think, is that not until the state of innocence has been recovered can sin be apprehended in its full horror. So long as any taint of sinfulness remains, there is always something in the soul that still assents to sin; only when the last, lingering vestige of unconscious assent has been purged away can one see one's own sin as it appears to God – as something unspeakably vile and hideous. The sight is unbearable to human nature (thus, in xxx. 76–87, Dante cannot endure to look at his own reflection in the stream); therefore, as soon as realization is complete and confession made, the remembrance of sin is mercifully drowned in oblivion.

NOTES. l. 12: *this water of oblivion*: i.e. Lethe.

ll. 22–4: *that desire of me ... to be eager for*: these lines are perhaps Dante's simplest and most definite statement of the quality and action of the love which finds the image of the Creator in the creature (the "Good" in question being, of course, God, as in many other passages).

l. 36: *your face*: this is the plural of respect.

l. 42: *backward against the edge we turn the wheel*: i.e. the edge of the grindstone is turned against the edge of the sword of justice, to blunt it.

l. 45: *the sirens' song*: see l. 34 and Images to Canto xix.

ll. 49–54: *nothing in art or nature*, etc.: the line of thought is simple: "Since the highest joy of earth turned out to be transitory, you should have known that there could not, *a fortiori*, be any satisfaction in lesser earthly joys." The interesting, and, to our minds perhaps rather unexpected, thing is the insistence on physical beauty as the source of the highest earthly joy.

l. 60: *some girl*: Between the sentimentalists who, in spite of Dante's own admissions and the evidence of his contemporaries, have determined to see in him a kind of Galahad (slightly embarrassed by the presence of a wife and four children), and, on the other hand, the sensationalists who have constructed a populous harem for him from the names of all the women he has ever mentioned, sober comment must be content to steer a middle course. It seems likely that he was an "average sensual man", and that, like most of his kind, he was frequently tempted and sometimes fell. *Allegorically*, of course, since Beatrice is here the image of the true Good, "some girl" is the obvious image of the false or secondary goods.

l. 68: *hold up thy beard*: The only contemporary and certainly authentic portrait we have of Dante is Giotto's fresco in the Bargello at Florence, which shows him as a beardless youth. Of the later representations (all clean-shaven) none can produce any clear title to independent authority. Boccaccio's description, and the anecdote about the women in the streets of Verona, who would say as he passed: "That is the man who has been to hell; see how the fires have grizzled and crisped his beard", agree with this line in indicating that at one period, at any rate, of his life, he wore a beard. It is, however, possible that Beatrice is here speaking only metaphorically (see below, ll. 74–5).

l. 71: *Iarbas' land*: the south wind from Africa. (Iarbas was a Libyan king, mentioned in *Aen.* iv. 196 as one of Dido's suitors.)

l. 75: *the venom the allusion hid*: Beatrice's pointed reference to his "beard" is a reminder that he is not a naughty child but a grown man.

l. 77: *those primal creatures*: the angels (cf. *Purg.* xi. 3 and note).

l. 92: *my first-met, lone-met lady*: i.e. Matilda.

l. 97: *asperges me* (thou shalt purge me): from *Ps.* li. 7 (*Vulg.* l. 9): "Thou shalt purge me with hyssop and I shall be clean; thou shalt wash me and I shall be whiter than snow." The *Asperges* is sung at the beginning of the Mass, when the priest sprinkles the people with holy water.

l. 102: *drink the water down*: i.e. the "water of oblivion", which blots out remembrance of sin (see Introduction, p. 68).

l. 104: *those fair four*: the Cardinal Virtues.

l. 106: *stars we are in heaven*: Cf. *Purg.* i. 23 and note.

l. 107: *ere she came down to dwell on mortal ground*: Dante is not suggesting that the flesh-and-blood Beatrice had a pre-natal existence, but that the Virtues were, in God's eternal counsel, foreordained to wait upon her. *Allegorically*, he means that the Natural Virtues were given to Man from the beginning, to attend on and prepare the special Revelation of Grace which entered the world at the Incarnation.

l. 109: *the threefold round, yon side*: the three Theological Virtues at the other side of the chariot.

l. 116: *the orbs of emerald*: the eyes of Beatrice. The phrase probably means no more than "shining like jewels"; though if we like to suppose that the eyes were of a greenish hazel, there is no reason why we should not.

l. 122: *the Twyform*: i.e. the Gryphon.

l. 123: *now in the one, now in the other guise*: in the mirror of Revelation (the eyes of Beatrice), Dante sees the double Nature of the Incarnate Love – now as wholly divine, now as wholly human; but he cannot as yet see the two as one thing and One Person: that is reserved for the Beatific Vision at the end of the *Paradiso*.

ll. 128–9: *fed of that food ... hungering*: literally, love; *allegorically* the "food" is Christ. (Cf. *Ecclus.* xxiv. 21: "They that eat me [the Divine Wisdom] shall yet be hungry, and they that drink me shall yet be thirsty.")

l. 138: *the second beauty*: Dante locates beauty particularly in the eyes and the mouth, because in these two places the soul most readily shows itself. A smiling mouth moves him especially to admiration, "for what is a smile but a coruscation of the joy of the soul, like the outward shining of an inward light?" (*Conv.* iii. 8). Elsewhere he says that "the eyes of Wisdom are her *demonstrations*, whereby the Truth is beheld with the utmost certainty; and her smile is her *persuasions*, whereby the interior light of Wisdom is seen as it were beneath a veil: and in these two we feel that supreme joy of beatitude which is known in its fulness in Heaven" (*Conv.* iii. 15). Throughout the *Paradiso*, the successive stages in the ascent from one heaven to the next are marked by the increasing loveliness of Beatrice's eyes and smile.

l. 139: *splendour of the living light eterne*: Beatrice; the word "splendour" in Dante always means *reflected* light: Beatrice is the reflected image of the Divine light.

l. 140: *beneath Parnassus' shade*, etc.: see xxii. 65, note.

# CANTO XXXII

THE STORY. *The Beatrician Pageant turns northward and comes, with Dante and Statius following, to the Tree of Knowledge. The Gryphon binds the Chariot-pole to the Tree, whose bare branches break into blossom. The sweetness of the heavenly anthem lulls Dante to sleep. When he awakes, he finds Beatrice alone except for the Seven Nymphs, sitting beneath the Tree; and is shown the Pageant of the Church.*

So fixed mine eyes were, in resolve entrenched
    So deep, their ten years' thirst to satiate,
    That all my other faculties were quenched;

4    And on this side and that of them were set
    High walls of unconcern, the holy smile
    So drew them to itself in the old net;

7    Until those goddesses in forceful style
    Turned my gaze leftward, for: "Too fixedly!"
    I heard one say, when I had looked awhile;

10    And that condition which we often see
    In eyes but lately smitten by the sun,
    For a short time thereafter blinded me.

13    But when to lesser lights the eyes had done
    Readjusting – lesser lights, I mean, compared
    With that great brilliance I'd been forced to shun –

16    Wheeled by the dexter flank, the glorious guard
    I saw, so turned that sun and sevenfold light
    Now both together in their faces flared.

19    As troops, for good defence, wheel their armed might
    Round under shield, the standards in the van,
    Before their march can change its front outright,

22    So moved the chivalry of heaven; each man
    Whose place was in the lead had passed us by
    Ere the pole turned and the car's march began.

25    Back to the wheels the ladies all drew nigh;
    Then moved the Gryphon with his hallowed load,
    Pacing unruffled, not a plume awry;

Then I, with Statius, and the fair who'd towed     28
   Me through the ford, following the wheel which made
   The smaller arc when turning on the road.

As thus we paced the lofty forest glade,     31
   Void through her fault that to the snake gave ear,
   To time our steps angelic music played.

Haply we had advanced about as far     34
   As three flights of an arrow might have spanned,
   When Beatrix descended from the car.

I heard all murmur "Adam": then their stand     37
   They took beneath a tree whose boughs were shred
   Bare of all flowers and leaves on every hand.

The more it rose, the wider still it spread,     40
   And Indians in their woods it well might fill
   With wonder to behold its lofty head.

"Blessed art thou, O Gryphon, that thy bill     43
   Plucks nothing from this tree of sweetest gust,
   Which wrung the belly with such griping ill."

Thus cried they all, circling the trunk august.     46
   Then spake the Beast in whom two natures met:
   "Thus is preserved the seed of all that's just."

And, turning to the pole he'd drawn, he set     49
   His strength to drag it to the widowed tree,
   And what came from it he left bound to it.

As our own plants, when the time comes to be     52
   That the great light falls joined with those that beam
   Behind the heavenly Carp immediately,

Burgeon and break in beauty, each a-gleam     55
   With its own hue, or ever the sun goes
   Under another sign to yoke his team,

Brighter than violets, deeper than the rose,     58
   Suffused with colour, fresh and green it grew,
   The tree that was so bare in all its boughs.

I sing not here – indeed, I never knew –     61
   What hymn resounded there on every tongue,
   Nor might I bear to hear the music through.

64  Could I describe how, hearing Syrinx sung,
     The pitiless eyes were lulled to slumber deep,
     Those eyes it cost so dear to watch so long,

67  Then, as a painter works with lines that keep
     Close to the model, I would show you how
     I drowsed: but whoso can let him paint sleep!

70  Therefore I'll pass to when I woke, and now
     Tell how sleep's veil by shining light was riven,
     And a voice calling: "Up! what makest thou?"

73  As, when a glimpse of the apple-bloom was given
     Which whets the angels' thirst for the fruit it bears,
     And makes perpetual marriage-feast in heaven,

76  Peter and James and John fell unawares
     On sleep, o'ercome, and were roused to wakefulness
     By the word that had broken deeper sleep than theirs,

79  To find their blessed company grown less
     By Moses and Elias being departed,
     And changed the texture of the Master's dress:

82  So I came to, and found that gentle-hearted
     Lady beside me who had been my guide
     When by the river-bank my journey started.

85  In some alarm: "Where's Beatrice?" I cried:
     "Lo where she sits upon the tree's roots, under
     The newly budded foliage," she replied.

88  "Take note of the companions who surround her:
     The rest of them are with the Gryphon risen
     Up, with a sweeter music and profounder."

91  If more than this she said, I did not listen,
     My eyes being set on her to whom my mind
     Was altogether subject and in prison:

94  Alone on the bare ground she sat reclined,
     As though left guardian of the chariot
     I'd seen the Beast of double nature bind;

97  The seven nymphs stood cloistering her about,
     Bearing in hand those lights no hurricane,
     Be it Aquilo or Auster, can put out.

"Here shalt thou rusticate awhile, and then          100
   Thou of that Rome where Christ a Roman is
   Shalt be with me perpetual citizen;

Therefore, to help the world that lives amiss,          103
   Fix on the car thine eye, and when thou hast made
   Return back yonder, write whate'er it sees."

Thus Beatrice; and I, devoutly laid          106
   Submissive at the feet of her command,
   Gave mind and eyes to whatsoe'er she bade.

Never so swiftly did the levin-brand,          109
   Sped from the farthest confine, dart to move
   Down through thick cloud to strike upon the land

As downward I beheld the bird of Jove          112
   Swoop on the tree, rending the bark and scattering
   All the new foliage and the flowers thereof;

With all his might he struck a blow so shattering          115
   That the car staggered like a storm-tossed ship
   Starboard and larboard rolled by billows' battering.

Next, on the car triumphal, I saw skip          118
   And lurk within, a fox all skin and bone,
   As though good food had never passed his lip;

But straight rebuking him for foul deeds done          121
   My lady sent him packing with such haste
   As could be got from such a skeleton.

Then once again, down on the chariot's waist,          124
   From the same place I saw the eagle dart
   And leave it plumed with plumes from his own breast;

And in the accents of a grieving heart          127
   A voice from heaven cried: "O my little keel,
   How laden with calamity thou art!"

And then, meseemed, the earth 'twixt wheel and wheel          130
   Gaped, and out came a dragon from below,
   And through the chariot's floor drove up his tail;

And as a wasp withdraws its sting, even so          133
   He pulled away barbed tail and bits of floor,
   And skimble-skamble off I saw him go.

136    And what remained grew covered as before,
    Like rich soil run to knot-grass, with the plumes
    Offered, perchance, with good intent and pure;

139    Feathered, the wheel-fellies and axle-drums
    And shaft, and feathered in less time the whole
    Than lips are held apart when a sigh comes.

142    And, thus transformed, the sacred vehicle
    Started to sprout forth heads all over it,
    One at each corner, three upon the pole;

145    These last were horned like oxen; the quartet
    Had each a forehead with one horn upon't –
    So strange a monster never was seen yet.

148    And throned there, like a keep on a high mount
    Secure, I saw a harlot, loosely dressed,
    Sit, with a rolling eye and brazen front;

151    And upright at her side, that none might wrest
    His prize away belike, a giant appeared,
    And many a time the pair embraced and kissed;

154    But soon, because her wanton glances veered
    To me, her brutal paramour grew vexed,
    And head to foot he drubbed her good and hard;

157    And, jealous-mad and cruel with rage, he next
    Unloosed and dragged the monster, thus released,
    Far through the wood, till the wood closed betwixt

160    Me and the harlot and the wondrous beast.

THE IMAGES. *The Interlude and the Second Masque*: The Pageant which
follows the dramatic human scene between Dante and Beatrice is
divided, as it were, into two acts. The first, which I have called for
want of a better name, "The Interlude", is theologically the more
important of the two, and provides the clue to the interpretation
of the whole series.

*The Interlude: The Chariot and the Tree*: According to tradition, the
Cross of Christ was made from the wood of the Forbidden Tree.
This legend supplies the richly allusive allegory of ll. 37–60.

As soon as we see the Tree, we recognize it, from its peculiar
shape (l. 40) as the "stock" from which the "scions" on Cornice
vi were taken: i.e. as the Tree of Knowledge (xxiv. 114–16). The
key to the whole passage is thus seen to be l. 51: "And *what came*

*from it* he left bound to it", which gives us to understand that the pole of the Church's chariot is the Cross itself. The murmur of the heavenly company (l. 37) has further identified the Tree, in its bare and ruined state, as an image of Adam in his fallen nature. We shall thus have no difficulty in identifying the Chariot-pole (Cross, or "Tree of Glory") as an image of Christ, the Second Adam, in His unfallen Humanity – each Adam being figured, that is, by his particular Tree.

These identifications made, the interpretation is quite straight-forward. When, by means of the Incarnation (the Gryphon), the Second Adam (the Chariot-pole) is united (bound) to the First Adam (the Tree) of whose race He came (l. 51) but whose fall He did not share (ll. 43–5), Man's ruined nature is redeemed and re-ceives new life from the perfect Nature of Christ (the dry Tree breaks into blossom).

*The Second Masque: The Pageant of Church and Empire*: As the first Masque showed the history of the Church up to and including the Incarnation, so the second Masque shows her history from Apos-tolic times to Dante's own day. The Tree now represents Man in his redeemed nature: in other words, it has become the image of Christendom, and, in an especial sense, of Rome, the spiritual and temporal centre of Christendom. Its condition is thus tragically affected by the relations between Church and Empire. The various episodes of the Masque will be best considered in the Notes, as they occur.

*Statius*: Throughout these last three cantos, Dante has an air of forget-ting Statius, only throwing in a casual reference now and again, to show that he is still there. We infer from l. 28 that he has crossed Lethe, and we are told (xxxiii. 133–4) that he drinks of Eunoë; but he is excluded altogether from the interview with Beatrice, who appears to pay no attention to him. Obviously, he could have no part in that intimate scene; yet, if the poet had found his presence embarrassing, he could easily have got rid of him earlier (by sup-posing, for example, that he needed to stay behind and do penance on the Ninth Cornice, or in some other way). He is doubtless here to show that the drinking of the two waters is part of the regular purgation of all spirits. But we may reasonably ask what the ap-pearance of Beatrice means to him, and whether he undergoes any experience corresponding to Dante's. My own conjecture (for it can be no more than that) is that what Statius beholds upon the Car is not Beatrice, but whatever is, for him, the personal God-bearing image; and that his experience is here as private from Dante as Dante's is from him. In which case, the reason why Dante (the Poet) tells us nothing, is that Dante (the Pilgrim) knew no-thing about it.

NOTES. l. 2: *their ten years' thirst*: i.e. the interval between Beatrice's death in 1290 and 1300, the date assigned to the vision.

l. 7: *those goddesses*: i.e. the Theological Graces. For the use of this term for Angels or Intelligences, cf. *Inf.* vii. 87.

l. 8: *too fixedly*: the Graces (more prudent in this matter than the Virtues, xxxi. 115) warn Dante against too intense and exclusive a concentration on Beatrice. This may be because his sight is not yet strong enough to bear her unveiled light (as we see, he is momentarily blinded); but it is rather, I think, a reminder that Beatrice, though a true image, is not the only nor the ultimate Image – thus anticipating Beatrice's own reminders in *Para.* xviii. 21, "Not in my eyes alone is Paradise", and *Para.* xxiii. 70–2, "Why does my face so enamour thee that thou turnest not to the fair garden which flowers beneath the rays of Christ?"

ll. 17–18: *so turned that sun and sevenfold light ... flared*: the procession was wheeling northward by the right, so that the torches in the vanguard were leading them into the rays of the sun, now coming up towards noon.

l. 28: *Statius*: we are not told when Statius crossed Lethe; presumably either during Dante's swoon (xxxi. 88–90), or while his attention was riveted on Beatrice. (But see Images.)

l. 29: *the wheel which made the smaller arc*: the inner (right) wheel.

l. 32: *void through her fault that to the snake gave ear*: because of Eve's sin, the Earthly Paradise has no inhabitants (see Images to Canto xxviii). This line would seem to dispose of the suggestion that the Earthly Paradise is the image of the Active Life.

l. 40: *the more it rose, the higher still it spread*: Cf. xxii. 133–5.

l. 41: *Indians in their woods*: Dante's conception of the great height of Indian trees is probably derived from Virgil's *Georgics*, ii. 122–4: "The Indian grove ... where arrows in their loftiest flight can scarcely reach the tree-tops."

ll. 43–5: *blessed art thou, O Gryphon*, etc.: i.e. "blessed is the Divine Humanity that never tasted the sweet but poisonous fruit of sin".

l. 48: *thus*: i.e. by the union of the Second and First Adams, which his next action symbolizes. (See Images.)

ll. 52–4: *when the time comes*, etc.: i.e. in spring, when the Sun ("the great light") enters the sign of Aries (the Ram), which follows the sign of Pisces (the Fishes – here called "the Heavenly Carp").

ll. 64–6: *hearing Syrinx sung*: Argus (see xxix. 95 and note) was sent by Juno to keep watch on Io whom, out of jealousy, she had turned into a cow. Argus could "watch so long", because he could rest some of his hundred eyes in turn while the others kept open. Mercury, however, being sent by Jove to Io's assistance, lulled all the monster's eyes to sleep at once, by singing to him the story of the nymph Syrinx and then cut off his head.

ll. 73–81: *when a glimpse*, etc.: i.e. at the Transfiguration (*Matt.* xvii. 1–8). The "apple-tree" as an image of Christ belongs to the allegorical interpretation of the *Song of Songs*, "as the apple-tree among the trees of the wood, so is my beloved among the sons" (*Cant.* ii. 3); *the word that had broken deeper sleep than theirs*: the word of Christ, which raised Lazarus from the sleep of death (*John* xi. 11–14; 43–4).

l. 95: *as though left guardian*: Beatrice (the earthly image of the Divine Wisdom) is left alone by the Tree of Christendom to guard the Church. It must be remembered that for Dante (as he says very plainly in *Para.* xxvii. 23–4), the Chair of Peter was "vacant in the sight of the Son of God", because of the usurpation of Boniface VIII and the corruption of his successors. Moreover, at the time when he was writing the *Purgatorio*, the Popes had actually left Rome for Avignon; so that the See was "vacant" in a double sense.

l. 98: *those lights*: i.e. the Seven Torches, which have now been transferred to the care of the Seven Nymphs (i.e. the Virtues and Graces).

l. 99: *Aquilo or Auster*: the North and South winds.

l. 101: *that Rome where Christ a Roman is*: i.e. Heaven.

ll. 109–60: *never so swiftly*, etc.: Here the Second Masque begins.

ll. 112–17: *the bird of Jove*, etc.: Jove's bird (the Eagle) here represents the Roman Empire of which it is the emblem. This passage figures the persecution of the Church by the heathen Emperors from Nero to Diocletian (A.D. 64–314). The persecution does damage, not only to the Church, but to Rome itself, maiming its new spiritual energy, and cutting off some of its best citizens from the life of the community.

ll. 118–23: *next ... I saw ... a fox*: the Fox represents the various heresies which troubled the early Church.

ll. 124–9: *once again ... I saw the eagle*, etc.: the next tribulation is the well-meaning (ll. 137–8) munificence of Constantine, the first Christian Emperor, who endowed the Church with the riches which led to her corruption (see *Inf.* xix. 115 and note); *A voice from heaven*: i.e. that of St Peter, the Fisherman; his "little keel" is the Church.

ll. 130–5: *then ... out came a dragon*, etc.: the dragon is variously interpreted as: (1) Anti-Christ; (2) the Devil; (3) the spirit of Cupidity; (4) the schism brought about in the sixth century by Mohammed. The reference in xxxiii. 34–5 seems rather to favour interpretation (2) or (3). The fact, however, that all the other episodes of the Masque allude to historical events is an argument in favour of interpretation (4), Mohammed being thus classed (as in *Inf.* xxvii. 31 *sqq.*) as a Christian schismatic who detached part of the Church from its allegiance ("pulled away ... bits of floor"). The image of the dragon is perhaps derived from *Rev.* xii. 3: "his tail drew the third part of the stars of heaven and did cast them to earth."

ll. 136–47: *what remained grew covered ... with ... plumes*: the corruption caused by riches now runs riot, and the Car of the Church turns into the Beast of the Apocalypse, "having seven heads and ten horns" (*Rev.* xvii. 3).

ll. 148–50: *throned there ... a harlot*: this is the image of the corrupt and usurping Papacy (cf. *Inf.* xix. 109–11), the "woman on the beast" of *Rev.* xvii. 3.

ll. 151–60: *at her side ... a giant*: this is the image of the Papacy "committing fornication with the kings of the earth" (cf. *Inf.* xix. 107–8 and *Rev.* xviii. 3). The Giant is France, and in particular King Philip the Fair (cf. *Inf.* vii. 109 and note), by whose connivance Pope Clement V (cf. *Inf.* xix. 83–5 and notes) transferred the Papal See to Avignon. (Since this did not happen till 1305, ll. 156–60 must be taken as a prophecy of what is to happen after the date assigned to the vision.)

ll. 154–5: *her wanton glances veered to me*: This is perhaps best taken in the *literal* sense, Dante being, as Charles Williams light-heartedly observes, "the only male thing about" – at any rate, the only one that is present in the flesh. If an *allegorical* interpretation is insisted on, one might say that the Papacy was trying to enlist political support by worldly and unworthy means, thus provoking Philip to assert his domination and remove the Papal See to a place where it would be under his thumb. This was, in fact, the case.

# CANTO XXXIII

THE STORY. *Beatrice, escorted by Matilda, the Seven Ladies, Statius, and Dante, sets off on foot through the Forest. Calling Dante to her side, she talks to him about the Pageants he has been shown, and prophesies the coming of one who shall avenge the wrong done to Christendom. He discovers that the Water of Oblivion has taken away all memory of his former faults. But now they come to the double fountain-head of Lethe and Eunoë, and Dante, drinking the water of Good Remembrance, feels himself renewed through and through, and ready for his ascent to the Heavenly Paradise.*

"*Deus venerunt gentes,*" thus a-weeping
   Those nymphs began their psalm melodious,
   By three and four alternate measure keeping;

The while, all pitying sighs and dolorous,      4
   Beatrice, listening, changed her aspect so
   That scarce more changed was Mary at the cross.

But when those other virgins, to bestow     7
   Room for her speech, made place, then up rose she
   And stood and spake, all in a fiery glow:

"*Modicum, et non videbitis me,*      10
   And once again, my sisters dear and kind,
   *Iterum modicum et videbitis me.*"

Then all the seven before her she aligned,     13
   And me, the lady, and the sage who'd stayed,
   She motioned with a nod to come behind.

So she advanced; nor yet, I think, had laid     16
   Her tenth step on the ground whereupon she paced,
   Ere her eyes smote on mine; and thus she said,

Looking upon me calmly: "Make more haste,     19
   So that if I have somewhat for thine ear
   Thou for the hearing wilt be better placed."

And then, when I had duteously drawn near:     22
   "Brother, hast thou no tongue to question with?
   Wilt thou not venture, since thou hast me here?"

25  Then, as with those who're too much awed to breathe
        Before their betters, and can scarce endure
        To drag the living voice across their teeth,

28  So was't with me; in accents insecure:
        "Madonna, all my need and what beseems
        My case, you know," I faltered out unsure.

31  Then she to me: "These hampering fond extremes
        Of fear and shame henceforth I'd have thee drop:
        So, prithee, talk no more like John-a-dreams.

34  Know that the vessel which the worm broke up
        Was, and is not; who bears the blame, I say
        Let him believe God's vengeance fears no sop.

37  Not without heirs for ever and a day
        Shall be the eagle that once plumed the car,
        Whence it turned monster first and then a prey.

40  Surely I see, and so foretell, not far
        Ahead now, stars that shall not heed to strive,
        But shall bring in, secure from let or bar,

43  The times when a Five-hundred-ten-and-five,
        God-sent, shall smite the thief, and smite the giant
        That sins with her, and leave them not alive.

46  If on my rede thou art the less reliant
        Because, like Sphinx or Themis, dark it is,
        And, darkening reason, leaves it uncompliant,

49  Yet soon events shall be the Naiades
        To solve the hard enigma, nor shall scathe
        Be done to flocks or corn because of this.

52  Take note, and as my speech delivereth
        The tale, deliver it again to those
        Who live the life that is a race to death.

55  And mark, when writings spare not to disclose
        The plight in which thou hast beheld the tree
        Twice in this place despoiled now where it grows.

58  Who robs or rends it, enacts blasphemy
        Offending God, by whom 'twas made and meant
        For His sole use, a thing of sanctity;

332

Yea, for one bite, in grief and longing pent,      61
    Five thousand years on Him the first soul yearned
    Who on Himself imposed the punishment.

Thy wit's asleep if it hath not discerned      64
    That for especial cause the tree's so high,
    And hath its top inverted thus and turned;

Had fancies round thy mind not come to lie      67
    Like Elsa's waters, nor their little span
    Of joy played Pyramus to thy mulberry,

Thy moral sense had told thee how to scan      70
    And recognize, by all these signs alone
    Wrought on the tree, God's justice in the ban.

But since I see thy mind is turned to stone,      73
    And dull as stone, so that it is not lit
    By my words' light, but dazzled and outdone,

In heart I'd have thee bear them – if not writ,      76
    Then at least pictured, for that cause which brings
    The potent home with palm-leaves bound on it."

Then I: "Like wax beneath the signet-ring's      79
    Pressure, which leaves a print unalterable,
    My brain is stamped by you with all these things.

But wherefore do your words, with such long zeal      82
    Desired, outshoot my sight so, that the more
    I strain to follow them, the less my skill?"

"That thou," she said, "may'st know that school whose lore      85
    Thou hast been following, and judge how near
    It can keep up when my word goes before;

And see these ways of yours, how they appear      88
    As far from God's way as this terrene ball
    Lies distant from the highest and swiftest sphere."

Here I protested: "But I can't recall      91
    That ever I estranged myself from you;
    For that, my conscience feels no twinge at all."

"And if thou hast forgotten it – go to,      94
    Remember" – she was smiling as she spoke –
    "Thou'st drunk to-day of Lethe; yea, and true

333

97     It is, if fire may be inferred from smoke,
       From this oblivion we may well adduce
       Proof of thy guilt – false will and fealty broke.

100    But from now on I promise thee to use
       A naked style of speech – that is, so far
       As truth unveiled befits thy sight obtuse."

103    More blazing, and with paces tardier,
       The sun was riding the meridian ring
       Whose whereabouts depends on where we are,

106    When, even as halts an escort travelling
       Ahead, if he should find confronting him
       Presence or trace of some unusual thing,

109    So those seven ladies halted at the rim
       Of such pale shadow as an Alp might shed
       Through green leaves and dark boughs on some cool stream.

112    Methought I saw, springing from one well-head,
       Euphrates there and Tigris intertwined
       And parting, as friends part with lingering tread.

115    "O light, O glory of all human kind,
       What water's this that, rising from one well,
       Doth self from self diverging ways unwind?"

118    My prayer found answer: "Let Matilda tell;
       Ask her." Whereon the lady fair replied,
       As one who swears she's no way culpable:

121    "All this I've told him, and much more beside;
       And sure I am that there was nothing there
       Which Lethe's wave had any cause to hide."

124    Beatrice then: "Belike some greater care,
       Which often is the thief of memory,
       Hath blanketed his mind's eye; howsoe'er,

127    Look, flowing yonder, there is Eunoë;
       Conduct him there, and in it, as thy use is,
       Restore his fainting powers' vitality."

130    With that good breeding which makes no excuses,
       But to another's will adapts its own
       At the first sign of what that other chooses,

The beauteous lady took my hand anon,        133
    Saying in tones of womanly sweet grace
    To Statius, "Come with him"; and so led on.

If for my writing, Reader, I'd more space,        136
    I'd sing – at least in part – those sweets my heart
    Might aye have drunk nor e'er known weariness;

But since I've filled the pages set apart        139
    For this my second cantique, I'll pursue
    No further, bridled by the curb of art.

From those most holy waters, born anew        142
    I came, like trees by change of calendars
    Renewed with new-sprung foliage through and through,

Pure and prepared to leap up to the stars.        145

THE IMAGES. *Eunoë*: the name (meaning "good-remembrance" or "good-mind") is "made up", as a modern commentator observes, "from Greek words which were well known to medieval culture." Oddly enough, they do not seem to have been known to Dante's son Pietro, who, in his Latin commentary on the *Comedy*, writes the name of the river "Aonius", and identifies it with the "Aonian waters" mentioned by Ovid: i.e. with the Muses' fountain of Aganippe in Aonia. Pietro, however, seems to have lacked the curiosity – or perhaps the courage – to ask his father all the questions that we should like to have answered, and at one point (the notorious passage about the three mirrors, *Para.* ii. 97 *sqq.*) is reduced to saying to the reader: "Work out the rest, in fact the whole thing, for yourself, for I see nothing and understand nothing." We may therefore ignore him and conclude that the name Eunoë (which is undoubtedly what Dante wrote) was either the poet's own invention, or derived from some medieval or post-classical Latin source which was unknown to Pietro and has escaped the search of later commentators.

For the significance of *Eunoë*, see Introduction, p. 68, and Canto xxvii, Images.

*Matilda*: The function of Matilda is now clearer to us: the handmaid of Beatrice, and of all that Beatrice signifies, she welcomes the soul, instructs it, cleanses it, and brings it, thus prepared, into the presence of the sacramental mystery. She thus figures as all levels the Active Christian life: (1) *morally*, the perfecting of Nature to receive Grace; (2) *historically*, the visible and institutional life of the Church as the means whereby it is enabled to become the "true body" of Christ; (3) *mystically*, the life of good works in the world which is the necessary basis for the life of contemplation.

NOTES. l. 1: *Deus, venerunt gentes*: "O God, the heathen are come [into thine inheritance]" (*Ps.* lxxix. 1; *Vulg.* lxxviii. 1): the Nymphs lament the usurpation of the Papal See and the carrying away of the Church into captivity.

ll. 10–11: *modicum, et non videbitis me ... iterum modicum et videbitis me*: "a little while, and ye shall not see me; and again, a little while, and ye shall see me" (*John* xvi. 16): in these words, spoken by Christ of His approaching death and resurrection, Beatrice prophesies the captivity and subsequent restoration of the Holy See to the centre of Christendom. (The return duly took place in 1377, 56 years after Dante's death.)

l. 14: *the sage who'd stayed*: i.e. Statius.

ll. 34–5: *the vessel which the worm broke up was and is not*: Cf. *Rev.* xvii. 8: "the beast thou sawest was, and is not". The *vessel* is the Car of the Church, corrupted and divided; the *worm* (Dante's actual word is "serpent") is the Dragon of xxxii. 130–5.

l. 36: *God's vengeance fears no sop*: this refers to the ancient Florentine belief that if an assassin could contrive, within nine days after the murder, to eat a sop of bread and wine on the grave of his victim, he would be safe from the vengeance of the family (to prevent this evasion of justice a watch was kept over the grave). Beatrice warns the author (or authors) of the crime against the Church that God's vengeance is not so easily evaded.

ll. 37–8: *not without heirs ... shall be the eagle*, etc.: Constantine, who established the Church within the Empire ("that once plumed the car") shall have an Imperial successor who will establish order and restore the Papal See.

l. 43: *a Five-hundred-ten-and-five*: the person thus mysteriously designated is undoubtedly the same as the "Greyhound" of *Inf.* i. 101, who is also alluded to in *Purg.* xx. 15. Critical ingenuity has exhausted itself over this numerical cipher, with no great success. Some have (with a good deal of juggling) extracted from it a rebus of Henry VII. If they are right, this passage must have been written before Henry's death in 1313 (see *Inf.* Introduction, p. 47), and also before *Purg.* vii. 96, which laments the failure of Henry's expedition into Italy. Since, however, Dante continued to the end to hope for the advent of an Emperor of the right sort, it is probably better to take the prophecy in a general sense. What the 515 was intended to mean, we shall now probably never know.

l. 44: *smite the thief and smite the giant*: the "thief" is the Harlot; the "giant" the corrupt papacy of Boniface the Usurper and his successors.

**l. 47**: *Sphinx or Themis*: the Sphinx was a female monster who proposed a riddle to the Thebans, and slew all those who could not guess it. The riddle was guessed by Oedipus, whereupon the Sphinx destroyed herself. The goddess Themis was a patroness of the Delphic Oracle, famous for its ambiguous prophecies.

**l. 49**: *the Naiades*: this is a very curious error. The passage of Ovid's *Metamorphoses* in which Dante found the story of the Sphinx refers to Oedipus simply as "Laïades", i.e. "the son of Laïus" (*Metam.* vii. 759). Owing to some early scribe's carelessness, all the MSS. of Dante's time read, corruptly, "Naiades"; this word he has taken to be a feminine plural, and rendered "the Naiads" (*le Naiade*). The Naiads were water-nymphs, who had nothing to do with solving riddles; but since Dante knew no Greek, he had probably no reason for supposing the text to be corrupt, and is scarcely to be blamed for taking what he read at its face value.

**ll. 50–1**: *nor shall scathe be done*, etc.: after the death of the Sphinx, another monster was sent against Thebes, so that the people feared the total destruction of themselves and their cattle (*Metam.* vii. 762–5).

**l. 57**: *twice in this place despoiled*: i.e. once by the sin of Adam, and once by the theft of the Car.

**l. 60**: *for His sole use, a thing of sanctity*: this applies to the Tree in all its significations: human nature; Christendom; Rome. (*N.B.* Much perplexity, argument, and ink could be saved by resolutely bearing in mind that Dante's allegory is meant to be interpreted on three different levels simultaneously.)

**ll. 61–3**: *for one bite*, etc.: "Adam, for tasting the fruit of the Tree (which was a crime against all human nature), spent five thousand years in longing for the coming of Christ, who took upon Himself the penalty of the Fall." The 5000 years is a round number. According to *Gen.* v. 5, Adam was 930 years old when he died; and in *Para.* xxvi. 118, Dante makes him say that he spent 4302 years in Limbo before Christ came to release him (cf. *Inf.* iv. 52–5). This makes 5232 years in all. Dante is using the chronology of Eusebius, which puts the birth of Christ 5200 years, and His crucifixion 5232 years, after the Creation.

**ll. 65–6**: *for especial cause the tree's so high*, etc.: i.e. it is made so in sign that it should be kept inviolate (cf. xxii. 135).

**l. 68**: *Elsa's waters*: the Elsa is a river in Tuscany, flowing into the Arno between Florence and Pisa, whose waters have petrifying properties.

**l. 69**: *played Pyramus to thy mulberry*: for the story of Pyramus, see xxvii. 37–9, note. Beatrice means that the brief pleasure of "false delights" have left a stain of sin on Dante's mind.

**ll. 70–2**: *thy moral sense*, etc.: if Dante's mind had not been thus hardened and clouded, he would have understood how right God was when He forbade Adam to eat of the Tree.

ll. 76–7: *if not writ, then at least pictured*: i.e. "if you cannot understand or remember what I say, at least remember the images of the truth which I have shown you." These lines are the classical *apologia* and justification for all religious art and symbolism.

l. 78: *the potent home with palm-leaves bound on it*: the "potent" (pilgrim's staff) was wreathed with palm-leaves to show that its owner had visited the Holy Land.

ll. 85–6: *that school whose lore thou hast been following*: controversy has raged about Dante's "school" and its inadequacies. As we saw in the Introduction to the *Inferno*, pp. 40–2, Dante's early tendency had been to separate Philosophy from Theology, and make it, in its own right, the means to the perfection of earthly felicity. In terms of the allegory, he has been following Virgil, and has now come to the point at which Virgil can see no further.

l. 90: *the highest, swiftest sphere*: the Primum Mobile, or first moving sphere, lying beyond all the celestial spheres; cf. *Isai.* iv. 8–9: "My thoughts are not your thoughts, neither are your ways my ways, saith the Lord. For as the heavens are higher than the earth, so are my ways higher than your ways, and my thoughts than your thoughts."

ll. 91–9: *I can't recall*, etc.: Dante's draught of Lethe has expunged from his memory not merely the *guilt*, but the *fact* of his sin. (See Introduction, p. 68.) Beatrice is amused, and observes (a Freudian before the time) that this odd gap in his memory is proof in itself that there was something there which would not bear examination.

l. 101: *a naked style of speech*: in the *Paradiso*, Beatrice (the reader may be glad to hear) keeps her promise: there are no more. Masques. She hints, however, that her "naked" speech may present some difficulties to the average intellect; (the reader is warned).

l. 104: *the meridian ring*: i.e. it was now noon in Purgatory. (The meridian varies according to the longitude of the place we are in.)

ll. 113–14: *Euphrates and Tigris*, etc.: the Euphrates (which rises in Armenia and flows into the Persian Gulf near Basra) and the Tigris (which rises in Kurdistan, and joins the Euphrates at Kurna) are mentioned in *Gen.* ii. 14–15 as two of the rivers which watered Eden (the river Hiddekel being identified with the Tigris). Boethius (*Consolations of Philosophy*, v. metr. i.) says of them: "Tigris from the same head doth with Euphrates rise,/And forthright they themselves divide in several parts." Dante, therefore, naturally supposes that this is what he is seeing.

l. 118: *let Matilda tell*: thus casually, for the first and last time, the "Fair Lady's" name is mentioned. See Images to Cantos xxviii, xxxiii, and Appendix, p. 347.

ll. 119–26: *the Lady fair replied*, etc.: The two ladies seem to be indulging in a little mirth at Dante's expense, because he is so pre-occupied with Beatrice ("belike some greater care ...") as to forget what Matilda told him. Readers of *The New Life* may be reminded of the party at which Dante made himself conspicuous (see *Inf.* Introduction, p. 27), and Beatrice – as he complained in a sonnet – "made fun of him with the other ladies" (*V.N.* xiv). This passage confirms my own belief that Matilda was a personal friend of Beatrice's, and probably one of the young women who joined in the laughter on that occasion.

l. 127: *Eunoë*: See Images. From this time on, Dante will remember all the past, but without shame or bitterness. Forgiveness, that is to say, is now both fully given and fully accepted.

l. 128: *as thy use is*: Dante implies that this ritual is carried out for every soul – by Matilda, or at any rate by the Handmaid of Grace, in whatsoever guise she may appear to the penitent.

l. 135: *Statius*: we infer, therefore, that Statius also drinks of Eunoë.

l. 139: *since I've filled the pages*: Dante has written his thirty-three cantos, and shows a laudable determination not to over-run the mould. He is almost unique among medieval writers in thus submitting to be "bridled by the curb of art": it is one of the reasons for his enduring readableness.

l. 145: *the stars*: these, the closing words of the *Inferno*, are also the closing words of both the *Purgatorio* and the *Paradiso*.

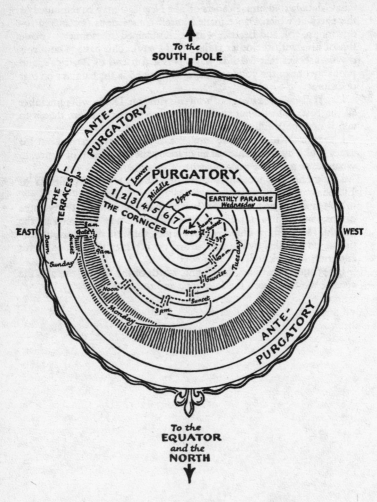

PATH OF THE POETS UP THE NORTHERN SIDE
OF THE MOUNTAIN

# APPENDIX

## NOTE A: THE NEEDLE'S EYE

THE text of ll. 7-12 is:

*Noi salivam per una pietra fessa,*
*che si movea d' una e d' altra parte,*
*si come l' onda che fugge e s' appressa.*

"*Qui si convene usare un poco d' arte,*"
*cominciò 'l duca mio, "in accostarsi*
*or quinci, or quindi al lato che si parte.*"

The plain and flat-footed translation which obviously presents itself
is: "We were climbing up through a cleft rock which was moving on
one side and the other, like to the wave which recedes and approaches.
'Here it is needful to use a little skill,' began my guide, 'in keeping
close, now hither, now thither, to the side which is going away.'"
This literal interpretation, though accepted by some translators and
commentators, is dismissed by modern writers with the (!) indicative
of derision. We are thus left with the difficulty of explaining why it
should have been needful to keep laboriously to the "side which is
going away", which, on the supposition that the rocks are static, can
only mean "the far side of the curve". Various suggestions have been
offered – as that the inner curve of the zigzag was the more precipitous,
or was encumbered with fallen stones.

I have succumbed to the pressure of opinion; for nobody is eager
to incur the stigma of a (!). But I am by no means persuaded that the
conception of a literally moving mountain is so contemptibly absurd
as that stigma would imply. The negotiation of a moving barrier, or
"pass perilous" of a similar sort is a commonplace of Other-World
Journeys, both in classical and romantic folk-lore, the most famous
instances being the Clashing Rocks through which the Argonauts
have to steer (Apollonius Rhodius, Bk. II. l. 317 *sqq.*, 549 *sqq.*) and the
falling portcullis past which Owain has to leap both in the Celtic
(*Mabinogion*: *Lady of the Fountain*) and the French (Chrestien de
Troyes, *Yvain*, ll. 921 *sqq.*) versions of the story.

I do not think that *Purg.* xxi. 40-60 could be cited to refute this inter-
pretation, since the motion, though undoubtedly occurring above
Peter's Gate, is clearly not of natural origin but occasioned, like the
"quaking" which accompanies the release of a soul, by "what of itself
Heaven for itself doth take"; the most one can say is that, if there were
such a motion, Statius ought to have mentioned it and has not done so.

# NOTE B: TITHONUS' LEMAN

## (ix. 1 *sqq.*)

THE other proposed interpretation of this passage affirms that the "dawn" here described is not the rising of the Moon (between 8 and 9 P.M.) but that of the Sun (about 6 A.M.). In that case the stars on Aurona's forehead ("set in the form of the cold-blooded animal") would be the constellation of Pisces (the Fishes), and night's "two ascending paces" are explained as "signs of the Zodiac" or "*watches* of the night". The argument is that to call the Lunar Aurora the "leman – *concubina*" of Tithonus, as opposed to his "lawful wife", the Solar Aurona, is (a) forced, (b) without classical precedent.

The arguments which seem to me conclusively in favour of Moonrise are: (1) *the constellation*: only *one* "cold animal" is mentioned; fishes do not "strike people with their tails" and scorpions do, and there seems to be an allusion here to *Rev.* ix. 10; there are no brilliant stars in Pisces; (2) the "steps" are *ascending* steps: i.e. night is still "going up the sky", and it is therefore before midnight (cf. the similar description of day "going up the sky" in xxii. 119); (3) *the parallelism of the three dreams*: on each occasion (cf. xviii. 87, 145; xix. 1–6; xxvii. 88–92, 94) the hour when Dante falls asleep is carefully distinguished from the hour (always just before sunrise) when he dreams; (4) *poetic expediency*: Dante's sleep is here an obvious poetic device for marking the passage of time; his explanation "that he still retained Adam's nature" – which is clearly an apology for his ill-mannered behaviour in thus dozing off in the midst of such distinguished company and so much edifying conversation – would have little point if he had actually remained awake until nearly 6 A.M.

# NOTE C: THE *SACRA FAME* RIDDLE

MUCH enjoyable mental exercise may be had from the effort to negotiate this notorious critical crux. The Italian is:

> *Per che non reggi tu, O sacra fame*
> *dell' oro, l' appetito de' mortali?*

This, if one reads the first two syllables as one word – *perchè* – makes obvious and very relevant sense:

> Why dost thou not control the appetite of mortals, O holy hunger for gold?

But if Dante is really taking that to be the original meaning of Virgil's line, then he has committed the biggest howler in history, beside which the "pink emu" looks pale, and the "sorrowful wolf" hides its diminished head.

I think we may safely dismiss the "howler" theory. It is true that Dante sometimes construes incorrectly (e.g. his rendering in *Conv.* II. vi. of *Aen.* i. 664–5), and is sometimes misled by a faulty text (e.g. *Naiades* for *Laïades* in Ovid: *Metam.* vii. 759; *Purg.* xxxiii. 43; or the confused rendering in *Conv.* IV. xxvii. of *Metam.* vii. 507–11; both of which can be traced to inaccuracies in the text available to him). But the present passage is one whose text has never been in dispute, and whose intention, despite the somewhat bold and unusual construction, is quite unmistakable in its context. That context is, moreover, one which Dante knew well, and alludes to at least twice in the *Commedia* (*Inf.* xiii. 28 *sqq.*; *Inf.* xxx. 12 *sqq.*). And if he could be supposed ignorant or forgetful of the ambiguous meaning of *sacer*, the parallel passage in *Aen.* iv. 412, *Improbe amor, quid non mortalia pectora cogis* would have served him as warning and guide.

It is much more likely that he was following the customary medieval method of dealing with inspired texts,[1] by which it was held legitimate, for the purpose of exegesis, meditation, or argument, to put upon a passage any interpretation which could be grammatically screwed out of it. This practice, though frowned upon by the pedant, is not unknown even to-day among popular preachers and religious apologists – or indeed among journalists and other persons addicted

---

1. The works of the "Prophet of the Gentiles" enjoyed, for such purposes, the honorary status of an "inspired" text; the method found its sanction in the theory (indirectly derived from Plato): *nomina consequentia rerum*: i.e. that words are not accidental or arbitrary symbols, but bear an actual relation to the things they denote.

to casual quotation. Every day we see "more honoured in the breach than in the observance" cited as though it meant "more often honoured"; or "one touch of nature makes the whole world kin", as though it meant "a single touch of natural feeling suffices to demonstrate universal human brotherhood." Yet a glance at their respective contexts would show that by the first Shakespeare intended "more *fitly* honoured", and by the second "there is one natural failing that all human beings share" (viz. a passion for gaudy novelties). A still clearer parallel is afforded by Ezra Pound, who frequently quotes from Latin poets with such distortion of sense and syntax as to invite precisely that accusation of illiteracy to which Dante here lays himself open.

On this hypothesis, the translation: *quid non cogis = perchè non reggi tu* is perfectly defensible. Though the sense given to *cogis* may be a little strained, the syntax is an entirely normal medieval construction, of a type inherited from the Vulgate (e.g. *quid hic statis tota die otiosi, Matt.* xx. 6), where the Latin *quid* represents the Greek τί. Advantage is taken of the ambivalence of *sacer* holy/unholy (like the English "devoted"), to give the passage a new and unexpected sense. Thus Statius, pondering on Virgil's text, suddenly sees the pattern of the words as it were white on black instead of black on white, and a fresh train of thought is started in his mind, leading to the conclusion that whereas an "unholy greed" of gold may "drive" mortals to extremes of wickedness a "holy hunger" for gold may equally operate to "control" the excesses of prodigality.

This solution of the problem – elegant, adequate, and wholly of the period from the philological point of view – is nevertheless open to one serious objection. It is not the Latinity but the sentiment that gives us pause. Is it conceivable that any medieval moralist – especially Dante, whose hatred of money-grubbing amounts almost to an obsession – could under any circumstances bring himself to speak of a "holy hunger for gold"? A reasonable financial prudence – yes; a proper respect for the worldly goods entrusted in one's care – most certainly; it is indeed made abundantly clear in *Inf.* xiii. that profligacy is mortal sin. But *hunger* for gold is another matter, for the phrase implies acquisitiveness. And it is, precisely, *acquisitiveness* that constitutes the sin of "Covetise" – whether it takes the form of acquiring in order to hoard (Avarice), or acquiring in order to spend (Prodigality). On this point Aristotle and St Thomas agree.

Perplexed by these considerations, various commentators have sought a fresh way out of the difficulty by exploiting certain ambiguities in the Italian. Setting aside the rather desperate expedient of taking "*dell' oro l' appetito*" together and understanding by "*sacra fame*" "hunger for holiness" (a sense quite impossible to extract from the Latin by any ingenuity whatsoever), it remains possible to read for *perchè* (why?), *per che* (by what?) and to construe:

# Note C: *The* Sacra Fame *Riddle*

> By what [crooked ways] dost thou not drive (guide, compel)
> human appetite, O accursed greed of gold?

This, to be sure, gives to *sacra* a sense which it does not normally bear in Italian, though the older commentators seem to accept it without difficulty and paraphrase it *esecrabile*. The rendering does at least contrive to make the lines into a plausible translation of the original, and so to save Dante's reputation both as a Latinist and as a moralist. On the other hand, it is certainly not elegant, neither does it explain why Statius should have seen in the passage a specific warning against prodigality.

If we modify this process by extending a similar principle of interpretation to the Latin, we may perhaps suppose that Statius, taking the *quid* as a kind of cognate accusative, and rendering *quid non cogis* as "with what [compulsion] dost thou not compel", was moved to understand this as: "is there any urge [whether of stinginess or of prodigality] by which thou dost not [contrive to] urge ...?" And if one then renders the somewhat equivocal *reggi* (drive/control) and the equivocal *sacra* (holy/unholy) by an equally equivocal "constrain" (or "sway") and "devoted", one obtains an English version which is ambiguous in almost exactly the same way as Dante's Italian. It is not impossible that the ambiguity was intended, and I have, with considerable searching of heart, so rendered the passage. But if I had before me any warrant or precedent in a medieval Catholic writer for applying the word "holy" to the greed of gold, I would gladly abandon these sophistries and render straightforwardly:

> O why dost thou not regulate the lust
> Of mortals, hallowed hunger after gold?

One must, in any case, remember that Dante had very effectually tied his own hands. Having determined, for reasons dictated by the plan of his poem, that Statius (*a*) was to appear on the Fifth Cornice, and not earlier or later, (*b*) that he was to have been a spendthrift rather than a (hopelessly unsympathetic) niggard, and (*c*) that he was to owe his first impulse for reformation to the *Aeneid*, he was obliged to cast about for some passage from that work which might operate as a rebuke to conspicuous waste. The available choice was not a wide one, and he will have the sympathy of every writer who, hunting the pages of his favourite author for an appropriate chapter heading, finds every passage that presents itself either too long, too involved, or maddeningly just off the point.

# NOTE D: DERIVATION OF LAW

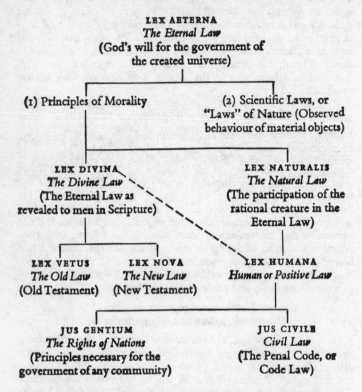

**LEX AETERNA**
*The Eternal Law*
(God's will for the government of
the created universe)

**(1) Principles of Morality**

**(2) Scientific Laws, or
"Laws" of Nature** (Observed
behaviour of material objects)

**LEX DIVINA**
*The Divine Law*
(The Eternal Law as
revealed to men in Scripture)

**LEX NATURALIS**
*The Natural Law*
(The participation of the
rational creature in the
Eternal Law)

**LEX VETUS**
*The Old Law*
(Old Testament)

**LEX NOVA**
*The New Law*
(New Testament)

**LEX HUMANA**
*Human or Positive Law*

**JUS GENTIUM**
*The Rights of Nations*
(Principles necessary for the
government of any community)

**JUS CIVILE**
*Civil Law*
(The Penal Code, or
Code Law)

(In Christian communities the LEX HUMANA and its derivatives are
of course directly and consciously influenced by the LEX DIVINA.)

DANTE's handling of his encounter with this lady is without parallel in the *Commedia*. Although he has a long conversation with her, he does not ask her name; nor, when it is casually supplied by Beatrice, does he show any recognition of it or her. It is, indeed, only the fact that she has this quite ordinary and earthly name, that precludes us from supposing that she is an embodied abstraction, or masquing Intelligence, like the persons of the two pageants.

By the early commentators it is unanimously assumed that she is Matilda of Canossa, the "Great Countess" of Tuscany (1046-1115) who was a friend of Pope Gregory VII and a lavish benefactor of the Church; and the main line of comment has accepted this traditional identification. Some have built upon it a theory that Matilda is a type of the Empire – rather perversely, since the Great Countess was an anti-Ghibelline, and always supported the Popes against the Imperial power. I am myself persuaded that it is a mistake to try and find in the *Commedia* that elaborate parallelism and antithesis between Empire/Church, and the felicity of the secular/spiritual life which is outlined in the *Convivio*; and if this identification is accepted should find no difficulty in supposing that the Countess Matilda represents the active life of the Church in the world.

There are, however, serious objections. The description of Matilda is, as d' Ovidio pointed out, a very highly idealized picture of "a fiery and imperious old woman of seventy, who had been twice married"; and it would seem, from his descriptions of, e.g. Manfred and St Bernard, that Dante's intention was to represent the shades as they appeared at the time of their death. Also, the parenthetical, and almost off-handed, mention of the Lady's name is entirely unlike his usual way with eminent historical personages.

Struck by these considerations, modern commentators have offered other suggestions. Some have urged the claims of one or other of the two thirteenth-century nuns, Mechthild of Magdeburg and Mechthild of Hackeborn, whose mystical writings severally contain passages showing some resemblance to parallel passages in the *Purgatorio* and *Paradiso*. Mechthild of Magdeburg died, however, at an even more advanced age than the Great Countess, and Mechthild of Hackeborn at the age of 58; neither is there any very good evidence that Dante had read either of them, or that either of them was so well known to her Italian near-contemporaries that her name would be recognized without further identifying details; and, in fact, it was not recognized.

A third suggestion is that Matilda – far from being a character so prominent that her mere name sufficed for her recognition – was a memory so personal to Dante that her identification would add nothing to the reader's knowledge; that she is, in fact, one of the ladies mentioned in the *Vita Nuova* – and probably that close friend of Beatrice's whose death is mentioned in *V.N.* viii, and concerning whom he wrote the sonnet *Morte villana*, with its enigmatical conclusion. It is true that Dante does not recognize her when he meets her; but in the *V.N.* he lays no claim to her acquaintance, saying only that he had seen her in Beatrice's company and had looked on her dead body. Matilda's position as an attendant and friend, to whom Beatrice speaks with a kind of intimate and smiling familiarity, lends a certain propriety to this identification, which seems to me much the most attractive of those proposed, although I am bound to confess that it has no more extraneous evidence to support it than any other.

The objection made (in the Scartazzini-Vandelli commentary) to *all* these identifications, on the grounds that Matilda must, like Cato, be a *permanent* functionary of the Earthly Paradise, and cannot therefore be anybody who died later than the institution of Purgatory, does not, I think, carry much weight. It might apply with equal force to Beatrice herself. To the penitent and purified soul the God-bearing Image (whatever it may be) appears, accompanied by its whole train of functionaries; but that vision is unique and personal to every man that sees it. For Dante, the Image is Beatrice whose handmaid is Matilda; for others, other Images will doubtless perform the like offices. This is, I think, the best reason there is for connecting the identity of Matilda directly and exclusively with that of Beatrice; since this hypothesis presents no incongruities or improbabilities, and is entirely consistent with the allegory at every level of interpretation.

# GLOSSARY OF PROPER NAMES

THIS list contains all the names of persons and places mentioned in the *Purgatorio*, together with references to the *Inferno* if they have already been mentioned there, with an indication of all the passages in which they occur. If sufficient information about them has already been given in the "Images" or "Notes", I have merely inserted the relevant reference; if not, I have included a brief description or explanation here. All references are given by Canto and Line (not by page); if the actual name is not mentioned in Dante's text, the reference relates to the line which identifies the person or place in question. Names of actual inhabitants, or places forming part of the geography, of Dante's Three Kingdoms are shown in capital letters, thus: BEATRICE; LETHE; names of persons and places which are merely referred to in the text or notes are shown in italic type, thus: *Haman*; *Arno*.

Where the English form of the name differs from the classical or Italian form, the form used in the English text is given first, followed by the original or more correct form in brackets, thus: JUVENAL (Decius Junius Juvenalis); *Peter Combseller* (Piero Pettinagno).

For the Italian personages the main entry will be found sometimes under the Christian name and sometimes under the family name, according to which is the more familiar, or figures the more prominently in the poem; but a cross-reference is given in every case. Thus, information about FORESE DONATI will be found under FORESE, with a cross-reference under DONATI; but information about *Can Grande della Scala* will be found under *Scala, della*, with a cross-reference under *Can Grande*.

> N.B. Both here and in the notes the myths and stories of antiquity are given as they were known in Dante's day, i.e. in versions that are frequently post-classical and, by modern standards of scholarship, garbled and debased. One god or hero is often confused with another who happened to have a similar name or attributes; the Greek legends in particular have, since the time of Homer, suffered many alterations and additions in passing through the hands of generation after generation of Greek and Latin story-tellers. Here and there I have pointed out a few of the more flagrant corruptions, but for the most part I have been content to tell the tale as it was known to Dante.

*Abydos*: on the Hellespont. (*Purg.* XXVIII. 74 and *notes* to 71 and 73.)

*Achan*: of the tribe of Judah. (*Purg.* XX. 109 and *note* 103–17.)

ACHERON: River of Hell. (*Inf.* III. 78 and Images to III; XIV. 116; *Purg.* II. 105.)

ACHILLES: Greek warrior, the hero of the *Iliad*. He was the son of Peleus by the Nereid Thetis. According to Homer, he was killed at the siege of Troy (*q.v.*); but a later tradition, which Dante follows, tells that he fell in love with Polyxena, daughter of King Priam of Troy, and was promised her hand on condition that he should join the Trojans. Deceived by this promise, he ventured unarmed into a Trojan temple, and was there assassinated by Paris. (*Inf.* V. 65; XII. 71; XXVI. 62 and *note* to XXVI. 55; XXXI. 4 and *note*; *Purg.* IX. 34 and *note*; XXI. 92.)

ADAM: father of mankind. (*Inf.* III. 116; IV. 55; *Purg.* IX. 10; XI. 44; XXIX. 85; XXXII. 37 and see Images to XXXII; XXXIII. 62 and *note* 61–3.)

*Adige*: river of Italy. (*Inf.* XII. 5 and *note*; *Purg.* XVI. 115 and *note*.)

ADRIAN V, Pope (Ottobuono dei Fieschi): (*Purg.* XIX. 89 and *note*, and Images to XIX.)

AENEAS: a Trojan prince, son of Anchises by the goddess Venus; the hero of Virgil's *Aeneid*. Troy having fallen, he escapes with his father, his young son Ascanius, and a number of followers, his wife Creusa having been lost in the confusion. He is told by the Penates (household gods), whose images he has piously brought away with him, that his destiny is to settle in Italy. After many wanderings by sea, in the course of which Anchises dies, his fleet is wrecked by the spite of Juno, but Aeneas with seven of his ships is saved by Neptune and brought to the coast of Africa. Here the Trojans are hospitably received by Dido, queen of Carthage, who, breaking her oath of fidelity to her dead husband, Sychaeus, falls in love with Aeneas, and, when he again sails for Italy at the bidding of Mercury, kills herself. Aeneas lands in Sicily, celebrates the funeral games of Anchises, and leaves some of his followers to found a colony there. The rest sail on and visit Cumae; here, guided by the Sibyl, Aeneas makes the descent into Hades, where he sees the punishment of the wicked and the placid after-life of the virtuous. Among the latter he meets Anchises and learns from him that he is destined to be the ancestor of the Roman people, who are to possess the empire of the world. (This is the famous Book VI of the *Aeneid*, from which Dante derived so much of the geography and machinery of his *Inferno*.) Aeneas then sails up the mouth of the Tiber and lands in Latium; here the fulfilment of an oracle shows that the Trojans have reached their destined goal. Latinus, the king of the country, welcomes Aeneas and offers him

# UNIVERSAL 24-HOUR CLOCK

## TO ILLUSTRATE DANTE'S
### *Purgatory*

Showing the corresponding times of the day
in the Northern and Southern Hemispheres,
with the movement of the
Zodiacal Signs

Cut out the circle of the Earth on this page and that of the Heavens on the page opposite, and paste each of them down on a circle of stiff card. Place the Earth-circle on the Heaven-circle and fasten the two together through the centre with a paper-clip or split-pin, so that the one will revolve upon the other.

Turn the apex of Mt Purgatory to the hour indicated in the text; the clock will then show the corresponding times at Jerusalem, at Rome, on the Ganges, and at the Pillars of Hercules (Morocco).

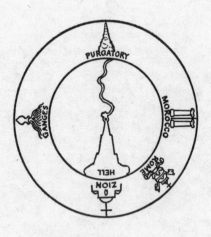

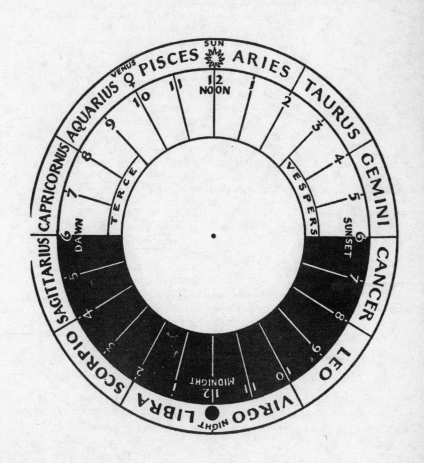

the hand of his daughter Lavinia, previously betrothed to Turnus, prince of the Rutuli. Juno, with the aid of the Fury Alecto, stirs up war between the Trojans and the Latins, and after a number of engagements, in which allies are called in on both sides, the Rutulians are routed. Turnus challenges Aeneas to single combat; and Juno at length comes to an agreement with Jupiter that Aeneas shall be the victor, on condition that Latium shall keep its own name. Thus in Aeneas and Lavinia the Trojan and Latian lines are united and the way is open for the foundation of the city and empire of Rome. (*Inf.* II. 32; IV. 122; XXVI. 93; *Purg.* XVIII. 137 and *note* 132–8; XXI. 97 (*Aeneid*).)

*Aeneid*: see AENEAS.

*Aeolus*: god of the winds. (*Purg.* XXVIII. 21 and *note* 19–21.)

*Africanus*: see *Scipio*.

AGATHON: born at Athens *c.* 448 B.C.; died *c.* 400 B.C.; Greek tragic poet, mentioned by Aristotle in the *Poetics* and the *Rhetoric.* (*Purg.* XXII. 108.)

*Aglauros*: daughter of Cecrops. (*Purg.* XIV. 139 and *note.*)

*Agobbio*: see *Gubbio*.

*Ahasuerus*: king of Persia, the story of whose marriage to the Jewess Esther is told in the Bible (*Bk. of Esther*); identical with *Xerxes* (*q.v.*). (*Purg.* XVII. 28 and *note* 25–30; (Xerxes) XXVIII. 71 and *note.*)

*Alagia*: niece of Pope Adrian V. (*Purg.* XIX. 142 and *note.*)

*Alagna* (Anagni): town in Latium about 40 miles S.E. of Rome. (*Purg.* XX. 86 and *note.*)

*Albert I of Austria*: emperor. (*Purg.* VI. 97 and *note.*)

ALBERTI, COUNT ORSO DEGLI: see ORSO DEGLI ALBERTI.

*Alberto della Scala*: lord of Verona. (*Purg.* XVIII. 121 and *note.*)

*Alcmaeon*: son of Amphiaraus (*Purg.* XII. 50 and *note* 49–51.)

*Aldobrandesco, Guillim (Guglielmo)*: nobleman of Tuscany, father of Humbert Aldobrandesco (*q.v.*). (*Purg.* XI. 59.)

ALDOBRANDESCO, HUMBERT (Omberto): nobleman of Tuscany. (*Purg.* XI. 67 and *note* to XI. 58–9.)

*Alessandria*: town of Piedmont. (*Purg.* VII. 135.)

ALFONSO III, KING OF ARAGON (reigned 1285–91): eldest son of Peter III of Aragon (*q.v.*). (*Purg.* VII. 115.)

ALIGHIERI, DANTE: see DANTE ALIGHIERI.

*Amata*: wife of Latinus. (*Purg.* XVII. 36 and *note* 34–9.)

*Anagni*: see *Alagna*.

*Anastagi*: a noble Ghibelline family of Ravenna, who during the first half of the 13th century played an important part in the political life of Romagna. In 1249 they helped to expel the Guelfs from Ravenna but were soon after expelled in their turn. About nine years later they made their peace with their opponents, and returned to Ravenna, under the protection of the Counts of

Bagnacavallo (*q.v.*); but the family rapidly fell into decay and had almost completely died out by 1300. (*Purg.* XIV. 107.)

*Anchises*: father of Aeneas (see AENEAS). (*Inf.* I. 74; *Purg.* XVIII. 137.)

*Andes*: ancient name of Pietola (*q.v.*).

ANGELS:

ANGEL (GABRIEL) OF THE ANNUNCIATION: (*Purg.* X. 34.)

ANGEL OF CHASTITY: guardian of the Seventh Cornice. (*Purg.* XXVII. 6 and *note*.)

ANGEL OF GENEROSITY (or MERCY): guardian of the Second Cornice. (*Purg.* XV. 34 and *note*.)

ANGEL OF HUMILITY: guardian of the First Cornice. (*Purg.* XII. 79 and *note*.)

ANGEL OF LIBERALITY: guardian of the Fifth Cornice. (*Purg.* XXII. 1 and *note*.)

ANGEL OF MEEKNESS: guardian of the Third Cornice. (*Purg.* XVI. 143; XVII. 47 and *note*.)

ANGEL-PILOT: steersman of the Ship of Souls. (*Purg.* II. 29 *sqq.*, *note* to II. 17–24 and Images; II. 94.)

ANGEL PORTER (Angel of the Church): at Peter's Gate. (*Purg.* I. 98; IV. 129; IX. 78 *sqq.*; XII. 134–5; XXI. 23, 54.)

ANGEL SENTINELS: guardians of the Valley of the Rulers. (*Purg.* VIII. 26 *sqq.*)

ANGEL OF TEMPERANCE: guardian of the Sixth Cornice. (*Purg.* XXIV. 136 and *note*.)

ANGEL OF ZEAL: guardian of the Fourth Cornice. (*Purg.* XIX. 46 and *note*.)

ANTENOR of Troy: (see Images to *Inf.* XXXII) reputed founder of Padua (*Purg.* V. 75.)

ANTIGONE: daughter of Oedipus, king of Thebes, by marriage with his mother Jocasta (*q.v.*); sister to Eteocles and Polynices (for whom see *Inf.* XXVI. 54 and *note*). When Oedipus had put out his own eyes and been expelled from Thebes, Antigone accompanied him on his wanderings until his death at Colonus. She then returned to Thebes, and, in defiance of King Creon, buried the body of Polynices, slain by Eteocles in the war of the Seven against Thebes. Creon had her imprisoned in a cove, where she took her own life. (*Purg.* XXII. 110.)

ANTIPHON: Greek tragic poet who *fl.* at the court of Dionysius I of Syracuse (*c.* 430–367 B.C.). He is mentioned by Plutarch among the greatest of the tragic poets, and also by Aristotle in the *Rhetoric*, which is presumably Dante's source. (*Purg.* XXII. 108.)

*Aquilo*: the North Wind. (*Purg.* IV. 60; XXXII. 99.)

AQUINAS, ST THOMAS (Tommaso d'Aquino) (*c.* 1225/7–1274): the greatest of the scholastic theologians, the "Common Doctor" of the Church, whose great work in systematizing Christian

Doctrine according to Aristotelian philosophic method dominated the thought of the Middle Ages, and is still officially accepted as fundamental to the exposition of Catholic theology.

Born at Rocca Secca in Campania, the son of the Count of Aquino; entered the Dominican Order at the age of 17; studied under St Albertus Magnus of Cologne; debated in Paris, 1245; taught in Cologne, 1248; Doctor of Theology (Sorbonne), 1257; lectured in Paris, Rome, Bologna, etc.; wrote exhaustive commentaries on the Works of Aristotle, and many theological works, including the *Summa contra Gentiles* (dealing with the principles of natural religion) and the monumental *Summa Theologica* – usually referred to briefly as the *Summa* – a complete systematization of Christian theology; died at Fossa Nuova, near Terracina, on the way to attend the Council of Lyons in 1274; canonized, 1323 (two years after Dante's death).

The work of St Thomas in "baptizing" secular philosophy into the Christian faith, and so reconciling reason with revelation, was of incalculable value, especially at that period, when the rediscovery of classical learning and literature was threatening to disturb people's minds by the apparent dilemma of having to choose between the two. St Thomas maintained and demonstrated that the knowledge that God exists could be arrived at by the reason, and that revelation, although transcending reason, at no time contradicted it.

Dante studied the works of St Thomas closely, and the theological structure of the *Comedy* owes more to him than to any other single theologian, although the poet supplemented his teaching by that of many other authorities, and did not hesitate to differ from him, now and again, in points of detail. References to relevant passages from St Thomas will be found from time to time in the *notes*.

Dante places St Thomas in Paradise, in the Heaven of the Sun, among the Doctors of the Church (*Para.* x–xiii). (*Notes, passim.*) (*Purg.* xx. 69 and *note*.)

*Arachne*: of Lydia. (*Purg.* xii. 43 and *note*.)

ARAGON, Kings of: see ALFONSO III, JAMES II, PETER III.

*Aragon*: ancient kingdom of Spain. (*Purg.* iii. 116.)

*Archian(o)*: river of Tuscany. (*Purg.* v. 95, 124, and *note* to v. 94.)

*Arezzo, Aretines*: city of Italy, in the S.E. of Tuscany; the Aretines were strongly Ghibelline, and in continual feud with the Florentines (see *Inf.* Intro., p. 30). (*Inf.* xxii. 5; xxix. 109; xxx. 31. *Purg.* vi. 13; xiv. 46 and *note*.)

*Arezzo, Guittone d'*: see *Guittone d'Arezzo*.

ARGEIA: daughter of Adrastus, king and sister to Deipyle (*q.v.*). (*Purg.* xxii. 110.)

# Glossary

*Argus*: hundred-eyed monster of class. myth. (*Purg.* XXIX. 96 and *note*; XXXII. 64–5 and *note*.)

ARISTOTLE: the great Athenian philosopher, founder of the Peripatetic School (384–322 B.C.). He was Plato's most brilliant pupil, but later diverged considerably from his master's teaching. His works were rediscovered and translated in the Middle Ages (largely through the work of the Arabian scholars), and became enormously influential. The work of St Thomas Aquinas incorporated the Aristotelian system of philosophy into Catholic theology. All Western philosophy derives ultimately from the twin Platonic and Aristotelian traditions.

The works of Aristotle were voluminous, and covered every branch of learning known in his day: Dialectics and Logic (the *Organon*); Philosophy (the *Physics* and other works on natural science; the *Metaphysics*; two treatises on *Mathematics*); Politics (the *Ethics*, the *Politics*, the *Economics*); Art (the *Poetics*, the *Rhetoric*). Only the major works are mentioned in this list, but there are many others.

For Aristotle, human thought proceeds by abstraction from the data provided by the senses; i.e. investigation into the nature of being starts from the observation of individual things sensibly existing. It is in this feature that his philosophy contrasts most forcibly with the Platonic idealism, for which (especially in its later developments) the world of existence is only the shadow of the world of essences. Aristotle analyses the individual existent into Matter (undifferentiated "stuff") and Form (structural organization), and the process by which a thing comes to attain its proper end (to be what it was intended to be) into the passage from Potentiality to Actuality. Neither Form nor Matter has any real existence by itself – every individual existent being a Form-Matter complex. The soul of the individual man is the "form" of the human body, both soul and body being thus considered as essential parts of the actualized personality. It is obvious that this concept lends itself readily to incorporation into orthodox Christian doctrine (e.g. of the sanctity of the material universe, sacramentalism, and the Resurrection of the Body) as opposed to the Gnostic doctrines of the inherent evil of matter derived from the Neo-Platonists. God is "the unmoved Mover", source of all change, motion, and process – a definition which has left its mark on Thomist theology. Dante was well acquainted with all the works of Aristotle that were available in Latin in his time, and refers to them many times. (*Inf.* IV. 131; VI. 106; (*Ethics*) XI. 80; (*Physics*) XI. 101; *Purg.* III. 43.)

ARNAUT DANIEL: Provençal poet. (*Purg.* XXVI. 142 and *note* to XXVI. 116.)

*Arno*: river of Italy. (*Inf.* XIII. 146; XV. 113; XXIII. 95; XXX. 65; XXXIII. 83; *Purg.* V. 126; XIV. 16; XIV. 24 and *note*.)

*Asopus*: river of Boeotia. (*Purg.* XVIII. 92 and *note*.)

*Assyrians*: (*Purg.* XII. 58 and *note*.)

*Athens*: city of Greece. (*Purg.* VI. 139; XV. 97.)

*Augustus* (*Caesar*): see CAESAR, AUGUSTUS.

*Aurora*: the Dawn. (*Purg.* II. 7.)

*Auster*: the South Wind. (*Purg.* XXXII. 99.)

AVERROES (Ibn Roshd): Arabian physician and philosopher. His famous commentary on Aristotle, translated into Latin, had a wide vogue in the Middle Ages, and did much to revive the study of Aristotelian philosophy. He taught a pantheistic doctrine of Universal Reason, and denied the immortality of the individual soul. He was born at Cordova and died in Morocco (1126–98). (*Inf.* IV. 144; *Purg.* XXV. 62 and *note*.)

*Azzo da Este*: see *Este, Azzo da*.

*Azzo, Ugolin(o) d'*: see *Ugolin, Azzo d'*.


*Bagnacaval(lo)*: town of Romagna. (*Purg.* XIV. 115 and *note*.)

*Barbagia*: district of Sardinia. (*Purg.* XXIII. 96 and *note*.)

*Barbarossa, Frederick*: Frederick I, 2nd Emperor of the Hohenstaufen line; born 1121; emperor 1152; died 1190. A vigorous upholder of the Imperial authority against the Pope and against the rebellious cities of Italy, he spent 25 years stubbornly opposing the Lombard League, capturing Milan (1162) and Rome (1167) and making himself master of Italy. The Lombard cities having again revolted, he was beaten at Legnano (1176) and reconciled (1177) with Pope Alexander III. Thereafter he exercised his rule with more mildness, and in 1183, at the Peace of Constance, recognized the independence of the Italian city-states. In 1189 he joined Richard Cœur de Lion and Philip Augustus in the Third Crusade, and was drowned while crossing a river in Cilicia (1190). No German prince was ever more dearly loved by his subjects. Legend maintains that he did not die, but sits asleep beneath the mountains in Thuringia. His red beard (which earned him his Italian nickname of "Barbarossa") has grown through the marble table before him; and one day he will come again (like British Arthur) to save his country in her direst need. Dante's epithet of "Good" probably refers partly to his reputation among his subjects and partly to his championship of the Imperial cause. (*Purg.* XVIII. 119.)

BEATRICE: daughter of Folco Portinari, born in Florence 1266. In the *Vita Nuova* (*New Life*) Dante says that he first saw and fell in love with her when she was 8 years and 4 months old and he was nearly 9. She was married to Simone dei Bardi, and died in 1290. See Intro., pp. 26 *sqq*. and The Greater Images, p. 67. (*Inf.* II.

53 *sqq.*; X. 131; XII. 89; XV. 89; *Purg.* I. 53, 91; VI. 47; XV. 77; XVIII. 49, 74; XXVI. 59 and *note*; XXVII. 36, 53; appears to Dante in XXX. 31 *sqq.*; names herself to him, XXX. 74; accuses him to the Intelligences, XXX. 103 *sqq.*; reproaches him, XXXI. 1. *sqq.*; the Twyform reflected in her eyes, XXXI. 121 and *note* 123; shows D the Masque of Church and Empire, XXXII. 104 *sqq.*; prophesies the DXV, XXXIII. 43 and *note*; directs Matilda to lead D to drink of Eunoë, XXXIII. 127.)

*Beatrice d'Este*: widow of Nino Visconti. (*Purg.* VIII. 73 and *notes* VIII. 71, 74, 79.)

*Beatrix* (*Beatrice*) *of Provence*: youngest daughter of Raymond Berenger IV, count of Provence; married (1246) Charles I of Anjou (cf. v.) by which marriage Provence became united to the French crown. (*Purg.* VII. 128.)

BELACQUA: Florentine maker of musical instruments. (*Purg.* IV. 122 and *note.*)

*Benevento*: town in Campania, N.E. of Naples, near which was fought the Battle of Benevento, 26 Feb. 1266 (see *Inf.*, Intro., p. 25). (*Purg.* III. 128 and *note* to III. 112.)

BENINCASA DA LATERINA: a judge of Arezzo who, while acting as assessor for the podestà of Siena, sentenced to death a relative of the famous highwayman, Ghino di Tacco (*q.v.*). On hearing of the sentence, the condemned man said to him: "May my soul remain in Purgatory no longer than thine in thy body!" Then Benincasa, learning who Ghino was, hastened to get himself transferred to Rome. But Ghino pursued him thither and coming into the papal audit office, disguised as a pilgrim, he made his way through the crowd to where Benincasa was sitting on the bench, and stabbed him. Then throwing off his disguise and drawing his sword, he made his way out of the palace, no one daring to hinder him. (*Purg.* VI. 14.)

*Berber*: native of Barbary. (*Purg.* XXIII. 104.)

*Bernardine of Fosco* (Bernardin di Fosco): i.e. Bernardo, son of Fosco, said to have been a "tiller of the soil"; a man of humble birth in Faenza, who rose to great wealth and authority, and by his generous and virtuous qualities made himself accepted by the native nobility of the city. In 1240 he played a prominent part in the defence of Faenza, against the Emperor Frederick II (*q.v.*). He was podestà of Siena in 1249. The date of his death is not known. (*Purg.* XIV. 101–2.)

*Bismantova*: mountain-peak in Emilia. (*Purg.* IV. 26 and *note.*)

BOHEMIA, OTTOCAR II and WENCESLAS IV OF: see OTTOCAR II, WENCESLAS IV.

*Bologna*: city of Italy, in the Romagna (see map, *Inf.*, p. 173). (*Inf.* XVIII. 58; XXIII. 104, 143; *Purg.* XIV. 100.)

*Bologna, Franco of*: see *Franco of Bologna*.

*Bolsena*: lake in Italy, near Viterbo. (*Purg.* XXIV. 24 and *note* to XXIV. 21.)

BONGIUNTA ORBICCIANI DEGLI OVERARDI: of Lucca. (*Purg.* XXIV. 20 and *note*.)

BONIFACE, Archbishop of Ravenna: (*Purg.* XXIV. 29 and *note*.)

BONIFACE VIII: Pope (Benedict Caietan) (*c.* 1217–1303); Pope, 1294–1303 (see *Inf.*, Intro., pp. 34 *sqq.*). (*Inf.* XV. 112; XIX. 53 and *note*; XXVII. 70, 85. *Purg.* XX. 87 and *note* 85–7.)

*Brabant, Mary of*: wife to Philip III of France (*Purg.* VI. 23 and *note* to VI. 22.)

*Brettinoro*, now Bertinoro: a small town in Emilia, between Forlì and Cesena. After being for some time under the lordship of the Malatesta of Rimini, it passed, towards the end of the 13th century, into the hands of the Ordelaffi (mentioned in *Inf.* XXVII). In its heyday Brettinoro was celebrated for the hospitality of its nobles, but Dante represents it as being now greatly degenerated. (*Purg.* XIV. 112.)

BRIAREUS: giant. (*Inf.* XXXI. 99 and *note*; *Purg.* XII. 28 and *note*.)

BRIE, SIMON DE: see SIMON DE BRIE.

*Brindisi*: see *Brundisium*.

BROSSE, PIER DE LA: see PIER DE LA BROSSE.

*Bruges*: city of Flanders. (*Inf.* XV. 5; *Purg.* XX. 46 and *note*.)

*Brundisium* (Brindisi): city of Italy. (*Purg.* III. 27 and *note*.)

*Burgundy, Margaret of*: see *Margaret of Burgundy*.

CAECILIUS (Caecilius Statius): born at Milan, died 168 B.C.; Roman comic poet, mentioned by Horace and St Augustine. (*Purg.* XXII. 98.)

CAESAR: (1) Caius Julius, Dictator of Rome (100–44 B.C.) – son of C. Julius Caesar the praetor, he liked to claim descent from the Trojan hero Aeneas (*q.v.*), founder of Rome. A brilliant general, and strong adherent to the democratic party, he was made Consul, 59 B.C.; his conquest of Gaul (59–51 B.C.) made him the idol of the people and the army. His rival, Pompey, jealous of his rising power, joined the aristocratic party and headed an armed opposition against him; but Julius, crossing the river Rubicon which separated his own province from Italy, marched upon Rome, and being everywhere received with acclamation, made himself master of all Italy (49 B.C.). After defeating Pompey's adherents in Spain, he crossed over into Greece and decisively overthrew Pompey at the Battle of Pharsalia (48 B.C.). He was made Dictator and, after a period of further military triumphs, was offered the kingship; this, however, he reluctantly refused, for fear of offending the people. On the Ides of March, 44 B.C., he was assassinated in the Capitol by a band of conspirators, led by Brutus and Cassius. His successor Augustus (*q.v.*) was the first Roman Emperor, and the name Caesar became part of the Imperial title. (*Inf.* I. 70; IV. 123; XXVIII. 97; see also Images to XXXI; *Purg.* XVIII. 101 and *note* 100–3.)

(2) Caesar Augustus (Caius Julius Caesar Octavianus): 1st Roman Emperor (63 B.C.–A.D. 14). He was the great-nephew of Julius Caesar and adopted by him as his heir. After the assassination of Julius, he assumed the name of Caesar, and became, with Lepidus and Mark Antony, one of the triumvirs who took over the government of the Republic. He gradually gathered all the great offices of state into his own hands; in 32 B.C. he accepted the title of Imperator. The defeat of Antony at Actium (31 B.C.) and the death of Lepidus (12 B.C.) left him in fact and in name sole master of the Roman Empire. The epithet "Augustus", conferred on him by the Senate in 27 B.C., was borne by his successors as part of the Imperial title. The "Augustan Age" was marked by a brilliant flowering of Latin literary genius. (*Purg.* VII. 6; XXIX. 116 and *note* 115–16.)

*Caesar* as imperial title denoting Albert of Austria (*Purg.* VI. 92).

CAIN: son of Adam. (*Purg.* XIV. 133–4 and *note.*)

*Calboli*: Fulcieri da, podestà of Florence. (*Purg.* XIV. 58 and *note.*)

CALBOLI, RINIER DEL: Guelf nobleman of Forlì. (*Purg.* XIV. 88–9 and *note* XIV. 7–8.)

*Calliope*: Muse of Epic Poetry (see Muses). (*Purg.* I. 9.)

*Campagnatico*: village and castle belonging to the Aldobrandeschi family, near Grosseto in the Sienese Maremma. (*Purg.* XI. 66 and *note* to 58–9.)

*Campaldino*: Battle of. (*Inf.* XXII. 1. and *note*; see also *Inf.*, Intro., p. 31; *Purg.* V. 92.)

*Canavese*: district on the borders of Monferrato (*q.v.*). (*Purg.* VII. 136.)

*Can Grande della Scala*: see *Scala, Can Francesco della.*

CAPET, HUGH, the Great: see HUGH CAPET.

*Capet, Hugh, the Younger*: see *Hugh Capet the Younger.*

*Capricornus* (the Goat): see *Zodiac.*

*Capulets* (Capelletti): family of Verona. (*Purg.* VI. 106 and *note.*)

*Carpigna, Guy of* (Guido di Carpigna): a nobleman belonging to a branch of the counts of Montefeltro (*q.v.*), which had been established in the town of Carpigna (now Carpegna) in Romagna since the 10th century; probably Guido the Younger, who was podestà of Ravenna in 1251 and died before 1289. He is said to have been famous for his liberality. (*Purg.* XIV. 97.)

CASELLA: musician and friend of Dante. (*Purg.* II. 91 and *note.*)

*Casentin(o)*: district of Tuscany. (*Inf.* XXX. 65 and *note*; *Purg.* V. 94 and *note*; XIV. 41 and *note*, XIV. 42).

CASSERO, JACOPO DEL: see JACOPO DEL CASSERO.

**Castel, Guy** (Guido da Castello): gentleman of Treviso. (*Purg.* XVI. 125 and *note*.)

**Castor and Pollux**: the semi-divine sons of Leda by Zeus (or Tyndareus), from whom the constellation of Gemini (the Twins) is named. See *Zodiac*.

**Castrocaro**: formerly a castle, now a village, in Romagna. The counts of Castrocaro, originally Ghibellines, submitted to the Church party in 1282. About 1300 the place passed into the hands of the Ordelaffi, and the original family, whose continued existence Dante deprecates, had become extinct by 1375, when Benvenuto da Imola was lecturing on the *Comedy* at Bologna. (*Purg.* XIV. 116.)

**CATO OF UTICA** (Marcus Porcius Cato the Younger): Roman statesman (95–46 B.C.). A strict republican of the old school, nurtured in the Stoic philosophy, he at first opposed both Caesar and Pompey, but when the civil war broke out (see CAESAR, JULIUS), found himself obliged to take sides with the latter. After the Battle of Pharsalia he escaped into Africa and, after a terrible march across the desert, joined forces with Metellus Scipio, who had the command of Pompey's African forces. Caesar defeated Scipio at the Battle of Thapsus, and Cato, rather than make terms with the victor, committed suicide. He became for the Romans the typical example of Stoic virtue. In the *Purgatorio* Dante makes him guardian of the approach to Mt Purgatory. (*Inf.* XIV. 15 and *note*; *Purg.* I. 31 *sqq.*, *note*, and Images.)

**CAVALCANTI, GUIDO DEI**: son of Cavalcante dei Cavalcanti, was born between 1250 and 1259. Dante, who calls him "the first of my friends", says that their friendship began when Guido wrote a reply to one of his sonnets, and it was with him that Dante went to the famous party where Beatrice mocked him (*Inf.* Intro., p. 27). Like Dante, he belonged to the younger school of poets, who wrote in the "sweet new style – *il dolce stil nuovo*" and, like his father, was an "Epicurean". Guido was a White Guelf, and his marriage to the daughter of the Ghibelline Farinata degli Uberti was one of the alliances frequently arranged in the hope of reconciling the two parties. He died in August 1300 (*Inf.* Intro., p. 34 and *note*). (*Inf.* X. 63 and *note*; *Purg.* XI. 97 and *note*.)

**CERBAIA, COUNT ORSO DEGLI ALBERTI DELLA**: see ORSO DEGLI ALBERTI.

**CHARLES I OF ANJOU** (1220–85): king of Naples and Sicily, count of Anjou and Provence, son of Louis VIII of France and Blanche of Castile. Invited by Pope Urban IV to assume the crown of Naples, and urged by Pope Clement IV to take possession of the kingdom, he entered Italy in 1265, was crowned King of Sicily and Apulia in 1265, and defeated Manfred (*q.v.*) at Benevento in 1265. The Sicilians, revolting against French rule, invited Conradin (son of the Emperor Conrad IV) to expel him. He defeated Conradin at Tagliacozzo in 1268, but in 1282 the Sicilian "underground movement" (surreptitiously aided, as was believed, by Pope Nicholas III and others) broke out into open insurrection, ending in a fearful massacre of the French (the "Sicilian Vespers") and the end of their rule in Sicily. Charles died in 1284 while trying to regain the kingdom. (*Inf.* XIX. 99 and *note* (see also *Inf.*, Intro., p. 25); *Purg.* VII. 109; XI. 137; XX. 67 and *note*.)

*Charles (Carlo) II*: king of Naples, count of Anjou and Provence (1243–1309); son of Charles I of Anjou and Beatrix of Provence. (*Purg.* V. 69; XX. 79 and *note*.)

*Charles of Valois*: brother of Philip the Fair, of France. (*Purg.* XX. 71 and *note*.)

CHASTITY, ANGEL OF: see ANGELS.

*Chiassi* (Classe): near Ravenna. (*Purg.* XXVIII. 19 and *note*.)

*Chiaveri*: town of Italy. (*Purg.* XIX. 100 and *note*.)

*Chilperic III*: king of France; perhaps referred to in *Purg.* XX. 54; see *note in loc.*

CHIRON: Centaur. (*Inf.* XII. 65 *sqq.* and *note*; *Purg.* IX. 38.)

CHRIST, JESUS: addressed as "most high Jove". (*Purg.* VI. 118 and *note*; XIII. 36 and *note*; XVI. 17; *Purg.* XX. 87 and *note*); XXI. 8; XXIII. 74; XXVI. 129; XXXII. 101.)

CHURCH, ANGEL OF: see ANGELS (Angel-Porter).

*Cimabue, Giovanni*: painter. (*Purg.* XI. 94 and *note*.)

*Circe*: the sorceress. (*Inf.* XXVI. 91 and *note*; *Purg.* XIV. 42.)

*Classe*: see *Chiassi*.

*Clement IV* (Guy Foulquois): Pope 1264–8. (*Purg.* III. 125.)

*Clio*: muse of history (see *Muses*). (*Purg.* XXII. 58 and *note*.)

*Colonna* (Colonnesi): a great Roman family, with whom Pope Boniface VIII had a feud for many years, and against whom he actually proclaimed a crusade. In 1297, Sciarra Colonna having robbed the Papal treasury, Boniface deprived his uncles, the Cardinals Jacopo and Pietro, of their dignities, excommunicated them and their whole house, and destroyed their palaces. The Colonnesi retired to their fortresses at Palestrina and Nepi. The Pope, having taken Nepi, proceeded, on the advice of Guido da Montefeltro, to procure the surrender of Palestrina and the submission of the Colonnesi by promising a full amnesty; which promise he treacherously broke. The Colonnesi rebelled again, were again excommunicated; and in 1303 it was Sciarra Colonna who, on behalf of Philip the Fair of France, made Boniface a prisoner at Anagni (*Inf.*, Intro., p. 35). The Pope's feud against the Colonna family is alluded to in *Inf.* XXVII. 86 *sqq.*; and his capture at Anagni (Alagna) by Sciarra Colonna and Guillaume de Nogaret (the "living thieves") in *Purg.* XX. 90 (and see *note*).

*Colonna, Sciarra di*: see above, *Colonna* (Colonnesi).

*Conio*: castle in Romagna, near Forlì; now totally destroyed. Its counts, said to have called themselves Conti da Barbiano, seem to have been mostly Guelfs. (*Purg.* XIV. 116.)

CONRAD (CURRADO) MALASPINA II: son of Conrad Malespina I. (*Purg.* VIII. 65, 118 and *note* to VIII. 118.)

*Conradin* (Curradino): last of the Hohenstaufen, son of the Emperor Conrad IV; born 1251; died 1268. On his father's death in 1254 he should have succeeded to the crowns of Sicily and Naples, but his uncle Manfred (*q.v.*) seized first the regency and then the crown, alleging that Naples could not be ruled by a three-year-old child, and promising to appoint C. his successor. After Manfred's defeat and death at Benevento in 1266 (see *Purg.* III. 112 *sqq.*), the Sicilies, with the support of all the Italian Ghibellines, called on C. to assume the crown and drive out the French (see under Charles I of Anjou). C. was beaten at Tagliacozzo and executed at Naples. (*Purg.* XX. 68.)

*Conrad Palazzo*: see *Palazzo, Conrad*.

*Constance*: daughter of Manfred, married Peter III of Aragon. (*Purg.* III. 143; VII. 127.)

*Constance* (Costanza): Empress, mother of Frederick II. (*Purg.* III. 112 and *note.*)

*Corsica*: (*Purg.* XVIII. 81 and *note* 79–81.)

*Corso Donati*: brother of Forese Donati, Florentine leader of the "Black" party. (*Purg.* XXIV. 82 and *note.*)

*Cosenza*: town of Calabria; the "Bishop of Cosenza" referred to by Manfred is probably Cardinal Bartolommeo Pignatelli (Archb. 1254–66). (*Purg.* III. 124.)

*Costanza* (Constance): Empress: see *Constance*.

*Crassus*: Marcus Licinius, Roman triumvir. (*Purg.* XX. 116 and *note* 103–17.)

*Cupid*: god of love, son of Venus (*Purg.* XXVIII. 65 and *note.*)

*Cyrus*: tyrant of Persia. (*Purg.* XII. 56 and *note* 55–7.)

*Cytharaea*: epithet of Venus, goddess of love, the planet Venus (*q.v.*). (*Purg.* XXVII. 94.)


DANIEL, ARNAUT: see ARNAUT DANIEL.

*Daniel*: prophet of the Jews. (*Purg.* XXII. 146 and *note* 140–54.)

DANTE ALIGHIERI: poet. Born in Florence in Tuscany, May–June 1265, son of Alighiero Alighieri, and his first wife Bella (family name uncertain). Baptized at church of San Giovanni Battista (St John Baptist).

First meeting with Beatrice Portinari (*q.v.*), May 1274. Fought on the Guelf side at Campaldino, 11 June 1289. Enrolled in Apothecaries' Guild, 1295 or 1296. Spoke in *Consiglio dei Centi*, 1296. Ambassador to San Gimignano, 1299.

Married, not later than 1298, Gemma Donati, by whom he had issue: Pietro, Jacopo, Giovanni (?), Antonia (?), Beatrice.

Elected to priorate to serve 15 June to 15 August 1300. Said to have been sent with embassy to Pope Boniface VIII, October 1301. Exiled from Florence with White Guelfs: 1st Decree, 27 January 1302; 2nd Decree, 10 March 1302. Joined Ghibelline party, but appears to have left them *c.* 1304 and taken refuge with Bartolommeo della Scala at Verona.

Lived a wandering life of which little record remains. With the Malaspini family, 1306–7; said to have visited Paris about this time; in Italy (probably as guest of Guido Novello), 1310–11, when he wrote letters in the Imperial cause to the Florentines and to the Emperor Henry VII. Excluded from decree of pardon the same year; 3rd Decree of exile (including his sons Pietro and Jacopo) published 6 November 1315. Refused to return to Florence under amnesty of 1316.

After visiting Verona again as guest of Can Grande della Scala, went to live at Ravenna, under the protection of Guido Novello, with his banished sons and his daughter Beatrice. Sent on embassy to Venice, July 1321. Died of fever on his return to Ravenna, 14 September 1321.

*Works* (dates conjectural, but order pretty certainly established): *La Vita Nuova* (*The New Life*), probably between 1292 and 1295; *Il Canzoniere* (*Song-book*), collection of lyrics of various dates; *Il Convivio* (*The Banquet*), *c.* 1307–9 (unfinished); *De Vulgari Eloquentia* (*Of Writing in the Vulgar Tongue*), probably about the same time as *Il Convivio*; *De Monarchia* (*Of Monarchy*), probably about 1311; various *Letters* (chiefly political) in Latin; two Latin *Eclogues* addressed to Giovanni del Virgilio, 1319; a scientific treatise, *Quaestio de Aqua et Terra*, of which the authenticity has been much disputed. A number of other minor works have been attributed to him from time to time.

The *Commedia* (the word "Divina" is not part of Dante's own title for the work) is thought by some to have been begun before Dante's exile, and Boccaccio states that the first draft of it was in Latin. As we have it, however, the *Inferno* cannot have been completed before 1314. The *Purgatorio* seems to have been partly or wholly written by 1319; some place its completion before 1312. Of the *Paradiso*, the twenty-seventh canto cannot have been written before 1316, and the poem was apparently finished only a short time before the author's death in 1321.

DAVID: king of Israel. (*Inf.* IV. 58; XXVIII. 136 and *note* to XXVIII. 134; *Purg.* X. 64–5 and *note*.)

Deïdamia: in class. myth., daughter of Lycomedes, king of Scyros. (*Inf.* XXVI. 62 and *note* to XXVI. 55; *Purg.* XXII. 114.)

DEIPYLE: daughter of Adrastus, king of Argos. Tydeus, king of
Calydon, and Polynices (see *Inf.*, XXVI. 154 and *note*), when in
exile, came to the court of Adastrus, who married Tydeus to
Deipyle and her sister Argeus to Polynices.

Adastrus then undertook to restore them to their thrones, and
began by leading an expedition on behalf of Polynices (the
"Seven against Thebes"). On the way to Thebes the army halted
at Nemea, where Hypsipyle showed them the way to water at
the fountain of Langeia. (*Purg.* XXII. 110.)

*Delos*: island of. (*Purg.* XX. 131 and *note*.)

DEVIL: The Devil is referred to by various names in the *Comedy*,
according to the speaker:

    (1) BELZEBUB (by Dante). (*Inf.* XXXIV. 127.)
    (2) DIS (by Virgil). (*Inf.* VIII. 68; XI. 65; XII. 39; XXXIV. 20.)
    (3) LUCIFER (by Dante). (*Inf.* XXXI. 143; XXXIV. 89.)
    (4) SATAN (by Pluto). (*Inf.* VII. 1.)
    (5) LORD OF MISRULE (by Conrad Malaspina). (*Purg.* VIII. 131.)
    Other refs: *Purg.* XII. 25 and *note*.

*Dian(a)*: (Greek Artemis): the virgin huntress-goddess. (*Purg.* XXV.
131 and *note* 128–35.)

*Diana*: river of Siena. (*Purg.* XIII. 153 and *note* 151–3.)

*Domitian* (Titus Flavius Domitianus Augustus): Roman Emperor.
(*Purg.* XXII. 83 and *note*.)

*Donati, Corso*: see *Corso Donati*.

DONATI, FORESE: see FORESE DONATI.

*Donati, Nella*: see *Nella Donati*.

DONATI, PICCARDA: see PICCARDA DONATI.

*Douay*: city of Flanders. (*Purg.* XX. 46 and *note*.)

DUCA, GUIDO DEL: Ghibelline nobleman of Brettinoro. (*Purg.* XIV.
81 and *note* XIV. 7–8.)


*Ebro*: river of Spain. (*Purg.* XXVII. 3 and *note*.)

*Elbe*: river of Bohemia and Germany. (*Purg.* VII. 99.)

*Elias*: see *Elijah*.

*Elijah*: prophet of Israel, who was taken up to Heaven in a fiery
chariot (2 *Kings* ii. 11). (*Inf.* XXVI. 34; *Purg.* XXXII. 80.)

*Elsa*: river of Tuscany. (*Purg.* XXXIII. 68 and *note*.)

ENGLAND, HENRY III OF: see HARRY III OF ENGLAND.

*Erysichthon*: Thessalian who offended Ceres. (*Purg.* XXIII. 25 and *note*.)

*Este, Azzo da*: (died 1308); son of Obizzo II (for whom see *Inf.* XII.
111, XVIII. 56 and Gloss.). Married Beatrice, daughter of Charles II
of Naples. (*Purg.* V. 77.)

*Este, Beatrice d'*: see *Beatrice d'Este*.

*Esther*: queen of Ahasuerus (Xerxes) king of Persia. (*Purg.* XVII. 29
and *note* 25–30.)

*Eteocles*: in class. myth. son of Oedipus. (*Purg.* XXII. 56 and *note*.)

*Ethiope*: (Ethiopia) Ethiop(ian). (*Inf.* XXIV. 89; *Purg.* XXVI. 21.)

*Eunoë*: river of the Earthly Paradise. (*Purg.* XXVIII. 130 and *note* to 121–6; Images to XXXIII; XXXIII. 127 and *note*.)

*Euphrates*: river. (*Purg.* XXXIII. 113 and *note*.)

EURIPIDES: born at Salamis 485 B.C., died in Macedonia 406 B.C.; great Greek tragic poet, eighteen of whose plays have come down to us, including the *Alcestis, Medea, Hippolytus, Electra, Orestes, Iphigenia in Aulis, Iphigenia in Taurus,* and *Ion.* His style, freer and more emotional than that of his great predecessors, Aeschylus and Sophocles, excels in pathos and in the representation of pathos and abnormal passions, and he has been blamed for his "romanticism" and for his outspoken criticism of the gods, as much as he has been praised for his warm humanity, and for the lyrical beauty of his choruses. His emphasis upon the human situation and the psychology of love make him the most "modern" of the great Greek dramatists. Dante, who knew no Greek, cannot have had a first-hand knowledge of his works, though he may have known the plays of Seneca, many of which are based upon those of Euripides. (*Purg.* XXII. 107.)

EVE: mother of mankind. (*Purg.* VIII. 99; XI. 63; XII. 71; XXIX. 24; XXX. 52.)

*Ezekiel*: prophet of the Jews. (*Purg.* XXIX. 100 and *note* to XXIX. 93 *sqq.*)

*Fabbro* (dei Lambertazzi): a Ghibelline of the noble family of Lambertazzi of Bologna. His birth-date is not known; he is mentioned in 1228 as being in charge of the city's *carroccio* (battle-chariot) in the war with Modena. He was three times podestà of Faenza, and held the same office in various cities many times during his busy and influential life. He died in 1259. Soon after, his sons became involved in conflict with the Geremei, which led to the ruin of the Lambertazzi family and of the Ghibelline party in Bologna. (*Purg.* XIV. 100.)

*Fabricius*, Caius: Roman consul. (*Purg.* XX. 25 and *note* 20–33.)

*Faenza*: town of Italy, on the Lamone, between Forlì and Imola, near Bologna. (*Inf.* XXVII. 49 and *note*; XXVII. 50; XXXII. 123. *Purg.* XIV. 101.)

*Falterona* (Monte): mountain in Romagna. (*Purg.* XIV. 16 and *note*.)

*Fano*: city of Ancona, on the Adriatic coast. (*Inf.* XXVIII. 77; *Purg.* V. 70.)

*Fantolin(i), Ugolin(o) de'*: nobleman of Faenza. (*Purg.* XIV. 121 and *note*.)

FARINATA DEGLI SCORNIGIANI: see SCORNIGIANI, FARINATA DEGLI.

*Fates*: in Greek and Roman mythology, the deities who preside over the destinies of mankind. According to the Greek poet Hesiod, there were three Fates: Clotho, who span the thread of a man's life; Lachesis, who wove it on the loom; and Atropos, who cut it at death. (*Inf.* IX. 97; (Atropos) XXXIII. 126; *Purg.* XXI. 27 (Clotho); XXV. 79 (Lachesis).)

FIESCHI, OTTOBUONO DEI: see ADRIAN V.

*Filippeschi*: family of Orvieto. (*Purg.* VI. 108 and *note* to VI. 106.)

*Fishes* (Pisces): see *Zodiac*.

*Florence*: in Italy, on the river Arno, chief city of Tuscany, and birthplace of Dante. (For history see *Inf.*, Intro., pp. 29 *sqq.*) (*Inf.* VI. 49 *sqq.*; VI. 61; X. 92; XIII. 143 *sqq.* and *note*; XVI. 75; XXIV. 144; XXVI. 1. *Purg.* VI. 127 *sqq.*; XIV. 51 and *note*; XX. 75; XXIII. 102 and *note* to XXIII. 101.)

*Florence*, denunciation of: *Inf.* XXVI. 1 *sqq.*; *Purg.* VI. 127 *sqq.*

FORESE DONATI: Florentine, brother of Corso and Piccarda Donati; friend of Dante. (*Purg.* XXIII. 48 and *note*.)

*Forlì*: town of Italy (see map, *Inf.*, p. 153). (*Inf.* XVI, 99; XXVII. 43 and *note*; *Purg.* XXIV. 32.)

*Fortune, Greater* (Fortuna Major): star-group. (*Purg.* XIX. 5 and *note*.)

*Fosco, Bernardine of*: see *Bernardine of Fosco*.

*Franco of Bologna*: painter. (*Purg.* XI. 83 and *note*.)

*Frederick I*: emperor. See *Barbarossa*.

FREDERICK II, KING OF SICILY: born 1272, reigned 1296–1337; third son of Peter III of Aragon (*q.v.*). On the death of Alfonso III in 1291, James, the second brother, succeeded to the throne of Aragon, leaving Sicily to Frederick, the youngest; but a few years later, ignoring this arrangement, he tried (at the instigation of Pope Boniface VIII) to hand Sicily over to Charles II (of Anjou), King of Naples. The Sicilians rose in protest, renounced their allegiance to James, and offered the crown to Frederick, who succeeded in holding it against all comers. Frederick seems to have been an excellent and well-loved ruler. He assisted the Emperor Henry VII (*q.v.*) against Robert of Naples; but, after Henry's death, ceased to interest himself in Italian affairs, devoting himself exclusively to the defence of Sicily. It is probably this preoccupation with his own kingdom, to the neglect of national and imperial interests, that accounts for Dante's poor opinion of him, and for the place assigned to him in Purgatory. (*Purg.* VII. 119.)

FREDERICK (FEDERICO) NOVELLO: of the Conti Guido family, son of Guido Novello of Battifolle and of Gherardesca, daughter of Count Ugolino della Gherardesca of Pisa (for whom see *Inf.* XXXIII. 13 and *note*). Killed in a fray at Bibbiena in 1289 by one of the Guelf Bostoli of Arezzo. (*Purg.* VI. 16.)

# Glossary

*Frederick (Federico) Tignoso*: see *Tignoso, Frederick.*
*Fulcieri da Calboli*: see *Calboli, Fulcieri da.*

GABRIEL, ANGEL: see ANGELS.
*Gallura*: Nino Visconti of: see *Nino Visconti.*
*Ganges*: river of India; regarded as eastern limit of horizon, reckoned from meridian of Jerusalem. (*Purg.* II. 5 and *note*; II. 1–9; XXVII. 4 and *note*.)
*Ganymede*: son of Tros. (*Purg.* IX. 22 and Images.)
*Garigliano, River*: see *Verde.*
*Gascony*: district of France. (*Purg.* XX. 66 and *note*.)
*Gemini* (the Twins): see *Zodiac.*
GENEROSITY, ANGEL OF: see ANGELS.
*Gentucca* (? Morla, wife of Bonaccorse Fondora): of Lucca. (*Purg.* XXIV. 39 and *note*.)
GERYON: monster of Hell (see Images to *Inf.* XVII.) (*Inf.* XVII. I. *sqq.*; XVII. 97 (descr. XVI. 131 *sqq.*); XVIII. 19; *Purg.* XXVII. 23.)
*Ghent*: city of Flanders. (*Purg.* XX. 46 and *note*.)
*Ghin(o) di Tacco*: famous highwayman of Siena, said to have been of noble family, and to have behaved like Robin Hood, robbing the rich and giving to the poor. Various exploits are narrated of him; Boccaccio places one of these during the papacy of Boniface VIII (1294–1303). (*Purg.* VI. 14.)
*Giacomo da Lentino*: see *Lentino, Giacomo da.*
GIANTS: according to Homer, were a huge and savage race in Trinacria, destroyed on account of insolence towards the gods; according to Hesiod, they sprang from the blood of Ouranos (Lat. Uranus, the sky), falling upon Ge (Lat. Tellus, the earth). Later poets confuse them with the Titans and say that they rebelled against Zeus (Jupiter) and attempted to storm Olympus. Dante, in placing the Giants round the edge of the infernal Well, seems to have the later legend in mind. (*Inf.* XXXI. 32, 43 *sqq.*; *Purg.* XII. 33 and *note* 31–3.)
*Gideon*: captain of the hosts of Israel. (*Purg.* XXIV. 125 and *note* 120–5.)
*Gilboa*: mountain range in Palestine. (*Purg.* XII. 41 and *note* 40–2.)
*Giotto di Bondone* (1266–1337): "father of modern painting", was discovered by the painter Cimabue, drawing on a piece of stone one of his father's lambs, which he was tending. Cimabue took him into his workshop, where the pupil soon learned to surpass his master. Among the extant works of Giotto are a series of frescoes in the Upper Church at Assisi illustrating the life of St Francis, and paintings on the ceilings of the Lower Church; a further series of frescoes in the Bargello in Florence, some of which are by his hand; the great frescoes in the Scrovegni (Arena) chapel at Padua;

and those in the Peruzzi chapel in the Church of Santa Croce in Florence. With Andrea Pisano he executed the statues for the façade of the Cathedral of Florence, and designed the Campanile. (*Purg.* XI. 95 and *note* to XI. 94–5.)

*Giovanna*: daughter of Nino Visconti. (*Purg.* VIII. 71 and *note*.)

*Giovanna*: daughter of Buonconte da Montefeltro: see *Joan*.

*Goat* (Capricornus): see *Zodiac*.

*Gomorrah*: "city of the plain". (*Purg.* XXVI. 40 and *note*.)

GRACES, Christian, or Theological VIRTUES: characters in Pageant of the Sacrament. (*Purg.* XXIX. 121 and *note*: see also *Purg.* VII. 35 and *note*; VIII. 89 and *note*, and Images to VIII.)

*Greater Fortune*: see *Fortune, Greater*.

*Gregory, St* (Pope Gregory I, the Great): born *c.* 540. Educated for the law, at the age of about 30 was elected Prefect of Rome, and held office for three years. On his father's death he retired from public life and devoted his fortune to founding monasteries and charitable institutions, eventually becoming a monk of the Order of St Benedict in a monastery which he had built in Rome. About 579 he was made abbot, and in 590 was elected Pope in succession to Pelagius II. He was an active and vigorous pontiff, checking the Lombard aggressions, tightening up ecclesiastical discipline in France and Italy and constantly combating paganism and heresy. Bede relates how, on seeing some Anglo-Saxon slaves in the market at Rome, he was fired with enthusiasm for the conversion of this fair-haired race – "not Angles, but Angels". His writings include the *Moralia* (a commentary on *Job*), *Homilies* (on *Ezekiel* and the Gospels), the *Dialogues* and *Letters*. He died at Rome in 604. (*Purg.* X. 74–5 and *note*.)

GUARDIAN ANGELS: see ANGELS (ANGEL SENTINELS).

GUBBIO (Agobbio): city of Umbria, about 30 miles E. of Arezzo. (*Purg.* XI. 80 and *note* to XI. 79.)

GUIDO CAVALCANTI: see CAVALCANTI, GUIDO DEL.

*Guido da Castello*: see *Castel, Guy*.

GUIDO GUINICELLI: see GUINICELLI, GUIDO.

GUINICELLI (or GUINIZELLI), GUIDO: poet. (*Purg.* XI. 97 and *note*; XXVI. 92 and *note*.)

*Guittone d'Arezzo* (Guittone del Viva): poet. (*Purg.* XI. 97 and *note*; XXIV. 56 and *note*; XXVI. 124 and *note*.)

*Guy* (*Guido*) *di Carpigna*: see *Carpigna, Guy of*.

*Guy of Prata* (Guido da Prata): a native, or resident, of Prata (now Prada), a village in Romagna, between Forlì, Faenza, and Ravenna. He seems to have been a man of considerable local importance, being mentioned in various documents between 1184 and 1228; he died probably between 1235 and 1245. (*Purg.* XIV. 105.)

*Haman*: vizier of King Ahasuerus. (*Purg.* XVII. 25 and *note*.)

HARRY (HENRY) III, KING OF ENGLAND: born 1216; reigned 1226–72. (*Purg.* VII. 131.)

*Harry Mainard*: see *Mainard, Harry*.

*Hebrews* (Jews): (*Purg.* IV. 83.)

*Helice*: nymph, attendant on Diana. (*Purg.* XXV. 132 and *note* 128–35.)

*Helicon*: mountain in Boeotia, sacred to the Muses; where sprang the two fountains of the Muses, Aganippe and Hippocrene. Either D. has mistaken Helicon for the name of a fountain, or he means, "all the waters of Helicon". (*Purg.* XXIX. 40.)

*Heliodorus*: chancellor to King Seleucus. (*Purg.* XX. 113 and *note* to 103–17.)

HENRY VII OF LUXEMBURG: (born 1268; emperor, 1308–13); elected emperor in 1308 at the instance of Pope Clement V, in opposition to the French candidate, Charles of Valois; crowned at Aix, 6 Jan. 1309. The following year he sent ambassadors to Florence, announcing that he intended to come to Italy to receive the imperial crown. (This ceremony had been neglected for the last sixty years, so that Dante had some grounds for maintaining that Frederick II was the "last Emperor of the Romans", his successors having been neither crowned nor anointed.) Henry crossed the Alps in 1310, and was at first well received, but presently encountered bitter opposition. On reaching Rome he found St Peter's in the hands of King Robert of Naples, and his coronation had to take place, without ceremonial, at St John Lateran. The violent opposition of the Guelfic League, headed by the Florentines, obliged him to ally himself with the Ghibellines and to hasten back to Tuscany, with the intention of besieging Florence; an enterprise to which Dante, who hoped great things from Henry's reign, passionately urged him, though refusing himself to bear arms against his native city. Under pressure from France, Clement V withdrew his support from Henry, and the siege had to be abandoned. Next year Henry set out with the intention of reducing Naples, but suddenly fell ill and died at Buonconvento near Siena (24 Aug. 1313).

Henry was a prince of great parts and piety, eager to heal the internecine feuds which devastated Italy, and to unite the Empire under a just rule; and in him Dante saw the promise of that ideal emperor by whom the civil government of the world might be established on a secure and peaceful basis (see *Inf.*, Intro., pp. 43–8). In the *Paradiso* he is shown the seat that awaits Henry in the Empyrean (*Para.* XXX. 133–8). (*Purg.* VII. 96.)

HENRY (ENRIQUE) I OF NAVARRE ("the Fat"): reigned 1270–4; son of Thibaut (Tibbald) I and brother of Thibaut II, whom he succeeded. His daughter Juana married Philip IV ("the Fair") of

France (*q.v.*), their son Louis X being the first sovereign of the united kingdom of France and Navarre. (*Purg.* VII. 104.)

*Hellespont* (Dardanelles): (*Purg.* XXVIII. 71 and *note*.)

*Holofernes*: captain of Nebuchadnezzar, king of Babylon. (*Purg.* XII. 59 and *note* 58–60.)

HOMER: the great epic poet of Greece, probably *fl. c.* 9th or 10th century B.C., author of the *Iliad* (siege of Troy) and the *Odyssey* (wanderings of Odysseus or Ulysses). He is said to have been blind; seven cities dispute the honour of being his birthplace. Dante knew no Greek, and in his day no Latin translation of Homer seems to have been available. He knew the poems only by reputation and by a few fragments quoted by Aristotle and Horace. (*Inf.* IV. 85 *sqq.*; *Purg.* XXII. 101.)

HUGH CAPET, the Great: (*Purg.* XX. 49 and *note*; also *note* to XX. 43, 52 and Images to XX).

*Hugh Capet the Younger*: king of France. (*Purg.* XX. 58, and *note* to XX. 49.)

HUMBERT ALDOBRANDESCO: see ALDOBRANDESCO, HUMBERT.

HUMILITY, ANGEL OF: see ANGELS.

*Hypsipyle*: daughter of Thoas, king of Lemnos. For the story of her betrayal by Jason see *Inf.* XVIII. 88 *note*. On her flight from Lemnos she was captured by pirates and sold to Lycurgus, king of Nemea, who gave her charge of his infant son. One day when she was with the child in a wood near Nemea the "Seven against Thebes" passed that way and asked her where they could find water. Hypsipyle led them to the fountain of Langeia, and while she was away a serpent killed the child (see *Purg.* XXVI. 94 and *note*). (*Inf.* XVIII. 91; *Purg.* XXII. 112; *Purg.* XXVI. 95.)

*Ilerda* (Lerida): city of Catalonia. (*Purg.* XVIII. 101 and *note* 100–3.)

*Ilium*: see *Troy*.

*Ind* (India), *Indians*: (*Inf.* XIV. 32; *Purg.* XXVI. 21; XXXII. 41.)

*Ismenus*: river of Boeotia. (*Purg.* XVIII. 92 and *note*.)

*Italy*: Dante refers several times to "Italy", but never uses the word "Italian" for its inhabitants collectively (see *note* to *Inf.* XXII. 65). (*Inf.* I. 106; IX. 114; XX. 61; XXVIII. 71; *Purg.* VI. 76, 124; XIII. 96; XXX. 86.)

JACOPO DEL CASSERO: of Fano. (*Purg.* V. 64 and *note*.)

JAMES II, king of (1) Sicily, (2) Aragon: second son of Peter III of Aragon (*q.v.*). On Peter's death in 1285 his eldest son Alfonso succeeded to the crown of Aragon, and James to that of Sicily. When Alfonso died in 1291, James succeeded to Aragon, leaving the government of Sicily in the hands of the youngest brother, Frederick (*q.v.*). James died at Barcelona in 1327. (*Purg.* VII. 119.)

JAMES, ST: the Apostle. (*Purg.* XXXII. 76 and *note* 73–81.)

*Jerusalem or Zion*: Holy City of Palestine: antipodal to Mt Purgatory.

JESUS CHRIST: see CHRIST, JESUS.

*Joan* (Giovanna): daughter of Buonconte da Montefeltro. (*Purg.* V. 89.)

*Jocasta*: mother and wife of Oedipus. (*Purg.* XXII. 56 and *note*.)

JOHN THE BAPTIST, ST: forerunner of Christ. (*Purg.* XXII. 152 and *note* 140–54.)

JOHN, ST: the Divine. (*Inf.* XIX. 106; *Purg.* XXIX. 104 and *note* to XXIX. 93 *sqq.*; XXXII. 76 and *note* to 73–81.)

*Jordan*: river of Palestine. (*Purg.* XVIII. 134 and *note*.)

*Joshua*: son of Nun. (*Purg.* XX. 111 and *note* 103–17.)

*Jove* (Jupiter): Roman deity, identified with the Greek Zeus, the son of Cronos and Rhea, "father of gods and men" and chief of the Olympian deities. His spouse was Juno (Greek Hera), and his weapon the thunderbolt. (*Inf.* XIV. 52; XXXI. 43, 92; *Purg.* XXIX. 120; XXXII. 112.)

*Jove*: as designation of Christ. (*Purg.* VI. 118 and *note*.)

JUDAS ISCARIOT: the disciple who betrayed Christ. (*Inf.* IX. 27; XXXI. 143; XXXIV. 62; *Purg.* XX. 74 and *note*; XXI. 84.)

*Jupiter*: see JOVE.

JUSTINIAN: surnamed "the Great", Emperor of Constantinople, A.D. 527–65. He made a valiant effort to hold together the decaying fabric of the Empire, and by the help of his famous generals, Belisarius and Narses, overthrew the Vandals in Africa and the Ostrogoths in Italy. He is chiefly renowned for his great codification of the Roman Law. His four compilations, the *Digesta* or *Pandectae*, the *Codex Justinianus*, the *Institutiones*, and the *Novellae Constitutiones*, known jointly as the *Corpus Juris Civilis*, contain a summary of the work of earlier jurists together with the Imperial Constitutions of his own time, and make up the "Roman Law", as received in Europe. Dante (to whom Justinian's figure must have been familiar from the great mosaics in the Church of San Vitale at Ravenna) places this great Christian Emperor in the Heaven of Mercury (*Para.* V. 121 *sqq.*, VI. 1 *sqq.*). (*Purg.* VI. 88.)

JUVENAL (Decius Junius Juvenalis): Roman poet. (*Purg.* XXII. 13 and *note*.)

*Lacedaemon*: city of Sparta. (*Purg.* VI. 139.)

*Lachesis*: see *Fates*.

*Lambertazzi, Fabbro dei*: see *Fabbro* (*dei Lambertazzi*).

*La Mira*: town of Venetia. (*Purg.* V. 79 and *note*.)

*Langeia*: fountain at Nemea. "She who led down the troops to the Langeia" is Hypsipyle (*q.v.*). (*Purg.* XXII. 112.)

LATERINA, BENINCASA DA: see BENINCASA DA LATERINA.

*Latian(s)*, *Latin(s)*, (Latino, Latini): Dante's name for the inhabitants of Italy, especially of Lower Italy (anc. Latium). (*Inf.* XXII. 65; XXVII. 26, 33; XXIX. 90, 92; *Purg.* VII. 16; XIII. 92.)

*Latona* (Gk. Leto): mother of Apollo and Artemis (Diana) by Zeus (Jupiter). (*Purg.* XX. 131 and *note*.)

LAVINIA: daughter of Latinus (see AENEAS). (*Inf.* IV. 126; *Purg.* XVII. 34; XVII. 37 and *note*.)

*Leah*: wife of Jacob. (*Purg.* XXVII. 101 and Images to XXVII.)

*Leander*: lover of Hero. (*Purg.* XXVIII. 73 and *note*.)

*Lentino, Giacomo da* ("the Notary"): poet. (*Purg.* XXIV. 56 and *note*.)

*Lerici*: town of Genoa. (*Purg.* III. 50 and *note*.)

*Lerida*: see *Ilerda*.

LETHE: river of the Earthly Paradise. (*Inf.* XIV. 130 *sqq.* and *note*; XXXIV. 130 and *note*; *Purg.* I. 40; XXVI. 108; XXVIII. 130 and *note* 121–6; XXXIII. 96 and *note* 91–9, 123.)

*Leto*: see *Latona*.

*Levi*: third son of Jacob and Leah. The Levites (tribe of Levi) were the consecrated tribe, one branch of which (the "sons of Aaron") constituted the hereditary priesthood of Israel (*Purg.* XVI. 132 and *note*.)

*Lewises*: kings of France of the Capetian dynasty. (*Purg.* XX. 50 and *note*.)

LIBERALITY, ANGEL OF: see ANGELS.

*Libra* (Scales): see *Zodiac*.

*Lille*: city of Flanders. (*Purg.* XX. 46 and *note*.)

*Lizio* (*da Valbona*): born in the first half of the 13th century, a nobleman of Brettinoro in Romagna; contemporary and adherent of Rinier da Calboli (*q.v.*). Though a Guelf, he served with Guido Novello, the Ghibelline podestà of Florence after the Battle of Monteperti (see *Inf.*, Intro., p. 30), in 1260; in 1276 he joined with Rinier da Calboli in the attack on Forlì which was defeated by Guido da Montefeltro. He is last heard of alive in 1279, and was presumably dead before 1300. (*Purg.* XIV. 98.)

LOMBARDO, MARCO: see MARCO LOMBARDO.

*Lombardy*, *Lombards*: northern part of Italy between the Alps and the Po, and bounded by Venice to the E. and Piedmont to the W. (*Inf.* I. 68; XXII. 99; XXVII. 20; *Purg.* VI. 61; XVI. 46.)

LUCCA, BONGIUNTA of: see BONGIUNTA ORBICCIANI DEGLI OVERARDI.

LUCY (St) (LUCÌA): she is traditionally associated with the especial gifts of the Holy Ghost, and it is possible that in the "Three Blessed Ladies" (Mary, Lucia, and Beatrice) who interest themselves in Dante's salvation we are to see an analogue of the Holy

Trinity of Father, Son, and Spirit – or, in St Hilary's phrase, Basis, Image, and Gift – Mary, the absolute Theotokos, corresponding to the Basis; Beatrice, the derived God-bearer, to the Image; Lucìa, the bond and messenger between them, to the Gift. (*Inf.* II. 97 and *note* and Images to II; *Purg.* IX. 55, 88 and Images.)

*Magpies* (Picae): daughters of Pireus. (*Purg.* I. 11 and *note*.)

*Mainard, Harry* (Arrigo Mainardi): a gentleman of Brettinoro (now Bertinoro) near Forlì. Little is known of him except that he was taken prisoner, along with Pier Traversaro (*q.v.*), by the Faentines in 1170 and was still alive in 1228. He is said to have been a man of great courtesy and liberality. The Mainardi family were for the most part Ghibellines, and adherents to the Traversari; but some took the Guelf side, one of them being killed with Rinier da Calboli (*q.v.*) in the assault on Forlì. (*Purg.* XIV. 97.)

*Mainardi*, family: see *Mainard, Harry*.

MALASPINA, CONRAD II: see CONRAD MALASPINA II.

MANFRED (Manfredi) (*c.* 1231–66): natural son of Emperor Frederick II. (*Purg.* III. 112 and *note*, and *note* to III. 121.)

MANTO: prophetess, daughter of Tiresias (see TIRESIAS.)

*Mantua* (Mantova); *Mantuan(s)*: city in N. Italy, birthplace of Virgil (*Inf.* I. 69; II. 58; XX. 93; *Purg.* VI. 71; VII. 85; XVIII. 83.)

*Marcellus*: Roman consul. (*Purg.* VI. 125 and *note*.)

MARCHESE: of the Argugliosi of Forlì. (*Purg.* XXIV. 31 and *note*.)

MARCIA: daughter of Lucius Philippus; second wife of Cato of Utica (*q.v.*). Lucan (*Phars.* II. 328 *sqq.*) relates that after she had borne three sons to Cato he ceded her to his friend Q. Hortensius, after whose death she returned to Cato, and was remarried to him. In the *Convivio* (IV. 28) Dante uses her story as an allegory of the noble soul returning to God at the end of life; in the *Purg.*, however, where she is mentioned as an inhabitant of Limbo, she seems rather to symbolize those natural aims and affections to which the Cardinal Virtues (when unregenerate) are directed (see *Purg.* I, Images under *Cato*). (*Inf.* IV. 128; *Purg.* I. 78, 85.)

MARCO LOMBARDO: gentleman of Venice. (*Purg.* XVI. 46 and *note*, and Images to XVI.)

*Maremma*: malarious and swampy district along the coast of Tuscany. (*Inf.* XXV. 19; XXIX. 48; *Purg.* V. 134.)

*Margaret of Burgundy*: eldest daughter of Raymond Berenger IV, count of Provence; married (1234) Louis IX of France. (*Purg.* VII. 128.)

*Mars* (planet): (*Purg.* II. 14.)

*Mars*: God of War – ancient patron of Florence. (*Inf.* XIII. 144 and *note* to XIII. 143; XXIV. 145; XXXI. 51; *Purg.* XII. 32 and *note* 31–3.)

MARTIN IV, Pope: see SIMON DE BRIE.

MARY, B. V.: (*Inf.* II. 94 and *note*; *Purg.* III. 39; V. 101; VIII. 37;

XIII. 50; XX. 97; *examples from life of*: Humility (Annunciation), X. 34–45 and *notes*; Generosity (Marriage at Cana), XIII. 28 and *notes* 25, 29; *Meekness* (Finding of Christ in the Temple), XV. 88 and *note* 87–9; *Zeal* (Visitation), XVIII. 100 and *note*; *Liberality* (Nativity), XX. 20 and *note*; *Temperance* (Marriage at Cana), XXII. 142 and *note* 140–54; *Chastity* (Annunciation), XXV. 128 and *note*.

*Mary of Brabant*: see *Brabant, Mary of.*

*Marzucco degli Scornigiani*: see *Scornigiani, Marzucco degli.*

MATELDA: see MATILDA.

MATILDA (MATELDA): friend and attendant to Beatrice; image of the Active Life. (*Purg.* XXVIII. 40 *et sqq.* and Images to XXVIII ("the Lady"); XXXIII. 118 and Images to XXXIII (Matilda).

MEEKNESS, ANGEL OF: see ANGELS.

*Meleager*: son of Oeneus, king of Crete. (*Purg.* XXV. 22 and *note*.)

*Michael, Saint*: the Archangel, chief of the angelic host. (*Inf.* VII. 11 and *note*; *Purg.* XIII. 51.)

*Michal*: wife of David, king of Israel. (*Purg.* X. 67 and *note* to X. 56.)

*Midas*: king of Phrygia. (*Purg.* XX. 106 and *note* 103–17.)

*Midian*: an Arabian people descended from Midian, son of Abraham and Keturah, and dwelling along the eastern frontier of Palestine. Their wars against Israel were brought to an end by their defeat at the hands of Gideon (*q.v.*). (*Purg.* XXIV. 126.)

*Milan*: Galeazzo Visconti of. (*Purg.* VIII. 79 and *notes* to VIII. 71, 74, 79.)

*Minerva*: see *Pallas Athene.*

MINOS: in class. myth., the legendary king of Crete who after death became a judge in the Underworld. (*Inf.* V. 5 *sqq.* and *note*; XX. 36; XXVII. 124; XXIX. 119; *Purg.* I. 77.)

*Miriam*: Jewess mentioned by Josephus. (*Purg.* XXIII. 30 and *note*.)

*Moldau*: river of Bohemia. (*Purg.* VII. 98.)

*Monaldi*: family of Orvieto. (*Purg.* VI. 107 and *note* to VI. 106.)

MONFERRAT(O), WILLIAM OF: see WILLIAM OF MONFERRAT(O).

*Monferrat* (Monferrato): district of N. Italy, between the Po and the Ligurian Apennines. (*Purg.* VII. 136.)

*Montagues* (Montecchi): family of Verona. (*Purg.* VI. 106 and *note*.)

MONTEFELTRO, BUONCONTE DA: (died 1289); son of Guido da Montefeltro (for whom see *Inf.* XXVII. 29 *sqq.* and Gloss.). (*Purg.* V. 88 and *note*.)

*Mordecai*: uncle of Esther. (*Purg.* XVII. 30 and *note* 25–30.)

*Morocco*: on N. coast of Africa; regarded as Western limit of horizon reckoned from meridian of Jerusalem. (*Inf.* XXVI. 103; *Purg.* IV. 139.)

MOSES: the Law-Giver of Israel. (*Inf.* IV. 57; *Purg.* XXXII. 80.)

*Muses*: the nine Muses, inspirers and patronesses of the Arts, dwelt upon Mt Parnassus, of which, according to Dante, one peak

(Nyssa) was dedicated to them, and the other (Cyrrha) to Apollo (see *Para.* I. 13–18). They were said to be the daughters of Zeus (Jupiter) and Mnemosyne (Memory). (*Inf.* II. 7; XXXII. 10; *Purg.* I. 8; XXII. 102; XXIX. 37.)

*Naiades* (erroneously written for "Laïades"): (*Purg.* XXXIII. 49 and note.)

*Naples*: city of Italy. (*Purg.* III. 27.)

*Nella (Giovanella) Donati*: wife of Forese Donati. (*Purg.* XXIII. 85 and note.)

*Nicholas, St*: Bishop of Myra. (*Purg.* XX. 32 and *note* 20–33.)

*Night*: point of Zodiac opposite to point where Sun is. (*Purg.* II. 4 and *note*; IV. 139.)

NIMROD: Biblical king. (*Inf.* XXXI. 77 and *note*; *Purg.* XII. 34 and note.)

NINO (UGOLINO) VISCONTI: justiciary of Gallura. (*Purg.* VIII. 54 and note.)

*Niobe*: wife of Amphion, king of Thebes. (*Purg.* XII. 37 and *note*.)

*Nogaret, William (Guillaume) de*: emissary of Philip the Fair. (*Purg.* XX. 90 and *note* 86–90.)

*Noli*: town of Piedmont. (*Purg.* IV. 25 and *note*.)

*Normandy*: district of France. (*Purg.* XX. 66 and *note*.)

*Notary, the*: see *Lentino, Giacomo da*.

NOVELLO, FREDERICK: see FREDERICK NOVELLO.


*Octavian*: (see *Caesar Augustus*).

ODERISI: painter, of Gubbio. (*Purg.* XI. 79 and *note*.)

*Olympus*: mountain at the extreme E. of the great chain forming the N. boundary of ancient Greece proper; in class. myth., the dwelling-place of the gods; used by Dante as a synonym for Heaven. (*Purg.* XXIV. 14.)

OMBERTO ALDOBRANDESCO: see ALDOBRANDESCO, HUMBERT.

*Orestes*: son of Agamemnon, who avenged the murder of his father upon his mother, Clytemnestra, and was haunted by the Furies. He appears, with his friend Pylades, in Aeschylus' dramatic trilogy, the *Oresteia*. (*Purg.* XIII. 33 and *note*.)

*Oriago*: village of Venetia. (*Purg.* V. 80 and *note*.)

ORSO DEGLI ALBERTI DELLA CERBAIA, COUNT: son of Napoleone degli Alberti and grandson of Count Albert da Mangona (see *Inf.* XXXII. 56 and *note*). He was killed by his cousin Alberto, son of Count Alessandro degli Alberti (see *Inf.* XXXII. 56); no doubt in pursuance of the blood-feud between Napoleone and Alessandro. (*Purg.* VI. 19.)

OTTOBUONO DEI FIESCHI: see ADRIAN V.

OTTOCAR II: king of Bohemia, 1253–78; see under RUDOLPH I OF HAPSBURG. (*Purg.* VII. 100.)

*Pagani*: noble family of Faenza. (*Purg.* XIV. 118 and *note*.)

*Palazzo, Conrad* (Currado di Palazzo): of Brescia. (*Purg.* XVI. 124 and *note*.)

*Pallas Athene* (identified with Lat. Minerva): Greek goddess of wisdom, patron deity of Athens; patroness of needlework and other arts. (*Purg.* XII. 32 and *note* 31–3; XII. 43 *note*; XXX. 68.)

*Paris*: capital city of France. (*Purg.* XI. 81 and *note*; XX. 52 and *note*.)

*Parnassus*: mountain of the Muses (*q.v.*). (*Purg.* XXII. 65 and *note*; XXXI. 140.)

*Pasiphaë*: wife of Minos, king of Crete; mother of the Minotaur (see *Inf.* XII. 13 and *note*) by a bull, to whom she was brought disguised in the wicker-work effigy of a cow. (*Purg.* XXVI. 41 and *note*.)

*Pelorus*: mountain in Sicily. (*Purg.* XIV. 33 and *note*.)

PERSIUS (Aulus Persius Flaccus): born A.D. 34, died A.D. 62, Roman satirist; six short poems of his survive, but Dante does not show signs of first-hand knowledge of them. He is quoted at second hand by Brunetto Latini (for whom see *Inf.* XV. 30 and *note*). (*Purg.* XXII. 100.)

*Peter Combseller* (Piero Pettinagno): hermit of Siena. (*Purg.* XIII. 128 and *note*.)

PETER III, KING OF ARAGON (reigned 1276–85): son of James I of Aragon; married 1262 Constance (see *Purg.* III. 143), daughter of Manfred, king of Sicily in whose right he assumed the crown of Sicily in 1282, after the revolt against the rule of the House of Anjou which ended at Palermo in the massacre of the French, known as the "Sicilian Vespers". Peter died in 1285, near Barcelona, as the result of a wound received in a skirmish with the French before Gerona. After the brief reign of his eldest son Alfonso III, the crowns of Aragon and Sicily passed to his younger sons, James and Frederick respectively. Villani says of him that he was "a good lord and valiant in arms, and very enterprising and prudent, redoubted by Christians and Saracens alike, above all the kings of his day" (*Chron.* VII. 103). (*Purg.* VII. 112.)

PETER, St: (*Inf.* II. 24; XIX. 91, 94; *Purg.* IX. 127; XIII. 51; XIX. 99 and *note*; XXI. 54 (Peter's Vicar); XXII. 63; XXXII. 76 and *note* 73–81.)

*Pettinagno, Piero*: see *Peter Combseller*.

*Phaeton* (Gk. Phaethon): son of Phoebus. (*Inf.* XVII. 107 and *note*; *Purg.* IV. 72; XXIX. 118.)

PHILIP III ("the Bold") OF FRANCE (Philippe le Hardi): born 1245, reigned 1270–85); son of Louis IX and of Margaret of Provence. He was succeeded by Philip IV, his second son by his first wife,

Isabella of Aragon. By his second marriage with Mary of Brabant (*q.v.*) he had two daughters: Margaret who married Edward I of England, and Blanche who married Rudolph of Hapsburg. (*Purg.* VII. 103 and *note*.)

*Philip IV* ("the Fair") of France (Philippe le Bel): born 1268, reigned 1285–1314; second son of Philip III and brother to Charles of Valois. By his marriage in 1284 to Juana, daughter of Henry I of Navarre, he became father of three kings of France and Navarre: Louis X, Philip V, and Charles IV. His reign was marked by a bitter quarrel with Pope Boniface VIII, which arose over the taxation of the clergy. By the Bull *Clericis Laicos* the Pope declared church property to be exempt from all secular obligations. Philip retorted that if the clergy were not to be tributary to France, then neither should France be tributary to the Pope; and promptly cut off papal supplies by prohibiting the export of money and valuables from France. Eventually, Boniface excommunicated Philip, who replied by seizing the Pope's person at Anagni (Alagna) (see *Purg.* XX. 86–90 and *notes*). After the death of Boniface, and the short pontificate of Benedict XI, Clement V succeeded, by Philip's influence, to the papal Chair, and became a mere tool in Philip's hands; during his pontificate the Papal See was transferred to Avignon (see *Purg.* XXXII. 151–60 and *note*). Dante also refers (*Purg.* XX. 93–5) to Philip's persecution and suppression of the Order of the Knights Templars (1313). Philip was killed in 1314 by an accident during a boar-hunt. (*Inf.* XIX. 87 and *note*; *Purg.* VII. 109 and *note*; XX. 86 *sqq.*; XXXII. 152.)

*Philips*: kings of France of the Capetian dynasty. (*Purg.* XX. 50 and *note*.)

*Philomena* (Philomela): sister of Procne. (*Purg.* IX. 13 and *note*.)

PIA (LA) DEI TOLOMEI: see PIETY.

*Picae*: see *Magpies*.

PICCARDA DONATI: sister of Forese Donati. (*Purg.* XXIV. 11 and *note*.)

*Pier(o) Traversaro*: see *Traversaro, Pier of*.

PIER(RE) DE LA BROSSE: surgeon to Philip III of France. (*Purg.* VI. 22 and *note*.)

*Pietola*: birthplace of Virgil. (*Purg.* XVIII. 82 and *note*.)

PIETY (LA PIA) DEI TOLOMEI: of Siena. (*Purg.* V. 133 and *note*.)

*Pignatelli, Bartolommeo*: see *Cosenza*.

PILA, UBALDIN DALLA: see UBALDIN(O) DALLA PILA.

*Pilate, Pontius*: governor of Judea. (*Purg.* XX. 91.)

*Pisa*, city of Italy; *Pisans*: (*Inf.* XXXIII, 30, 79; *Purg.* XIV. 53 and *note*.)

*Pisces*: see *Zodiac*.

*Pisistratus*: tyrant of Athens. (*Purg.* XV. 101 and *note* 94–105.)

PLATO: the great Athenian philosopher, pupil of Socrates and founder of the Academic school (*c.* 428–347 B.C.). His *Dialogues*

had not, for the most part, been translated into Latin by the
beginning of the 14th century, and Dante seems only to have read
the *Timaeus*, though some of the influence of the Platonic philo-
sophy reached him through the works of St Augustine. (*Inf.*
IV. 134; *Purg.* III. 43; his doctrine of the multiple soul, *Purg.*
IV. 5 *sqq.* and *note*.)

PLAUTUS (Titus Maccius Plautus): born in Umbria 245 B.C., died
184 B.C.: Roman poet, author of many comedies, of which
twenty-one are extant. Dante shows no signs of first-hand
acquaintance with his works, but would have known his name
from the lists of Latin poets given by Horace and St Augustine.
(*Purg.* XXII. 98.)

*Plough*: see *Wain*.

*Po*: river of N. Italy (see map, *Inf.*, p. 153). (*Inf.* V. 98; XX. 78;
*Purg.* XIV. 91; XVI. 115 and *note*.)

*Poitou*: see *Ponthieu*.

*Polyclete* (Polycletus): Greek sculptor. (*Purg.* X. 32 and *note*.)

*Polydorus*: son of Priam, king of Troy. (*Inf.* 19 and *note* to XXX. 13;
*Purg.* XX. 115 and *note* 103–17.)

*Polymnestor*: king of Thrace. (*Purg.* XX. 115 and *note* 103–17.)

*Ponthieu* (Poitou): district of France. (*Purg.* XX. 66 and *note*.)

*Prata, Guy of*: see *Guy of Prata*.

*Pratomagno*: mountain-chain in Italy. (*Purg.* V. 116 and *note* to
V. 94.)

*Procne*: wife of Tereus. (*Purg.* IX. 13 and *note*; XVII. 19 and *note*.)

PROSERPINE (Gk. Persephone): in Greek and Roman myth., the
daughter of Ceres (Gk. Demeter), the Earth-Mother. She was
stolen away by Dis (Pluto) while gathering flowers in the vale of
Enna, in Sicily, and carried off to be his queen in Hades. She is
identified with the Moon, as being one of the manifestations of
the "Triple Goddess" Hecate – Luna in Heaven, Diana on earth,
and Proserpine in Hades. (*Inf.* IX. 44 and *note*; X. 80; *Purg.* XXVIII.
51 and *note*.)

*Provence*: district of France. (*Purg.* XX. 62 and *note*.)

*Provence, Beatrice of*: see *Beatrix of Provence*.

PROVENZAN(O) SALVANI: Sienese nobleman. (*Purg.* XI. 121 and
*note*.)

*Pygmalion*: brother of Dido. (*Purg.* XX. 103 and *note*.)

*Pylades*: friend of Orestes. (*Purg.* XIII. 33 *note*.)

*Pyramus*: lover of Thisbe. (*Purg.* XXVII. 37 and *note*; XXXIII. 69 and
*note*.)

RACHEL: wife of the Patriarch Jacob and mother of Joseph and
Benjamin. (*Inf.* II. 102 and *note*; IV. 60; *Purg.* XXVII. 104 and Images
to XXVII.)

*Red Sea*: (*Inf.* XXIV. 90; *Purg.* XVIII. 134.)

*Rehoboam*: king of Israel. (*Purg.* XII. 46 and *note*.)

*Reno*: river of Italy. (*Inf.* XVIII. 61 and map, p. 173; *Purg.* XIV. 91.)

*Rhipean mountains*: (*Purg.* XXVI. 44 and *note*.)

RINIER DEL CALBOLI: see CALBOLI, RINIER DEL.

*Romagna*, province of Italy lying between Bologna and the Adriatic; *Romagnols*: (*Inf.* XXVII. 28, 37; XXXIII. 154; *Purg.* V. 69; XV. 44.)

*Rome, Romans*: (*Inf.* I. 71; II. 20; XIV. 105; XV. 77; XVIII. 28; XXVI. 60; XXXI. 59; *Purg.* VI. 113; XVI. 106 and *note*; XIX. 108; XXI. 89; XXII. 145; XXXII. 101.)

*Rubaconte*: bridge in Florence. (*Purg.* XII. 100 and *note*.)

RUDOLPH I OF HAPSBURG: (born 1218, emperor, 1272–92); eldest son of Albert IV, count of Hapsburg; founder of the Imperial House of Austria. While serving in Germany under Ottocar, king of Bohemia, he heard that he had been elected emperor in preference to Ottocar and Alphonso of Castile. Ottocar refused to acknowledge Rudolph, but was defeated in battle and obliged to cede Austria and other provinces. A second rebellion led to Ottocar's defeat and death in 1278. Rudolph allowed Ottocar's son Wenceslas to succeed to the throne of Bohemia, but retained Austria and the other ceded provinces for his own sons, Albert and Rudolph. (*Purg.* VI. 103; VII. 94 and *note*.)

SALVANI, PROVENZAN(O): see PROVENZAN SALVANI.

*Samaria*: woman of. (*Purg.* XXI. 3 and *note*.)

*San Leo*: town of Urbino. (*Purg.* IV. 25 and *note*.)

SAN ZENO'S ABBOT: see ZENO, SAN.

*Santafior(a)*: country in the Sienese Maremma. (*Purg.* VI. 111 and *note* to VI. 106.)

*Sapìa*: lady of Siena. (*Purg.* XIII. 110 and *note*.)

*Sapphira*: wife of Ananias. (*Purg.* XX. 112 and *note* 103–17.)

*Sardinia*: (*Inf.* XXII. 90; XXVI. 104; XXIX. 48; *Purg.* XVIII. 81 and *note* 79–81; XXIII. 94 and *note*; XXIII. 95.)

*Saturn*: planet. (*Purg.* XIX. 3 and *note* XIX. 1–3.)

*Saul*: king of Israel. (*Purg.* XII. 40 and *note*.)

*Scala, della* (or in its Latin form *Scaliger*): noble family of Verona. Their name means "of the Ladder", and they bore the canting arms: a ladder surmounted by an Imperial eagle. They first rose to prominence in the middle of the 13th century, when Mastino della Scala was appointed first podestà of Verona and then (1262) Captain of the People. Their sovereignty over Verona lasted for 100 years, during which time Verona enjoyed unexampled peace and prosperity. The three sons of Alberto (*q.v.*) all succeeded him in the government of the city, and Dante, during the period of his exile, owed, and expressed, a great debt of friendship to the family. See below under Bartolommeo and Can Grande.

*Scala, Alberto della*: lord of Verona, 1277–1301; father of Dante's patrons, Bartolommeo and Can Grande (see below). (*Purg.* XVIII. 121 and *note*.)

*Scala, Alboino della*: second son of Alberto della Scala; lord of Verona, 1304–11.

*Scala, Bartolommeo della*: eldest son of Alberto della Scala; lord of Verona, Sept. 1301–Mar. 1304. He was Dante's host at Verona during the early years of his exile (see *Inf.*, Intro., p. 38) and is alluded to by him in *Para.* XVII. 62.

*Scala, Can Francesco della*: commonly called *Can Grande*: third son of Alberto della Scala; born 1291; died 1329. Joint lord of Verona with his brother Alboino 1308. On Alboino's death in 1311 he became sole lord of Verona. Imperial Vicar-General in Verona (1311), Vicenza (1312), Vicenza and Verona (1317). A great Ghibelline prince; a patron of the arts and a generous friend to the exiled members of his party, including Dante and Guido da Castello (*q.v.*) (see *Inf.*, Intro., p. 50). He is thought by many commentators to be the "Greyhound" of *Inf.* I. 101–11 and (possibly) the DXV of *Purg.* XXXIII. 43–5. In *Para.* XVII. 78 *sqq.* Dante speaks of him in the highest terms of praise. It was to Can Grande that Dante sent the first "fair copy" of the *Comedy*, about half a dozen cantos at a time, as it was completed; and to him that he dedicated the *Paradiso*, in a letter (known as Epistle X) which explains his purpose in writing and the manner in which the allegory is to be interpreted (see *Inf.*, Intro., pp. 14–15); it opens with a fervent eulogy of his bounty and magnificence. Can Grande is said to have been tall, handsome, gracious in act and bearing and also in speech, and a bold warrior. His equestrian statue is to be seen at Verona.

*Scala, Giuseppe della*: bastard son of Alberto della Scala. (*Purg.* XVIII. 124 and *notes* 121–6, 129.)

*Scales* (Libra): see *Zodiac*.

*Scaliger*: see *Scala, della*.

*Scipio* (Publius Cornelius Scipio Africanus Major): Roman general, (234–*c*. 183 B.C.); fought against Hannibal at Cannae (cf. *Inf.* XXVIII. 11 *note*); was appointed to the command of the army in Spain, captured New Carthage (Cartagena) (210 B.C.), and drove the Carthaginians out of Spain; crossed into Africa and there gained a decisive victory over Hannibal at the Battle of Zama (202 B.C.). For these services he earned the title of Africanus. After being twice consul, and serving in the war against Antiochus the Great, he was accused of accepting bribes, and eventually left Rome and died in exile. (*Inf.* XXXI. 116; *Purg.* XXIX. 115 and *note*.)

*Scirocco*: the S.E. wind which blows across Italy from Africa, producing sultry and oppressive weather. (*Purg.* XXVIII. 21.)

# Glossary

SCORNIGIANI, FARINATA DEGLI: son of Marzucco degli Scornigiani of Pisa (*q.v.*). (*Purg.* VI. 17.)

*Scornigiani, Marzucco degli*: a Pisan doctor of laws who, after an active legal career, became a Franciscan in 1286. The story of his fortitude over the murder of his son Farinata is told in two different versions: (1) Farinata having been killed by a Pisan citizen, Marzucco went with other brothers of his order to fetch away the body, and, after preaching upon the Christian duty of making peace with one's enemies, kissed the murderer's hand and forgave him. (2) Farinata was beheaded by order of Count Ugolino and the body left to rot in the Piazza. Marzucco went to the count and said: "Sir, may it please you to let the body of that unhappy man be buried, lest it poison the air of the city." Ugolino, recognizing him, replied: "Thy fortitude has overcome my determination and my hardness of heart; go, and do as thou wilt." (*Purg.* VI. 18.)

*Sennacherib*: king of Assyria. (*Purg.* XII. 53 and *note* 52–4.)

*Sestos*: on the Hellespont. (*Purg.* XXVIII. 74 and *notes* to 71 and 73.)

*Sestri*: town of Italy. (*Purg.* XIX. 100 and *note*.)

*Shinar*: ancient name of the plain through which the Tigris and Euphrates run; later known as Chaldaea or Babylonia; site of the Tower of Babel. (*Purg.* XII. 36.)

SICILY, Kings of: see MANFRED, JAMES II, FREDERICK II.

*Sicily*: kingdom of. (*Purg.* III. 116.)

*Siena*, city of N. Italy, in Tuscany; stronghold of the Ghibelline party; *Sienese*: (*Inf.* XXIX. 109, 122, 134; *Purg.* V. 134; XI. 65, 111, 123, 134; XIII. 106.)

SIMON DE BRIE: Pope Martin IV. (*Purg.* XXIV. 21 and *note*.)

SIMONIDES: born in island of Ceos, 556 B.C.; died at Syracuse 467 B.C.; Greek lyric poet. In 489, at Athens, won, in competition with Aeschylus and others, the prize for an elegy upon the men who fell at Marathon. A few of his elegies, epigrams, etc., have been preserved. (*Purg.* XXII. 107.)

*Siren*: the Sirens in class. myth. were sea-nymphs, who by their song bewitched mariners and lured them from their course to perish upon the rocks. Homer places their island on the S.W. coast of Italy, near the rock of Scylla; but Latin poets, off the coast of Campania. (*Purg.* XIX. 19 and *note*, and Images to XIX.)

*Sodom*: a "city of the plain", near the Dead Sea, destroyed by fire from heaven because of the notorious vice of its inhabitants (*Gen.* xix). (*Inf.* XI.; 50; *Purg.* XXVI. 40 and *note*.)

SORDEL(LO): troubadour. (*Purg.* VI. 74 and *note*; VIII. 43, 62, 94; IX. 58.)

*Spain*: (*Inf.* XXVI. 103; *Purg.* XVIII. 102 and *note* 100–3.)

*Sphinx*: monster of Greek myth. (*Purg.* XXXIII. 47 and *note*.)

*Stars, Four*: alleged S. Polar constellation typifying the Cardinal Virtues (*q.v.*). (*Purg.* I. 23 and *note*; I. 37.)

STATIUS (Publius Papinius): poet. (*Purg.* XXI. 91, Images to XXI); overtakes Dante and Virgil, XXI. 10; explains release of spirits from purgation, XXI. 40–72; acknowledges his poetic debt to the *Aeneid*, XXI. 94–103; is rebuked for kneeling to Virgil, XXI. 130–6; attributes to Virgil his release from spendthrift covetousness, XXII. 37–54, and to Virgil's 4th *Eclogue* his conversion to Christianity, XXII. 64–73; describes his conversion, XXII. 76–93; his discourse on the natural and aery bodies, XXV. 34 *sqq.*; goes behind Dante through the fire, XXVII. 47–8; accompanies the car of Beatrice, XXXII. 28; is invited to drink of Eunoë, XXXIII. 134–5.

*Stephen, Saint*: the first martyr. (*Purg.* XV. 107 and *note* 106–14.)

*Syrinx*: nymph. (*Purg.* XXXII. 64 and *note*.)


*Tacco, Ghin(o) di*: see *Ghin(o) di Tacco*.

*Talamone*: port in the Maremma. (*Purg.* XIII. 152 and *note* 151–4.)

*Tarpeia*: the Tarpeian rock on the Saturnian hill (later called the Capitoline) in Rome; so named from Tarpeia, daughter of the governor of the citadel, who betrayed the fortress to the Sabines. (*Purg.* IX. 136 and *note*.)

TEMPERANCE, ANGEL OF: see ANGELS.

*Temple* (Knights Templars): (*Purg.* XX. 93 and *note*.)

TERENCE (Publius Terentius Afer): born at Carthage 195 B.C., died in Greece 159 B.C. Latin poet, author of six comedies (all extant). Dante mentions him in his *Epistle to Can Grande* in connexion with the definition of a "comedy" as a play with "a prosperous ending", but does not show any first-hand acquaintance with his work, though he may, of course, have read them, or passages from them, since T was often quoted by medieval writers, including Brunetto Latini (for whom see *Inf.* XV. 30 and *note*.) (*Purg.* XXII. 97.)

*Tereus*: king of Thrace. (*Purg.* IX. 13, *note*.)

*Thaumas' daughter*: Iris. (*Purg.* XXI. 50 and *note*.)

*Thebes*, city of Boeotia; *Thebans*: Thebes is celebrated in many classical myths and legends, to several of which Dante alludes in the *Inferno*. Its walls were fabled to have built themselves to the music of the great musician Amphion; it was the birthplace of the prophet Tiresias and one of the cities which claimed to be the birthplace of Bacchus. It was the scene, among other episodes of vengeance and horror, of the tragic story of Oedipus and the consequent war of the "Seven against Thebes", and of the infanticidal madness of Athamas. (*Inf.* XIV. 69 and *note* to XIV. 51; XX. 33, 59; XXV. 15; XXVI. 52 *sqq.* and *note*; XXX. 2 *sqq.* and *note*; XXXII. 11 and *note*; XXXIII. 88; *Purg.* XVIII. 93; XXI. 92; XXII. 89 and *note*.)

*Themis*: Greek goddess. (*Purg.* XXXIII. 47 and *note*.)

*Theseus*: legendary king (or, as Dante calls him, "Duke") of Athens. Greek hero, son of Aegeus, king of Athens, and of Aethra, daughter of Pittheus, king of Troezen. Among his many exploits are the slaying of various robbers and monsters, and his attempt to carry off Persephone (Proserpine) from Hades. (*Inf.* IX. 53 and *note*; XII. 17 and *note* to XII. 13; *Purg.* XXIV. 123 and *note* 120–5.)

THETIS: wife of Peleus and mother by him of Achilles (*q.v.*). According to class. myth. she was a Nereid (sea-divinity), but Dante treats her as a mortal and places her in Limbo. (*Purg.* IX. 37 and *note*; XXII. 114.)

*Thisbe*: lover of Pyramus. (*Purg.* XXVII. 38 and *note* to XXVII. 37.)

THOMAS AQUINAS, ST: see AQUINAS, ST THOMAS.

*Thymbraeus*: epithet of Apollo. (*Purg.* XII. 31 and *note*.)

*Tiber*: river on which Rome stands. (*Inf.* XXVII. 30; *Purg.* II. 101 and *note*.)

*Tignoso, Frederick* (Federico Tignoso): a noble of the Tignoso family of Rimini, noted for his wealth and hospitality. He probably flourished in the first half of the 13th century; but next to nothing is known of him. (*Purg.* XIV. 106.)

*Tigris, River*: (*Purg.* XXXIII. 113 and *note*.)

TIRESIAS, daughter of: the daughter of Tiresias (for whom see *Inf.* XX. 40 and *note*), was Manto (see *Inf.* XX. 55 *sqq.*). In naming her as an inhabitant of Limbo, Dante seems to have forgotten that he had already placed her in Hell, in the Bowge of the Sorcerers. Various ingenious explanations have been offered for this discrepancy, but the simplest is that, for once, his memory played him false. (*Purg.* XXII. 113.)

*Tithonus*: son of Laomedon, and brother of Priam, king of Troy. His wife Aurora (the Dawn) obtained for him from the gods the gift of immortality, but forgot to ask also for perpetual youth, so that he shrank into an everlasting decrepitude. Having no hope of release by death, he was turned by Aurora into a cicada. (*Purg.* IX. 2.)

*Titus* (Flavius Sabinus Vespasianus): Roman Emperor. (*Purg.* XXI. 82 and *note*.)

*Tomyris*: queen of Scythia. (*Purg.* XII. 56 and *note* 55–7.)

*Toulouse*: city of S.W. France, on the Garonne; former capital of Aquitaine. (*Purg.* XXI. 89 and *note*.)

*Tours*: city of France. (*Purg.* XXIV. 23.)

TRAJAN (M. Ulpius Trajanus): Roman Emperor A.D. 98–117; born at Italica near Seville A.D. 52. After serving with distinction in the East and in Germany he was made Consul in 91, and in 97 was adopted by the Emperor Nerva and given the title of Caesar. He succeeded Nerva as Augustus in 98, being the first emperor who was born out of Italy. A good commander, he was loved and respected by his troops, whose fatigues and privations he shared, and was victorious in his wars against the Dacians (102–3), (104–6) and the Parthians (115–16). As a ruler he won the affection of his people by his simple and laborious life, his love of justice, and his sincere concern for their welfare. He constructed a number of great roads in the Empire, built libraries and a theatre in Rome, and laid out the Forum Trajanum, in the centre of which stood the famous Column of Trajan, commemorating his victories. He was succeeded by Hadrian. (*Purg.* X. 76 and *note* to X. 74.)

*Traversaro, House of*: see *Traversaro, Pier of.* (*Purg.* XIV. 106–7.)

*Traversaro, Pier of*: born *c.* 1145, died 1225; member of the great Traversari family of Ravenna, and several times podestà of the city. He was a distinguished Ghibelline, in great favour with the Emperor Frederick II (for whom see *Inf.* Intro. p. 25). He is described as a man "magnanimous and magnifical", who married his daughter to King Stephen of Hungary and was a great patron of troubadours. He was succeeded by his son Paolo who deserted to the Guelf faction, and after whose death in 1240 the splendour of the House of Traversari departed. The family were expelled from Ravenna, and their place taken by Dante's friends and patrons the counts of Polenta. (*Purg.* XIV. 97–8.)

*Troy* (or Ilium; Gk. Ilion), ancient coast-town in Asia Minor; *Trojans*: Troy was taken and sacked by the Greeks under Agamemnon, after ten years' siege for the recovery of Helen. The siege is described in Homer's *Iliad*, and the sack in Virgil's *Aeneid* (*q.v.*). (*Inf.* I. 74–5; XIII. 11; XXVIII. 10 and *note*; XXX. 14, 22, 97, 113; *Purg.* XII. 61, 62.)

*Turbìa*: village of Genoa. (*Purg.* III. 50 and *note*.)

*Turk*: (*Purg.* XXIII. 104.)

*Tuscany, Tuscans*: that district of Italy which lies, for the most part, between the Apennines and the Mediterranean, extending roughly from the Gulf of Genoa in the N. to Orbitello in the S. It is watered by the Arno, and Dante's birthplace, Florence, was its chief city. Many Tuscan towns are mentioned in the *Comedy*, and on two occasions the spirits of Hell recognize Dante by his Tuscan speech. (*Inf.* X. 22; XXII. 99; XXIII. 76, 91; XXIV. 122; XXVIII. 108; XXXII. 66; *Purg.* XI. 59, 110; XIII. 149; XIV. 17, 103, 124.)

*Twins* (Gemini): see *Zodiac*.

UBALDIN(O) DALLA PILA: Florentine. (*Purg.* XXIV. 28 and *note*.)

*Ugolin, Azzo d'* (Ugolino d'Azzo): probably Ugolino degli Ubaldini, son of Azzo degli Ubaldini da Senno, a member of the great Ubaldini family frequently mentioned in the *Comedy*. He was a man of property and influence, whose name occurs many times in contemporary documents from 1218 onwards; he died at a great age in 1293. (*Purg.* XIV. 105.)

*Ugolin(o) de' Fantolin(i)*: see *Fantolin(i) Ugolin(o)*.

ULYSSES (Odysseus): prince of Ithaca; hero of Greek mythology, renowned for his cunning. His exploits at the siege of Troy are recounted in Homer's *Iliad*, and his wanderings in the *Odyssey*. (*Inf.* XXVI. 55 *sqq.* and *notes*; *Purg.* XIX. 22 and *note*.)

*Urania*: Muse of Astronomy. (*Purg.* XXIX. 41 and *note*.)

*Ursa Major*: see *Wain*.

*Utica*: scene of Cato's suicide (see CATO). (*Purg.* I. 74.)


*Valbona, Lizio da*: see *Lizio (da Valbona)*.

*Valdimagra* (Val di Macra): valley of the R. Macra, in Lunigiana, a district in the N.W. of Tuscany ruled over in Dante's time by the Malaspina family. (*Inf.* XXIV. 145 and *note* to XXIV. 142; *Purg.* VIII. 116.)

*Venus* (goddess of love): (*Purg.* XXVIII. 65 and *note*.)

*Venus* (planet): (*Purg.* I. 19 and *note*; XXV. 132; XXVII. 94 and *note*.)

*Verde*: river of Italy, now the Garigliano. (*Purg.* III. 131.)

*Vernaccio wine*: a rich, sweet white wine, said to have been produced from the rough-skinned grape cultivated in the mountains near Genoa. (*Purg.* XXIV. 24.)

*Verona*: city of Italy in Venetia. (*Inf.* XV. 122 and *note* to XV. 121 [see map, *Inf.*, p. 153]; XX. 68; *Purg.* XVIII. 118.)

VIRGIL (P. Vergilius Maro): Roman poet (70–19 B.C.). Born at Andes, near Mantua. His great epic, the *Aeneid*, tells the story of Aeneas, and celebrates the origins of the Roman people and empire (see AENEAS). Author also of the *Georgics* and of the *Eclogues*, one of which (*Ec.* iv) looks forward to the birth of a Wonder-Child who should restore the Gold Age, and was held in the Middle Ages to be an unconscious prophecy of Christ (*Purg.* XXII. 70–2). In medieval legend, V. had the reputation of being a White Magician. In the *Divine Comedy* he is the image of Human Wisdom; he guides Dante through Hell and accompanies him through Purgatory. First meeting with Dante, *Inf.* I. 62; recognized by him, I. 79; visited by Beatrice, II. 53; his place in Limbo, IV. 39; his companions there, IV. 67 *sqq.*; his "words of power", III. 95, V. 23, VII. 11, XXI. 83; his conjuration of the spirits, XXVI. 79; prophecy of Greyhound, I. 101 *sqq.*; discourse on Luck, VII. 73 *sqq.*; on arrangement of Hell, XI. 16 *sqq.*; on origin of infernal rivers, XIV. 94 *sqq.*; on origin of Mantua, XX. 61 *sqq.*; opposed at gates of Dis, VIII. 112 *sqq.*; deceived by demons, XXI. 106 *sqq.*; carries Dante in his arms, XIX. 34 *sqq.*, 124 *sqq.*, XXIII. 37 *sqq.*, XXXIV. 70; explains fall of Satan and geography of Antipodes, XXIV. 106; and *passim*. Rebuked by Cato, *Purg.* I. 49 *sqq.*,

II. 115 *sqq.*; on the aery body and the *quia* and *quid*, III. 25 *sqq.* and *notes*; on efficacy of prayer, VI. 37 *sqq.*; embraced by Sordello, VI. 70 *sqq.*; inquires concerning the Rule of the Mountain, VII. 49 *sqq.*; challenged at Peter's Gate, IX. 85 *sqq.*; his first Discourse on Love, XV. 40 *sqq.*; explains arrangement of Cornices, XVII. 91 *sqq.*; his second Discourse on Love, XVIII. 19 *sqq.*; appears in Dante's dream of the Siren, XIX. 28 *sqq.*; is made known to Statius, XXI. 94 *sqq.*; and rebukes him for falling at his feet, XXI. 131; is acknowledged by Statius as his guide to Christ, XXII. 64 *sqq.*; encourages Dante to pass through the fire, XXVII. 20 *sqq.*; resigns his guardianship of Dante, XXVII. 127–42; "crowns and mitres" him, XXVII. 142; vanishes in the presence of Beatrice, XXX. 49.

VIRTUES, Cardinal (or Natural): characters in the Pageant of the Sacrament (*Purg.* XXIX. 130 and *note.*) (see also *Purg.* I. 23 and Images to I; VII. 36 and *note*).

VIRTUES, Theological: see GRACES, Christian.

*Visconti, Galeazzo,* of Milan: see *Milan, Galeazzo Visconti of.*

VISCONTI, NINO: see NINO VISCONTI.

*Wain* (the Plough, or Great Bear; Ursa Major): N. Polar constellation. (*Inf.* XI. 114; *Purg.* I. 26, 30; IV. 65; "Septentrion of the First Heaven", XXX. 1 and *note.*)

WENCESLAS IV: king of Bohemia, 1278–1305; see under RUDOLPH I OF HAPSBURG. (*Purg.* VII. 101.)

WILLIAM OF MONFERRAT(O): Marquis (marchese). (*Purg.* VII. 134 and *note.*)

*Xerxes:* king of Persia, 485–465 B.C. On the death of his father Darius (485) his first task was the suppression of a revolt in Egypt. This done, he turned his attention to the subjugation of Greece. In the spring of 480 he set out from Sardis, crossed the Hellespont (the Dardanelles) by a bridge of boats, and marched through Thrace, Macedonia, and Thessaly without much effective opposition, until he was faced by Leonides, king of Sparta, at the famous Pass of Thermopylae. Here he was repulsed again and again, until, a traitor having shown him a pass through the mountains, he was able to fall upon the Greeks from behind, and destroy them to a man. Meanwhile, his fleet, which had suffered heavy losses in a storm off the coast of Magnesia, had been attacked by the Greek navy at Artemisium. After two days of stubborn combat, with considerable losses on both sides, the Greeks retired to Salamis opposite the W. coast of Attica. By this time Xerxes with his land forces had marched through Phocis and Boeotia and entered Athens. The Greeks were thus in a position of the utmost peril;

but the situation was saved by the resounding defeat of Xerxes'
naval forces in the Bay of Phalerum off Salamis. Xerxes, who had
witnessed the disaster from Mount Aegaleos, thereupon quitted
Greece, leaving his general, Mardonius, with 300,000 troops to
carry on the war. The bridge of boats having been destroyed by
storms, he returned to Sardis by sea. In the following year the
Greeks defeated the Persian armies at Plataea and Mycale and in
478 recaptured Sestos, the last of the Persian possessions in Europe.
Xerxes was murdered in 465 by his rival Artabanus. He is generally
thought to be identical with the Biblical Ahasuerus (*q.v.*). (*Purg.*
XXVIII. 71 and *note.*)

ZEAL, ANGEL OF: see ANGELS.
ZENO, SAN, Abbot of: (*Purg.* XVIII. 118 and *note.*)
*Zion*: see *Jerusalem.*
*Zodiac, signs of*:
   *Aquarius* (the Water-Carrier): (Sun in Aq. mid-Jan. to mid-
      Feb.) (*Inf.* XXIV. 2, *note.*)
   *Aries* (the Ram): (Sun in A. mid-Mar. to mid-Apr.) (*Inf.* I. 37
      and *note.*)
   *Pisces* (the Fishes): (Sun in P. mid-Feb. to mid-Mar.). (*Inf.*
      XI. 113 and *note*; *Purg.* I. 21 and *note*; XXXII. 54 and *note* 53-4.)
   *Libra* (the Scales): (Sun in L. mid-Sept. to mid-Oct.). (*Purg.*
      II. 5 and *note*; XXVII. 3 and *note.*)
   *Capricornus* (the Goat): (Sun in C. mid-Dec. to mid-Jan.)
      (*Purg.* II. 56 and *note.*)
   *Gemini* (the Twins): (Sun in G. mid-May to mid-June) (*Purg.*
      IV., 61, 62 and *note.*)
   *Scorpio* (the Scorpion): (Sun in S. mid-Oct. to mid-Nov.).
      (*Purg.* IX. 5.)

# BOOKS TO READ

## GENERAL

UMBERTO COSMO: *A Handbook to Dante Studies*, translated by David Moore (Basil Blackwell, 1950). This excellent manual by a distinguished Italian Dante scholar, now happily available in English, gives briefly and clearly the most modern conclusions about Dante's life and works, and contains useful bibliographies for every branch of the subject.

DOROTHY L. SAYERS: *Introductory Papers on Dante* (Methuen, 1954). These papers, originally delivered as lectures to students, aim chiefly at clearing away some of the obstacles which six hundred years have interposed between us and the ready appreciation of Dante.

## PURGATORY

SAINT CATHERINE OF GENOA: *Treatise on Purgatory*, etc. (Sheed and Ward, 1946). Although St Catherine lived nearly 200 years later than Dante, her doctrine has so much in common with his that she is well worth comparing with him, if only to show that his views are not peculiar to him, but belong to the main stream of Catholic tradition.

## MEDIEVAL PHILOSOPHY

D. J. B. HAWKINS: *A Sketch of Medieval Philosophy* (Sheed and Ward, 1946). A handy book of reference covering the great names and major developments from the 9th century to the Renaissance. Short, sound, clear, Catholic.

S. J. CURTIS: *A Short History of Western Philosophy in the Middle Ages* (Macdonald, 1950). This deals with the subject in a good deal more detail, and is written in a lucid and readable style for the "ordinary reader" who, though not a trained philosopher, feels an intelligent interest in those medieval Schoolmen who laid the foundations of modern thought.

ÉTIENNE GILSON: *The Spirit of Medieval Philosophy*, translated by A. H. C. Downes (Sheed and Ward, 1950). Those choice spirits who have got bitten by the thing, and would like to pursue their researches at "top-level", will find this completely fascinating; but it is not a beginner's book.

### DANTE'S POLITICS

A. P. D'ENTRÈVES: *Dante as a Political Thinker* (Clarendon Press, 1952).

JOSEPH LECLER: *The Two Sovereignties*: A Study of the Relationship between Church and State (Burns Oates and Washbourne, 1952).

These are the two books referred to in the Introduction (pp. 47, 48).

### COURTLY LOVE

C. S. LEWIS: *The Allegory of Love* (O.U.P., 1938). A unique study of the doctrine of *amour courtois* and its allegorical expression. It does not deal specifically with Dante, but is indispensable for the background.

### MEDIEVAL ASTRONOMY

M. A. ORR: *Dante and the Medieval Astronomers* (Gale and Inglis, 1913; new edition (Allan Wingate) 1955). Quite the best guide available to Ptolemaic Astronomy and to Dante's handling of celestial phenomena.

# READ MORE IN PENGUIN

In every corner of the world, on every subject under the sun, Penguin represents quality and variety – the very best in publishing today.

For complete information about books available from Penguin – including Puffins, Penguin Classics and Arkana – and how to order them, write to us at the appropriate address below. Please note that for copyright reasons the selection of books varies from country to country.

**In the United Kingdom**: Please write to *Dept. EP, Penguin Books Ltd, Bath Road, Harmondsworth, West Drayton, Middlesex UB7 ODA*

**In the United States**: Please write to *Consumer Sales, Penguin USA, P.O. Box 999, Dept. 17109, Bergenfield, New Jersey 07621-0120.* VISA and MasterCard holders call 1-800-253-6476 to order Penguin titles

**In Canada**: Please write to *Penguin Books Canada Ltd, 10 Alcorn Avenue, Suite 300, Toronto, Ontario M4V 3B2*

**In Australia**: Please write to *Penguin Books Australia Ltd, P.O. Box 257, Ringwood, Victoria 3134*

**In New Zealand**: Please write to *Penguin Books (NZ) Ltd, Private Bag 102902, North Shore Mail Centre, Auckland 10*

**In India**: Please write to *Penguin Books India Pvt Ltd, 706 Eros Apartments, 56 Nehru Place, New Delhi 110 019*

**In the Netherlands**: Please write to *Penguin Books Netherlands bv, Postbus 3507, NL-1001 AH Amsterdam*

**In Germany**: Please write to *Penguin Books Deutschland GmbH, Metzlerstrasse 26, 60594 Frankfurt am Main*

**In Spain**: Please write to *Penguin Books S. A., Bravo Murillo 19, 1° B, 28015 Madrid*

**In Italy**: Please write to *Penguin Italia s.r.l., Via Felice Casati 20, I–20124 Milano*

**In France**: Please write to *Penguin France S. A., 17 rue Lejeune, F–31000 Toulouse*

**In Japan**: Please write to *Penguin Books Japan, Ishikiribashi Building, 2–5–4, Suido, Bunkyo-ku, Tokyo 112*

**In South Africa**: Please write to *Longman Penguin Southern Africa (Pty) Ltd, Private Bag X08, Bertsham 2013*

# PENGUIN AUDIOBOOKS

### A Quality of Writing that Speaks for Itself

Penguin Books has always led the field in quality publishing. Now you can listen at leisure to your favourite books, read to you by familiar voices from radio, stage and screen. Penguin Audiobooks are ideal as gifts, for when you are travelling or simply to enjoy at home. They are produced to an excellent standard, and abridgements are always faithful to the original texts. From thrillers to classic literature, biography to humour, with a wealth of titles in between, Penguin Audiobooks offer you quality, entertainment and the chance to rediscover the pleasure of listening.

You can order Penguin Audiobooks through Penguin Direct by telephoning (0181) 899 4036. The lines are open 24 hours every day. Ask for Penguin Direct, quoting your credit card details.

*Published or forthcoming:*

**Emma** by Jane Austen, read by Fiona Shaw

**Persuasion** by Jane Austen, read by Joanna David

**Pride and Prejudice** by Jane Austen, read by Geraldine McEwan

**The Tenant of Wildfell Hall** by Anne Brontë, read by Juliet Stevenson

**Jane Eyre** by Charlotte Brontë, read by Juliet Stevenson

**Villette** by Charlotte Brontë, read by Juliet Stevenson

**Wuthering Heights** by Emily Brontë, read by Juliet Stevenson

**The Woman in White** by Wilkie Collins, read by Nigel Anthony and Susan Jameson

**Heart of Darkness** by Joseph Conrad, read by David Threlfall

**Tales from the One Thousand and One Nights**, read by Souad Faress and Raad Rawi

**Moll Flanders** by Daniel Defoe, read by Frances Barber

**Great Expectations** by Charles Dickens, read by Hugh Laurie

**Hard Times** by Charles Dickens, read by Michael Pennington

**Martin Chuzzlewit** by Charles Dickens, read by John Wells

**The Old Curiosity Shop** by Charles Dickens, read by Alec McCowen

# PENGUIN AUDIOBOOKS

**Crime and Punishment** by Fyodor Dostoyevsky, read by Alex Jennings

**Middlemarch** by George Eliot, read by Harriet Walter

**Silas Marner** by George Eliot, read by Tim Pigott-Smith

**The Great Gatsby** by F. Scott Fitzgerald, read by Marcus D'Amico

**Madame Bovary** by Gustave Flaubert, read by Claire Bloom

**Jude the Obscure** by Thomas Hardy, read by Samuel West

**The Return of the Native** by Thomas Hardy, read by Steven Pacey

**Tess of the D'Urbervilles** by Thomas Hardy, read by Eleanor Bron

**The Iliad** by Homer, read by Derek Jacobi

**Dubliners** by James Joyce, read by Gerard McSorley

**The Dead and Other Stories** by James Joyce, read by Gerard McSorley

**On the Road** by Jack Kerouac, read by David Carradine

**Sons and Lovers** by D. H. Lawrence, read by Paul Copley

**The Fall of the House of Usher** by Edgar Allan Poe, read by Andrew Sachs

**Wide Sargasso Sea** by Jean Rhys, read by Jane Lapotaire and Michael Kitchen

**The Little Prince** by Antoine de Saint-Exupéry, read by Michael Maloney

**Frankenstein** by Mary Shelley, read by Richard Pasco

**Of Mice and Men** by John Steinbeck, read by Gary Sinise

**Travels with Charley** by John Steinbeck, read by Gary Sinise

**The Pearl** by John Steinbeck, read by Hector Elizondo

**Dr Jekyll and Mr Hyde** by Robert Louis Stevenson, read by Jonathan Hyde

**Kidnapped** by Robert Louis Stevenson, read by Robbie Coltrane

**The Age of Innocence** by Edith Wharton, read by Kerry Shale

**The Buccaneers** by Edith Wharton, read by Dana Ivey

**Mrs Dalloway** by Virginia Woolf, read by Eileen Atkins

# READ MORE IN PENGUIN

## A CHOICE OF CLASSICS

| | |
|---|---|
| St Anselm | **The Prayers and Meditations** |
| St Augustine | **The Confessions** |
| Bede | **Ecclesiastical History of the English People** |
| Geoffrey Chaucer | **The Canterbury Tales** |
| | **Love Visions** |
| | **Troilus and Criseyde** |
| Marie de France | **The Lais of Marie de France** |
| Jean Froissart | **The Chronicles** |
| Geoffrey of Monmouth | **The History of the Kings of Britain** |
| Gerald of Wales | **History and Topography of Ireland** |
| | **The Journey through Wales and The Description of Wales** |
| Gregory of Tours | **The History of the Franks** |
| Robert Henryson | **The Testament of Cresseid and Other Poems** |
| Walter Hilton | **The Ladder of Perfection** |
| Julian of Norwich | **Revelations of Divine Love** |
| Thomas à Kempis | **The Imitation of Christ** |
| William Langland | **Piers the Ploughman** |
| Sir John Mandeville | **The Travels of Sir John Mandeville** |
| Marguerite de Navarre | **The Heptameron** |
| Christine de Pisan | **The Treasure of the City of Ladies** |
| Chrétien de Troyes | **Arthurian Romances** |
| Marco Polo | **The Travels** |
| Richard Rolle | **The Fire of Love** |
| François Villon | **Selected Poems** |